ALBERTA
A New History

Howard Palmer
with
Tamara Palmer

Hurtig Publishers
Edmonton

Hurtig Publishers Ltd.
1302 Oxford Tower
10235–101 Street
Edmonton, Alberta
Canada T5J 3G1

Canadian Cataloguing in Publication Data

Palmer, Howard, 1946–
  Alberta, a new history

  Includes biographical references.
  ISBN 0-88830-340-8

  1. Alberta—History. I. Palmer, Tamara
Jeppson. II. Title.
FC3661.P34 1990   971.23   C90-091302-9
F1078.P34 1990

Editor: Nancy Marcotte
Design: David Shaw & Associates Ltd.
Maps: Marta Styk (pages vi, 2, 40, 52, 75, 145, 206, 356, 369)
      Rick Checkland (page 326)
Composition: Attic Typesetting Inc.
Manufacturer: Friesen Printers

Edited, designed, typeset, printed, and bound
in Canada for Hurtig Publishers Ltd.

Contents

Maps

Acknowledgements

A number of colleagues have provided helpful comments on different chapters of *Alberta: A New History* at various stages in the writing. They include John Foster of the Department of History, University of Alberta; Donald Smith, Doug Francis, and Henry Klassen of the Department of History, University of Calgary; Hugh Dempsey and Doug Cass of the Glenbow-Alberta Institute; David Jones of the Department of Educational Policy and Administration, University of Calgary; Roger Gibbins of the Department of Political Science, University of Calgary; Alvin Finkel of the Department of History, Athabasca University; David Elliott and Frank Dabbs.

Jean Burnet and Joanna Buhr both read the entire manuscript and made many helpful suggestions.

Marta Styk drew most of the maps, based on information provided by the authors.

We also appreciate the research assistance of Joanna Buhr, Bob Hromadiuk, and Lauretta Nelson.

The Alberta Foundation for the Literary Arts provided research funding for this project, and the Alberta Historical Resources Foundation provided funding for another project on the oral history of immigrants and ethnic minorities in southern Alberta, which provided a wealth of useful information on a number of topics.

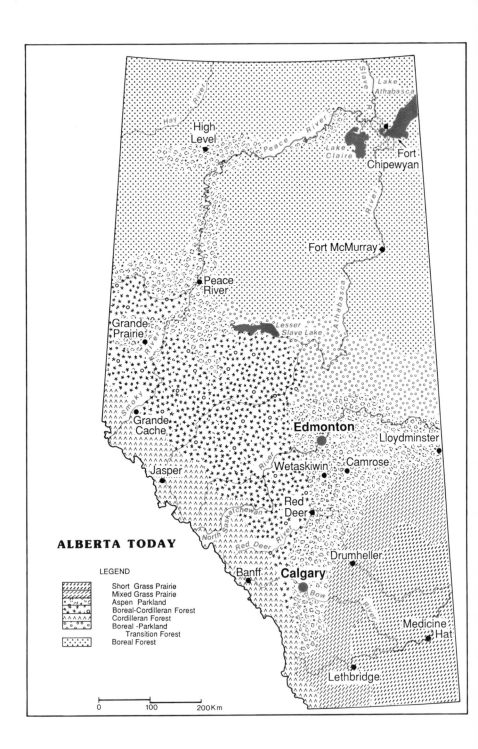

ALBERTA TODAY

LEGEND

Short Grass Prairie
Mixed Grass Prairie
Aspen Parkland
Boreal-Cordilleran Forest
Cordilleran Forest
Boreal -Parkland
    Transition Forest
Boreal Forest

0   100   200Km

Introduction

For most Canadians, Alberta is not a neutral word. It conjures up a variety of images and often evokes strong emotions, both positive and negative. Capable of commanding intense loyalty from its inhabitants, Alberta also irritates and puzzles those both inside and outside its borders. What gives it this power to both attract and repel? What forces have fashioned its economic, political, and social institutions, its provincial cultures and images? What lies beneath its contemporary surfaces? *Alberta: A New History* attempts to find some of the answers to these questions by exploring a variety of subjects and sources—traces, however fragmentary, of a complex and only partially retrievable past. Ultimately, this exploration has been in search of two things: a tangible sense of the events and personalities that are Alberta's past, and the nature of the connections between that past and what is perhaps an even more complex and equally elusive present.

We begin with a brief overview of the history of the native peoples and the fur trade. The nomadic way of life of the Plains and Woodlands Indians changed with the arrival of French and British fur traders in the 1700s. Two rival fur-trading empires challenged each other for control of the fur trade until 1821, when they merged under the name of the Hudson's Bay Company (HBC). During the 1860s and 1870s the advance of the central Canadian frontier challenged the fur trade's economic control over the West and led to radical changes in the native way of life. The coming of the North-West Mounted Police, the signing of Indian treaties, changes in Indian culture and growing Indian unrest, the arrival of a transcontinental railway, and the development of ranching and agricultural settlement were the mixed legacy of this advance.

From the late nineteenth century to the present, Alberta has experienced remarkably rapid social, demographic, and economic change. From a society that was until the 1940s predominantly rural and agricultural, Alberta has become overwhelmingly urban and industrial, and strongly dependent on the oil and gas industries. Today three out of five Albertans live in either Calgary or Edmonton. Alberta is now linked in multiple ways with the world's most advanced post-industrial economies.

Insight into contemporary Alberta depends on an understanding of the past. How has Alberta differed historically from the rest of Canada, and what makes it distinctive today? An important part of Alberta's story has been its unique political history, marked by the rapid rise and fall of political movements, one-party dominance, and political alienation from central Canada. *Alberta: A New History* highlights the interplay amongst economics, the environment, class, ethnicity, religion, and individual personalities that produced this short but complex and distinctive political history.

Since 1905 Alberta has witnessed the rise of four different political parties that have, in turn, dominated its political life. In the boom period of early settlement, and during World War I and the years immediately after, the Liberals were ascendant. They were replaced in 1921 by the United Farmers of Alberta (UFA), a dynamic farmers' cooperative movement. The UFA collapsed in 1935, when the scandal-ridden party was swept aside by a Social Credit landslide. During Social Credit's thirty-six-year reign, the voices of rural and smalltown Alberta dominated provincial politics. This era ended abruptly in 1971, when the movement was overpowered by an urban-based Conservative party. Social Credit, like the UFA and the Liberals before it, quickly faded into oblivion. Both shaping and reacting to these events was a cast of fascinating people who crossed Alberta's political stage—Frederick Haultain, R. B. Bennett, Frank Oliver, Henry Wise Wood, Louise McKinney, Nellie McClung, William Irvine, John Brownlee, William Aberhart, Ernest Manning, Peter Lougheed, Joe Clark, and many others—and in the process influenced the political history of the entire country.

Dramatic political changes have been parallelled by rapid shifts in the province's economic base, from fur and buffalo hides, to beef, then to wheat and other crops, and finally to oil and gas, and tourism. The development of Alberta's resource-based economy has been characterized by recurring boom-and-bust cycles, their causes complex, their consequences profound.

In addition to political and economic change, *Alberta: A New History* highlights the shifting ethnic composition of the region and Alberta's emergence as a multicultural society. The diversity of nine Indian tribes was augmented by successive waves of immigration. Alberta's people now trace their origins to over one hundred different groups, from American to Ukrainian and Vietnamese. *Alberta: A New History* explores the origins, development, and economic, social, and political consequences of this diversity. It also examines the closely related issue of the role of religion, its diversity and strength, and the reasons why in Alberta, religion, ethnicity, and politics have often been closely interwoven. Though frequently viewed from the outside as monolithic, Alberta has been shaped by recurring regional, class, religious, and ethnic divisions.

The telescoping of social, economic, and political change that has occurred in Alberta is evident in the variety of images it has had over the past 120 years. The images of "Fur-Trade Wilderness", "Cattle Kingdom", "Last Best West", "Dust Bowl", "Bible Belt", "Red Neck Country", and "Home of the 'Blue-Eyed Arabs'" have, successively or overlappingly, provided symbols of the essential Alberta. Each image has, however, expressed only a limited reality at any particular time. Moreover, change has been so rapid that each has quickly become outdated. Nevertheless, each of these greatly oversimplified labels has in part embodied Alberta's uniqueness. This book explores the evolution of Alberta's identity, finding continuity as well as change.

Alberta has developed against the backdrop of four quite distinct regions. The Rocky Mountains, foothills, Alberta plains, and Canadian Shield have all had a part in determining the nature of economic activity and the limits of human settlement. These landforms together with climate, soil, and natural vegetation have also interacted to create several distinct biophysical regions, including both short-grass and mixed-grassed plains, parkland, boreal and mountain (cordilleran) forests, and transitional zones between regions. A crucial and often painful process throughout Alberta's history has been that of people gradually understanding and coming to terms with each region's possibilities and limitations.

The prairie of southern Alberta includes both the dry shortgrass region in the southeast and a more moist mixed-grass region stretching in an arc to the west and north of the shortgrass area. The settlement and abandonment of the drybelt of southeast Alberta from the 1880s through the 1930s, the continuing struggle against drought and soil erosion, and the introduction of irrigation are central to the story of settlers adapting to this region. The parkland areas of central Alberta and the Peace River district have fertile soils and ample moisture, though productivity in Peace River is limited by a cooler climate. The central Alberta parkbelt provides an ideal locale for cereal, livestock, and dairying.

The boreal region of northern Alberta contains a wide variety of forest vegetation (predominantly aspen and white birch) and wildlife that sheltered and sustained the woodlands natives for thousands of years, and provided the basis for the fur trade that first attracted

Europeans to the area. As far as non-native settlement is concerned, the North is both the oldest and the youngest region of Alberta, since European fur traders went there first. Nonetheless, Alberta's ranching and farming settlement began in the south, and human settlement in the north remained very sparse until after World War II, when oil, gas, and forestry development accelerated.

The mountain (cordilleran) forest region contains fir, spruce, and pine, and peaks and lakes known around the world for their beauty. The resources and scenery of the mountains have supported a mixed economy of trapping, mining, foresty, and tourism, creating a sub-region culturally distinct from the agrarian society of the prairies.

This is a "new" history in several different senses. The last overview of Alberta, J. G. MacGregor's *A History of Alberta*, was published in 1972. We bring the account up to 1990, synthesizing a great deal of new research published since 1972. Given McGregor's focus on exploration and the fur trade, we cover those topics more generally, while emphasizing subjects not treated in depth in his book. At the same time, being realistic about what can be covered in a single volume, we have not attempted to provide a definitive survey covering all topics in depth. Our concern has been to highlight and explain the major trends and patterns in Alberta's history, rather than to examine in detail developments in every region and community in the province.

This is also a new history since it draws on the results of twenty years of new research not only on political, economic, ethnic, and religious history, but also on coal mining, the oil industry, organized labour, education, sport and leisure, tourism, popular culture, the arts, women, and natives, among other topics, many of which have only recently been addressed by historians. *Alberta: A New History* synthesizes many existing books, articles in historical journals, government documents, and unpublished theses, as well as our own research in archives and interviews with Albertans. We are deeply indebted to many other scholars and authors, specialists in a variety of fields, and we have attempted to acknowledge their invaluable contributions in the bibliography for each chapter.

Finally, *Alberta: A New History* tells the story of the creation of a new society out of the interaction among varied personalities and a myriad of economic, political, and social forces. We hope that our account of this process will help Albertans to better understand their own history, and others to more fully appreciate a sometimes enigmatic, but ever fascinating, part of Canada.

CHAPTER ONE

Native Peoples and the Encounter with the European Frontier

The human history of Alberta begins with the story of the native peoples who lived in the area for thousands of years before the arrival of European settlers. Recent research by archaeologists has provided many new insights into ways of life that slowly emerged as nomadic native hunters adjusted to the changing climate and game of the region. As long as twelve thousand years ago, they lived in an ice-free corridor along the Rocky Mountains between two ice masses. Then, over thousands of years, the climate changed to virtual desert-like conditions because of higher temperatures and drought.

In the last few thousand years, natives gradually adapted to the varying climate and resources of the plains and the woodlands we know today. Different tribes became associated with each of these environments. Those on the plains who relied on the buffalo for food and for many other material aspects of their culture left evidence of their way of life, particularly at buffalo jumps where, with skill and ingenuity, they herded bison over cliffs. Living in a desolate land where food supplies were often uncertain, the Woodland Indians farther to the north had to be hardy and resourceful to survive.

Centuries of gradual change in response to changing climate, and to the contact and conflict amongst different native tribes, gave way to accelerated change with the arrival in the 1700s of white traders, who brought European ironware and guns. Rival fur trade companies, directed from London and Montreal, expanded rapidly across the region in the late 1700s. They were led by a series of remarkable fur traders and explorers, men such as Anthony Henday, Peter Pond, Alexander Mackenzie, and David Thompson, whose feats of daring, endurance, and skills at diplomacy with natives, often with the aid of their native wives, are justly renowned as vital to the exploration and development of western Canada.

FUR TRADE POSTS
and
THOMPSON'S EXPLORATION ROUTE

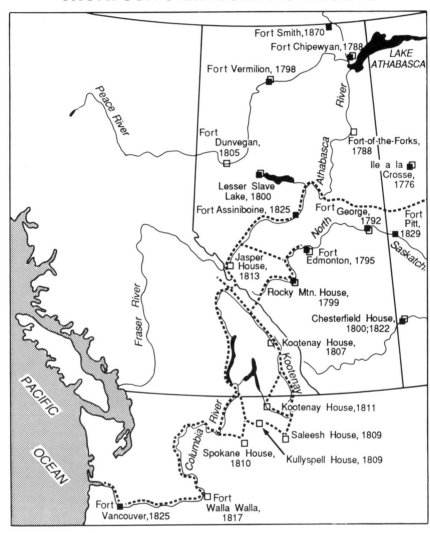

LEGEND
TRADING POSTS

- ■ Hudson's Bay Company
- □ North West Company
- ▣ Hudson's Bay Co. & North West Co.
  operating separately in the same vicinity

••••••• Thompson's Route (1805 - 1807)

Indians and traders became dependent on each other in a relation-ship based on cooperative exploitation of the region's fur resources. The Indians trapped the furs and transported them to posts where they exchanged furs for European goods, many of which were adapted to native tastes and needs.

The fur-trade posts, dotted across the river systems of the region, particularly in what is now northern Alberta, were tiny centres of western society, with their own seasonal rhythms. Their social struc-ture emerged from the intermingling of French, English, Scots, and natives and the consequent formation of a new mixed-blood people, the Métis. Some of these posts, for example Fort Edmonton, were located in such strategic locations that they remained important settlement sites even after the economy shifted away from the fur trade. Other posts, located at sites that were strategic during the days of river transportation, faded away during the 1800s with the transi-tion to a new economy.

The fur traders were joined during the 1840s by Christian missionaries, who added to the complexity of European impact on native culture and accelerated the pace of change in the West. These missionaries represented a variety of Christian denominations, and included Methodists Robert Rundle, George and John McDougall, and Henry Steinhauer, and Catholics Alexander Taché, Vital Grandin, and Albert Lacombe, among many others. They felt it was their duty to "civilize" the natives. Their work of exploration, linguistic understanding, diplomacy between whites and natives, and directed cultural change left a mixed legacy, which is still being assessed by both natives and whites.

The Aboriginal Peoples

Alberta's original inhabitants have lived in what is now Alberta for at least twelve thousand years. Basing their views on the spiritual insights passed on in sacred myths, dreams, and visions, many Indian elders believe that their people in fact were created on this continent. In contrast, archaeologists generally contend that the first North Americans crossed over the Bering Strait from Asia during the last ice age, following large Asian animals across a land bridge that linked Alaska and Siberia. Many archaeologists also believe that during this ice age, there was an ice-free corridor between the mountains and the continental ice masses along the eastern slope of the Rockies, and that animals and people travelled south along this corridor. Archaeologists have found traces of hunting bands at Vermilion Lakes in what is now Banff National Park (in what was the ice-free corridor) from at least 10,500 years ago. These hunters lived during the final years of the Pleistocene Epoch, which ended ten thousand years ago. Toward the end of the ice age, the large Pleistocene mammals—mammoths, camels, lion-like cats, giant bison, and others—mysteriously died out, for reasons still hotly debated by scientists. Did people with superior hunting technology wipe out the game, or did the climate change? Or did both factors contribute to the extinction of these mammals?

From five to eight thousand years ago, because of higher temperatures and less moisture, the numbers of animals and people in the northern plains region of North America declined. For several thousand years this area, which includes present-day Alberta, was a virtual desert. Archaeologists differ in their views of how disastrous the effect of this drying was on the bison, the major food supply for native peoples living in the region.

Evidence of people having been in Alberta for thousands of years comes from many sources. There are hundreds of thousands of stone rings, or teepee rings—rocks placed in a circular pattern and used to hold down the edges of hides. Alberta also has at least sixteen different rock art sites. Pictograph paintings or petroglyphs (drawings etched, incised, or pecked into a rock surface) show humans, animals, and abstract figures. The largest site is at Writing-On-Stone, which is east of Milk River, near the present-day border between Montana and Alberta. Writing-On-Stone has an intriguing array of petroglyphs with native symbolism and depictions of native life dating back one to two thousand years. Huge, mysterious medicine wheels, usually on top of high hills, also show the antiquity and ingenuity of Alberta's native peoples. About forty-five medicine wheels have been discovered in the province. Some have over twenty spokes radiating from a central cairn, all enclosed within a circle. Some have no spokes at all, only concentric circles. They may have been used for religious ceremonies, or for commemorating people or events, or perhaps they are evidence of an early interest in astronomy.

Stone, bone, and ceramic artifacts provide archaeologists with clues to Alberta's past. Basing their analysis on differing types of projectile points (sharp stone pieces placed at the ends of spears, darts, and arrows), archaeologists have divided Alberta's ancient past into a series of phases, thereby showing the movements of different peoples, the length of their residences, their trade patterns, their influence on each other, and their shifting patterns of tribal dominance. Thanks to provincial protection of Alberta's archaeological heritage, the past thirty years have brought much new archaeological research in all regions of the province and, with the aid of sophisticated dating techniques, researchers are constantly revising their views of the past, thereby generating lively debate. Basic questions related to the social organization and religious beliefs of early native peoples are difficult to answer, however, because of the fragmentary nature of the evidence.

The buffalo jumps are among the richest sources of information for archaeologists. The Head-Smashed-In Buffalo Jump near present-day Fort Macleod is one of the largest, with evidence of occupation for over five thousand years, ending in the 1850s. Lines of rock cairns lead away from the edge of the cliff, extending for miles; these served as V-shaped driveways that funnelled the unsuspecting buffalo to the cliff's edge. Young men would go out as far as ten miles to begin herding buffalo toward the funnel. When the buffalo came closer to the edge, the young men speeded them up. The older men and boys on the side then moved to frighten the animals and stampede them over the cliff. Many of the buffalo died immediately; those only wounded were killed with spears, arrows, and stone hammers. After the stampede, the area at the base of the cliff became a vast, well-organized abattoir, as families skinned and treated the hides, and butchered and processed the meat. Much of the meat was dried and made into pemmican, a greasy but nourishing mixture of buffalo flesh, fat, and berries that the natives, and later the fur traders, carried in hide bags and relied on for food. Sometimes natives also drove the buffalo into corrals or pounds for the slaughter.

The buffalo served as the basis for a native lifestyle on the plains that extended across the southern part of what is now Alberta, Saskatchewan, and Manitoba, and into the United States. Estimates of the numbers of buffalo on the Great Plains when this culture was flourishing range from twenty to eighty million, with about two million in Alberta.

As part of their annual cycle of migrations, during the winter Plains Indians such as the Blackfoot gathered amongst the trees of the parkland or in sheltered river valleys, where they found protection, fuel, and buffalo. During the long winters, the elders had ample time to pass on oral accounts of their history and conduct religious rituals. These rituals constantly reminded them of their dependence on nature. On mild days, they ventured out and drove buffalo into snowdrifts or ravines, where they could be killed. In spring the Plains

Indians packed their belongings and moved onto the grasslands, where they held communal buffalo kills. During the late summer, large groups broke into small bands to hunt. In fall, the bands would gather for another communal buffalo kill.

The tribes of northern Plains Indians such as the Blackfoot were usually divided into separate hunting bands with twenty to thirty families in a band, or one to two hundred men, women, and children. Bands needed to be large enough to enable their members to encircle a small herd of buffalo, and large enough to defend themselves from raiding enemy tribes. They also needed to be small enough to permit survival in times of scarcity. Each band, composed primarily of relatives, was led by the most respected able-bodied man in the group.

As they followed the buffalo herds from one temporary encampment to another, the largest and heaviest possession was their shelter, the tipi. In the period before the arrival of the horse in the early 1700s, its size was limited to the weight a strong dog could carry on a travois, or about 75 pounds (34 kilos). The painted tipi was a prized possession among the Blackfoot. "Connected with it [the tipi] were the sacred songs and rituals bought from the previous owner, obtained through bravery in battle, or given in a holy dream."[1]

The buffalo provided almost everything the Plains Indians needed, from food and shelter to utensils. They fashioned bison bones into tools such as scrapers and needles, and made horns into spoons. Buffalo hides provided material for tipis, as well as for shields, robes, and blankets. Hair and tails were braided into ropes or used as ornaments; sinews were dried and stripped into strands for thread; internal organs were used as containers. Buffalo tongues were used as a form of communion in the Plains Indians' most important religious ceremony, the annual summer Sun Dance. This expressed in ritual their belief that the sun was an intermediary through which the creative forces of the world could be addressed.

The arrival of horses in the early eighteenth century revolutionized the Plains Indians' way of life. The largest of the Plains Indian groups in Alberta, the Blackfoot nation, consisted of three tribes, the Blackfoot, Blood, and Peigan. They shared similar traditions, customs, and language, and united to protect each other's hunting territory. The Blackfoot obtained horses (which had originally been brought to Mexico by Spaniards) by the 1730s, two decades before the arrival of whites in present-day Alberta. Horses enabled the Indians to transport four times as much and travel twice as far as when they relied on dogs for transportation. Better transportation also enabled

6

them to acquire more possessions. A relatively classless society began to change to one of three classes, with status based on the number of horses a person owned. The desire for horses to hunt buffalo and transport baggage, as well as for wealth and status, led to horse raiding against enemy tribes and to more warfare. Personal bravery and zeal in war became ideals for young men. With more warfare, conducted with bow and arrow, lance, club, knife, and eventually gun, came more casualties.

While there were many variations among Plains tribes, there were some similarities in the native customs connected with the life cycle. Usually after a baby was born, it received its first name from its mother. This name was changed frequently in response to later events in the child's life. For example, the great Blackfoot warrior and chief, Crowfoot, born in southern Alberta around 1830, was known as Shot Close, then Bear Ghost, then Packs a Knife. It was only after he proved his bravery in a battle against the Crow Indians in Montana that he received the name Crowfoot. He later became chief of one of the Blackfoot bands and in 1870 became one of the three head chiefs of the Blackfoot tribe.

Young boys and girls were looked after by their mothers and other close female relatives, who taught them legends that usually conveyed moral lessons. After boys reached the age of seven or eight, male relatives began to take a greater interest in them, making them their first bows and arrows, and encouraging them to play games, often war games, and stage mock attacks. Boys usually began going to war at about age thirteen, first as servants to experienced warriors, for whom they would make fires, mend moccasins, and cook food. At about the same time they would join a warriors' society, each of which had its own songs, face paint, and special religious objects or medicine bundles. Young girls were taught by their mothers or other close relatives. They learned bead work and quill work, and they performed chores such as going for water or wood. By the time they were thirteen or fourteen, young girls had begun the difficult tasks of cooking, skinning, and tanning.

Men usually married in their early twenties and women in their late teens. Parents arranged their children's marriages. The surplus of women, caused by the loss of men who died in warfare, led to the practice of polygamy.

Adult males were responsible for hunting, weapon making, and religious rituals. Though warriors were usually in their late teens or twenties, some fought longer. Crowfoot, for example, went to war nineteen times and was wounded six times. His fearlessness in battle was one of the main reasons he was chosen as chief.

The treatment of the elderly varied from tribe to tribe, but usually until they were infirm or disabled, they were respected and were treated as wise elders with a lifetime of experience. In a nomadic, hunting culture, the very old became a detriment to the camp, and would sometimes be left behind. Abandoning mothers, fathers, or grandparents was extremely traumatic, but doing so was essential if the group were to remain mobile. Among the Plains Indians, the dead were placed on a scaffold on a high hill. They did not bury their dead underground since they believed this would trap their spirits.

Impact of European Fur Traders

When the Europeans first reached present-day Alberta in the 1700s, the native peoples had two distinct ways of life: that of the plains and that of the woodlands. There were three linguistic families, the Athapaskan (which included the Chipewyan, Slavey, Beaver, and Sarcee), the Algonquian (including the Cree and the Blackfoot nation), and the Siouan (including the Assiniboine or Stoney).

At the time of European contact, the tribes on the plains of present-day central and southern Alberta included the Blackfoot nation and their allies, the Sarcee and Atsina (Gros Ventre). Another tribe, the Kootenai, a mountain people, lived along the slopes of the Rockies, but during the late 1700s they were driven westward across the mountains by the Blackfoot. While the Plains Indians relied primarily on the bison, the Indians of the woodlands in northern Alberta, including the Slavey, Beaver, and Chipewyan, lived by fishing and hunting deer, moose, or caribou, supplementing their diets with berries, roots, wild plants, and the inner bark of certain trees.

The largest of the Woodland Indian tribes, the Chipewyan, depended on the the caribou as their main source of food. They adopted a variety of means to hunt them: "during the summer, one of the favorite means of killing them was by spearing them from canoes as they swam across rivers or lakes. On other occasions they were driven into traps where they were killed with arrows. In winter they were snared or caught in deep snow."[2] Since the northern Indians usually travelled in small family groups they did not have a structured form of leadership, other than the head of a family, in contrast to the system of tribal chiefs of the Plains Indians.

The arrival of fur traders in western Canada, following the establishment of the Hudson's Bay Company in England in 1670, led to many changes in the native ways of life. One of the first of these changes was a great displacement of Indians in western Canada by those from farther east. The Cree, Assiniboine, and Chipewyan near Hudson Bay, anxious to obtain European ironware, added the trapping of furs to hunting. As their trapping grounds became depleted, many migrated westward. These Indians became the middlemen of the fur trade, exchanging metal tools (particularly iron goods with their fine cutting edges) and weapons for furs gathered by other tribes farther inland. Their expansion was aided by European guns, which often gave them a great advantage over the people they displaced.

The westward migration of the Cree and Assiniboine (or Stoney) drove a wedge westward up the North Saskatchewan River to the Rockies, pushing interior tribes to the north and south. The Stoneys established themselves along the foothills in central and southern Alberta. The Cree forced the Blackfoot southward from the North Saskatchewan River. One of the largest tribes in Canada, the Cree included the Plains Cree in the central part of Alberta and the Woods Cree in the north. The Plains Cree, armed with European guns, developed the reputation of being fierce warriors.

The Chipewyan also pushed the Beaver westward, a movement that stopped only when the Beaver obtained their first guns from European traders in 1782. Now armed, the Beaver stopped the Cree advance into their territory, and in turn pushed the weaker Sekani Indians out of the upper waters of the Peace River and into the mountains.

Though the fur traders brought new technology that made native life easier in many ways, they were also forerunners of changes that would forever alter the native ways of life. The fur trade had an impact on natives across the province, but nowhere was it stronger than in the north, where the Europeans concentrated their fur trade posts because of the higher incidence of fur-bearing animals. Historian Hugh Dempsey describes some of the advantages the fur traders brought to the Woodland Cree of northern Alberta:

> The gun soon replaced the bow and arrow in hunting; sinew or rawhide nets were abandoned in favor of European ones; and the availability of knives, metal pots, axes, and other utensils made life much easier. Similarly, the tedious task of tanning hides was sometimes eased when shirts, blankets and other cloth objects were bought.[3]

But the traders' presence also led to problems. The northern Indians began placing more emphasis on trapping rather than hunting. As they became more dependent on the trading posts for survival, they also became more influenced by European practices. Alcohol and disease began to make serious inroads. The Plains tribes farther south did not feel the same weight of European influence as early because trapping for them was not as profitable. Indeed, the period from the mid-1700s to the early 1830s was something of a "Golden Age" for the Plains Indians, who had access to European trade goods. Dependent on the buffalo, they still lived very much as they chose.

Fur Trade Rivalry and Exploration

Lured by the promise of tremendous profits, the French and the English challenged each other for control of the fur trade. The trade consisted primarily of beaver pelts. These were used to make felt hats, which were very popular in Europe in the seventeenth and eighteenth centuries.

The Hudson's Bay Company (HBC) was formed in 1670 when a group of London businessmen secured a charter from the English crown to trade in "Rupert's Land." This included all the region that drained into Hudson Bay, which was 1.5 million square miles (3.9 million square kilometres), covering most of present-day Canada between the Rocky Mountains and Labrador, and part of the northern U.S. Similarly the French, who had an established colony in New France, claimed sovereignty over the lands of present-day western Canada. In reality, for almost two hundred years neither power controlled any territory outside of its trading posts. The Europeans relied on the native peoples to supply furs and provisions.

The French and British set up competing posts on Hudson Bay in the late 1600s. The French challenged the British militarily on Hudson Bay until the French gave up their posts in the Treaty of Utrecht in 1713, one of the temporary peaces in the long series of imperial wars between Britain and France. After 1713 the French challenged the English in the Northwest by using the long trade route through the St. Lawrence and Great Lakes system, connecting with Lake Winnipeg and the Saskatchewan River, the best access route to the interior.

French traders such as Pierre La Vérendrye and his sons established fur-trading posts inland in what is now Manitoba during the 1730s. The HBC traders, however, for decades did not travel inland from their posts on the Bay. Because of the company's conservative trading practices and their inexperience with transportation into the interior, the Hudson's Bay Company traders waited for the Indians to bring furs down river to the posts on the Bay. By the mid-eighteenth century, the French were siphoning off most of the best furs. French traders were likely the first whites to have contact with native peoples in what is now Alberta, though the Peigan, the southernmost of the Blackfoot-speaking tribes, likely also had contact with a few Spaniards much farther south. The French were likely the first European group to meet the Blackfoot; the word for "Frenchman" in their language means "real White Man."

Anthony Henday, sent out by the Hudson's Bay Company to report on interior natives and the potential of drawing their trade to the Bay, wrote the first account of the region that is present-day Alberta. Henday, a labourer, netmaker, and one-time smuggler, left York Factory on Hudson Bay in the spring of 1754. Travelling with a band of Cree, he arrived in Alberta in September, witnessed the buffalo hunt, and visited one of the main camps of the Blackfoot, near present-day Red Deer. While the Cree had no horses and generally travelled by canoe, the Blackfoot had become equestrians. Using an interpreter, Henday invited the Blackfoot to go to Hudson Bay to trade, but they were not interested. They were unfamiliar with canoes, the main means of transport along the river system, and feared starvation on the long trip. Instead, they traded their furs to the Cree, who then transported them and sold them to the French traders in the interior.

After the British conquest of New France in 1760, French traders abandoned their posts in the Northwest. However, they were soon replaced by a new trading system, again centred in Montreal. Initially the individual traders were known as Pedlars. In the 1780s a large grouping of partnerships became known as the North West Company (NWC). The Nor'Westers re-established the fur-trade routes through the St. Lawrence and Great Lakes. They established fur-trading depots at the head of Lake Superior, and from there took their trade goods into the western interior. After spending the winter trading with the natives, they returned to their annual meeting point at Fort William and paid off their Montreal-based suppliers with their accumulated furs. Most of the company's managers were of British (predominantly Highland Scots) origin, but the transporting of furs was still done by French Canadian canoemen called voyageurs.

The rivalry between these companies intensified until they

merged in 1821. The Hudson's Bay Company, with its much shorter supply route and greater financial reserves, came to the conclusion that it would have to compete inland to assert its charter and obtain quality furs. The demand for more fur-bearing animals forced both companies farther inland, with the Nor'Westers being far more aggressive.

Nor'Wester Peter Pond built the first fur-trading post in present-day Alberta on the Athabasca River in 1778. Pond, a New Englander, moved in 1775 from the area southwest of the Great Lakes to the Canadian West. He was the first trader to take goods from the lower Saskatchewan River into the Athabasca country via Methye Portage. Pond returned several times to the Athabasca country as a partner for the NWC, but he left the fur trade after being implicated in the murder of two competitors. Before he left, it was clear that Pond's fur-trade work had been successful, and the NWC built a number of posts up the Peace River. Nor'Westers built Fort Chipewyan on nearby Lake Athabasca in 1788, and this fort became their central post in the Athabasca region. It also served as the departure point for Nor'Wester Alexander Mackenzie on his exploration trip down the Mackenzie River to the Arctic Ocean in 1789, and across the Rockies to the Pacific in 1793.

Alexander Mackenzie, one of the great personalities of the fur trade, was born in Scotland and came to America as a young man. He left for Montreal in 1778 because of the Revolutionary War. There he entered the fur trade, and in the mid 1780s, as a partner in the North West Company, wintered with Peter Pond. Mackenzie was ambitious, and at times ruthless. Because of his blend of sternness and kindness in his dealings with his voyageurs, they served him well and helped make his arduous explorations possible.

Pond must have shared with Mackenzie his knowledge of the northland, and told him of a broad river flowing westward. They hoped the river would lead to the "Western Sea," opening up new fur-trade areas and a transportation route shorter than the Great Lakes-St. Lawrence River system. In his epic voyage in 1789, Mackenzie discovered that the river now bearing his name (which he called the "River of Disappointment") did not empty into the Pacific, and was thus of little use for the fur trade. But his appetite for exploration had been whetted. In 1792 he set out again, up the Peace River this time, searching for a route to the Pacific.

As he proceeded up the Peace River beginning in October 1792, Mackenzie passed a number of small posts built over the previous five years by NWC men operating out of Fort Chipewyan. These included Fort De Tremble, built by John Finlay forty miles (64 kilometres) up river from present day Fort Vermilion, and a post built by Archibald McLeod thirty miles (48 kilometres) downriver from the present-day town of Peace River. Mackenzie wintered at Fork Fort, about twelve miles (19 kilometres) above the mouth of the Smoky River. His crew numbered ten—seven French Canadians, two Indians, and a Scot.

Mackenzie crossed the Rockies, descended the Fraser, and portaged to another river, which led him to the Pacific. Mackenzie was the first European to cross the broad North American continent overland. It was clear, however, that this passage was too arduous to become an important trade route.

Mackenzie was convinced of the need to reorient the trade westward to the Pacific, where furs could be shipped to China. When he could not obtain the backing of the NWC, in 1800 he threw in his lot with a group of upstart traders known as the XY Company.

By the 1770s, the Hudson's Bay Company had also decided it would have to compete fiercely inland to survive; consequently, it established its first post inland at Fort Cumberland (in present-day Saskatchewan) in 1774. The company's employees gradually gained experience with canoes and snowshoes, and the HBC evolved a system of York boats. These heavy wooden boats lacked the beauty and speed of canoes, but were sound and economical and could carry almost twice as many packs of fur. The HBC also sent surveyors Peter Fidler and David Thompson to explore and map the Athabasca and Saskatchewan rivers.

During the 1790s, the NWC and HBC established competitive posts across what is now central and northern Alberta. In 1792 the NWC built Fort George, the first fur post on the Alberta portion of the Saskatchewan River. In 1795 a young trader of the NWC, Angus Shaw, established Fort Augustus at the confluence of the Sturgeon and North Saskatchewan rivers, near present-day Edmonton. The area was, according to one report, "a rich and plentiful Country, abounding in all kinds of animals, especially Beavers and otters which are said to be so numerous that the Women and Children kill them with sticks and hatchets."[4] The HBC soon followed with a nearby post, Edmonton House, built within a musket shot of the NWC post. The post was reputedly named either after an estate owned by the Deputy Governor of the HBC, or after the hometown of an HBC clerk at the new post. The two posts, the first of a series of fortified trading posts near present-day Edmonton, were built on the north

Fort Edmonton, as depicted by artist Paul Kane in the late 1840s. Strategically located on a major river, Fort Edmonton was the centre of the Alberta fur trade. The fur trade era was a period of relative equality between Indians and whites. *(Royal Ontario Museum 912.1.38)*

bank of the Saskatchewan River to reduce the danger of attack from the south by Plains Indians. The closeness of the posts enabled the companies to keep an eye on each others' activities, but also to provide some joint protection from attacks by natives.

The NWC set up another important trading centre at Rocky Mountain House in 1799, followed closely by the HBC's Acton House. Despite the HBC's advantage of having a much shorter trade route through Hudson Bay, the NWC clearly outdistanced them through their aggressiveness and their French Canadian and Métis employees' superior mastery of the rivers, forests, and prairies of the Northwest.

The NWC, HBC, and XY companies were ruthless competitors. Their rivalry often led to violence and debauchery as the fur trade became soaked in rum. The north branches of the Saskatchewan and Athabasca rivers were the main battlegrounds. Traders could expect to have their trading goods and canoes destroyed and their tents slashed to ribbons. They fought to sabotage each others' food supply lines and fired shots at each others' canoes. This fierce competition, which was economically and morally ruinous, was not entirely eradicated by the union of the NWC and the XY Company in 1804.

One of the consequences of the amalgamation between the XY Company and the NWC was renewed exploration westward toward the

Pacific. This was partly to make use of surplus traders by opening up fur-rich areas where the native demand for European commodities had not yet been satisfied. Exploration westward might also lead to the discovery of the better and shorter trade route from the interior that had eluded Alexander Mackenzie. Nor'Wester Simon Fraser was placed in charge of the company's operations west of the Rockies in 1805. He discovered that the river that now bears his name was too perilous to serve as a trade route.

David Thompson, a fellow Nor'Wester, made Rocky Mountain House his base of exploration. He was looking for a navigable route to the Pacific. A trader, mapmaker, and surveyor, Thompson headed the NWC drive to reach the Columbia River from the North Saskatchewan. Born in London and raised in poverty, Thompson had an aptitude for mathematics. He was quiet and observant, with a simple, unaffected manner and great skill as a surveyor and mapmaker. His journal, *Narrative of Explorations in Western America, 1784–1812*, written in the 1840s, was based on his daily note-taking. It is a detailed and insightful record of native peoples and geography in the Northwest. Thompson opposed the use of liquor as a trade item with the natives, and neither drank nor traded liquor with his customers.

When he was twenty-nine, Thompson married a young Métis, Charlotte Small. Charlotte was the daughter of an Indian mother and a partner of the NWC who had left his Indian family in the wilderness when he returned to "civilization," a common practice among those in the upper echelons of the fur trade. Charlotte travelled with Thompson on many of his trips, as did their children, of whom there were eventually thirteen.

Beginning in 1793, first as an employee of the HBC, Thompson travelled most of Alberta's rivers. He left the HBC in 1797 because of lack of support for his surveys, and the NWC eventually posted him at Rocky Mountain House. Here he pursued his passion for exploration and mapmaking, with important consequences.

From 1807 to 1812, Thompson surveyed the Kootenay and Columbia rivers, setting up posts in the Windermere Valley and south of the 49th parallel (near present day Kalispell, Montana, and Spokane, Washington) before Britain and the United States had determined their claims over the area. In 1810 Thompson was blocked by the Peigan in his movements westward across the mountains because he was supplying guns to their enemies. He had to get around them and find another pass through the Rockies. He crossed northward to the Athabasca River, then set out over the Athabasca Pass and finally made his way to the mouth of the Columbia River in 1811. Thompson had found the key to a new route across the Rocky Mountains. His explorations opened up a vast new fur-trading region for the NWC.

Rivalry between the HBC and the NWC climaxed after 1812 with the establishment of the Red River Colony. Lord Selkirk, a Scottish philanthropist, gained financial control of the HBC and attempted to establish an agricultural colony in what is now Manitoba. The colony fell across the main transportation lines of the NWC, which responded with unprecedented violence. This renewed rivalry spilled over into the Athabasca region. When the HBC sent a group there under John Clarke and constructed Fort Wedderburn, near NWC's Fort Chipewyan, the NWC men persuaded their native allies to drive game away from the areas where the HBC men travelled. Thirteen HBC men died of starvation. The HBC retaliated in 1818 by sending an expedition of twenty-six officers and 160 men led by Colin Robertson to the Athabasca region to re-establish their presence.

Concerned about the violence and wanting to assert sovereignty in the Northwest to prevent possible American and Russian expansion, the British government pressured the two companies to come together. In 1821 the companies joined under the name of the Hudson's Bay Company. After the merger, Fort Edmonton, Rocky Mountain House, and Fort Chipewyan became the leading centres of the new Hudson's Bay Company's reorganized fur trade in Alberta.

George Simpson, a Scot, was governor of the HBC from 1821 to 1860. Simpson first came to the Northwest in 1820 during the period of intense competition, and spent his first winter on Lake Athabasca competing with the Nor'Westers. Simpson's style of leadership earned him the nickname "Little Emperor"; this was perhaps an appropriate title, since his hero was Napoleon. He loved ceremony, and hired someone to play the bagpipes whenever he entered a post. A competent administrator, able to unite warring factions, he had tremendous energy. On his cross-country journeys, he travelled at breakneck speed from three in the morning until ten at night. On one famous trip in the spring of 1825, he travelled from Fort Vancouver to the Red River in two and a half months. But he was also vindictive and particularly insensitive toward native women. When he decided that respectability required that he and other company officers have white wives, Simpson arranged for his common-law native wife to marry a company employee; he encouraged other officers to do likewise.

After he took charge of the HBC in 1821, Simpson reorganized the fur trade. He improved transportation, cut down on presents, liquor, and credit to the Indians, closed posts, reduced wages, and tried to make interior posts more self-sufficient by having the staff grow their own food. In 1822 he attempted to make use of excess staff by sending out the Bow River expedition to re-establish Chesterfield House (first established temporarily in 1800) on the South Saskatchewan River. But the eighty men sent on the expedition found the Blackfoot unwilling to trade because the English traders had given guns to their enemies, the Cree and the Assiniboine. The American Fur Company, in contrast, trading out of northern Montana, was more successful in establishing trade links with the Peigan.

When Simpson moved to Montreal, an old Nor'Wester named John Rowand took over in 1826 as chief trader at Edmonton House, the fur-trade headquarters for all the western prairies. Rowand was second only to Simpson in his dominance over the fur trade. In his early years in the trade, Rowand had rubbed shoulders with the great explorers of the Northwest, and had worked his way up the fur-trade administrative hierarchy. He spoke Gaelic, English, French, and Cree, all of which were needed in the fur trade. Rowand could be a charming host, but he also believed that fisticuffs was a necessary persuasive skill.

In 1832, following one of the frequent floods on the North Saskatchewan River, Rowand rebuilt Edmonton House on higher ground immediately below where the provincial legislature stands today. Here he constructed his "Big House," which was both residence and office. It measured thirty by eighty feet and had three storeys and glass windowpanes. Rowand intended to impress the natives with the building's size and novelty. Because of this memorable structure, Edmonton was known as "Big House" in Cree and Blackfoot.

Rowand faced growing competition from the Americans, who by 1832 had steamboats far up the Missouri River. This enabled them to provide trade goods cheaply, carry furs quickly, and trade for the heavy buffalo robes that the HBC could not handle. Responding to the American presence, in 1832 Rowand sent his men to establish Peigan Post on the Bow River near present-day Morley. The Peigan regarded the post as an unwelcome intrusion, and it closed within two years.

Rowand saw many changes during his tenure, which lasted until his retirement in 1854. These included the devastation of Indian wars, the ravages of disease, and the arrival of Christian missionaries.

Fur Trade Life

The fur traders built posts that were simple structures made from materials on the site. The buildings were surrounded by stockades for protection. The traders placed cannons in the bastions, but these were often so antiquated that they posed a greater danger to the men firing salutes than to a potential enemy. Buildings were set in a cleared quadrangle beside the river. The "main house," often two storeys high, was split into a trading room and living quarters for the senior men. Other buildings contained the men's quarters, storerooms, and workshops. Outside the stockade was a vegetable garden, a corral for livestock, and an area where the Indians pitched their tents when they arrived to trade.

Life at the trading posts was marked by long periods of monotony and isolation broken by short periods of intense activity. At mid-nineteenth-century Fort Edmonton, the hub of the fur trade, the season began in late September or early October with the arrival of the brigade. Ten boats manned by fifty men would arrive from York Factory on Hudson Bay, loaded with trade goods. After the goods were stored, the men appeared for their reward of rum and an all-night dance at the chief factor's house. A fiddler or two among them would play lively music, and native and Métis women would join them in Red River jigs and other spirited dance steps. As described by fur trade historian A. S. Morton in *The History of the Canadian West to 1870-71*:

> The gaiety of the occasion was all the keener because the post was a dull place through the summer with the men away, and little business doing. All the society of the place, from the Chief Factor's family to the Orkney blacksmith and his household. . . took part in this joyous opening of the season at the fort.[5]

The men then moved quickly to arrange the "outfits" of goods for the other posts. The officers allocated men and pack horses to various expeditions. A large outfit headed for Fort Assiniboine, northeast of Edmonton on the Athabasca River. This post was the point of departure for brigades both west and north. From Fort Assiniboine, goods were taken upstream by boat to the post on Jasper Lake, and from there by horse through the passes into what is now British Columbia. Other outfits left Edmonton by horse and then boat for the Lesser Slave Lake post, and by boat for Rocky Mountain House.

Once the outfits were off, the Indians, who had been arriving for days, began trading. The trade itself, at Fort Edmonton and other posts, was accompanied by an elaborate ceremony, which emphasized equality between the whites and natives. The chief factor shook hands with the chiefs as they arrived. Then a flag was raised, and a salute fired. The pipe of peace was lit and passed around. Speeches took up the rest of the day. Gift-giving was very important, and the tobacco, powder, and liquor that the natives received symbolized their tie with the traders. The traders honoured the leaders of bands by giving them scarlet coats, trousers, and hats, and extra presents of tobacco and liquor. The next day trading began.

The Indians, already experienced traders from centuries before the Europeans arrived, refused to do business if they were unsatisfied. Before the amalgamation of the HBC and NWC in 1821, they played one company against another. Credit was an important part of the trade: Indians were entrusted with a certain quantity of goods in the fall on the understanding that they would repay their debt in the spring. From the company's standpoint, this kept them in debt and obligated them to deal with the company. But in practice, the Indians sometimes refused to pay up, pleading either poverty or sickness. Or they might simply leave the area and go to another post. A lively debate continues among fur-trade historians over whether shrewd traders exploited the natives, or whether the natives themselves controlled the terms of the trade.

Those employees who stayed all year at the trading posts spent much of their time hunting for buffalo, moose, or deer to supply the post with fresh meat. In addition, Indian and Métis hunters killed buffalo on the plains to supply meat. At Fort Edmonton during the winter, native and Métis women made snowshoes, cut and made shirts for the trade, and made pemmican to supply the brigades that carried the furs to Hudson Bay by boat in the spring. When spring finally arrived, trains of horses and boats began arriving from other posts, and incoming furs were inspected, packed, and loaded onto boats for their long journey to the sea. By mid-May, the brigade was dispatched to York Fort on Hudson Bay, and most of the men departed for the summer.

The fur-trade era was a period of equality between whites and Indians, when the Indians went about their own lives. The two groups met briefly at the posts, and exchanged goods. Each received from the other what it could not produce.

The Rise of the Métis

Traders in both fur-trade companies took Indian wives for companionship, for possible trading alliances with Indian bands, and for survival. The Indian women made the traders' clothing, footwear, snowshoes, and toboggans, repaired their canoes, and cooked their meals. The traders learned the customs and languages of the tribes from their wives. The mixed-blood children of the European traders and their Indian wives became known as Métis in French, and half-breeds in English.

Their culture had its roots in both European and Indian traditions. Bilingual and bicultural, the Métis were an indispensable part of the fur trade. They also adapted European technology to the prairies. Their two-wheeled ox-drawn carts, called Red River carts, could carry loads of a thousand pounds roughly twenty miles a day. An adaptation of the small cart used by the French Canadians in the St. Lawrence Valley, Red River carts transported furs and other trade goods between the Red River and Fort Edmonton.

While most Métis in the early nineteenth century lived at the junction of the Red and Assiniboine rivers in what became Manitoba, there were Métis settlements from the 1790s at Lac La Biche, 140 miles (224 kilometres) northeast of Fort Edmonton, and from the 1830s at Lac Ste. Anne, 50 miles (80 kilometres) west of Fort Edmonton. During the 1860s, Métis buffalo hunters left the Red River and moved west, increasing the numbers of Métis in the region that became Alberta.

In 1853, when Father Albert Lacombe joined the Roman Catholic mission at Lac Ste. Anne (first established in 1842), he found the land was swampy and subject to early frosts. In 1861 he founded a new mission for the Métis north of Fort Edmonton, which was named St. Albert after his patron saint. He hoped to educate the Métis in agriculture to prepare them for the day when they could no longer rely on the buffalo. An economic as well as spiritual adviser, Lacombe organized a brigade of Red River carts to transport goods to and from Red River. By 1870, St. Albert had become the largest settlement west of Red River, with a population of a thousand settlers, both Métis and white. Another Métis settlement flourished seasonally during the winters from 1872 to 1877 at Buffalo Lake in central Alberta. Here Métis hunted the rapidly diminishing buffalo herds for robes to trade as well as for meat.

Father Albert Lacombe, a French Canadian Roman Catholic missionary, with Blackfoot chiefs Crowfoot, left, and Three Bulls in 1886. Lacombe had a long and varied career in Alberta. His relationship with the Blackfoot was particularly close. Missionaries were important intermediaries between whites and natives during the 1870s and 1880s, as larger numbers of whites began moving West. (*Glenbow Archives NA-1654-1*)

Native Religion and the Christian Missionaries

While the cultural impact of the fur trade on Indians was indirect, the impact of the missionaries was direct and intentional. The missionaries, who arrived beginning in the 1840s, represented a number of different denominations. They worked to replace the fur trade with agriculture, as they believed that a settled, agricultural existence was essential to both "civilization" and Christianity. There are varying assessments of the missionaries' cultural impact, but it is fair to say that it was limited and that Indian culture remained largely intact until the end of the Great Plains buffalo herds and the onset of large-scale white settlement.

The natives had their own religion, which shaped all aspects of their lives. They believed that all living things were inhabited by spirits, and that all things had been created with a purpose by the Great Spirit. A key event in the religious lives of men was the vision quest. Young men left the camp for an isolated, lonely place, often near a mountaintop, where they fasted and prayed in search of a vision, or an encounter with a guardian spirit. If a young man were blessed, a supernatural being appeared and gave the vision seeker prayers and special powers, and imposed various restrictions on his behaviour. These spirit helpers could be game animals, birds, or other natural beings. Spirits such as the sun, birds, and animals were friendly, while others were believed to be evil.

The Plains Indians made sacred bundles called medicine bundles, which they believed helped them to ward off danger. These bundles contained articles that were regarded as having been assigned to the bundle owner by a spirit power, including such items as buffalo horn bonnets, skins of owls or eagles, or bear paws. A bundle, including the rituals, songs, and items that went with it, such as pipes, sweet grass, and paint, could be transferred through gift or purchase.

Among the Blackfoot, Cree, and Stoney, the most important religious ceremony was the Sun Dance, held in the summer. This ceremony embodied their religious world view, and was an annual renewal of faith in their place in the universe. Each year, they asked the sun to return with its warmth and life. The Sun Dance marked the high point of the year. People who had been separated for the long, cold months of winter joined together in a joyous reunion to feast, play games, and socialize. Tribal societies met to select new members and reinforce tribal ties among smaller bands.

The Sun Dance lasted for several days, and was conducted around a circular medicine lodge with a sacred centre pole. At the Sun Dance camp, men sometimes underwent self-inflicted torture, seeing their pain as an offering to the spirit powers. Other religious rituals included taking sweatbaths (which were a form of spiritual cleansing), and smoking sweetgrass.

Some men and women became shamans because of their special gifts, which, it was believed, enabled them to contact the supernatural world. Shamans could cure others by invoking the power of spirit helpers, or by dispensing potions from plants. Views of an afterlife varied among native peoples. The Chipewyan and Slavey believed that the souls of the dead were helped by spirits of otters and loons as they travelled through the earth and crossed a lake to a place where life began again.

The missionaries encountered native religions and cultures with world views very different from their own. Misunderstandings created by the differences between the natives' world view and that of the missionaries were profound. Shamans and missionaries vied with each other for influence, just as Roman Catholic and Protestant missionaries competed with each other. Though they faced vast cultural and linguistic differences, the missionaries had the advantage of being linked with their culture's more sophisticated technology. Whites were possessors of potent "supernatural" powers such as copper kettles, guns, compasses, telescopes, magnets, writing, and mirrors. Anyone with such potent "medicine" deserved at least to be listened to, even if only out of curiosity. The Blackfoot, who associated the origins of whites with the supernatural, believed that Robert Rundle, the first Methodist missionary in Alberta, had stepped from a piece of paper that had fallen from the sky.

In Red River, the first missionaries were Roman Catholics in 1818, followed by Anglicans and then Methodists. Roman Catholic missionaries travelled through the Alberta region in 1838, but the first long-term missionary was the Methodist Robert Rundle, who arrived from England in 1840. The HBC originally hoped that Methodist missionaries might help relieve the company of caring for destitute Indians, and maintain a cheap and docile labour force for the fur trade. But Rundle quickly came into conflict with Rowand over the issue of Sabbath observance, as Rundle did not want Indians working on Sunday. Rowand saw the clergy as meddlesome, noting that "The worst thing for the trade is these ministers and priests—the natives will never work half so well now—they like praying and singing."[6] The greenhorn Rundle struggled to learn Cree and eventually mastered it. He worked in the area for eight years, spending time at Lesser Slave Lake Fort, Fort Assiniboine, Rocky Mountain House, and Gull Lake under hardships that tested his physical and emotional endurance. He made two trips south into Blackfoot country, but his only lasting success was with the Cree and Stoney, among whom he made a few converts. Though his own impact was slight, partly because of effective competition from Roman Catholic missionaries, his follower, Benjamin Sinclair, started a mission at Pigeon Lake in 1848.

The Methodist work remained largely dormant until the mid-1850s. It was revived with the arrival in 1855 of missionaries Thomas Woolsey at Edmonton and an Ojibwa convert from Ontario, Rev. Henry Steinhauer. When he was about ten, the Methodists had changed Steinhauer's name from his original native name in honour of an American benefactor who provided money for his education. At Whitefish Lake, Steinhauer encouraged native families to become self-sufficient farmers. He believed that once the natives were Christianized, they would "naturally crave and desire the blessing and comforts of civilized habits."[7] By "civilized habits," Steinhauer meant agriculture, literacy, and European forms of dress, manners, medical practices, and household customs. He hoped his mission station could become a "little Jerusalem," a beacon of light to Indians conforming to traditional lifestyles and religion. He believed Christianity could redeem natives from what he called their "dark and chaotic mind."[8] Though his missionary work was slow and often discouraging, Steinhauer helped prepare his followers for the disappearance of the buffalo.

Steinhauer was followed by the father-and-son team of George and John McDougall, who came from Ontario in 1862. George McDougall was appointed the Methodists' western superintendent in 1862. The McDougalls built a new mission seventy miles (112 kilometres) downstream from Edmonton and named it Victoria in honour of the British Queen. Here they attracted many settlers of mixed ancestry, mainly English-speaking. George McDougall ran the mission from 1863 to 1871, and built a complex with a house, school, and church.

One of the native leaders who helped the Methodists in the mid-nineteenth century was Maskepetoon ("Broken Arm"), a prominent Cree leader whom Rundle had converted to Methodism. In the early 1840s, Maskepetoon, who had previously been known as an important warrior, had a dream that convinced him needless killing was wrong, and he began seeking peace with the Blackfoot. He courageously entered into a pact to end the constant fighting; the pact was concluded near present-day Wetaskiwin, which means Hills of Peace. In 1869, Maskepetoon was killed by a Blackfoot when he and a small party of Cree were seeking another peace pact with the Blackfoot.

John McDougall, who had a long and prominent career in the west, first established a mission among the Stoney in the 1860s. In 1864 the young McDougall married Abigail Steinhauer, daughter of Henry Steinhauer, and her native background undoubtedly gave McDougall more credibility as a missionary to the natives. But Abigail died in 1871, leaving him with three small children. McDougall returned to Ontario. There he met and married Eliza Boyd, whom he then took on a honeymoon trip back into the Northwest. They finished their journey to Alberta in winter on a horse-drawn toboggan.

In 1873 the McDougalls, father and son, chose Morley, one of the traditional Stoney winter camping grounds, as the site of a mission station. There they built a church and school. George McDougall's efforts were cut short in January 1876, when he became lost on the prairies during a buffalo hunt and froze to death.

John McDougall continued the missionary work and played a prominent role in a number of transitions in the region. In his efforts to establish agriculture among the Indians, McDougall was responsible for bringing the first cattle to southern Alberta. His reports of the disastrous impact of American whisky traders on the Plains Indians in the 1860s helped convince the Canadian government to establish the North-West Mounted Police (NWMP) in 1874. He also helped prepare the Indians for the arrival of the NWMP, was present at the signing of Treaty No. 7 in 1877, and later served on federal government commissions of inquiry on Indians and the Russian pacifist sect, the Doukhobors.

The Methodist missions to the Cree and Stoney had a permanent effect, but it was the Roman Catholics who would have a much greater impact on Alberta's natives. (Today, three-fifths of Alberta's natives are nominally Catholic.) The first Roman Catholic missionary in the province was Father Jean-Baptiste Thibault, who arrived in 1842. Methodist Rundle recorded his distressed reaction to his competitor:

> Several of my old friends among the Indians, both men and women, keep away from me. I went to some of their tents but it was no use. O my God! when shall these things end! The Priest was telling them yesterday that neither the Governor or the Queen had any right to send missionaries, the power belonged to the Pope.[9]

The French-based Oblate Order provided the manpower for the Catholic missions in the West, and a string of illustrious missionaries left their marks, and their names, as witnessed by the towns of Lacombe, Leduc, Vegreville, and Grouard, among others. Father Alexander Taché, who was to become one of the great leaders of the Roman Catholic Church in western Canada, followed Thibault into northern Alberta and began missionary work among the Chipewyan and Cree Indians at Fort Chipewyan in September 1847. The Oblates established other missions at Lac La Biche in 1853 and at Dunvegan in 1866.

The mission at Lac La Biche, established among a number of Métis families, was astride one of the important fur-trade routes linking the Churchill and Athabasca river systems, one of the routes between Hudson Bay and British Columbia. The Oblates subsequently turned the mission at Lac La Biche into a key point in a chain of communication linking the south with missions in the Mackenzie watershed. Father Taché pioneered in testing the navigability of the middle portion of the Athabasca River as he set out by canoe from Lac La Biche to Fort Chipewyan. From the 1860s through the next three decades, scows and barges conveyed supplies northward from the waterfront warehouses at Lac La Biche to distant Arctic missions.

Perhaps the best-known and best-loved Oblate was Father Albert Lacombe, a French Canadian born in 1827. Raised on a farm near Montreal, he had learned to do everything for himself, the perfect training for the rugged life he led on the plains. While studying for the priesthood, he had talked to a missionary from the West and determined to work there. After journeying to Fort Edmonton in 1852, he learned Cree, worked in the nearby mission of Lac Ste. Anne, and in 1861 established St. Albert as a home for Métis.

From 1865 to 1871, this "Man of the Good Heart," as he was known by the Blackfoot, travelled among the Blackfoot and Cree, gained their confidence, and learned Blackfoot. He tried to reconcile the two tribes and stop warfare between them. Because of the trust he inspired, Lacombe was an important intermediary among police, government authorities, railway personnel, and the Blackfoot during the 1870s and 1880s, when significant numbers of whites came West. Before his death in 1916, Lacombe also established an agricultural mission, St. Paul de Métis, among the Métis, promoted French Canadian immigration to the West, fought to protect Roman Catholic schools, and established an Indian "industrial school" among the Blackfoot on the Highwood River and an Old Folks Home in Midnapore. The industrial school was a residential school that took native children away from their parents to teach them skills that theoretically would enable them to succeed in the settlers' world.

As a French Canadian, Lacombe was exceptional among the Oblates, since most of them came directly from France. For much of his life in Alberta, Lacombe reported to the French-born Vital-Justin Grandin, who in 1871 became the Roman Catholic bishop of the newly created diocese of St. Albert, which covered much of present-day Alberta, Saskatchewan, and northern Manitoba. Grandin had arrived in the west in 1854 to work among the Indians and Métis, and despite his poor health, dedicated himself to bringing Roman Catholicism to them. From the 1870s onward, he lobbied the Canadian government for funding to aid agriculture, education, and health care among the native peoples, and until his death in 1902, led the battle for the preservation of state-supported Roman Catholic schools in the Northwest.

The Oblates worked closely with the Grey Nuns, a Canadian religious order that began in New France. Together they established mission posts across northern Alberta and preserved a French Catholic presence in the West. In 1859 three Grey Nuns arrived by Red River cart at Lac Ste. Anne. There they began a school for native children. They moved to St. Albert in 1863, following Father Lacombe, and started a convent, school, and orphanage, and later (in 1891) a hospital. Their work among natives eventually expanded to include French Canadian and other Roman Catholic settlers. The nuns were among the first educated white women in western Canada, and their legacy remains in the many schools and hospitals that they founded, such as the General Hospital in Edmonton and the Holy Cross Hospital in Calgary.

The Anglicans, like the Methodists and Catholics, depended on large missionary organizations to support their activities. The British Church Missionary Society in London, motivated by the reform impulse of the Victorian era, sent out missionaries to bring a settled, agricultural life to potential native converts. The Anglicans concentrated their work with Alberta natives among the Blackfoot Confederacy and in the northwest. During the 1880s, they began mission farms at Fort Vermilion, Fort Dunvegan, and Shaftesbury Flats (near the present town of Peace River).

Of the three major missionary denominations, the Roman Catholics were by far the most successful, particularly in the North. Their ties to the French-speaking Métis provided a link to the latter's Cree relatives and gave them a better understanding of native culture. They arrived early and were well-organized. Single priests and nuns, with their vows of poverty, were dedicated labourers, willing to engage in strenuous itinerant work with a high level of commitment. Many Roman Catholics were also more willing than Protestants to accommodate native religion, and placed less stress on eradicating all elements of native culture and religious belief.

The missionaries were agents of cultural change who attempted to transform the native's world view and way of life. Missionary work by different Christian religious groups created divisions within and between bands, and undermined the authority of established native leaders. But the missionaries also tried to protect natives from many of the worst aspects of white civilization, including the impact of disease and alcohol. Missionaries undermined the natives' way of life, but they also contributed to an understanding of native languages, and to the study of native culture.

Fur traders and missionaries were forerunners of western "civilization." While native society could absorb, and even benefit from, changes introduced by the fur traders, and could pay little heed to the missionaries, they were totally unprepared for the changes that swept across the West in the late nineteenth century.

Alberta's natives lived in the region for at least 12,000 years before the arrival of Europeans. The arrival of horses in the 1730s changed the Plains Indians' way of life, making possible easier transportation and hunting but also leading to more intense intertribal warfare. *(Glenbow Archives NA 1700-9)*

People in central Canada, who had previously ignored the West, began casting covetous eyes. Momentous changes were in the offing as western Canada began to be seen as part of a vision of national and imperial greatness.

By the 1850s, 1860s, and 1870s, the pace of cultural and economic change in the region had increased and the relationship of relative equality between whites and Indians that had marked the fur-trade era changed dramatically. The dominance of the great fur-trading company, the Hudson's Bay Company, began to break down as new elements, particularly independent American traders, began making inroads. Game declined dramatically, at the same time that white intrusion accelerated, undermining the basis of cooperation between Indians and whites that had developed in the late 1700s and early 1800s. The evolution of the economy and society in the region that eventually became known as Alberta, sparsely populated and limited to an economy of hunting, fishing, and gathering for thousands of years, was about to accelerate dramatically. The tide of western "civilization" swept into the region, changing forever the native way of life.

CHAPTER TWO

"Civilizing" the Northwest: 1850–1885

The advance of the central Canadian frontier challenged the control of the Hudson's Bay Company (HBC) over the West and threatened the native way of life. During the 1850s and 1860s, several new developments changed central Canadians' ideas of the West. Once viewed as a wasteland suited only to the fur trade, the Northwest gradually came to be seen as an unspoiled wilderness with much potential. Expansionist forces in Ontario came together to push for the acquisition of the West; Confederation in 1867 was partly a response to these forces.

With the cooperation of the British government, the new Canadian nation purchased Rupert's Land from the HBC in 1869. Subsequently, as part of the new Canadian government's efforts to settle the area and create a viable transcontinental economy, the federal government sent the North-West Mounted Police (NWMP) westward to establish law and order. It also arranged for treaties with the natives, prepared the way for settlement, and gave massive support to the building of a transcontinental railway, the Canadian Pacific Railway (CPR). The railway was completed through Alberta in 1883. The period from the 1850s to 1885 brought many changes that set the stage for the displacement of the fur-trade economy by an agricultural economy. The failed Métis and native resistance against the Canadian government in 1885 was centred in Saskatchewan, but it had strong reverberations in the area that was to become Alberta. It marked the end of native power in the Northwest.

Expansionism, Confederation, and the West

Recent historical studies have stressed how, during the 1850s, a group of Canadians (mostly in Canada West, now Ontario) convinced themselves that acquiring and developing the Hudson's Bay Company territories was essential to the future of Canada. Since the West had great economic potential and a railway was crucial to possessing it, and since only a union of British North American colonies could afford such a transcontinental scheme, the desire to acquire the West was one of the driving forces behind Canadian Confederation in 1867.

Prior to the 1850s, central Canadians had seen the Northwest through the eyes of fur traders, who approached it through the Hudson Bay or Great Lakes fur-trade routes. Canadians consequently saw the Northwest as predominantly cold, desolate, and isolated. They saw the grassland of the southern prairies as a northern extension of a Great American desert. The absence of trees they took as a sign that the area was infertile. The HBC perpetuated this image of the region as suitable for fur trading only.

A number of factors in the 1850s revised the negative image of the Northwest. Writers and artists such as Paul Kane, who visited the West in the mid-1840s, romanticized the West, stressing its natural beauty, solitude, and majesty, and portraying the native peoples as noble savages in harmony with nature. These images of a romantic, pristine wilderness enhanced its attractiveness and heightened interest in settlement.

During the 1850s a small group of expansionists began demanding that the Canadas (the union after 1840 of parts of present-day Ontario and Quebec) acquire Rupert's Land from the HBC. They worried about Canada's economic future once reciprocity with the United States ended. They also worried about possible American designs on the Northwest. The commercial elite of Ontario began thinking of the West as a potential hinterland for eastern industrial interests: an area that could supply the East with raw materials and provide a market for manufactured goods. They also began thinking of a transcontinental railway that would unite Canada economically and serve as a link to Asia for the British Empire. One of the strongest reasons for a new interest in the Northwest came with the disappearance in the 1850s of Ontario's agricultural frontier and the resulting exodus of farmers to the American Midwest. As one of the expansionists put it, the Canadas' decision concerning westward expansion would determine "whether this country shall ultimately become a petty State, or one of the Great Powers of the earth."[1]

In 1857 a committee of the British House of Commons studied the question of the renewal of the HBC charter. The HBC officials found their views of the unsuitability of the West for agriculture challenged by Canadian expansionists. Because of the contradictory evidence that the committee heard, more scientific information was needed. Consequently, in 1857, both the Canadian and British governments sent scientific expeditions westward.

Captain John Palliser, a wealthy member of the Irish gentry with influential government friends, led the British expedition. His main qualification for doing so seemed to be his enthusiasm for the West, gained from a hunting trip to the western United States a few years earlier. Palliser secured the support of the Royal Geographical Society, and then the British government, for his plans to explore the potential of the plains south of the North Saskatchewan River and determine the nature of the southern passes through the Rocky Mountains. The Palliser Expedition, which worked from 1857 to 1860, included among others Dr. James Hector, geologist and naturalist, and Lieutenant Thomas Blakiston, magnetical observer. The group collected geological, magnetic, and other scientific data, and provided information on the native peoples. Their report predicted the difficult problems of transportation from the Great Lakes to the prairies and through the Rockies. They warned that there was a semi-arid belt, now known as Palliser's Triangle, that stretched across the American border into the prairies, but they also reported that there was a fertile belt well suited for stock-raising and agriculture to the north of this arid triangle.

The expedition of the government of the Canadas in 1857 and 1858, headed by geologist Henry Youle Hind, was more enthusiastic than Palliser's about the agricultural potential of the West. Despite their reservations about the southern plains, both reports encouraged those who wanted to open the West. They confirmed the view that although there were difficulties, the area had substantial agricultural potential.

After Confederation in 1867, the Canadian government negotiated with the British government and the HBC for the transfer of Rupert's Land. By the 1860s, the HBC was more amenable to surrendering control since it was under new owners, who believed that land sales might be more profitable than the fur trade. In 1869 negotiations were completed by the three parties for the transfer of land to the Canadian government. The company received a cash payment of 300,000 pounds and one-twentieth of the land in the fertile belt, and was free to carry on its trade as a private corporation. In 1870 the area that would become Alberta became essentially a colony of the Canadian government. It was administered as part of the North-West Territories (NWT) by a federally appointed lieutenant governor and council.

In 1870, by central Canadian standards, this area was relatively unpopulated. In addition to the few thousand natives, whose numbers were rapidly being depleted by disease and the effects of the whisky trade, there were ten Hudson's Bay Company fur-trade posts and eight mission stations, including the Roman Catholic centre at St. Albert. Edmonton House, the largest and the administrative centre for eight of the fur-trade posts, had a population of only 150.

The Plains Indians, the Whisky Trade, and the North-West Mounted Police

In 1870, without their knowledge, the natives of the Northwest became part of Canada. Simultaneously they faced a smallpox epidemic. The Plains Indians had already suffered huge losses from a smallpox epidemic in 1780–81, during which the Indian population on the prairies had decreased by an estimated half. Another epidemic, in 1837-38, carried away perhaps as many as three-quarters of the Blackfoot, Blood, Peigan, Sarcee, and Assiniboine. The Cree had been spared this latter epidemic because neighbouring HBC traders had vaccinated them before the disease spread into their territory. When John Palliser crossed the plains in 1857-59, he estimated that there were 600 Blackfoot, 2800 Blood, 4400 Peigan, and 1100 Sarcee. The last smallpox epidemic, in 1869-70, killed 2200 of the Blackfoot Confederacy.

Sensing the weakness of the Blood because of disease and the impact of American whisky traders, in October 1870 a large Cree and Assiniboine war party attacked a band of Blood on the banks of what is now known as the Oldman River, within the present city limits of Lethbridge. The Cree were unaware of the presence of the Blood's allies, the Peigan, who had fled from their Montana hunting grounds because of the violence of American army troops. The Peigan, armed with repeating rifles, joined the battle against the Cree and defeated them, killing three hundred. The Peigan and Blood lost forty men and women. This terrible slaughter was one of the last large Indian battles in North America, and further weakened the Indians just as they were facing the onslaught of white "civilization."

The growing impact of whisky traders from Montana was even more lethal to the Blackfoot than intertribal warfare. During the 1850s and early 1860s, the Blackfoot traded with both the HBC to the north and the American Fur Company to the south, although the bulk of their trade was in buffalo robes with the Americans. The Americans had established Fort Benton, Montana Territory, on the Missouri River in 1846. From Fort Benton they shipped buffalo robes that were used to make buffalo coats. (By the 1870s, buffalo hides were also being used to make belts for eastern industrial machinery.) The Blackfoot were never as dependent as the Woodland Indians on traders' goods, but the fur trade still effected many changes in their way of life. It had an impact on their culture, social organization, and intertribal warfare. All these changes could be absorbed, but the whisky trade, which began in the 1860s, threatened to destroy their way of life, just at the crucial time when the Canadian government extended its power westward.

The collapse of the American Fur Company in 1864 created a power vacuum that American whisky traders, many of them hardened Civil War veterans, soon filled. Partial enforcement of laws against the whisky trade by U.S. marshals during the 1860s prompted Montana whisky traders to move northward into the southwest part of the North-West Territories, where constituted authority was absent. The promise of gold in the Northwest also attracted prospectors, particularly those who had grown restless in the Montana goldfields. One expedition in 1868 consisted of twenty-five men, including the colourful J. J. Healy, Irish immigrant, Indian war veteran, and frontiersman, who soon turned to whisky trading.

In 1869 Healy and his partner Alfred Hamilton (a frontiersman and trader) built the first whisky-trading post, Fort Hamilton, at the junction of the Belly and St. Mary rivers, near present-day Lethbridge. The fort at first consisted of a series of log huts linked by a picket fence. After it accidentally burned to the ground, Healy and Hamilton replaced it with a much larger one, which became known as Fort Whoop-Up. It included a fourteen-foot stockade topped by sharpened stakes, two bastions with brass cannons and loopholes for rifles, and roofs covered with earth. They placed iron bars over doors, windows, and chimneys to protect them from the Indians. During the first winter's trade, Healy and Hamilton netted $50,000. The size of the trade grew from about five thousand robes in the first full year of Whoop-Up's operation to over sixty thousand by 1875. (When the Mounted Police sent Healy packing in 1874, he became an editor, sheriff, and hotel owner in Montana, before reappearing in Canada during the Yukon Gold Rush in the late 1890s as a miner and manager of a transportation and trading company. Hamilton later became a Montana sheriff and member of the Montana legislature.)

With the success of this whisky-selling venture, scores of independent traders crossed into British North America in search of the buffalo that were vanishing in the western United States before the

Blood Indians at Fort Whoop-Up in the early 1870s. The post was first established by American whisky traders in 1869, one of forty whisky posts in southern Alberta. These posts debauched the natives, exchanging rot-gut whisky for buffalo robes and furs, with devastating results for native society. (*Glenbow Archives NA 550-18*)

guns of the buffalo hunters. The "Whoop-Up Trail," linking Fort Benton with a score of remote whisky trading posts, became well-travelled and deeply rutted as bull and mule trains moved north with supplies and back with robes and furs. Most of the approximately forty whisky posts in southern Alberta were located along the Oldman and Belly rivers. They consisted of shanties—rough sod-roofed log structures that could be quickly built and just as quickly abandoned. The "supplies" included watered-down liquor with added tea leaves and tobacco. The deadly concoction also might contain pain-killer, red peppers, ginger, soap, red ink, and molasses mixed in with the spirits to give it "body" and colour.

The Blackfoot had never made alcohol and had no social controls to deal with it. Facing disease and the gradual disappearance of the buffalo, many Blackfoot succumbed to the drug and turned on each other in the aftermath. In the winter of 1872–73, an estimated seventy Blood died in violent conflicts. In the five-year period of the whisky trade, Red Crow, a noted warrior who became chief of the Bloods in 1870, killed his own brother and two fellow tribesmen in drunken quarrels, and saw the deaths of two uncles, his father-in-law, his father, and his wife.

Traders were callous in their dealings with the natives. Twenty-five-year-old Donald W. Davis, an American veteran of the Indian wars who had come west anxious to make a fortune, worked at Fort Whoop-Up. In 1873 he wrote home to his father in Vermont in an offhand fashion that his "work is not without danger as it is trading with Indians altho I have never been hurt or scared yet had to kill 2 last winter on act of stealing horses."[2] Davis, who in 1887 became the first member representing Alberta in the Canadian Parliament, was by no means the worst offender.

The devastation wrought by the whisky trade and the lack of legal authority in the West was impressed upon the government by the HBC, by missionaries such as John McDougall, and by Captain William Francis Butler of the British army and Colonel Patrick Robertson-Ross of the Canadian militia. The latter two were commissioned by the government in the early 1870s to report on Indian tribes and the degree of violence in the West. Prime Minister John A. Macdonald had been planning a force of mounted riflemen since 1869. He wanted to avoid costly Indian wars like those that had marked American expansion westward because they discouraged settlement. The plans had to be postponed because of the troubles in Red River in 1870, and it was not until 1873 that the government introduced an act creating the North-West Mounted Police. The event that finally forced the government to take action was the massacre of thirty Indians in the Cypress Hills (near the present southeast boundary of Alberta) by ten American and Canadian "wolfers" in the spring of 1873.

Wolfers poisoned buffalo carcasses as bait for wolves, whose skins they sought. They formed a particularly vile group among the frontiersmen operating in southern Alberta, and they angered the Indians because their bait also killed many Indian pack dogs. After a group of Indians (probably Blackfoot) raided a camp of wolfers and made off with about forty horses, the wolfers returned seeking revenge. Without provocation, but with repeating rifles, they attacked a camp of Assiniboine Indians, killing and wounding men, women, and children.

When Macdonald received news of the massacre, he had already decided to recruit a mounted police force to send West to eliminate the whisky trade. This news made him act. He hoped the police could prevent conflicts between whites and natives, awe potentially rebellious Métis, and assert Canadian sovereignty over the Indians and over the region.

In a march that has assumed mythic significance in Canadian history, three hundred men (recruited mostly from central Canada and Britain) trekked west from Manitoba in July 1874. They wore the red tunic of the British Army, which the government believed would be of great symbolic significance to the Indians. They were led by the Commissioner of the North-West Mounted Police, George Arthur French, a military officer on loan to the Canadian government from Britain. Other officers included Colonel James Macleod, a thirty-seven-year-old Scot who had come to Ontario with his family as a boy, become a lawyer, and then joined the military. Macleod later replaced French as commissioner, and subsequently had a distinguished career as a judge in the North-West Territories.

Most of the officers in the first years of the force were Canadian-born upper-class men with some military background. Many owed their appointments to Conservative patronage. They thought of themselves as an elite, and their strong sense of social hierarchy influenced the social structure that eventually emerged in southern Alberta. The enlisted ranks included clerks, tradesmen, former British soldiers, and farmers. Although many were Canadians, there were also many Britishers anxious for adventure in the colonies, including Inspector Francis Dickens, a son of English novelist Charles Dickens. Dickens was a small, morose, and introverted man who was later described by his superiors as "a very poor officer of no promise, physically weak in constitution, his habits not affording a good example."[3]

The NWMP trek westward, which began in July 1874 from Dufferin, Manitoba, was almost a disaster. Riding westward were 275 officers and men accompanied by 310 horses, 142 oxen, 93 cattle for slaughter, 114 Red River carts with 20 Métis drivers, 73 wagons, two field guns, two brass mortars, several mowing machines for hay cutting, portable forges, and field kitchens. Partly because of poor planning, lack of food, water, and fuel made their journey across the southern prairies harrowing. When they first arrived in what is now southern Alberta, ragged and starving, they could not even find Fort Whoop-Up. The Mounties' Métis guides knew the territory only as far west as the Cypress Hills. The country of their enemies, the Blackfoot, was unknown to them. Desperately needing supplies, French led a group south to Fort Benton, Montana, and bought provisions on credit. The Fort Benton merchants, including I. G. Baker and T. C. Power, who in fact had supplied the illegal whisky trade, now saw a new source of business, and promised to help the

North-West Mounted Police at Fort Saskatchewan in the early 1890s. The police were well established before settlers began arriving. Following their prominent role in putting down the 1885 North-West Rebellion, the Mounted Police began turning their attention to the problems of incoming white settlers. *(Glenbow Archives NA 1177-4)*

Fort Macleod in 1878. This was the centre of Mounted Police operations in the Northwest until 1882. The Mounted Police asserted sovereignty over the Northwest, drove out American whisky traders, tried to establish friendly relations with the natives, and prepared the way for the signing of treaties. *(Glenbow Archives NA 354-12)*

Mounted Police find Fort Whoop-Up. French returned east to Manitoba to his headquarters, leaving Macleod in charge.

Power provided Macleod with the services of a mixed-blood guide named Jerry Potts. Short and laconic, Potts, who became legendary in early NWMP history, had been born in Montana about 1840 to a Scots fur trader and a Blood woman. He had lived with and fought alongside the Blackfoot, but later worked at various whisky posts. He served the NWMP for the next twenty-two years.

In October the NWMP, with the aid of Potts, located Fort Whoop-Up. The one trader there invited Macleod to dinner. The rest of the traders, warned of the NWMP arrival, had cached their alcohol and cleared out. On Pott's recommendation, the NWMP decided to build their fort on an island in the Oldman River, where there were trees for building materials and pasture for horses. They named it Fort Macleod.

The arrival of the NWMP led to the rapid decline of the whisky trade. The police soon established other posts to help suppress the trade. In August 1875, fifty Mounted Police under a French Canadian, Inspector Ephrem Brisebois, opened a Mounted Police post, Fort Calgary, at the junction of the Bow and Elbow rivers.

The police made a few arrests for whisky trading, and most of the traders either left or changed their business. One of the most notable of these was whisky trader D. W. Davis, who became manager of northern trade for I. G. Baker and Company and, among other activities, helped the NWMP build Fort Macleod. Davis also managed the I. G. Baker store in Calgary during the late 1870s. He later turned to ranching, and from 1887 to 1896 served in Ottawa as Alberta's Member of Parliament. A Conservative, he became a strong spokesman for the ranching industry and part owner of the *Calgary Herald*, the voice of the cattlemen.

While one column of the Mounted Police was marching westward toward Fort Whoop-Up, another column, led by Inspector W. D. Jarvis, had split off and marched northwest toward Edmonton, travelling by way of the old HBC forts of Fort Ellice and Fort Carleton. They pushed past the Methodist mission at Victoria in October 1874, struggling through bogs where wagons became so deeply mired in mud that they all but disappeared. Two weeks after the Mounted Police reached Fort Whoop-Up, this northern wing was finally welcomed at Fort Edmonton by Chief Factor Richard Hardisty of the HBC.

Hardisty was a fur-trade veteran whose father and grandfather had previously worked for the HBC. He was responsible for the Saskatchewan district of the HBC, a huge area that included much of present-day Alberta and Saskatchewan. He welcomed the police since they could discourage the independent traders, who were bringing whisky to the natives. Hardisty and his brother-in-law, Methodist missionary John McDougall, had previously been asked by the government to explain to the natives that the police were being sent out to protect them and to disperse the whisky traders.

Hardisty and Inspector Jarvis disagreed about where the Mounted Police should build their new post. Hardisty urged them to build across the river from the HBC post on land now occupied by the University of Alberta, but Jarvis chose a site twenty miles (thirty-two kilometres) farther downstream at Fort Saskatchewan. Because of its terrain, this spot appeared to be the logical one for the proposed transcontinental railway to cross the North Saskatchewan River.

Whatever the location of their posts, the arrival of the Mounted Police marked a new era in the history of the West. But their arrival was just one of many developments that were irreversibly changing the region. By October 1874, steamboats were beginning to ply the North Saskatchewan River, and a government contract had been given for a telegraph line from Red River to Edmonton. Government surveyors were also fanning out west of Edmonton, probing possible routes through the Rocky Mountains for the proposed transcontinental railway. While white expansionists saw these developments as the inevitable march of progress, many Indians and Métis worried about what the future might bring.

Indian Treaties and the End of an Era

The arrival of the NWMP saved the Blackfoot Confederacy from further destruction at the hands of the whisky traders. Chief Crowfoot of the Blackfoot welcomed the NWMP as saviours of the Indians from the ravages of the whisky trade. He soon established a strong personal relationship with Colonel Macleod. Forcefully Macleod conveyed the message that once either of them gave his word, he would have to keep it, and that there was one law for both Indians and whites. The NWMP explained that they were there not to steal the land but to protect the inhabitants, and to stop intertribal warfare and horse stealing. The end of the liquor trade did lead to a new era of peace during the late 1870s. The Blackfoot constructed new lodges and began to build up their herds of horses to replace those sold to the whisky traders.

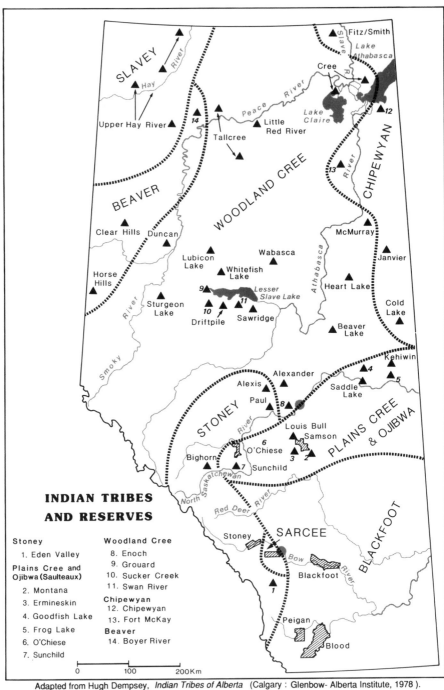

INDIAN TRIBES AND RESERVES

Stoney
1. Eden Valley

Plains Cree and Ojibwa (Saulteaux)
2. Montana
3. Ermineskin
4. Goodfish Lake
5. Frog Lake
6. O'Chiese
7. Sunchild

Woodland Cree
8. Enoch
9. Grouard
10. Sucker Creek
11. Swan River

Chipewyan
12. Chipewyan
13. Fort McKay

Beaver
14. Boyer River

0   100   200Km

Adapted from Hugh Dempsey, *Indian Tribes of Alberta* (Calgary : Glenbow- Alberta Institute, 1978).

40

The Canadian government and the natives both wanted treaties, but for different reasons. In the Royal Proclamation of 1763 (following the British conquest of New France), the British government had established the policy that Indians must agree to the surrender of their territory before settlement could proceed. Despite the view common among settlers that Indians had no title to land because they had failed to farm it, the British practice assumed that aboriginal occupants had certain rights. Under this policy, Indian lands had to be purchased by the government with the consent of the respective band. The government hoped these treaties would formalize the surrender of land and confirm the friendship between the natives and the government, and thereby both protect the Indians and clear the way for a transcontinental railway and white settlement. Once the treaties were signed, the government planned to place the Indians on reserves and work to assimilate them.

The government was particularly concerned about formalizing this friendship so that there would be no chance for the Canadian Plains Indians to join the hostile Sioux who, under Sitting Bull, took refuge in southwestern Saskatchewan in 1876. Several thousand Sioux fled to Canada following their victory over the American General Custer and his troops following Custer's attack on their camps on the Little Big Horn River in Montana.

The NWMP and the missionaries encouraged the Indians to sign treaties. The Indians agreed, partly because of the rapid decline in the game population. Chief Sweetgrass of the Cree, for example, asked the HBC factor in Edmonton to draw up a petition to the government on their behalf in 1871: "Our country is getting ruined of fur bearing animals, hitherto our sole support, and now we are poor and want help."[4]

Under the treaties, in return for the surrender of land and a guarantee to maintain peace, the Indians retained small reserves of land, and were promised hunting and fishing rights and annuities. Treaty No. 6, signed in 1876, covered the Cree land in central Alberta and Saskatchewan. Big Bear, one of the Cree chiefs, saw little value in Treaty No. 6 and refused to sign it. Big Bear had been born about 1825 near Fort Carlton, in present-day Saskatchewan, and by the 1870s was chief of about sixty-five lodges. Athletic and muscular, Big Bear had been fearless and successful on the warpath against other tribes. He felt the treaty would ensure poverty and the destruction of his people's way of life. Fiercely independent, he was not ready to submit to the HBC or any other authority, and following the treaty, he tried to rally other Indians to demand better terms.

Treaty No. 7, signed in September 1877, included the roughly ten thousand Blackfoot, Blood, Peigan, Sarcee, and Stoney in southern Alberta. Many Blackfoot were hesitant, sensing that the treaty meant subjugation to the whites. But Chief Crowfoot and many other tribal leaders trusted the NWMP, and in particular Colonel Macleod, one of the treaty commissioners. They felt their options were shrinking. Crowfoot was a conciliator and diplomat who foresaw the disappearance of the buffalo and knew his people would have to rely on the whites for help. He helped convince other chiefs, such as Blood Chief Red Crow, of the wisdom of signing.

In retrospect, it seems clear that the whites and Indians had different understandings of the meaning of the treaties. The idea of land ownership and disposal of land was foreign to native peoples. To them, land could not be sold. It could no more be given away than the wind. Nor did the Indians have any idea of the numbers of settlers who would come. The Blackfoot believed the treaties would solve the short-term problems of Métis and Cree hunting buffalo on Blackfoot lands, and traders and settlers using land and firewood without payment. Different interpretations by the government and natives of the meaning of the treaties have continued to the present day, and are still the bases of disagreements regarding native land claims.

The late 1870s was a period of great hardship for the Plains Indians. The disappearance of the buffalo on the Canadian side of the border by 1879 had totally undermined their way of life and demoralized them. The destruction of the buffalo transformed a people that was strong, mobile, and independent into one that was culturally dislocated and dependent. Prairie fires drove the remaining buffalo herds southward across the border, and in 1879 many Blackfoot, Blood, Peigan, and Cree, with police encouragement, followed the buffalo into Montana in a last desperate effort to hold onto their way of life. Those remaining in Canada were reduced to hunting rabbits and gophers.

With the final destruction of the buffalo in Montana, the natives returned home. Crowfoot and his followers travelled on foot, having sold their horses to American whisky traders. In 1880 the newly formed Department of Indian Affairs took advantage of the food shortage to induce Indians to go to their reserves. The Indians had to select their reserve lands before they would receive rations of beef and flour.

During the Treaty No. 7 negotiations, Crowfoot had suggested a common reserve for Blackfoot, Blood, and Sarcee. Macleod agreed to this, but the Blood under Red Crow opposed the idea, since the area was distant from their traditional hunting grounds. Eventually they received a new reserve farther south, between the Belly and St. Mary rivers. Chief Bull Head of the Sarcee also objected to a joint reserve, and after a showdown with the NWMP over the issue, in which the Sarcee refused to go to the assigned reserve and the police refused them rations unless they did so, the police gave in and the Sarcee were placed on a reserve along Fish Creek, southwest of Calgary.

Once the Indians were on the reserves, the Canadian government proceeded with its policy of trying to assimilate them to Canadian society. Under the Indian Act, the Indian agent had dictatorial control over the reserve, and Christian churches had similar control over reserve schools. State and church worked together to eliminate the native way of life and replace it with a civilization that they saw as superior. For example, they attempted to stop native religious ceremonies, such as the annual Sun Dances. The agents began teaching agriculture and stock raising, but the system of farming education seldom succeeded, particularly since much of the land was marginal for farming. Schools were plagued by inadequate salaries, incompetent teachers, and irregular attendance.

By the early 1880s, a range of forces converged to bring native discontent to a head. Colonel Macleod had retired in 1880, leaving the natives without the staunch advocate they had come to trust. Administration of Indians was transferred in 1880 from the NWMP to the new Department of Indian Affairs, one that was staffed by political appointees with little or no knowledge of Indians. Chief Crowfoot was also upset in 1883 when surveyors arrived on the Blackfoot Reserve to lay railway lines for the CPR on land to which he felt his tribe had a claim. Only the arrival of Father Lacombe and Edgar Dewdney, Lieutenant Governor of the North-West Territories, convinced Crowfoot to make a new agreement with the government, permitting the railway to cross the reserve.

Government economizing, including a cutback in food rations to Indians, led to widespread hunger in 1883-84, though not outright starvation. This short-sighted policy of economizing led a small number of Indians to join in the Riel Rebellion of 1885. They decided that they had nothing to lose in making a stand against white encroachment.

The Riel Rebellion of 1885

Despite the tremendous displacement that the Indians and Métis in Alberta experienced, very few joined the 1885 North-West Rebellion, led by Métis Louis Riel. In the north, the two Cree bands of Big Bear and Poundmaker took up arms. In the south, Crowfoot and the Blackfoot seriously considered joining in, but in the end stayed out of the conflict.

The bitterness felt by the Métis toward the Canadian government, which had led to the Red River Resistance of 1869–70, erupted again in 1885. This time, it was farther west in the NWT, around the settlement of Batoche (northeast of present-day Saskatoon). Once again, the Métis asked Riel to lead their protest against the federal government's apparent indifference to their grievances. In exile in Montana, Riel had dreamed of a new chosen people, the Métis, led by a prophet of the new world who had a special religious mission. Impatient with an unresponsive federal government and dreaming of a new western nation, in March 1885 Riel led his people into an armed rebellion.

The focus of the rebellion was in Saskatchewan, but for a while it appeared that some Indians in Alberta might join Riel. White newcomers, many of whom had arrived after the completion of the trancontinental Canadian Pacific Railway (CPR) through Alberta in 1883, were afraid that the rebellion might spread and endanger them. Many joined volunteer efforts to both protect themselves and put down the rebellion.

The only large-scale violence in present-day Alberta occurred at Frog Lake, north of what is now Lloydminster. The Cree there had been led by Big Bear. This fiercely independent native leader, after his early rejection of the government's treaty plan, finally had been forced by starvation to sign Treaty No. 6 in 1882, when he and his band took up land near Frog Lake. Big Bear tried to unite the Indians to demand better terms and in 1884 held a thirst dance near Battleford, which brought together over 2000 northern Cree. But Big Bear's hopes for better terms were destroyed as events overtook him.

As the Indians' discontent grew, Big Bear's authority waned. Younger and more aggressive warriors demanded confrontation with the whites. In March 1885, a group of Métis led by Gabriel Dumont ambushed a force of a hundred settler volunteers and NWMP at Duck Lake, killing twelve and wounding many more. When they got word of this, many of Big Bear's warriors decided to join in the uprising. As one of them later explained, "We are doomed, and will be killed one after another by the whites. But before we die, or disappear altogether . . . we must plunder stores and kill as many white people as we can."[5]

The news of the Métis outbreak proved to be the necessary

catalyst for violence. Against Big Bear's objections, the young warriors took several whites hostage and then opened fire, killing nine people, including two priests. The young warriors, recently arrived from the plains, held grudges against the Indian agent, the priests, and other whites. There were other incidents of pillaging of stores at Lac La Biche, Saddle Lake, Beaverhill Lake, Lac Ste. Anne, Bear Hills, and Beaver Lake, but only at Frog Lake did the tension turn to murder.

After the massacre, Big Bear's camp was bitterly divided between the warlike Plains Cree and the more peaceful Woodland Cree. They disagreed about what further action to take. They intimidated NWMP Inspector Francis Dickens into abandoning the nearby fur-trade post of Fort Pitt, and took several traders and their families captive.

Big Bear's warriors hoped the Métis in the Edmonton area would join in the rebellion. Undoubtedly some support existed for Riel among the French-speaking Métis at the mission villages, but there were important differences between them and the Métis 300 miles (480 kilometres) farther east at Batoche. Most of the Métis in the Edmonton area had been born in the region. They had not served with Riel in Red River in 1869–70. Nor had the Métis at St. Albert been angered, like those at Batoche, by government land policy. The St. Albert Métis were also more closely tied to the Roman Catholic Church and more willing to follow their priest's counsel not to join in the rebellion. They were bitter about the killing of the two priests by the Cree at Frog Lake.

Riel and the two bands of Plains Cree who had joined the rebellion tried to convince Crowfoot and the Blackfoot to join. Crowfoot listened to Riel's messengers but refused. He had visited Winnipeg, with its population of 15,000, the previous year, and he knew the power and numbers of the whites. Missionaries and government officials, extra rations, and the visibility of troops also convinced him to remain at peace. His decision was confirmed when Red Crow of the Bloods also refused to take up arms. Although some Blood sympathized with the rebellion, there were also several Blood warriors who offered to fight for the government because of their long-standing hatred of the Cree and Métis.

Response to the Rebellion

The government's earlier reaction to Métis and Indian discontent in the period leading up to the rebellion had been slow, but their response to the outbreak of violence proved swift and decisive. The government mobilized a military force of 8000 men under General Middleton. Middleton marched on the Métis stronghold at Batoche. A second column under Colonel Otter headed to relieve Battleford, which was threatened by a Cree band under Poundmaker, the adopted son of Crowfoot. A third force, the Alberta Field Force, under General Thomas Bland Strange, was sent to reassure panic-stricken residents in Calgary and Edmonton, and to march north to capture the perpetrators of the Frog Lake massacre.

People in Fort Macleod, Calgary, and Edmonton, adjacent to large Indian reserves, were terrified. Of Medicine Hat, established in 1883 on the CPR line, the *Macleod Gazette* of April 11, 1885, reported that "the excitement was intense. Volunteers were enrolled, scouts sent out, and guards put on all over the town. An attack was expected at any moment." Panic was particularly intense in Edmonton, which had a white population of just 125, no train connection, and was surrounded by Métis settlements and Indian reserves. Its telegraph line went dead shortly after the rebellion began. Citizens in Edmonton strengthened the stockade at the Hudson's Bay Company fort, moved most of the town's families into the fort, and began drilling a home guard and moulding lead balls for ammunition.

Strange, who directed military operations in Alberta, was a retired British army officer ranching on a 90,000-acre (36,000-hectare) lease immediately west of the Blackfoot Reserve. He had served in India, and later had headed an artillery school in Quebec. When the rebellion broke out, the rather eccentric and devoutly imperialistic Strange offered his services. He spoke French, which was a decided advantage since the government wanted to include French Canadian soldiers in the military operation. Middleton did not want them to have to fight directly against Riel, but under Strange they could be directed against the Indians.

Strange was authorized to raise a force (which came to be known as the Alberta Field Force) and to take military command of the District of Alberta. He quickly took charge. At a town meeting in Calgary, he directed the organization of a home guard. He also organized thirty-five cowboys into the Alberta Mounted Rifles under Major Hatton, his ranch foreman.

By April 15, when the first of his troops set out for Edmonton, Calgary was alive with soldiers and the merchants did a brisk trade outfitting the expedition. The Field Force included two units of the NWMP, the 65th Militia Battalion from Montreal, the Winnipeg Light

Troop of Rocky Mountain Rangers at Medicine Hat during the North-West
Rebellion in 1885. Made up mostly of cowboys and ranchers, the Rangers patrolled
southern Alberta without incident. Chief Scout "Kootenai" Brown is on the far
right. *(Glenbow Archives NA 619-2)*

Infantry, and the 9th Battalion from Quebec City. Sam Steele, one of
the veteran officers of the NWMP, was placed in charge of the scouts of
the Field Force. Another 150 men from the Fort Macleod area,
including cowboys, ranchers, and "Kootenai" Brown, the trader and
mountain man from the Waterton area, received government authori-
zation to form themselves into the Rocky Mountain Rangers. They
patrolled the area between High River and Medicine Hat, including
the telegraph line then under construction between the two new
towns of Medicine Hat and Lethbridge.

Irish-born and well-educated, John George "Kootenai" Brown
was an example of a Briton who had been attracted to the life of the
frontier in the western territories and who, when crisis arose, sided
with the forces of British "civilization." He had served in the British
army in India in the 1850s and had moved to the British Columbia
goldfields in 1861, where he worked as a miner and constable. Later he
became a buffalo hunter in Manitoba, and a pony express rider for the
United States Army. In this hazardous occupation, he was captured by
Sitting Bull and his Sioux Indians. He avoided death by escaping
naked at night. Brown moved to Montana, where he joined a band of
Métis buffalo hunters and married a young Métis woman. His life as a
wolfer led to violence when he killed a fur trader at Fort Benton. He
was acquitted of the charge of murder, and in 1877 he decided to cross
the border with his family. He settled in Waterton (originally

47

Kootenai) Lakes, where he ran a trading post. Brown hunted, fished, and served as a guide for travellers. His stint as a scout in the Rocky Mountain Rangers was relatively uneventful because the Blackfoot remained peaceful. After three months of patrolling, the Rangers disbanded. Brown returned to Waterton, where he would later be important in developing the area as a national park.

Farther north, with eight hundred men under his command, Strange left a few infantry to garrison the towns while he set off in pursuit of Big Bear. The Calgary-Edmonton Trail, which would become so central to Alberta life, had until now scarcely been used. The men (and 175 wagons) had to cross several rivers, and the second half of the two-week journey was through heavy bush and swamp. Along the way, a few settlers at Red Deer Crossing profited hand-somely from the exorbitant prices they charged the troops for bread and eggs. Strange arranged for a display of force at Hobbema, where some Cree had raided HBC stores. Strange arrogantly refused to shake hands with the Cree chiefs, Bobtail and Ermineskin, who came to proclaim their loyalty. He told the chiefs he would shake hands with them on his return—if they behaved themselves in the meantime.

Upon reaching Edmonton Strange divided his forces, and they fanned out to capture Big Bear and his tribe. About a third of the troops went down the North Saskatchewan River in specially built scows, while the others marched along the river. Downstream Strange found that the Indians and English-speaking mixed bloods around Victoria had been strongly influenced by the Methodist missionaries, and had no desire to become involved in the rebellion.

Strange and his men finally caught up to Big Bear's band at Frenchman's Butte, southeast of Frog Lake. There were about 370 natives, including women and children, along with forty white hostages. By this time, depressed by the train of events, Big Bear had given up all leadership of his band, and war chief Wandering Spirit led the Indian warriors.

The battle of Frenchman's Butte in late May was inconclusive. The outgunned Cree were ensconced in rifle pits, and Strange's forces occupied badly exposed positions, so were reluctant to press their advantages in manpower and weaponry. A two-hour battle led to the wounding of several on both sides and the death of one Indian warrior. Strange decided to withdraw to await supplies and reinforce-ments. The Cree, unnerved by the shells from the field gun, simulta-neously decided to beat a hasty retreat into the dense bush.

The one thousand troops sent into the bush after Big Bear and his followers could not capture him or his force. Finally, six weeks after Riel gave himself up, Big Bear surrendered on July 2. For their part in the rebellion, Big Bear and Poundmaker were sentenced to three years in jail. Poundmaker's health deteriorated quickly and after he had spent less than a year in jail, authorities released him. He died while visiting his adoptive father, Crowfoot, in July 1886. Big Bear's sentence was commuted after two years when he was released, a broken and sick man, to die in January 1888. Government treatment of other Cree Indians was also harsh. Some were condemned to death, and others were deprived of annuities and horses, their arms and ammunition taken from them, and their movement restricted. Riel was hanged for treason in Regina on November 16, 1885.

During the short period from 1870 to 1885, the native majority on the Canadian Plains had become a dominated minority. The year 1885 is crucial in the history of the Northwest since it marks the end of native power. With the overwhelming military suppression of the rebellion, the Métis and Plains Indians lost their power to resist. No longer did the government have to worry about the threat of an armed native uprising. After 1885, the North-West Territories could be settled on the federal government's terms.

CHAPTER THREE

The Northwest Frontier: Economy and Settlement, 1880–1896

Settling the West was part of a "national policy" aimed at creating a viable transcontinental nation. Both Conservative and Liberal federal governments hoped that through massive immigration into this potentially rich agricultural land, the West would become a supplier of natural products for eastern Canadian and international markets, and a consumer of eastern manufactured goods. A transcontinental railway had to be built, and a tariff established to keep out American goods and build up Canadian manufacturing. An aggressive immigration policy was also essential, since it was clear that Canada alone could not populate the West. Sending the NWMP, signing treaties, and attempting to get the natives to settle on reserves were all preliminaries to achieving this larger objective.

The plan of settlement was based on a largely agrarian vision. To implement it, Macdonald's Conservative government decided early that the prairies should be surveyed and the land distributed according to the pattern already in use in the U.S. In 1871, the government sent surveyors to divide the land into townships of thirty-six square miles (93.24 square kilometres). Each township was divided into thirty-six sections of one square mile, and each section was divided into four quarter sections. The Dominion Lands Act of 1872 allowed settlers who were male, twenty-one or older, or the heads of families (the only way a woman could qualify for a homestead grant) to apply for a homestead of 160 acres (64 hectares) upon payment of a $10 registration fee. After three years of residence, settlers received title and could buy a neighbouring quarter section.

Completed through Alberta in 1883, the transcontinental Canadian Pacific Railway (CPR) set the stage for the settlement and economic development of southern Alberta. Railway transportation meant a decisive shift away from the river systems as the key means of penetrating the region. Edmonton's position as hub of the fur trade had been based on its location on the North Saskatchewan River and

Calgary in 1885. Located strategically on the transcontinental CPR, Calgary developed during the 1880s and early 1890s as the capital of the southern Alberta cattle kingdom. (*Glenbow Archives NA 4035-77*)

its proximity to the river systems leading into the North. The railway shifted the focus of population and economic activity southward. During the 1880s and 1890s Calgary, located strategically on the new transcontinental railway system, replaced Edmonton as the largest centre. However, despite the Canadian government's efforts to attract immigrants, a variety of factors hindered the quick fulfilment of the vision of a West peopled with millions of contented farmers.

Although there was much debate about the suitability of southern Alberta for agriculture, an economy based on farming, largely of wheat, came to dominate the region during the late 1890s and after the turn of the century. Like the fur trade, wheat production implied close economic ties with Europe, the major market. Also like the fur trade, the wheat economy was subjected to both unpredictable price changes and unpredictable supplies. But wheat had several major economic advantages over fur as the staple base of the economy: it was not subject to the same rapid depletion, it was not a luxury item, and it provided the base for large-scale settlement.

The transition from a fur-based to a wheat-based economy took place over two decades; in the meantime, a transitional economy emerged in southern Alberta. Here, ranching temporarily reigned supreme during the 1880s and 1890s, before being pushed back to the foothills by the wheat economy.

The Ranching Frontier

The semi-arid climate of southern Alberta raised serious doubts about its potential for sustaining a farming population. Ranching, however, emerged as a major industry in southwestern Alberta in the 1880s and 1890s, and beef became an important export item. Ranching was

LEASES OF MAJOR CATTLE COMPANIES, 1885

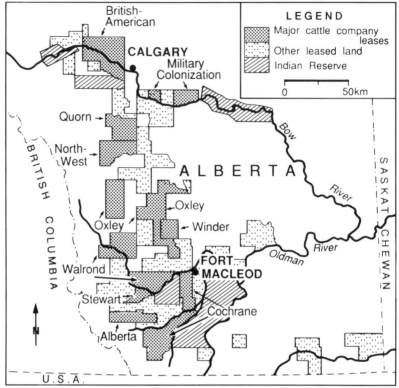

Courtesy S. M. Evans, "The Passing of a Frontier : Ranching in the Canadian West 1882-1912", Ph.D. thesis, University of Calgary, 1976.

made possible by the disappearance of the buffalo and the end of the traditional native way of life.

A new government leasing policy under Prime Minister John A. Macdonald opened the West to ranchers through large grazing leases. The Canadian government also played a dominant role in guiding and shaping virtually all aspects of the ranching industry. This government involvement and the strong British and Anglo-Canadian cultural influences of the ranching elite account for the unique characteristics of the Canadian as compared to the American ranching frontier. For a period of over twenty years, before the onset of large-scale settlement, the cattlemen dominated southwest Alberta.

The Palliser Expedition in the late 1850s, and later the NWMP, believed that southwestern Alberta was too dry for farming, and this perception worked to the advantage of ranchers. As well, the presence of the NWMP ensured protection for the ranchers from natives, and from squatters who wanted to farm. The warming effects of chinook winds, conditions that made possible the natural curing of hay, and a large number of mountain streams and coulees affording cattle a natural shelter against the elements created an ideal setting for ranching. From the perspective of the government, the area was vacant, and ranching could provide immediate economic development and traffic for the railway.

The foundations of the ranching industry were laid in the 1870s by three groups. A few early settlers, such as Irishmen Sam Livingstone and John Glenn, two of Calgary's first farmers and permanent residents, had shown the potential of stockraising. After 1877, when their first term of service was over, some former members of the NWMP went into the cattle business in the Fort Macleod and Pincher Creek areas. Montana trading companies also saw the potential for a cattle industry. The powerful I. G. Baker and T. C. Power Companies of Fort Benton, Montana, brought in stock, capital, and expertise, and provided beef to both the NWMP and the natives. Indeed one of the reasons the federal government decided to encourage an indigenous ranching industry during the 1880s was that so much of the money going to support the NWMP was ending up in the bank accounts of these Fort Benton merchants. Large-scale ranching would allow the government to meet the pressing problem of supplying the Mounted Police and providing enough beef to keep the Indians at least temporarily content.

The government was aware that the "Beef Bonanza" in the western U.S. was attracting British capital, and they wanted to bring some of this to western Canada. Large cattle leases could also provide possibilities for political patronage. The British government's decision in 1879 to impose an embargo on live cattle imported from the U.S. gave Canadian cattle a privileged position in the British market and ensured the economic potential of the southern plains.

In 1881 the federal government amended the Dominion Lands Act to permit the leasing of large acreages for grazing. The 1881 regulations granted leases to British subjects of up to a hundred thousand acres (forty thousand hectares) for twenty-one years at a rate of $10 per thousand acres (four hundred hectares)—one cent per acre per year. Furthermore, only the lessees could homestead on the land. Investors in eastern Canada and Britain snapped up these incentives.

Not surprisingly, the 1880s saw the growth and eventual dominance of the industry by a few very large ranches. By 1894, two-thirds of all stocked land was controlled by ten companies. The federal government's policy also put a damper on the influx of American ranchers. Thus, during the 1890s, about two hundred large-scale cattlemen controlled the region. With their business and political friends, they formed a powerful economic, social, and political elite. At the top of this hierarchy was a wealthy elite composed principally of Britons and eastern Canadians, usually with Conservative political ties.

One of these early cattle barons was Conservative Senator Matthew Cochrane, a cattleman and stock breeder from Compton, Quebec. Cochrane was politically well-connected; in fact, the Macdonald government drafted the 1881 regulations in response to his recommendations. He acquired six leases equalling 360,000 acres (144,000 hectares), mainly along the Bow River near the present town of Cochrane. In 1881 and 1882, his company purchased several thousand cattle in Montana and trailed them to his ranch. After early reverses caused by devastating winters, the Cochrane Ranche became profitable.

The British-born Governor General, the Marquis of Lorne, toured the West in the summer of 1881. Lorne was married to Princess Louise Caroline Alberta, Queen Victoria's fourth daughter, and it was after her that Alberta was named (first as one of four provisional districts in the North-West Territories). The correspondents from several leading British papers who travelled with Lorne publicized the foothills ranch country, helping to attract British investors.

Several huge ranches, such as the Oxley, Walrond, and Quorn, became homes-away-from-home for the sons of the English upper middle class. The Oxley ranch was founded in 1882 by Alexander Stavely Hill, a Conservative member of the British Parliament. The Walrond ranch was founded in 1883 by Sir John Walrond, a former British politician, along with several other British investors. By 1890, each of these enterprises had over two million acres (eight hundred thousand hectares) of leased land. The Quorn Ranch, owned by the Quorn Hunt Club in England, specialized in raising horses for the English hunting market. Many of the ranch managers, unlike the owners, were from eastern Canada.

With British agriculture slumping during the 1880s, many landed upper-middle-class Britons came to Alberta. Retired British military personnel, like General Strange, had enough capital to establish ranches. Many of the young men who came had gone to private schools in England. The eldest sons took over their families' estates;

the second sons found little room in the military, law, civil service, or clergy, so many came to Canada. Some received a monthly allowance or remittance. Many of these newcomers were industrious and succeeded in their new life; however, some had difficulty adjusting to the ranching frontier, and unfairly, the term "remittance man" was often considered virtually synonymous with alcoholism, laziness, and waste.

Along the foothills in Alberta, from the Priddis-Millarville area to Pincher Creek, in a few other rural areas around Pine Lake, and in the Alix area east of Lacombe, these Englishmen—and a few young Englishwomen—created a transplanted British Victorian lifestyle that lasted until World War I. The nature of the ranching enterprise, which required large amounts of capital and a division of labour between management and working cowboys, enabled them to develop a class-conscious community, tempered by western influences. A close community of values and interests developed between the ranchers and the NWMP, particularly since so many former members of the NWMP became ranchers.

The ranchers gradually established traditional social pastimes such as formal balls, formal dress dinners, fox hunts (with a coyote substitute), and polo, cricket, and tennis. One of the first sports in the Priddis-Millarville area was horse racing, and horses became a significant measure of social status. Some families imported British governesses or sent their children to private schools. They watched events in Britain closely, supported the Anglican Church, and backed the Conservative party (which they saw as pro-British). Their social orientation was east to central Canada and Britain rather than south to the U.S. The intensity of the imperial orientation was strongly evident at the time of royal or vice-regal visits and during wartime. Enlistment rates from the ranching community during the Boer War (1899-1902) and World War I (1914-1918) were extremely high.

The ranching frontier was not solidly British. American cowboys were part of the ranching industry from the 1870s onward, and there were several American ranch foremen such as George Lane of the Bar U. Most of the methods and technology for ranching came from the American west. One of the most interesting of the American cowboys was John Ware, atypical in that he was black. His life and career provide an example of both the opportunities and limitations that existed for blacks in Canada's northwest. Born a slave on a plantation in South Carolina, Ware was nineteen when the American Civil War ended in 1865, and he decided to move to Texas. There his youth,

Cowboys mounted for a roundup west of Okotoks in 1892. Ranching developed as a major industry in southwest Alberta during the 1880s and 1890s. *(Glenbow Archives NA 2084-50)*

physical strength, and skills with horse and lariat qualified him to join a cattle drive north to Montana. In 1882 he herded cattle farther north to Canada. His willingness to endure long hours in the saddle under severe conditions impressed the local cattlemen, and his warm personality, sense of humour, and willingness to help soon made him popular.

After working on the Quorn ranch, Ware acquired land on Sheep Creek near Millarville and bought a small herd of cattle. He married the daughter of a black farmer from Ontario in 1892. Ten years later, Ware moved his wife and five children to the isolated Brooks district, where his wife died in 1905. Shortly after, Ware was fatally injured in a fall from his horse. While not finding complete racial equality in Alberta, he had been able to advance well beyond the possibilities offered blacks in the American South.

From 1882 to 1891, the big ranches dominated southwestern Alberta. They were gradually challenged by farmers who resented both the ranchers' domination and the federal Conservative government's strong backing of the ranching community. The stock growers joined to prevent "sodbusters" from coming into the region, bringing ranchers and farmers on a collision course. An Alberta Settlers' Rights Association was formed in Calgary in April 1885 to force the government to open up land around Calgary for settlers. The settlers who met at the farm of John Glenn on Fish Creek to denounce government policy included several who had been evicted by the NWMP from their land as "squatters." They threatened violence, and demanded that the cattle leases be opened to settlement.

This pressure occurred at the same time as the North-West Rebellion of 1885, led by Louis Riel in Saskatchewan, and Ottawa didn't want more unrest. The federal government responded in small measure by cancelling some leases and opening two townships near Calgary for settlement. It also reassured the ranchers by reaffirming their control over previously leased land. The NWMP continued to evict squatters and the government excluded settlers from water reserves, which were set aside for ranchers.

The ranchers throughout this crisis had a strong champion in Calgary-based William Pearce, the senior western official in the Department of the Interior, who believed the southwest to be ideally suited for ranching and too dry for large-scale agriculture without irrigation. But as settlement gradually expanded, political pressure increased to end the privileged position of ranchers and to open the south to farmers. This pressure increased further in 1896 with the election of the federal Liberals, who were tied to settlers' interests. In Alberta, pro-settler Frank Oliver, editor of the *Edmonton Bulletin*, defeated rancher T. B. H. Cochrane for the federal seat from Alberta. Oliver's election symbolized the shifting balance in political forces as growing numbers of farmers gradually chipped away at the ranchers' power.

The development of the ranching industry, the arrival of the railway in Alberta in 1883, and the growth of Calgary were all closely linked. During the late 1870s, Fort Macleod's central location on the north-south transportation route to Fort Benton made it the heartland of the ranching country. But after the arrival of the railway, Calgary emerged as the largest centre in Alberta. By 1891 it had a population of 3900, compared to less than 700 in Edmonton.

Calgary became the capital of the cattle kingdom. It was the main shipping point for livestock, and its merchants catered primarily to the ranchers. The ranchers located their main organization, the Western Stock Growers Association, in the city. Calgary's first newspaper, established in 1883, was the *Calgary Herald, Mining and Ranch Advocate and General Advertiser*. It was a voice for the policies of the ranchers, the CPR, and the federal Conservative Party, whose interests were all closely linked. The town also became the financial centre for the ranchers, and its stockyards and meat processing plants gradually became major employers.

Pat Burns helped turn Calgary into a major centre for meat processing. A poor, uneducated young man from Ontario, he came west to Manitoba and went into the cattle business. In 1890 he came to Calgary and built a meat-packing firm that supplied beef to railway construction workers, and later to markets in B.C. and the Yukon.

Burns gradually established an integrated company that controlled all phases of production from growing livestock to delivering frozen dressed meats. In doing so, he built one of the first great fortunes in the region.

The ranching influence permeated almost all aspects of Calgary's business and cultural life. Ranching capital established many of Calgary's manufacturing concerns, such as the Calgary Brewing and Malting Company, formed in 1892 by ranchers including ex-Montrealer A. E. Cross, William Roper Hull, and John Lineham. Cattlemen also shaped the social and cultural life of the city. The centre of the city's elite social life, the Ranchmen's Club, was founded in 1891 on a set of rules based on those of an exclusive men's club, the St. James Club in Montreal. This male preserve brought together ranchers and the town's business elite. The ranchers helped maintain ties among Calgary, eastern Canada, and Britain through letters, visits, newspapers, and magazines. They expressed this eastern orientation in housing styles, literary societies, debating clubs, and entertainment.

Railways and the Origins of Alberta's Urban Network

The arrival of the transcontinental railway in 1883 gave a tremendous boost to ranching and to Calgary, and changed economic and settlement patterns throughout Alberta. The location of the railway decided where towns would be situated and which towns would grow, through decisions about where maintenance shops and divisional points would be placed. By their placement of stations and grants of free land for hospitals and town halls, the CPR also helped determine spatial growth in western urban centres. As well, the CPR, through its influence on immigration and settlement, helped to decide who would come to Canada, and where they would settle. CPR railway hotels and tourist promotion in the Rockies set a still-evident pattern for tourism development. The CPR, with two subsequent transcontinental railways built after the turn of the century, helped determine the rise and fall of coal mining and the towns dependent on it.

The transcontinental railway carried a huge burden of national objectives. Politicians hoped it would improve communication, colonize the prairies, forestall American expansion, and serve as a spine of Empire, linking Britain with the Far East. It would also open up a new economic hinterland for central Canada.

But the railway had trouble getting started. The first efforts by the Macdonald government to put together a group of investors foundered on the Pacific Scandal of 1873, which brought down the Conservative federal government. Their Liberal successors regarded the transcontinental railway with less enthusiasm than the Tories, but they allowed the surveys searching for the route to go on. The descriptions by Palliser and Hind of a fertile belt to the north of a semi-arid region led to the original plan to push a route along the North Saskatchewan River Valley and through the Yellowhead Pass, west of Edmonton. But when the Macdonald government returned to power in 1878, with its promises of pushing ahead with the railway as part of a "national policy," the question of the route was reopened.

In his search for a new sydicate to take over the construction of the railway, Macdonald became interested in a group of entrepreneurs who had taken over a bankrupt railway meant to run from St. Paul, Minnesota to Emerson, Manitoba, and made it successful. The entrepreneurs included, among others, J. J. Hill, a former Canadian who ran a steamship company out of St. Paul; Donald Smith, chief commissioner of the HBC; and George Stephen, president of the Bank of Montreal. They were persuaded to undertake the project. Under the terms of the contract signed with the Canadian government in 1880, the Canadian Pacific syndicate received, among other concessions, a subsidy of $25 million and 25 million acres (10 million hectares) of land. In addition they received tax exemptions; their freight rates were temporarily free of government regulations, and a monopoly clause, promised for twenty years, stipulated that no other rail line was to be constructed on the prairies south of the CPR main line. The monopoly clause prevented American railways from pushing branch lines into the southern prairies. While the generous terms of the contract seemed necessary at the time to get the railway built, they would for generations be a major source of grievance for prairie farmers, who felt they had to pay for the government's generosity.

The CPR management pushed ahead boldly. One of their first decisions was to change the proposed route of the railway to cross the southern prairies. Some of the managers were concerned about American railways encroaching on the southern prairies after the monopoly clause ran out. Assuming that a pass through the Selkirk Mountains in B.C. could be found, a southern route would also be shorter. Fewer bridges would have to be built, and coal for fuel was available in southern Alberta. Botanist John Macoun also publicized his view that Palliser's Triangle was not a barren wasteland, as previously believed. Macoun claimed it was ideally suited for agricul-

View of Medicine Hat in 1885. The arrival of the CPR in 1883 had first brought
Medicine Hat into being. The railways decisively shaped Alberta's urban network
and settlement patterns. The steamboats at the dock were briefly used to ship coal
from the Galt mines at Lethbridge to the railway at Medicine Hat. *(Notman
Collection, McCord Museum; Glenbow Museum NA 2003-13)*

ture; he both convinced and confirmed the CPR management in their
decision to move the route southward. Since land speculators had
most of their holdings in the North Saskatchewan River valley, the
CPR could also outflank them by moving southward.

The CPR hired William Cornelius Van Horne, an American
engineer, as general manager of the railway. Under Van Horne's
organizational genius, the railway spanned the prairies with amazing
speed. Surveying barely kept ahead of grading and laying track as
7600 men worked fifteen-hour days with horses, mules, crude graders,
shovels, and wheelbarrows.

The CPR arrived in Alberta in June 1883. At Medicine Hat, a
youthful group of squatters had gathered in the fall of 1882 where they
anticipated the railway would span the South Saskatchewan River. As
the railway crews arrived, the town sprang up with hotels, general
stores, saloons, and a veritable city of tents. The CPR then pushed into
Calgary and the boom repeated itself. Once the CPR decided on its
station site and townsite, Calgary's merchants, who had in 1881 and
1882 squatted around Fort Calgary on both sides of the Elbow River,
shifted westward. A committee including as chairman James Walker,
a former member of the NWMP and unofficial mayor, spearheaded the
drive for town incorporation. This would make possible taxation,
which would pay for services such as firefighting. In November 1884
Calgary, with a population of somewhere between 350 and 500
people, was incorporated as the second town in the North-West
Territories.

The coming of the CPR gave a huge boost to the coal industry at

Coalbanks (now Lethbridge), and permanently shifted the focal point of southwest Alberta's economy away from the ranching and police centre at Fort Macleod. Coal mining had first been started in Coalbanks in 1874 by Nicholas Sheran, an Irish-American Civil War veteran and former whisky trader. He had supplied coal by the wagonload to the NWMP at Fort Macleod and to the Fort Benton merchants.

Central Canadian capital and entrepreneurship, brought by the well-connected Galt family, soon transformed the Lethbridge region. Elliott Galt, son of Alexander Galt (one of the fathers of Confederation and a former Conservative cabinet minister), worked as an Indian commissioner in the West. After visiting Sheran's mine in 1879, Elliott helped interest his father in the region's potential for coal production. As Canada's High Commissioner in London from 1880 to 1883, Alexander Galt was responsible for promoting immigration and attracting British capital to western Canada, and he secured some of it for his own enterprises.

Once it was clear that the railway would go by the southerly route, it became easy to get capital for a colliery. Among the investors who were lured were bookseller W. H. Smith, and William Lethbridge, a friend and employee of Smith for whom the community was renamed. Galt, along with Smith, Lethbridge, and several other investors, formed the North-Western Coal and Navigation Company (NWC & NCo). With generous concessions from a Conservative government that wanted speedy development by private corporations, the Galt interests developed the townsite, recruited miners (including many Hungarians who had been working in Pennsylvania), and built barges to ship the coal down the South Saskatchewan River to the CPR main line. When this means of transportation failed because of low water levels, the Galts received a government subsidy for a narrow-gauge railway to Dunmore on the CPR main line near Medicine Hat. The first train rolled into Lethbridge on October 15, 1885, and by 1887, with a population of about 1000, Lethbridge had outstripped Macleod as the economic centre of southwestern Alberta.

One of the key figures in the early history of Lethbridge and Alberta was Ontario-born C. A. Magrath, a land commissioner and later manager for the NWC & NCo. As a company official and community leader, he saw the potential of the Lethbridge region not only for coal, but for irrigation, which could lead to colonization. As the first mayor of Lethbridge (1891), member for Lethbridge in the territorial legislature (1891–1902), minister without portfolio in the territorial cabinet (1898–1901), and Conservative Member of Parliament (1908–11), Magrath was an important economic and political force in the development of southern Alberta.

The Galt interests dominated the local economy. Because coal mining did not immediately lead to the economic bonanza they expected, they became convinced that irrigation and colonization of their sizable land grants was the key to economic survival. Partly because of their close ties with the Conservative government, the company received over a million acres (four hundred thousand hectares) as a land subsidy for building railways to their coal mines. In October 1890, the company completed a railway to Montana to market their coal. Their land subsidy encouraged the Galts to think of irrigation as a means of settling the vast dryland, and their attention soon turned to the nearby settlement of experienced irrigators, the Mormons at Cardston.

While Calgary and Lethbridge were growing relatively quickly, Edmonton and northern Alberta had been temporarily left behind by the building of the CPR along the southern route. Because of the difficulties of transportation and other factors, during the late 1870s growth had been slow; the 1881 census counted only 263 residents in Edmonton. Nonetheless, as the predominance of Hudson's Bay Company employees declined along with the fur trade, the character of the population changed. Newcomers arrived from Quebec and Ontario, hoping to cash in on future agricultural expansion. One of the young migrants from Ontario was Frank Oliver, who had begun his career as a journalist at the touchstone of Canadian agrarian Liberalism, George Brown's *Globe* in Toronto. In 1876, after a sojourn in Winnipeg, Oliver brought a few trade goods by oxcart to Edmonton and began trading. In 1880 he set up the *Edmonton Bulletin*, the second newspaper in the North-West Territories, and began a long career as a journalist and politician promoting the interests of farmers, Edmonton, and the West.

Other newcomers to Edmonton included Richard Secord and John A. McDougall (both from Ontario), who set up general stores and began fur trading and general merchandising (and eventually entered a long and lucrative parternship), and Richard Ottewell, whose Clover Bar homestead became the focus of a variety of enterprises including coal mining, sawmilling, and flour milling. Edmonton's business and professional people were rudely surprised when the railway was rerouted southward, and their dreams of quick profits in a real estate boom faded. In June 1887, when the new Presbyterian minister, the Reverend D. G. McQueen, arrived from Ontario, beginning a long and vital career in Edmonton's civic life, Edmonton's population was only 350. McQueen later recalled his first impressions of the young settlement:

There were six mercantile establishments. . . .There was also a butcher-shop, a baker's, a blacksmith shop, a land office, the *Edmonton Bulletin* printing establishment, a boat-building establishment, and a carriage-maker's shop, four churches, two schools, four hotels, a post office, telegraph office, grist-mill, saw-mill, and a brick-yard. Small settlements of homesteaders at Namao, Belmont, Stony Plain, Clover Bar, and eastward at Beaver Lake, gave to the little village its promise of a widening agricultural industry to take the place of the receding fur-trade.[1]

Edmonton was not cut off from the railway for long. In 1891 the CPR-owned Calgary and Edmonton Railway built a spur line northward. Elation gave way to dismay when Edmontonians realized that the CPR had no intention of spanning the North Saskatchewan River, but instead created the rival railway town of South Edmonton (later renamed Strathcona). After the railway rolled in on August 10, 1891, Edmonton residents rallied to halt their settlement's apparently imminent demise since it now appeared that commercial development would be on the south side of the river. Spearheaded by the Edmonton Board of Trade, a movement was launched to have the hamlet incorporated as a town in February 1892. Matt McCauley, who in 1881 had originally led the drive for Edmonton to have a school, became the first mayor. The Edmontonians' most dramatic action was forcibly preventing the relocation of government offices to Strathcona. When the land agent arrived with team, wagon, and teamsters to move the office, a milling crowd of two hundred, despite NWMP intervention, physically prevented anyone from moving anything. In the face of determined city officials and an aroused citizenry, who formed a "Citizens' Guard" to protect their threatened building, Ottawa backed down. Nonetheless, the railway connection enabled Strathcona to build an industrial and commercial base with flour mills, meat packing, lumber mills, and breweries.

The Calgary and Edmonton Railway, like the railway that was completed between Calgary and Macleod in 1893, opened up a new agricultural region. The arrival of the railways made possible the development of rural towns and villages along the axis from Edmonton to Calgary to Macleod, catering to the needs of settlers who were beginning to trickle in. However, settlement proceeded slowly. By 1891 there were 9,000 Indians and 17,500 Métis and white settlers in Alberta.

Railways and Tourism

One other consequence of the arrival of the CPR was the opening of the Rockies as a tourist attraction that would over the long term be a steady, if limited, part of the Alberta economy. As the railway pushed farther west into the Rockies, it opened up the Banff area, which became Canada's first national park and Alberta's prime tourist attraction from the 1880s to the present. Van Horne, travelling to the end of the CPR line in 1883, had been struck by the high cost of mountain construction, the low volume of expected traffic, and the magnificent scenery. He quickly concluded that "If you can't export the scenery, you have to import the tourists."[2] He began envisioning a series of luxurious hotels in the most scenic settings along the railway to attract tourists and increase traffic. Van Horne then spoke to William Pearce of the Department of the Interior about establishing a park system along the railway that would attract the wealthy from Europe and the United States.

Three CPR construction workers prospecting on their day off made a chance discovery that encouraged the government to act quickly. The trio of three young easterners, Franklin McCabe and brothers William and Thomas McCardell, noticed warm water and the strong smell of sulphur on the slope of a mountain on the south side of the Bow River. Their discovery of the Cave and Basin hot springs attracted immediate attention to the area, since hot water was a much-desired luxury and mineral waters were believed to have great medicinal value. Though the three set about "improving" the site by building a log hovel, which they labelled a hotel, a spate of subsequent claims and counterclaims about rights of discovery and ownership led to a government decision to retain ownership of the springs and their surroundings.

After visiting the hot springs in September 1885, William Pearce used his influence to have the area protected, and on November 25, 1885, the federal government set aside a tract of about ten square miles (25.9 square kilometres) as Canada's first park reserve. On the recommendation of George Stewart, a Dominion Land Surveyor and later the first park superintendent, the reserve was soon expanded to twenty-six times its original size. On June 23, 1887, the Rocky Mountains Park Act established Banff as Canada's first national park.

64

By 1887 a good deal of private and public development had already taken place in Banff. As Superintendent, Stewart laid out a townsite, bridged the Bow River, and built roads for access to the hot springs and the new CPR hotel, the Banff Springs. Van Horne chose as a site for the hotel a promontory above the confluence of the Bow and Spray rivers. He also chose a noted New York architect, who drew up plans inspired by sixteenth-century French châteaux. The opening of the Banff Springs Hotel in June 1888, which Van Horne advertised as the "Finest Hotel on the North American Continent," and a series of other railway hotels through the mountains, encouraged the development of the park as a major destination for the wealthy of eastern Canada, the United States, and Britain. In 1890, the CPR built a chalet at Lake Louise. The government set aside the area around Lake Louise as a government reserve in 1892, and it became part of Rocky Mountains Park in 1902.

Banff attracted not only tourists but photographers, artists, mountain climbers, naturalists, and writers. The CPR brought a whole series of distinguished Canadian landscape painters to the West, and their views of the dramatic effects of light and spectacular mountain peaks are an important part of Canadian art history. Over the next three decades, American Quaker writer, artist, and naturalist Mary Schäffer Warren (one of the "discoverers" of Maligne Lake near Jasper); German American painter Carl Rungius, who specialized in wildlife painting; American landscape painter John Singer Sargent, and many others used their talents to capture the natural beauty of the area. Since then, many English, American, and Canadian artists have continued to be attracted to the area.

Immigration and Settlement

The completion of the CPR did not lead immediately to large-scale migration, but it opened the possibility. Most newcomers to Alberta during the 1880s were of British origin, either from central Canada (mainly Ontario) or Britain. The majority of the newcomers from Ontario settled in the villages and towns of the Northwest, where their knowledge of the language and of Canadian institutions, as well as their educational background, made it possible for them to set up small businesses and to dominate the teaching, legal, and medical professions, and political life.

In the late nineteenth century, most of the politicians in the North-West Territories, men such as C. A. Magrath, Frank Oliver, and Macleod lawyer F. W. G. Haultain, were from Ontario. Haultain, representing Macleod, was first a member of an advisory council of four to the lieutenant governor of the North-West Territories, and later the dominant member of the assembly. Haultain led the long struggle with the federal government that preceded the territories' being granted responsible government in 1897. Haultain became premier, which made him the leading political figure in the North-West Territories until 1905, when Alberta and Saskatchewan became provinces.

The British immigrants and Ontarians were overwhelmingly Protestant. Anglicans, Presbyterians, and Methodists dominated the social, economic, and political life of Fort Macleod, Medicine Hat, Lethbridge, Calgary, and Edmonton, although there was also an important Roman Catholic minority. Despite rivalry among Protestant clergymen (particularly among Protestant missionaries to the natives), the main religious cleavage in the population was between Protestants and Catholics.

Alberta's ethnically diverse frontier society made anti-Catholicism less socially and politically potent than it had been in either Ontario or Manitoba. This was partly because priests such as Father Van Tighem in Lethbridge and Father Lacombe had been pioneers and were respected as community founders.

Nonetheless, anti-Catholic feeling occasionally surfaced in the late 1880s and early 1890s over the contentious issue of government support for separate schools. Catholics were largely natives, French Canadian farmers, or working-class Slavic immigrants, and (with the partial exception of the Irish) had a lower social status than Protestants. Except for the French Catholic clergy, which fought a desperate public battle to preserve state support and church control of Catholic schools, Catholics kept a low profile. Outside of Edmonton and the rural communities of French Canadian Catholics in northern Alberta (which developed in the 1890s), Catholics seldom became involved in Alberta's political life until the 1940s.

Although most Ontario settlers came west as individuals or in small groups, there were some larger group settlements. One was started near Red Deer in the early 1880s by Methodists from London, Ontario. They were led by Reverend Leonard Gaetz, who arrived from Ontario in 1884 with his wife and ten children, and attracted many other Methodists to the area. Gaetz determined Red Deer's location by persuading the Calgary and Edmonton Railway Company to cross the Red Deer River on his property in return for a donation of land for a townsite. The Gaetz family played a prominent role in Red Deer's commercial and political life for decades. Gaetz's eldest son, Raymond, was a successful businessman, first president of the board of trade, and in 1901 Red Deer's first mayor.

Another Ontario group settlement was started east of Fort Saskatchewan in 1892 by three hundred farmers from Parry Sound, Ontario, who were looking for better farmland. Despite initial hardships, the Parry Sound colony succeeded and over the next decade attracted over two hundred relatives and friends.

Though outnumbered by British and Americans after 1896, Ontario settlers continued to come in large numbers until World War I. There were many more settlers from Ontario than from other provinces.

From the 1880s onward, English-speaking settlers from Ontario greatly outnumbered French-speaking settlers from Quebec. The Roman Catholic clergy in the Territories encouraged French Canadians from Quebec to migrate westward, but without any real success. Instead, the *Québéçois* moved southward to nearby New England. Unsuccessful in attracting settlers from Quebec, the French Roman Catholic clergy in the North-West Territories turned their attention to attracting French-speaking immigrants from the U.S. and Europe.

Colonization priest Abbé Morin brought out the first group of French Canadian farmers in 1891. They settled just north of the original St. Albert, naming their town Morinville. This settlement, followed by many others in the region (including Vegreville, Beaumont, Villeneuve, Rivière Qui Barre, Legal, Vimy, and Picardville), brought together repatriated French Canadians from the U.S. with newcomers from Quebec, France, and Belgium.

The small numbers of the French-speaking settlers to the prairies threatened their language privileges in the Northwest. In 1877, an amendment to the North-West Territories Act had given equality to French and English in the courts and in the records and proceedings of the NWT council. However, the Ontarians were anxious to see the West develop as an English-speaking region, British in sympathy. In 1892 the territorial assembly (the expanded, and elected, successor of the earlier appointed council), dominated by the English-speaking members and led by Haultain, largely eliminated the legal rights of the French-speaking population. Henceforth the French-speaking community had to rely on rural isolation, large families, and strong parish organizations to keep their language and religion alive.

The waves of immigrants who arrived during the 1890s, and in larger numbers after the turn of the century, came to an area modelled on Ontario, and one largely governed by Ontarians. To the Ontarians, the English language was the instrument of forging a new, united Canadian community; and the public school was the institution by which Anglo-conformity would be imposed. F. W. G. Haultain's opposition to both separate schools and bilingualism reflected the views of many other Ontarians who moved westward. They wanted to see a new Ontario in the West, undivided by language or religion.

Although the largest number of newcomers to Alberta during the 1880s and early 1890s came from Ontario and Britain, the region also attracted immigrants from Europe, the U.S., and even Asia. The new federal government after 1867 had oriented immigration policy largely toward promoting British immigration. However, during the 1870s the response of British farmers was slight. The government consequently began to encourage emigration from other parts of Europe. Mennonites fleeing assimilation pressures in Russia came to southern Manitoba in 1874, and Icelanders arrived in 1875. During the 1880s the Canadian government encouraged Americans, Russian Jews, Hungarians, and Germans to immigrate to the West.

Nevertheless, settlement proceeded slowly. Fearing the impact of farming, ranchers in southern Alberta actively discouraged settlement, playing on the idea that Palliser's Triangle was too dry for farming. Agricultural depression, the North-West Rebellion of 1885, the absence of CPR branch lines, and the hardships of pioneering also slowed settlement. Extensive land was withheld for speculation by the HBC, the CPR, and colonization companies, thus further frustrating potential settlers. Since land policy was almost as liberal south of the Canadian border, most westward-moving farmers turned to the U.S.

There were, however, some important agricultural settlements during the late 1880s and early 1890s. During the middle to late 1880s, some American, Scandinavian, and German farmers arrived. Most of the Americans came individually and settled after 1891 on land along the newly opened Calgary-Edmonton and Calgary-Macleod railways.

The largest single group of Americans were Mormons from Utah seeking refuge from persecution by the American government. They were Alberta's first large body of successful farmers. Fleeing anti-polygamy laws, they came in 1887 under the leadership of Charles Ora Card and established farms in the area around present-day Cardston. A much larger group of Mormons came for economic reasons in the late 1890s and early 1900s.

Along with a number of other theological and social innovations, polygamy had been introduced among the Mormons in the 1840s as a practice of the Old Testament prophets and part of God's law. Following the assassination of founder Joseph Smith in Illinois, the Mormons had moved to Utah in the 1840s under the leadership of Brigham Young. In Utah and surrounding territories, they had grown and flourished. During the 1880s the American government passed harsh anti-polygamy laws. These laws imposed heavy fines on polygamists, declared the children of polygamist unions illegitimate, sent 1300 Mormons to jail, and dissolved the Mormon Church as a corporate entity.

Card was a prominent Mormon leader in northern Utah. Born in 1840, he grew up in New England. After his family had converted to Mormonism, he travelled with a handcart company across the plains to Utah. A community and church leader, he married four times, though he was divorced from his first wife. He was arrested in July 1886 for practising polygamy.

Card escaped from custody and went to see John Taylor, the president of the Mormon Church and successor to Brigham Young. Taylor, who was also in hiding, had been born in England. He had lived in Ontario until his conversion to Mormonism. He directed Card to go north to Canada to find "British justice." Taylor's son, Mormon apostle John W. Taylor, was an unrepentant polygamist, entrepreneur, and visionary. He and Card became the two key leaders in the early development of the Mormon settlements in southern Alberta.

In the fall of 1886, Card and a small party of colonizers chose southwestern Alberta as their new home. The region had good land, water for irrigation, accessible timber and coal, and was near the Blood Indian reservation, where the Mormons hoped to do missionary work. Card returned to Utah to report, and barely escaped arrest again. In the spring of 1887, he left for Canada at night, disguised by a short haircut, a close shave, a pipe, and an Irish brogue. He was joined by several others, who left with him for southern Alberta.

The Mormons arrived when the battle between homesteaders and ranchers was underway, and when the political and economic influence of the ranchers still held sway. The first Mormon settlers met considerable opposition from the press and many politicians elsewhere in Canada. Public views had been shaped by the prolonged conflict between the American government and the Mormons during the 1870s and 1880s. But the Canadian government and local boosters were glad to have skilled irrigation farmers settle in an area of the Territories known for its dryness. Two former Mounties, C. E. D. Wood, the editor of the *Fort Macleod Gazette*, and E. T. Saunders, editor of the *Lethbridge News*, gave voice to economic interests that were crying out for new settlers. When the Mormon leaders travelled to Ottawa in November 1888 and asked for permission to bring their existing plural families to Canada, the government quickly moved to outlaw polygamy. Most public opposition to the Mormons declined after 1890, when the Mormon Church itself officially abandoned polygamy.

The previous experience of the Mormons helped them meet the difficult problems of pioneering. The Cardston Company, a joint-stock cooperative store organized by Card and other church members, mobilized capital for community projects including a flour mill, cheese factory, steam threshing outfit, sawmill, and several other enterprises. The economic success of the Mormons, their achievements with small-scale irrigation projects, and the series of dry years in the early 1890s, which showed the necessity of irrigation, broke down the isolation that separated them from the local society.

Some of the early capital for the Cardston Company and other ventures came from Zina Card, third wife of Charles Ora Card, who travelled with him to southern Alberta. Zina, a daughter of Brigham Young, was a former college teacher and suffragette. She served as a role model for other Mormon women. In her ongoing attempts to bring civilization and gentility to the frontier, she emphasized the values of piety, submissiveness, and domesticity. The Mormons' village settlement pattern enabled Mormon women to avoid some of the intense loneliness that characterized the lives of other pioneer women. Frequent visiting from house to house and joint activities in their own religious organization, the Relief Society, brought Mormon women together in a strong sisterhood.

Nonetheless, like those of other western pioneers, the lives of Mormon men and women were often shaped by their differing experiences and consequently differing perceptions and expectations. What, for pioneer Richard Harvey, was "paradise indeed," meant to wife Millie distance from food supplies, medical help, schools, and companionship. Even the tall prairie grass threatened her children; their girls grew up wearing red sunbonnets so as not to be lost in the fields. All her life Millie longed to return home to Utah.[3]

While Mormons were helping to shift the balance from ranching to farming in southwest Alberta, Scandinavian American farmers were coming to the parkbelt of central Alberta. The groups of Icelanders, Swedes, and Norwegians who arrived in Alberta came from immigrant settlements in the American Midwest.

Icelanders came from North Dakota to central Alberta in 1888 and settled in the Markerville area, where there was feed for livestock, wood for homes and fuel, and readily available water and fish. One of the early Icelandic settlers was Stephan Stephansson, a political and religious radical who came to be considered by many people in Iceland as the greatest Icelandic poet of the twentieth century. Stephansson homesteaded, and authored six large books of poetry and scores of articles in Icelandic.

Stephansson had migrated to North America from Iceland in 1873, one of many who were fleeing a system of tenant farming, crop failures, and volcanic activity. He first pioneered in Icelandic settlements in Wisconsin and North Dakota before population pressure, rising land prices, debt, and drought in North Dakota drove him and many other Icelanders to central Alberta.

After his arrival in Markerville in 1889, Stephansson was active in many of the early community organizations and a member of the Icelandic Literary Society. He was also a member of the cooperative creamery, which was an economic mainstay of the community. Stephansson spent his nights writing poetry by the light of a coal-oil lamp. Some of his poetry drew its inspiration from Norse sagas, but much of it arose as a response to the natural landscape of Alberta and community and family life.

Norwegians came from Wisconsin to Calgary in 1886 to work for the Eau Claire Lumber Company, which by the early 1890s was the largest producer of lumber in the North-West Territories. Norwegians also began farming in 1893 at Bardo, in the Camrose area, under the leadership of P. B. Anderson, the first Norwegian Lutheran pastor in western Canada. Norwegians established over twenty settlements within a fifty-mile radius of Camrose, making it the most concentrated area of Norwegian settlement in Canada.

The Swedes, who also came via the U.S., took up land in the area around Wetaskiwin. New Sweden, Malmo, Water Glen, Falun, Westerose, and Calmar were all established by Swedish-American settlers in the early 1890s. By the turn of the century, the Scandinavian-American settlements, which would eventually make up at least half the population in parts of central Alberta, were firmly established.

People of German origin also began arriving in the 1880s. Most did not come directly from Germany, but from German-speaking areas in eastern Europe. Attracted by offers of land, local self-government, and linguistic freedom, German-speaking colonists had settled in eastern Europe in the late 1700s and early 1800s. Growing nationalism in the late nineteenth century, which brought pressures on them to assimilate, and a scarcity of land, caused many to leave for the American and Canadian Wests. Of the Germans who came to the prairies before World War I, only 12 per cent came from Germany; 44 per cent came from Russia; 24 per cent came from other parts of eastern Europe; 18 per cent came from the U.S.

German-speaking peoples became one of the largest groups in Alberta. They established several settlements during the late 1880s and early 1890s. Based on religious affiliation, these settlements were to become the nuclei for much larger German-speaking communities after the turn of the century. By 1900 people of German origin were the third largest ethnic group, after those of British and native origin. Through subsequent migrations and a high birth rate, Germans became the second largest ethnic category. A number of factors, including cultural and religious diversity, geographic dispersion, religious sectarianism, and the impact of two world wars, prevented them from being as visible or as well-organized as some other ethnic groups, such as the Ukrainians.

The first German settlers in Alberta came to the Pincher Creek area in 1883. In 1889 settlements were established near Medicine Hat when nearly a hundred families arrived from two neighbouring German villages in eastern Galicia in the Austro-Hungarian Empire. The three German settlements in the Medicine Hat area were short-lived. They encountered severe drought conditions, and the CPR relocated them to farming areas around Edmonton in 1891. German Lutherans began farming around Stony Plain, where they were the first settlers. Members of the Reformed faith moved to the Fort Saskatchewan area around Josephsburg. After the turn of the century, the Medicine Hat area became one of the largest concentrations of Germans per capita in Canada.

With the completion of the Calgary and Edmonton railway in 1891, German Protestants established thirteen communities (Lutheran, Reformed, Baptist, and Moravian) within a thirty-mile radius of Edmonton. From this beginning, the rural areas south and west of Edmonton—centred around Leduc and Stony Plain—became strongholds of German settlement. In 1894, German-speaking Moravians from Ukraine, seeking free land and religious freedom, established settlements that they named Bruderfeld and Bruderheim ("brethren's home"), both near Edmonton. The original pioneers were later joined by Moravians from Poland and Brazil, just as many other German group settlements, whether Mennonite, Baptist, or Lutheran, brought together co-religionists from many countries. Since virtually all of these early settlements of German-speaking peoples were started along religious lines, much of their early organizational life centred around their churches.

The eastern European origins of the German-speaking settlers shaped the settlement patterns of Ukrainians in Alberta. The Germans at Josephsburg were instrumental in encouraging their former Ukrainian neighbours in Galicia to come to Alberta.

Ivan Pylypiw, a Ukrainian peasant of moderate means, had heard about Canada from former German neighbours. He and a former employee, Vasyl Eleniak, came to Canada in 1891 and inspected the unsettled prairie lands. After filing for a homestead, Pylypiw returned to Ukraine to tell his story of opportunities in Canada. Austrian authorities arrested and jailed him briefly for promoting emigration. His trial effectively advertised Canada. Between 1892 and 1894, through Pylypiw's promotional efforts, the Edna-Star area became the main destination for the Ukrainian immigrants to Canada. In 1895 Dr. Josef Oleskiw, an agricultural expert in Galicia, toured Canada and met with government officials. His promotional booklets encouraging immigration publicized Canada widely. These early efforts by Pylypiw and Oleskiw eventually led to the arrival of tens of thousands of Ukrainians, who came to Alberta from the late 1890s onward.

The completion of the CPR also made possible the settlement in Alberta during the 1880s and early 1890s of a small number of Chinese immigrants, who were fleeing poverty and overpopulation in southern China. Chinese workers, having just completed the British Columbia section of the CPR, came east to open restaurants and laundries in villages and towns across the prairies. By 1885 there were a few Chinese living in Calgary and Lethbridge, by 1887 in Medicine Hat, and by 1889 in Edmonton. In the Calgary region, which had the largest number of Chinese, they were also employed as ranch cooks and domestic servants. However, restrictive immigration regulations and prejudice discouraged their coming, and by 1891 there were only thirty-one Chinese in Alberta. Nonetheless, this handful of settlers were the forerunners of many other Chinese who, against great odds, contributed to the development of Alberta's economy and society and who, through their presence, helped lay the foundation for Alberta's becoming a multiracial and a multicultural society.

The slow but steady influx of settlers from Ontario and Britain during the 1880s and early 1890s firmly established their cultural dominance in the Northwest. After the North-West Rebellion of 1885, the North-West Territories was controlled by white people. After 1892, with the imposition of a unilingual territorial legislature, it was officially an English-speaking area.

By 1896 the ranching frontier, which had dominated the economic and political life of southern Alberta throughout the 1880s and early 1890s, was under threat. After 1896, with new economic conditions and a new Liberal government committed to settling the West, agricultural expansion began on a large scale. The early settlements of Mormons, Germans, French Canadians, Scandinavians, Ukrainians, Chinese, and others became the nuclei of much larger settlements of co-religionists and fellow countrymen. Many other immigrants were also becoming aware of the potential of the "last best west," North America's last agricultural frontier. By the late 1890s, Alberta would be transformed into a society that was even more ethnically and religiously plural, and one that was rapidly growing and changing. This growing diversity would eventually challenge and change the British- and Ontario-dominated patterns of politics, religion, and education first established in the West in the late nineteenth century.

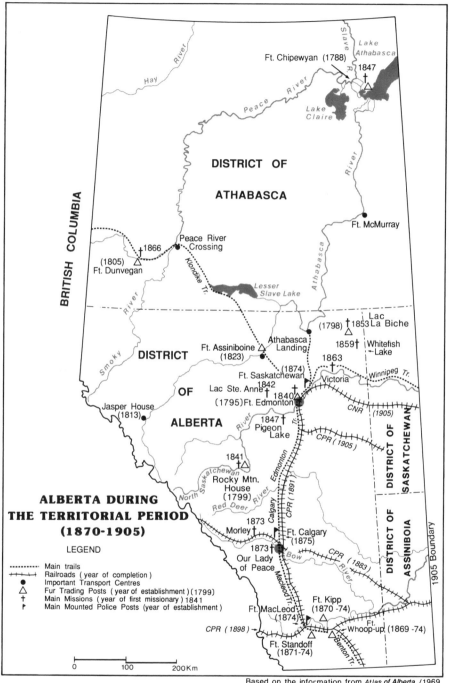

ALBERTA DURING
THE TERRITORIAL PERIOD
(1870-1905)

LEGEND

- - - - - - - - Main trails
+++++ Railroads (year of completion)
● Important Transport Centres
△ Fur Trading Posts (year of establishment) (1799)
✝ Main Missions (year of first missionary) 1841
⊧ Main Mounted Police Posts (year of establishment)

DISTRICT OF
ATHABASCA

Ft. Chipewyan (1788)
1847

Ft. McMurray

BRITISH COLUMBIA

Peace River
Crossing
1866
(1805)
Ft. Dunvegan

Lesser
Slave Lake

DISTRICT

OF

ALBERTA

Jasper House
(1813)

Ft. Assiniboine △
(1823)

Athabasca
Landing

(1798) ✝ 1853 Lac
La Biche

1859 ✝ Whitefish
◄ Lake

1863
✝

(1874)
Ft. Saskatchewan
1842
Lac Ste. Anne ✝
1840 ✝
(1795) Ft. Edmonton

Victoria

Winnipeg Tr.

CNR (1905)

1847 ✝
Pigeon
Lake

1841
✝ △

Rocky Mtn.
House
(1799)

CPR (1905)

DISTRICT OF
SASKATCHEWAN

1873
Morley ✝
1873 ✝
Our Lady
of Peace

Ft. Calgary
(1875)

CPR (1883)

DISTRICT OF
ASSINIBOIA

1905 Boundary

CPR (1898)

Ft. MacLeod ⊧
(1874)

Ft. Kipp
(1870 -74)
△

Ft. Standoff
(1871-74)

Ft.
Whoop-up (1869 -74)

0   100   200 Km

Based on the information from *Atlas of Alberta* /1969

75

CHAPTER FOUR

Peopling the "Last Best West": 1896-1913

The North-West Territories did not attract large numbers of settlers until the end of the nineteenth century. In the 1890s, however, the opportunities of the new agricultural frontier, combined with an expansive Canadian immigration policy and conditions in Europe, prompted many people to seek a new life in Canada.

The years between 1896 and World War I were formative ones for Alberta. During this time, homesteaders took up most of the province's farmland. Alberta's towns and cities grew dramatically, and hundreds of new communities began from scratch. Patterns of urban dominance and of ethnic and religious concentration solidified. Class divisions also emerged clearly.

Two new transcontinental railways, the Grand Trunk Pacific and the Canadian Northern, were pushed westward across the province toward Edmonton and through the Rockies. Branch lines were also built from the main settlement spine of the province between Edmonton and Fort Macleod.[1] The branch lines were arranged almost like an anatomical nervous system east and west of this main corridor, and settlement expanded quickly along these routes. Towns sprang up along the railways to meet the needs of the farmers.

Rapid population growth and increased economic activity fed upon each other to produce a boom atmosphere. A booster press and business interests hyped all the economic developments, real and imagined, producing inflated expectations about Alberta's potential. These expectations would eventually come crashing down, only to rise again in later decades in Alberta's continual cycle of booms and busts.

Alberta in the early years of the twentieth century was an immigrant society. Until the 1930s, half of its population was foreign-born. The immigrants' children were also caught up in the often difficult process of adaptation to a new culture. The interplay and clash of the newcomers' ideals and values provides much of the drama and excitement of Alberta's history in the early twentieth century.

Immigration Policy and Public Attitudes

After 1896, migration to Alberta increased dramatically. The agricultural depression of the early 1890s was ending. The new federal Liberal government, elected in 1896, inaugurated an aggressive campaign to promote immigration. Clifford Sifton, a Manitoba lawyer, was the cabinet minister responsible for immigration. The most powerful western voice in Prime Minister Wilfrid Laurier's cabinet, Sifton dedicated his political career to peopling the West. Laurier and Sifton were guided by the economic and nationalistic motives that had fueled Macdonald's national policy. Sifton altered the land-grant system, through which speculators and colonization companies had tied up much of the best land. He simplified the process of securing homesteads and placed new emphasis on the campaign to attract immigrants.

Sifton's immigration policy was aimed at attracting farmers. He believed that the most desirable immigrants were industrious, self-sufficient farmers and peasants. While the Ontario-born Sifton recognized that his fellow Anglo-Canadians preferred that the West be settled with people from Ontario, Great Britain, and north-western Europe, he knew these places could not supply enough immigrants. He turned as well to central and eastern Europe for potential settlers. When steamship companies began circulating information about 160 acres (64 hectares) of free land in Canada, many peasants could not resist.

Sifton's campaign was helped by favourable economic circumstances. Due to growing demand from a rapidly urbanizing Europe, the prices of western staple products rose while transportation costs to Europe fell. At the same time, new inventions in farm machinery, the building of mechanical grain elevators, and the development of an early-maturing wheat made it possible to cultivate, seed, harvest, and market vast expanses of land. Most important of all, the American frontier had been largely settled by the mid-1890s. By the turn of the century, Canada's North-West Territories were becoming widely known as North America's "last best west."

Immigrants flooded into Canada. A nation of only 5,000,000 in 1900 absorbed over 1,250,000 immigrants in the next ten years. During the following decade, 2,050,000 newcomers arrived even though the outbreak of the World War I in 1914 curtailed immigration. Between 1901 and 1911, the country's population increased by one-third, and Alberta's population increased 5.5 times, from 73,000 in 1901 to 374,000 in 1911.

Widely held notions of a world-wide racial hierarchy based on social Darwinism, which circulated as scientific fact in the English-speaking world in the late nineteenth century, were firmly embedded in Canada's immigration policy. During this period of British imperial ascendancy, British immigrants were considered "best." Anglo-Canadians gloried in the exploits of the British Empire, believing in loyalty to God, king, and country. They had been taught that the Anglo-Saxons and the British government were the apex of biological evolution and human achievement. The *Edmonton Bulletin* of January 10, 1906, expressed this widely held view: "The ideal of the West is not only greatness, but greatness achieved under the British Flag and stamped and moulded by the genius of race." Anglo-Saxon nativism, or hostility to non-British immigrants, which emerged among many people of British origin in Alberta as elsewhere in English-speaking Canada in the late 19th century, was based both on Anglo-Saxon racial thinking, and a strong colonial emphasis on preserving the cultural aspects of British traditions. It was assumed that British immigrants could help maintain these traditions. Americans were also thought to be ideal settlers, although there were concerns, particularly in central Canada, that they might "Americanize" the West. Scandinavians, Germans, and other northern and western Europeans were also considered desirable, while Slavs, Jews, and southern Europeans were regarded as questionable. Blacks and Asians were considered inferior and undesirable. These racial and ethnic prejudices were also reinforced by strong religious prejudices, particularly anti-Catholic prejudice.

The reaction of the Anglo-Canadian opinion leaders in Alberta to the new immigration suggests that they shared a common set of assumptions about the future role that non-Anglo-Saxon immigrants should play in prairie society. Virtually all subscribed to the tenets of Anglo-conformity, or the belief that it was the obligation of newcomers to conform to the already fixed values and institutions of Canadian society. These assimilationist assumptions had already been clearly revealed in the popular campaign against French-language rights and Roman Catholic schools in the 1890s, which had led to the abolition of bilingualism in the territorial legislature. In the public opposition to bilingualism, the argument was consistently

Settlers leaving their ox-drawn wagons for their new homestead land at Oyen, in eastern Alberta. Immigrants, usually attracted by "free land," came from all over Europe, North America, and parts of Asia, to build new lives for themselves and their families. *(Glenbow Archives NA 3081-16)*

made by politicians and the press that "if the French were to receive language rights, why not Norwegians, Germans, Icelanders, and Hungarians."[2] Most Anglo-Albertans judged minority groups on the basis of how quickly they could be assimilated, and European immigrants who were not quickly assimilated were thought to be in need of a "Canadianization" campaign. At the very least, their children should be assimilated through public schools. Even those Liberal politicians who favoured an open door policy on European immigration were confident that assimilation was not only possible but inevitable. Most agreed that non-whites could not be assimilated, so they would either have to be excluded or their numbers kept at a minimum.

British and American Immigrants

Although the immigration boom brought people from all over Europe and North America, by 1914 over half of the population of Alberta could trace their roots to Britain. This majority came mostly from Ontario, the U.S., and Britain in roughly equal numbers. There were some examples of conflict amongst the three. American farmers often regarded the British as effete and impractical, while the British tended to think of the Americans as brash, aggressive, and materialistic. Overall, through common religious, social, and political ties, the three groups came together to fashion the province's dominant economic, political, and social institutions.

79

Sifton's efforts to promote British immigration were only partially successful. While British farmers resisted the lure of immigration propaganda, many working-class people from cities saw little hope for advancement in a class-ridden Britain. Between 1900 and 1914, over one million people migrated from the United Kingdom to Canada. By 1911, just over 18 per cent of Alberta's population was British-born. The English were by far the largest group, the Scots a distant second. Though most of the farm-bound British immigrants came as individuals and were widely scattered, some were part of group settlements. These ventures were not successful because few of the British immigrants had farming experience.

One of the most ambitious attempts at British group settlement was the Barr Colony, located at what is now Lloydminster on the Alberta-Saskatchewan border. The Barr colonists were led by two Anglican clergymen. Isaac Barr was from Ontario, and had served briefly as a preacher in the North-West Territories before running through a series of conflict-ridden posts in parishes in the U.S. Englishman George Exton Lloyd was a fiery orator and veteran of the North-West Rebellion. He had run a boy's school in New Brunswick before returning to England to work for a church missionary society. In 1902 Barr went to London, where he began developing a scheme to promote British immigration to Canada. Barr and Lloyd developed a plan to bring thousands of Britishers to the Prairies to "keep it [Canada] as much as possible in the hands of people of British birth."[3] Barr advertised the farm colony in English newspapers. In 1903 almost two thousand people, mostly young city dwellers from the lower middle class with no farming experience, boarded a ship for Canada.

Unfortunately, Barr proved to be a poor organizer. On the ship the settlers contended with overcrowding and poor food, on the railway journey with uncomfortable trains and lost baggage, in Saskatoon at the railhead with merchants who overcharged mercilessly. They blamed Barr and turned to Lloyd, who had come along as chaplain, as their leader. Barr, under heavy criticism, including threats on his life, deserted the group in early May. But the problems the settlers encountered were only partly due to Barr's mismanagement. They were also a result of the settlers' exaggerated expectations and lack of pioneering experience.

Lloyd took over Barr's homestead and turned it into the townsite. The settlers decided to call the village Lloydminster. By March 1904, one hundred homes were under construction in the village, which, on Lloyd's insistence, forbade the sale of liquor.

The pioneer experience of the Barr Colonists was similar to that of many other immigrant groups. Their common migration experience and their self-help projects gave them a strong sense of identity. Until the 1920s, the Barr colonists dominated the community and controlled over half of the seats on the town council, hospital board, school board, and agricultural societies.

The British had their greatest impact as merchants, professionals, civic officials, and skilled workers in small towns and cities. Many British immigrants who started off as homesteaders eventually became postmasters, policemen, and merchants in smalltown Alberta. Skilled British workers also built many of the public buildings and homes in the prewar real estate boom in Alberta's cities. In Alberta's mines, British miners and mining engineers controlled the management positions as engineers, foremen, and pit bosses. British immigrants were also leaders in the labour movement in Alberta.

Many young British "gentlewomen" from the middle and upper-middle classes also came west to carve out a life for themselves. They not only came with husbands and children but many set out on their own. In Victorian Britain, there was a "surplus" of females because of the large numbers of males who had emigrated or left for military service. In addition, where ideals prescribing women's lives were rigidly bound by notions of correct, polite behaviour, and where "gentlewomen" were "removed from all form of productive labour except child-birth," there was a keen interest in the possibilities that immigration to Canada seemed to offer: adventure, opportunities for economic improvement, and often marriage. Female emigration societies in Britain such as the British Women's Emigration Association encouraged emigration to Canada, picturing Canada as a "cultural backwoods, desperately in need of the refining touch of British gentlewomen."[4]

Once they arrived in Alberta, the transition of British "gentlewomen" was often difficult and, like other immigrant women, they faced loneliness and homesickness. To ease their adjustment, they kept strong ties with home through letters, and through British magazines and newspapers. Many added to the preponderantly British tone among Calgary's economic and social elite and in the ranching district along the foothills in communities such as Millarville and Priddis. Their domestic tastes, from silver candelabra to pictures, curtains, lamps, linens, carving sets, and even pianos, transformed many Alberta homesteads. Recent studies of these women suggest that despite their trials of adjustment to a new land, which turned out not to be just an extension of British society, they often found a new sense of independence and self-worth in their new homeland. They joined community groups, supported hospitals, and joined groups with a strong British orientation such as the Imperial Order of the Daughters of the Empire and the Red Cross.

British workers, who were predominantly male, brought their working-class culture with them. In Calgary and Edmonton they had their own boarding houses, sports clubs, men's organizations, and even some residential concentrations. The Odd Fellows, Sons of England, Caledonian and St. Andrew's Societies, Orange Order, Sons of Wales, and regional associations all provided sociability, insurance benefits, and job networks to working-class and middle-class immigrants. Though they thought of themselves as different from other immigrants, the British in the cities created many of the same kinds of ethnic institutions as those established by other groups.

Because the Canadian government did so much to encourage British immigration, by 1911 British immigrants in Alberta were second in number only to the Americans. Their influence was evident in the creation of a skilled labour force, in the numerical and social prominence of the Anglican, Presbyterian, and Methodist churches, and in lingering class distinctions in urban areas. English and Scottish place names such as Banff, Calgary, and Airdrie predominate in Alberta. Names of villages dotted along railway branch lines such as Coronation, Throne, Veteran, Loyalist, Consort, and Monitor recall the importance of the British tie to many of the railway officials who named them.

British investors, adventurers, tourists, and royalty kept British interest in the Canadian West alive. Writers Arthur Conan Doyle and Rudyard Kipling both visited Alberta. British mountaineers Edward Whymper and Norman Collie explored many unclimbed peaks in the Rockies; Collie was one of the first white people to explore the Columbia Icefield. Well-publicized and lavishly staged royal and vice-regal trips by the Duke and Duchess of York (the Duke was eventually King George V) in 1901, the Duke and Duchess of Connaught in 1912, and Edward, Prince of Wales, in 1919 reminded Albertans of their British ties. British adventurers escaping "civilization," such as John George "Kootenai" Brown in Waterton, and Justin James "Jimmy" Simpson and E. William "Bill" Peyto in Banff, pioneered as trappers, guides, and conservationists in the Rockies.

Although there was a large influx of British immigrants elsewhere in the region, the cultural and political influence of the Conservative-oriented British and Anglo-Canadian ranchers in southern

American immigrants from Colorado arriving in Bassano in 1914. Americans, who came in large numbers to central and southern Alberta in the period up to 1914, played a key role in pioneer Alberta. *(Glenbow Archives NA 3060-1)*

Alberta waned after the settlement-oriented Liberals came to power in Ottawa. Also, with the outbreak of World War I, many of the young Britons returned to Europe to fight.

Sifton made great efforts to attract American farmers. They were considered desirable because they were predominantly of British background, and they brought machinery, money, and farming experience. The many American farmers who responded had a significant economic, social, and political impact on central and southern Alberta.

By the turn of the century, good land was becoming scarce and expensive in the American West. Between 1898 and 1914, nearly 600,000 American immigrants, mostly farmers from the Midwest, came to western Canada. By 1911, 22 per cent of Alberta's population was American-born, making them the largest immigrant group. By the 1920s, in the southern region, up to half of the farmers were Americans.

Perhaps as many as one-third of those coming from the U.S. were actually European-born. They had immigrated to the U.S. in the 1860s, 1870s, and 1880s, and now sought land for their children. The Canadian government hired special agents in the U.S. to encourage group settlements of Welsh, Norwegians, Danes, Dutch, Belgians, French Canadians, German Russians, and several religious minorities, including Mormons.

The Canadian government did not, however, want American black settlers to come to western Canada. When a few hundred blacks from Oklahoma, who were fleeing racial persecution, came to the

Edmonton area in 1910 and 1911, the federal government, responding to a hostile public, prevented further entry. Drawing on existing racist myths and stereotypes, several boards of trade in the Edmonton area, the Edmonton Trades and Labour Council, women's organizations, and newspapers peppered the federal government with resolutions, petitions, and editorials opposing an influx of blacks. They warned that western Canada would be importing the racial problems of the American South. The boards of trade petition as printed in the *Edmonton Capital* on April 25, 1911, stated directly, "We submit that the advent of such negroes as are now here was most unfortunate for the country, and that further arrivals in large numbers would be disastrous."

Before the government slammed the door, a thousand black Americans had arrived in Alberta and established several small farming communities in northern regions, including settlements at Amber Valley, Campsie, Wildwood, and Breton, all within a 100-mile (160-kilometre) radius of Edmonton. All were in isolated, bush-covered areas where the farm land was of marginal productivity and the climate was cool and moist. The black pioneers deliberately picked isolated areas because they wanted to be independent of white racism, and wanted to have large enough tracts of land to establish predominantly black settlements. Their isolation protected them from discrimination and helped give them a strong sense of community. However, the marginal land and harsh climate contributed to economic stagnation and the eventual decline of their communities.

The largest of the rural black settlements, and the only one that remained virtually all-black until after World War II, was Amber Valley, east of Athabasca. The history of this pioneer settlement, aside from its unique racial character, is representative of the history of nearly all small northern Alberta hamlets removed from major transportation routes. The first settlers began arriving in Amber Valley in 1910. They were joined the next year by other family members and friends, some of whom came in a group of ninety-three adults and fifty-six children brought from Oklahoma by a black clergyman, Parson H. Sneed. Even prior to their settling in the area, a sense of community existed among some of the blacks, since they came as families who had been neighbours in Oklahoma, or who had belonged to the same fraternal organizations, the Masons and Oddfellows, which had organized the groups of emigrants.

The first tasks awaiting new settlers were building homes and preparing land for crops. Covered with heavy brush, the land had to be cleared by hand with axes and grub hoes. The spruce stumps were often as large as a metre in diameter, making the work arduous and exhausting. Given these difficulties, only small amounts of land could be cultivated; by 1920 the average cropped land per farm in Amber Valley consisted of only thirty-three acres (thirteen hectares). In order to supplement their incomes, a number of men ventured to Edmonton to work in meat-packing plants or on construction; others hired themselves out as loggers, or worked as freighters to northern trading posts at Wabasca, Fort McMurray, and Fort Chipewyan, or worked with construction crews building the railroads.

Isolated from the outside world, the early black settlers soon established social institutions and developed a strong sense of community. A school was begun in 1913 and a church in 1914. Social activities included parties, dances, and (after 1915) the famous Amber Valley picnic, a two- or three-day event that drew people from a seventy-five-kilometre radius for foot and horse races, games, greased pig chases, pulling contests, good food, and dancing. The community became known throughout the North for its baseball team and boxers. The strong sense of solidarity in the community was reinforced by intermarriage among the Canadian-raised generation. At the community's peak during the 1930s, there were 350 blacks, about 95 per cent of the area's population.

However, isolation, the cold climate, and primitive conditions disillusioned many with farming, and there was a continual exodus of people who either returned to the U.S. or moved to Edmonton. Farm mechanization during the 1920s and 1930s meant that bigger farms were necessary to make economical use of expensive equipment, so many marginal farms were sold. During World War II, many young men left to join the armed forces, and young men and women left for better wages in the city. Though only a few black families are still in Amber Valley, the community remains a spiritual home for hundreds of people who grew up there and are now scattered across western Canada and the United States.

A few blacks also settled in urban areas, particularly Calgary and Edmonton, where they recreated in miniature the social and religious life centred around lodges and churches that blacks had created in American cities. Blacks who chose the cities, or were forced to the cities by lack of economic opportunity in the rural areas, found their opportunities limited by prejudice and discrimination. Unbending stereotypes confined them to service roles as railway porters and domestics, and one minor anti-black riot took place in Calgary during

World War II. Not until the postwar period did a public battle against racism and the emergence of black pride bring new opportunities and considerable social mobility to blacks in Alberta.

Although several settlements of transplanted European Americans developed in Alberta between 1896 and 1914, most American immigrants did not constitute a closely knit group. They came as individuals or in small family groups. Throughout central and southern Alberta, Americans immediately became involved in local politics and education, and established local fraternal and service organizations. They also organized sports such as baseball, basketball, and rodeo, which became community-wide institutions.

The Americans were less likely than some other groups to leave their home place names on the landscape. However, there are still many reminders of this large immigration scattered across rural Alberta. These include New Dayton and Usona (United States of North America). In the early years of settlement, Fourth of July celebrations were common across southern Alberta, although they often combined symbols that indicated their growing attachment to Canada. The *Lethbridge Herald* of July 6, 1914, described one such event. It brought together four hundred former Americans and included a dinner and baseball game:

> The most noticeable feature of the whole proceeding was the predominance of the Union Jack, and although the Stars and Stripes were very much in evidence, the British colors flew from the top of each mast, which goes to show that though there is still a love for the great republic from which these people came, they are now true Canadians.

Although most Americans joined with eastern Canadians and British immigrants to establish the major Protestant denominations, they also brought to western Canada a great diversity of religious groups from the American Midwest. They brought at least twenty-eight evangelical sects, and helped establish several Bible colleges, which exert a continuing influence on prairie religion.

Probably Americans' greatest impact was through the farmers' organizations and new political groups that they helped to establish before the 1920s. Much of the ideology and leadership of the new agrarian reform organizations came from the U.S. Two of Alberta's earliest farm organizations, the Society of Equity (begun in 1905) and the Non-Partisan League (begun in 1917) were brought directly from the U.S. Henry Wise Wood, Alberta's most important farm leader, was from Missouri. He moved to Alberta in 1905. The Carstairs farmer developed many of his ideas out of his experience with populist farm protest movements in the U.S. Like Wood, many of the other directors of the United Farmers of Alberta (UFA) after its formation in 1909 were American-born. Direct legislation (including referendums and the recall of public officials), the single tax, proportional representation, the abolition of an appointed senate, and monetary reform were all populist reforms advocated by Americans who believed in the ideal of a more democratic society.

Northern and Western Europeans

Many migrants from the U.S. came from the Scandinavian settlements in the American Midwest. Just as in the late 1880s and early 1890s, Scandinavians who came in the early years of the twentieth century settled primarily in central Alberta along the edge of the park belt, where they appreciated the presence of wood, hay, and water, and built a thriving dairy industry. More Icelandic immigrants joined the original settlers at Markerville. Scandinavians, such as the Danes at Standard and Dalum, the Norwegians at Claresholm, and the Swedes at Scandia and Stavely, also developed sizable settlements on the open prairies. Lutheran churches or church-related organizations often helped organize the migration.

H. N. Ronning, a Norwegian Lutheran minister and father of renowned Canadian diplomat Chester Ronning, founded a Norwegian settlement in the Peace River district in 1912. Ronning had been a missionary in China but, forced out of China by the Boxer Rebellion of 1900, he had fled to Iowa. In 1907 the family joined many other Norwegian Americans and moved to the Camrose area. Ronning soon saw Norwegian families leaving for the Peace River district because of land pressure and felt he should guide them. As he later recalled, "I was grieved that our Norwegian people seeking land scattered so widely. Neither church nor government lent them any guidance...I felt fully convinced that our church ought to do more to guide and gather our people in the founding of new settlements."[5]

After a scouting expedition to the Peace River district, he chose land with "wide, sweeping slopes; the whole landscape looking like an immense park. The grass was abundant. There was running water and a fine piece of timberland near by. Small wonder that we called it Valhalla, the home of the Gods...I was at once fully convinced that there was the place where God wanted us to settle."[6] Many more

Norwegian immigrants, attracted by the Norwegian Lutheran character of the settlement, came from the U.S., Norway, and other parts of Canada. The Lutheran clergy discouraged dancing, drinking, and cardplaying in the settlement.

Scandinavian settlers built churches that continue to play an important role in the communities. They also established several educational institutions, such as Camrose Lutheran College, opened by the United Norwegian Lutheran Church of America in 1911.

The Finns were a contrast to the largely church-going Danes, Norwegians, and Swedes. Leftwing and anticlerical ideas appealed to many Finnish immigrants, who had come from American mining communities marked by political radicalism. After the Canadian government set aside a tract of land west of Wetaskiwin and Red Deer for Finns, Finnish immigrants first came to Alberta from Montana in 1899 and 1900. To Finns working as unskilled labour in dangerous mines, the lure of free land in Alberta was irresistible. In coal-mining areas such as Canmore and the Crow's Nest Pass,[7] and in several scattered farming communities such as Sylvan Lake, Eckville, Trochu, and Thorhild, Finnish workers and farmers set up several branches of leftwing Finnish groups. The socialist hall was often more important than the Finnish Lutheran or Presbyterian Church as the focal point for community activities. The Finnish halls combined athletics, music, drama, dance, socializing, and politics.

Despite their large numbers (8 per cent of Alberta's population by 1911), the Scandinavians were not a highly visible group. They did not develop large concentrated blocs like the Ukrainians, nor were they as anxious to preserve a distinctive identity. Their previous American residence had already accustomed them to North America, and they were readily accepted by the English-speaking settlers. Nevertheless, the Scandinavians left a tangible legacy in Lutheran, Evangelical Free, Swedish Evangelical Covenant, and Swedish Baptist churches and Scandinavian place names and surnames.

Scandinavians made up by far the largest number of immigrants of northern and western European origin. However, Alberta also attracted Dutch, Belgian, and French immigrants. The Canadian government and the general public considered all three nationalities as part of the culturally and racially desirable northern European peoples, and the government and CPR immigration agents made special efforts to attract them.

Dutch farmers established a few widely scattered farming communities at Granum, Nobleford, Monarch, Strathmore, and Neerlandia, centred around either Reformed or Roman Catholic churches. The settlement at Neerlandia, eighty miles (128 kilometres) northwest of Edmonton, was begun in 1912 by seventeen Dutch settlers who had originally come to Edmonton from either the U.S. or Holland, but who wanted to become independent farmers. A group of Dutch Christian Reformed immigrants in Edmonton secured a tract of land where a Dutch Reformed community could be established. To attract immigrants, they wrote articles about Alberta for church newspapers in the U.S. and Holland. When the settlers arrived in Neerlandia after a week-long oxcart ride from Edmonton, their first chore was to build log cabins. Isolation forced the settlers to become self-sufficient, and before long they could depend almost entirely on game and their own gardens for food. In the first years of settlement, each pioneer family had to be its own butcher, veterinarian, blacksmith, shoemaker, and carpenter, since none of these services was within twenty miles (32 kilometres) of their settlement. Despite financial hardship, they were able to supplement their income by working at logging camps at Barrhead, the nearest major town. Through cooperative labour, in 1915 they built a church and two years later a school to serve the growing number of children in the settlement, which by then numbered about 150 people.

French-Speaking Albertans

Immigrants from France and Belgium, being culturally very diverse and few in number, formed only a few short-lived settlements. Beginning in 1903, one group of former French cavalry officers established ranches at Trochu, named after its founder, Armand Trochu. Most returned to France at the beginning of World War I, and the French influence was short-lived. Another notable French immigrant was farmer and writer Georges Bugnet (1879–1981), who came to Canada in 1905 and homesteaded at Rich Valley, northwest of Edmonton. He became known for his novels and poetry in French, particularly the novel La Forêt, published in 1935, which tells of the struggles of a young urban French couple homesteading in northern Alberta.

French Canadians rather than French or Belgian immigrants made up the vast majority of French-speaking Albertans. Many of them came from overcrowded French Canadian settlements in industrial New England, though economic conditions in rural Quebec also led some to seek a new home in western Canada. The French

Canadians rather than the French or Belgian immigrants established the only long-term and viable French-language cultural institutions in the province. While St. Albert remained the religious centre of French Canadian life, Edmonton emerged as the cultural, educational, and political capital for Franco-Albertans. In 1894 French Canadians in Edmonton established their own branch of the Saint-Jean-Baptiste Society, the leading French Canadian patriotic organization, and in 1894 began publishing L'Ouest canadien, the first of many newspapers that spoke out for French language and Roman Catholic rights in Alberta. Franco-Albertans had some political influence in the larger society, particularly during the period of Liberal ascendancy from 1905 to 1921. At the height of their influence, in 1913, five French-speaking members, mostly from northern Alberta, and all Liberals, were returned to a fifty-six seat legislature. In 1905 Edmonton doctor Philippe Roy became the first of several French Canadians from northern Alberta appointed to the senate.

Germans, Mennonites, and Hutterites

German-speaking settlement accelerated after 1896 as Germans established more rural and church-centred communities. Though a majority of them were Lutherans, they also brought more than ten new German American Protestant denominations. In addition, German Catholics established several settlements, including one in the Peace River district at Friedenstal, just south of the present community of Fairview, between 1911 and 1916. From 1900 to the outbreak of World War I, German-speaking settlers opened nearly ninety previously unsettled areas. These communities often brought together co-religionists of German background from a wide variety of geographical areas. The settlement at Friedenstal brought together ethnic Germans from Russia, Germany, the U.S., Argentina, and other parts of Canada. A German-speaking working class, with its own distinct neighbourhoods, and a small German-speaking business class, also developed in several Alberta cities. Due to their high degree of religious sectarianism, diverse origins, and geographic dispersion, the German settlers did not constitute an integrated German community.

One of the German-speaking settlers from Switzerland was Carl Stettler, who came to Alberta from the U.S. in 1903. He established a small German Swiss community near what is now the town of Stettler and tried to convince other Swiss to join him. The detailed German-language promotional literature that he sent out to prospective homesteaders told of the advantages of the settlement:

Conditions here are more orderly than in many places I have seen in the United States. Your life is safer here than there, nobody carries firearms with the exception of the police...laws are obeyed better...altogether the people are more decent and better mannered...Who has courage, good will, enthusiasm for work and push will advance quicker here than anywhere else, as this country is only in a state of development and excellent chances are offered to those who keep their eyes open.[8]

Several German Swiss families joined him at Blumenau, where he was postmaster, and they developed a village with two general stores, a lumberyard, blacksmith shop, bakery, and feed store. When the CPR built a line through the region in 1905, they decided to locate a townsite two miles (3.2 kilometres) east of Blumenau. Though disappointed, Stettler and the rest of the village moved to the new site in 1906. The enterprising Stettler became postmaster, CPR land agent, and owner of a large hotel, and the new town was named in his honour.

Despite their isolation and religious sectarianism, the German-speaking settlers were well accepted before World War I. German settlers became involved at an early stage in local politics. By 1914, one of every ten persons in Alberta was of German background, and twenty-six towns, hamlets, or post offices, and twenty school districts bore German names.

Among the German-speaking settlers before World War I were four different sects of Mennonites. Named after a Dutch religious reformer, Menno Simons, they were an Anabaptist, pacifist group that believed in adult baptism, plain living, and remaining separate from the world. The Alberta Mennonites, who were mostly German-speaking, came from settlements in the U.S., Ontario, and Russia (by way of Manitoba). The largest group of Mennonites settled in Didsbury beginning in 1892. By 1914 there were fifteen small Mennonite settlements. They did not live in concentrated blocs as in Manitoba and Saskatchewan, and since most were willing to make compromises with the larger society, they avoided conflicts with the state over the education of their children, an issue that had dominated their early history in Manitoba.

The Hutterites, another Anabaptist sect, named after sixteenth-century religious reformer Jacob Hutter, came to Alberta during

91

World War I. Like the Mennonites, they believed in adult baptism, a voluntary and disciplined community, pacifism, separation from the world, and simple living. With their community of goods, communal living, distinctive clothing, and use of the German language over several generations, they went further than most Mennonites in their efforts to remain separate from the world.

The Hutterites had come from Russia to South Dakota in 1874. They moved to Canada in 1918 because of wartime persecution in the U.S. The Canadian government promised them exemption from military service and permission to live communally. In 1918 the Hutterites established ten colonies in southern Alberta, making it the area with the highest concentration of Hutterite colonies in the world. Their arrival during World War I sparked a flurry of protest from groups who worried about their use of German, their pacifism, and their communal living at a time when wartime hysteria meant that dissent or unorthodoxy of any kind was suspect. Later expansion of the Hutterite colonies aroused fears of a possible negative impact on the social and economic life of rural Alberta.

The Hutterites erected buildings in their familiar pattern with houses and a dining hall in the centre, and farm buildings on the outside. Their commitment to hard work, cooperative labour, self-denial, and communal pooling of capital made them ideally suited to adapt to the rigours of prairie agriculture.

Central and Eastern Europeans

Sifton's decision to look to central and eastern Europe for farmers changed the development of Alberta. In the late 1800s in central and eastern Europe, most peasants had only tiny tracts of land, too small to support their families. They faced mounting debts. Their sons had to do military service for alien governments, and hostile governments often restricted the use of their mother languages.

The central and eastern Europeans who came to Alberta made a major contribution to agriculture, developing large tracts of farmland in east-central Alberta. After the turn of the century, they also did much of the railway building, coal mining, and hard manual labour in the cities. By 1911 they had arrived in such large numbers that one in nine Albertans could trace his or her roots to Slavic, Hungarian, and Romanian groups from central and eastern Europe.

The cultural patterns of the central and eastern Europeans in Alberta were a blend of Old World traditions and pioneer pragma-

Russian Orthodox Church at Smoky Lake. The cross-topped churches with their onion-shaped domes are characteristic landmarks throughout central and northern Alberta. The Russian Orthodox, Ukrainian Catholic, and Ukrainian Greek Orthodox churches vied for support among the Ukrainians. Churches were important forces of continuity and stability for uprooted immigrants. *(Provincial Archives of Alberta U.V. 16)*

tism. They maintained their traditional architecture in homes and their Greek Catholic, Russian Orthodox, and Ukrainian Orthodox churches. They celebrated holidays and festivals associated with European peasant life, and the first generation kept the styles of food and clothing of their homelands. Their rural bloc settlements, their cultural distinctiveness, their initial inability to speak English, and prejudice against them kept them on the margins of western Canadian society for decades. As a result, they kept their languages and cultures alive much longer than many other European immigrant groups.

By far the largest group of central and eastern Europeans were Ukrainians from the provinces of Galicia and Bukovina in the Austro-Hungarian Empire. Once Sifton decided to advertise and encourage immigration from the region, the number of immigrants increased rapidly. Between 1896 and 1914, approximately 170,000 Ukrainians came to Canada, the vast majority settling in the prairie provinces. Closely related to them by language and culture were the Poles, also from Galicia, who in Alberta settled primarily in the predominantly Ukrainian bloc. Romanians, who came from Bukovina, were also closely linked with the Ukrainians by culture and religion. They established a community at Boian, in the midst of the Ukrainian bloc.

Both the immigrants from central and eastern Europe and government agents felt that the parkbelt was an ideal location for settlement for Ukrainian peasant farmers. The wooded and lake-dotted regions north of the drier prairies provided wood for homes and fuel and water for livestock, and the meadowland provided hay for cattle. The area was also well-supplied with fish and game. The bloc settlements enabled the newcomers to take care of each other in case of illness, accidents, or death.

The Ukrainians gradually extended their original settlement eastward along an axis from Star to Vegreville. By 1905 the Ukrainian bloc was expanding north of the North Saskatchewan River and west in the direction of Two Hills and Myrnam. In later decades, with further immigration and expansion of families, the bloc expanded eastward and northward.

While the countryside in this region was populated largely by Ukrainian farmers, the towns that emerged along the railway, such as Mannville, Vegreville, and Mundare, were mostly dominated, socially and numerically, by English-speaking settlers until the 1920s and 1930s. The English-speaking businessmen and professionals provided the medical, legal, and educational facilities, and ran the grain elevators, banks, lumberyards, and creameries, which were usually branches of national corporations. There were also some Jewish merchants, who established themselves in the towns along the railway in the Ukrainian bloc; their eastern European background and language skills helped them relate to the Ukrainian majority. But by the 1920s, Ukrainians were settling in the railroad towns in larger numbers. Many second-generation Ukrainians established small businesses.

Central and eastern Europeans also formed an important part of the working class in the coal-mining camps and the largest cities. In addition to the Ukrainians and Poles who went into mining, many Hungarians, Czechs, and Slovaks came to Alberta by way of coal-mining communities in the U.S.

Czarist Russia also provided immigrants to the Prairies. German Russians constituted the largest group, but smaller numbers of other minorities—Byelorussians, Estonians, Latvians, Lithuanians, and two religious minorities, Jews and Doukhobors—also came to Canada. Many fled Russian military conscription and persecution of non-Russian minority groups, and they all sought better economic conditions in Canada.

94

Polish and Slovak miners in Bankhead during a Christmas religious procession. For some miners, religion and ethnicity provided an important form of solidarity in a new land, where they faced constant danger from mining accidents. Coal miners banded together to provide not only sociability, but also insurance in case of sickness, accident, or death. Some immigrant miners also turned to unions and left-wing ethnic organizations to help them face their new circumstances. (*Provincial Museum and Archives of Alberta 71.141*)

In the mines and cities, the central and eastern Europeans held less skilled jobs and made less money than most English-speaking workers. Alienated from their fellow Albertans by cultural and linguistic differences and discrimination, some of them turned to radical political and labour groups to try to change their living conditions. Left-wing political refugees from the Czarist Empire formed Russian, Lithuanian, Estonian, and Ukrainian organizations that urged radical political action.

The central and eastern Europeans faced more prejudice and discrimination than the Scandinavians or Germans. A negative public stereotype included images of their being dirty, immoral, unintelligent, lazy, politically corrupt, overly fond of alcohol and fighting, religiously deficient, and a threat to "British institutions." The Conservative press campaigned for restriction of "Galician" immigration. The *Calgary Herald* of January 19, 1899, demanded to know why Sifton was handing the Northwest over to "dirty hordes of half-civilized Galicians who come lacking everything but dirt."

The Doukhobors, rural peasants like the Ukrainians and Poles, were pacifists and believed in the communal ownership of property. The Russian government persecuted them because of their pacifism. Through the help of admirers in Russia (including novelist Leo Tolstoy), England, and Canada, over seven thousand Doukhobors came to Canada in 1899. The Canadian government promised them blocks of land, exemption from military service, and religious freedom.

The Doukhobors first went to Saskatchewan, where they established several communal agricultural villages. They came into conflict with the Canadian government when they opposed individual land holdings and objected to the oath of allegiance required to receive title to their land. They also objected to what they viewed as attempts to interfere with their religious lives through laws regulating marriage, divorce, and vital statistics. Because of conflict over the land issue, in 1907 the federal government confiscated the Doukhobors' land. As a result many of them moved to B.C., where they purchased private land.

The Doukhobors began their first colonies in Alberta in 1916 as offshoots of the B.C. settlement. They were located at the nearest points in Alberta's foothills where they could grow wheat profitably— Cowley and Lundbreck. Here, three hundred Doukhobors established thirteen communal villages, and maintained close economic and cultural ties with the Doukhobors in B.C. Doukhobors in Alberta have been plagued by controversy because of internal factionalism, and stigmatized because of the activities of the violence-prone Sons of Freedom Doukhobors in B.C. Nevertheless, individual Doukhobors in Alberta have struggled for decades to keep alive their belief in the sacredness of life through pacifism and vegetarianism, and have tried to illuminate the dangers of excessive individualism and materialism.

Unlike the rural Doukhobors, the Jews in Alberta went mostly to the cities. Jews in eastern Europe, prevented by law from owning farmland, had been craftsmen, teachers, or pedlars. Most Alberta Jews, largely from Russia and Poland, made a successful adjustment to urban life, usually in small business.

Jews began arriving in Alberta in the 1880s, fleeing religious persecution and seeking economic opportunity. The first Jews in Alberta were brothers Jacob and William Diamond. Jacob Diamond was a Russian Jew who immigrated to rural Ontario, then came to Calgary in 1888. He entered the hides business, pawnbroking, and eventually the liquor trade. William joined his brother in Calgary in 1892 and opened a tailoring shop. Abe Cristall, a Ukrainian Jew, arrived in Edmonton from Montreal as a young man in 1893. He began a cartage-drayman operation, went into the liquor business, and in 1895 opened a general store. This enterprise became the basis of a successful career that included ownership of several Edmonton hotels. All three men were instrumental in the early years in helping to bring an organized religious life to Jews in the two cities.

The first Jewish farming settlement began in 1893, when seventeen Jewish families came to central Alberta. These were eastern European Jews who had first gone to Chicago, where they had been recruited by a colonization agent to farm near Pine Lake. Though they received financial help from a Jewish relief agency in London, England, the group was destitute and lived in dugouts in the side of a hill overlooking a lake. Because of lack of capital and farming experience, they practically starved, and most left for the U.S. within two years.

Among the thousands of Jewish immigrants who came to Canada in the late nineteenth and early twentieth centuries, most stayed in the large urban centres of central Canada, particularly Montreal and Toronto. By 1901 there were only seventeen individual Jews left in Alberta territory. By 1911 the number had increased to 1505.

Between 1904 and 1911, Jews began farming settlements at Trochu, Rumsey, and Sibbald with the help of the European-based Jewish Colonization Association. These settlements were more successful than the Pine Lake disaster. The largest Jewish colony, at Rumsey, formed a major segment of the community's population, and Jews took an active part in community affairs. The population of these Jewish agricultural colonies declined during the 1920s and 1930s because of drought and debt, and because many of the settlers wanted to live in cities, which had more Jewish institutions.

There was little public enthusiasm for Jewish immigration. Yet anti-Semitism, based on notions of Jewish racial inferiority or inability to assimilate, was limited. Because of their small numbers, Jews who settled in Alberta encountered relatively little overt prejudice.

In Calgary and Edmonton, where roughly two-thirds of the province's 3200 Jews lived in 1921, they developed a community network with a wide variety of religious, cultural, and educational institutions. The communities were divided between the religiously conservative Hebraist group, and a smaller predominantly left-wing group, which wanted to maintain the Yiddish language and culture. They were united, however, in their support for the Zionist movement.

Mediterranean Immigrants

Since Canada's immigration policy was designed to attract farmers, the Canadian government discouraged supposedly urban-bound and racially "unpreferred" Mediterranean groups. Consequently the numbers of Greeks, Arabs, and Italians remained small. By 1921 there were only 350 Greeks, 200 Arabs, and 4000 Italians in the province. They did not farm because they had limited financial resources, and they had come to North America to escape agricultural life. Each of these groups developed its own niche in the provincial economy. The Greeks concentrated in small business—candy and ice cream stores, theatres, and restaurants. Like the Greeks, the Arabs were young and mostly male, with limited education and capital. Most began as pedlars, selling drygoods door-to-door. The Arab pedlars in northern Alberta usually used their profits from peddling and trading furs to establish drygoods and clothing stores in Edmonton, forming the nucleus of a Muslim community sufficiently large and active by 1938 to build a mosque, the first in Canada. One Arab community gradually developed in Lac La Biche, beginning in 1905 when two Lebanese immigrants began peddling drygoods and trading furs. While their numbers remained small until after World War II, the early Lebanese businessmen provided the nucleus of a postwar community. By the 1960s the Lebanese community constituted 10 per cent of the population and was able to support its own mosque and imam (clergyman).

Italians came as railroad workers and soon moved into coal mining and urban construction. The largest numbers lived in the coal mining areas of the Crow's Nest Pass, Drumheller, Nordegg, and Lethbridge, where they developed strong Italian mutual benefit organizations. Though the first Italian immigrants often came as sojourners intending to return to Italy, they gradually put down roots, arranged for wives or girlfriends to join them, and began raising families. In the Crow's Nest Pass and Calgary, there were enough Italians to develop small neighbourhoods or "little Italies," where they lived and had their own food stores. While most of those who lived in the Pass were miners, some later began small construction or logging businesses.

Most of the Italians avoided farming; however, there were some exceptions. North of Edmonton, groups of Italians established two farming communities, which they named Naples (begun in 1905 near Barrhead) and Venice (started in 1914 near Lac La Biche). These areas were heavily wooded and the settlers were isolated, but through cooperative effort the pioneers carved out successful farms for themselves. The railway, which passed through Venice, provided easy access to seasonal work in Edmonton, and on the railway. One of the descendants of these pioneer Italian farmers at Venice was Mike Maccagno, who became provincial Liberal leader in the late 1960s. He drew attention to the educational, health, and transportation needs of rural northern Alberta.

Chinese and Japanese

The numbers of Chinese and Japanese in Alberta remained small because of racist immigration regulations aimed at limiting their numbers. The Chinese continued to move into prairie cities and small towns, where they specialized in running restaurants and laundries that catered to the needs of a bachelor frontier society. During the pioneer years, there were far fewer Chinese women than men in Alberta. The Chinese men did domestic work, such as laundry and cooking, that other men were unwilling to do. Restaurants and laundries could be established with little capital and limited English language skills. Some Chinese also started market gardens. What these jobs required was a willingness to work incredibly long hours with little security and low pay despite very little chance for either wealth or social acceptance.

Very few of the Chinese had families in Canada. By 1921 there were nearly 3500 Chinese in Alberta, but less than 200 were women. Some left their families in China because they planned to return. The Canadian government also passed a special head tax, which after 1903 was $500. This made it very expensive for them to bring their families, since $500 amounted to almost two years pay for many workers. It was widely believed that the Chinese could not be assimilated, and that they provided unfair competition to white workers.

In small prairie towns, the Chinese lived lonely lives. Their isolation was relieved only by occasional visits back to China. Sometimes they were liked and accepted, but more often their speech, manners and dress provoked ridicule. The *Banff Crag and Canyon* of July 20, 1920, deplored the hostile treatment of the Chinese who, the editor believed, were looked on in "the light of an ox or ass to be beaten and kicked whenever the inclination arises."

In the largest cities, the Chinese congregated to form Chinatowns. Here they set up clan, regional, and political organizations that provided jobs, lodging, and credit. They also settled disputes,

Japanese sugar beet workers, Raymond, 1911. The Japanese had been brought by the Knight Sugar Company to work on sugar beet farms in the predominantly Mormon town of Raymond in 1908. *(Provincial Museum of Alberta PH75.7.396)*

encouraged Chinese economic interests, and tried to influence political developments in China. The Chinese lived together partly out of choice, because they spoke the same language and wanted to help each other, but also because of white discrimination.

Prior to World War I, there were attempts in several of Alberta's cities to keep the Chinese residentially segregated and to prevent them from voting. Hostility occasionally erupted into violence. In 1892, there was an anti-Chinese riot in Calgary, triggered by the outbreak of smallpox among a few of the city's Chinese residents. Three hundred men, after a cricket match and dinner, attacked the Chinese, hoping to run them out of town. They badly wrecked one of the laundries and "visited" three others, where they "roughed up" the Chinese proprietors. The town police did not appear during the early stages of the riot, partly because the mayor was in sympathy with the rioters. Only after the appearance of the NWMP did the crowd disperse.

The Chinese became a political issue. In southern Alberta in the 1908 federal and 1909 provincial elections, both parties strained to be the most anti-Chinese. Conservative MP and rancher John Herron told the press he would rather be left home than elected by Chinese votes. The *Lethbridge Herald* of October 17, 1907, demanded that the Chinese be disfranchised, arguing that they had no right to compete with either white labour or white votes. Calgary's Conservative heavyweight R. B. Bennett told his audience that "we must not allow our shores to be over-run by Asiatics and become dominated by an alien race."[9]

The Japanese began coming to Canada later than the Chinese, and most remained in B.C. A few came to the Lethbridge region, where they worked as coal miners or as farmers in the sugar beet fields around Raymond. Although strong pressures developed in B.C. to restrict Japanese immigration, there were not as many restrictions on Japanese immigrants as on the Chinese, making it easier for them to bring their families. By 1921, a quarter of the nearly five hundred Japanese in Alberta were women.

During the 1920s, tighter immigration regulations brought the number of newcomers from China and Japan to a virtual halt. Culturally distinctive, socially segregated, and victims of white prejudice, the Chinese and Japanese remained on the fringes of Albertan society until after World War II.

Native Peoples

With the massive influx of settlers, the Indians and Métis, who had constituted the majority of the population less than thirty years before, became a small minority numbering by 1911 only 3 per cent of Alberta's population. While white newcomers were building a new settler society, white teachers and missionaries were trying to destroy the natives' culture. Government-supported Indian industrial and residential schools, run by Christian churches, were bent on "civilizing" the Indians. These schools separated Indian children from their parents, and banned the use of their tribal languages and the practice of their native religious rituals. They taught native children to renounce their culture and history, with longterm social and psychological effects on those who were taught that they were inferior. Overcrowded and unsanitary living conditions and poverty on the reserves contributed to malnutrition and disease. Serious epidemics, particularly tuberculosis, killed many. Forced onto reserves and closely supervised by police and government agents, the Indians lost the last remnants of their cherished freedom.

Some of the younger people, educated in the residential schools run by Christian missionaries, did manage to adjust to the newcomers' ways. Most, however, found it extremely difficult, if not impossible, to make the transition to a settled agricultural way of life.

The influx of whites into northern Alberta led the Canadian government to extend its Indian policy northward in 1899-1900. When people going overland to the Klondike gold rush in 1897 and

1898 bogged down in their attempt to get from Edmonton, at the head of steel, to the Klondike, some stayed in the Peace River district. Natives were concerned about the growing illegal liquor traffic and white trappers' use of poison bait, which killed Indian hunting dogs. The natives wanted the government to deal with these problems. The federal government, anxious to get full title to this region of mineral and agricultural potential, sent a treaty party in 1899-1900 to nego-tiate Treaty No. 8. Encouraged by the NWMP and missionaries, woodland Indians in various parts of the region including the Wood-land Cree, Chipewyan, Beaver, and Slavey signed the treaty.

The influx of settlers into Alberta threatened the Indians' land base. As white settlers pressed for more land, the federal government encouraged Indians to sell their "idle" lands to make way for white settlement. In return, the Indians would receive money that could be used to improve their living conditions. From 1900 to 1914, several bands accepted the federal government's offers of cash for land, and Alberta bands gave up roughly five hundred (1295 square km.) out of three thousand square miles of land. In the long run, reserves that surrendered land and received money showed little apparent advance-ment over those that did not.

The Métis also faced a difficult transition, though without trea-ties, reserves, and special legal protection and status. After the 1885 rebellion, the federal government awarded them scrip that entitled them to 240 acres (about 100 hectares) of land or $240 dollars. Most took the cash scrip, which was soon gone.

On the initiative of Father Albert Lacombe, the Roman Catholics established an agricultural mission, St. Paul de Métis, among the Métis to help them adjust to the new society in the West. This mission began in 1896 on four townships of land near the Saddle Lake Indian reserve. The government and church promised land, equipment, livestock, and schools for the Métis settlers. But inadequate financial support from governments and the church, and Métis inexperience with farming, led to disillusionment among the Métis and the early end of the project. In 1908 the settlement was thrown open to other settlers and many French Canadians came to the area, while most of the Métis moved on.

With the decline of the buffalo and the fur trade, the Métis' traditional ways of earning a living were seriously eroded. Some took up trapping in northern Alberta, where game was still plentiful. Many Métis wandered from place to place, looking for occasional jobs on the fringes of white society—repairing fences, stacking hay, working on threshing gangs, cutting wood. Their homes were often small tents heated by tin stoves. Because they lived in remote areas or moved around so much, their children seldom went to school. As a result, there was little opportunity for them to break out of a way of life characterized by poverty, malnutrition, disease, and discrimination. They were often scorned, not only by white society, but also by Indians, who sometimes called them "half people."

A new society was developing in Alberta, but it would be the newcomers who shaped it. Indians and Métis had become outsiders in the land that had once been theirs.

The Role of Religion

The diverse ethnic backgrounds of immigrants, and the selective migration of religious minorities to the Alberta frontier, meant that there would eventually be over one hundred different religious denominations in the province. Virtually no new religious groups emerged in Alberta, yet the new frontier provided an ideal setting for the flourishing of many religions brought from elsewhere. The interplay of immigration, religion, and the frontier had a profound effect on the way Alberta developed.

Several developments strengthened the influence of organized religion. As noted, many churches and clergymen organized the movement of immigrants to Alberta. Other factors included the migration of persecuted religious minorities, and the competitive struggle for new territory among many religious groups. The cultural and intellectual vacuum on the frontier, the need for personal security and a sense of community, and the close tie between religion and ethnicity, all strengthened the power and appeal of organized religion.

Despite Alberta's reputation as a centre for religious eccentricity and fundamentalism, the vast majority of the population in the province's formative years belonged to religious groups with which Canadians were already very familiar. By 1921 the largest groups, as indicated by census figures, were the Presbyterians (21 per cent of the population), Anglicans (16 per cent), Catholics (16 per cent), Methodists (15 per cent), Lutherans (10 per cent), and Baptists (5 per cent). Together they constituted 83 per cent of the population.

The large number of evangelical sects in the province reflected primarily the migrations from the religiously plural American Midwest. Although they made up only about 10 per cent of the population, the evangelical sects were eventually influential out of proportion to their numbers; their membership was active and dedicated, and their organizational activity and evangelizing changed Alberta society in the 1920s and 1930s.

Given immigration patterns, Alberta was basically a Protestant province. Outside the frontier mining and lumber camps, Protestant ministers usually had a great deal of respect as community leaders. They occupied prominent roles in educational and service organizations, and their views on social and political questions commanded attention.

One of Alberta's early Presbyterian clergymen, Charles Gordon (who used the pen name Ralph Connor), began writing short stories for Presbyterian magazines about his experiences as a missionary in Banff and Canmore from 1890 to 1894. Born in Ontario and educated at the University of Toronto, Gordon had come west to help the Presbyterian Church in its effort to prevent the development of what his mission superintendent, James Robertson, termed a "wild and godless west."[10] Though he later moved to Winnipeg, his fiction based on experiences in Alberta helped turn him into Canada's most successful novelist in the early twentieth century, and his books had an enormous popular impact. *Black Rock* and *Sky Pilot* (1899) tell of a Protestant missionary's experiences on the frontier. Gordon's frontier was a region where society reverted to a primitive state, but where, with the guidance of policemen and clergymen who could convert frontiersmen to Christianity, new ideals and institutions would emerge, revitalizing the whole nation. One of the other themes that he discussed in his writing and sermons, along with many other Protestant clergymen, was the potential threat to a Protestant Canada of the new immigration to the West.

Two of the largest Protestant denominations, the Methodists and Presbyterians, long associated with the social and political elites of English-speaking Canada, worried about the social impact of the massive new immigration to the Canadian West. They saw it as their special duty to both "Canadianize" and "Christianize" the new immigrants. In their view, getting immigrants to join their Protestant churches was synonymous with Canadianizing them. The two churches established "home missions" among Ukrainians, Mormons, and Chinese. The most active work was among Ukrainians in Edmonton and in the rural Ukrainian bloc east of Edmonton. Both churches established residential homes, where they taught children English, Protestantism, and British Canadian nationalism. By 1914 the Methodists alone had seven missions and twenty-four workers in the Ukrainian bloc. The missions made few converts, but the amount of energy and money poured into them and the degree to which immigration became a major topic at church synods and in church periodicals reflected the great anxiety the two main Protestant denominations felt concerning these issues.

Whether Protestant, Catholic, Orthodox, Mormon, Jewish, or Buddhist, Alberta's religions had much in common. As well as giving meaning to life's central events, they were also the focus of cultural and social life for many communities. For many ethnic groups, the religious organization helped keep alive their language and cultural traditions. Their extensive social network included organizations for men, women, and youth. Scouting, the YWCA, and YMCA were closely linked to the churches.

The maintenance of religious traditions was so important to many Albertans that they devoted much time and money to establishing schools that reflected their denominational perspectives. A great deal of the energy of Catholic priests and nuns went into Alberta's Catholic separate school system. Many other religious groups, including Lutherans, Anglicans, Mennonites, Seventh Day Adventists, and Mormons, at various times set up their own private schools. Most of these were short-lived because they were expensive and because of the attraction of public schools. By 1916 various religious groups had also established six private denominational colleges. Even today there are many remnants of the educational institutions that church people established. These include Mount Royal College (originally Methodist) in Calgary, Concordia College (Lutheran) and College St. Jean (Catholic) in Edmonton, and Camrose Lutheran College.

The contours of the ethnic and religious mix and the major settlement patterns of Alberta had been established by 1914. There were some minor changes during the 1920s with the influx of new European groups, but the overall ethnic mix and settlement patterns would not significantly change until after World War II. In their ethnic and religious make-up, both rural and urban Alberta still show the impact of the boom period of immigration and settlement at the turn of the century.

By design, the educational, religious, and political institutions of the new society were based largely on a central Canadian model. However, out of the interaction of diverse peoples whose traditions were circumscribed by climate, geography, and the constraints of the Canadian economic and political system, a new society gradually emerged on the prairies, and in Alberta, different from those in other regions of Canada.

CHAPTER FIVE

The Pioneer Moment: Building the Rural Core

By far the largest number of immigrants to Alberta, particularly the non-British, went to rural areas. In 1911 almost three-quarters of Alberta's farmers were immigrants. Prior to World War II, 70 per cent of all Albertans lived in rural areas. Agricultural issues dominated political life, and the governing political parties, first the Liberals, then the United Farmers of Alberta (UFA) and Social Credit, had to be extremely sensitive to the province's farm constituency. The values of rural Alberta set the tone for much of the social and political debate in the province. The imagery of Alberta as an agricultural province was central both to its self-concept and to the perception of Alberta held by the rest of the world. Even after World War II, when Alberta changed dramatically and became predominantly urban, it was largely people who had grown up in small towns and on farms who populated the booming cities, and their rural backgrounds helped shape the nature of urban life.

From 1896 to World War I was an era of tremendous expansion and change in rural life. Scattered settlement and subsistence farming gave way in much of the region to massive grain production for export. By 1911 there were 60,559 farms in the province. By 1921 farms numbered 74,000 and covered 29,293,000 acres (11,717,200 hectares). The growth of the West's agricultural economy depended on the development of an elaborate system of railway transportation, grain handling, and marketing to carry grain for export. Advances in farm technology and agricultural science, including the development of early maturing strains of wheat, contributed to prosperity. The newspapers and farm magazines glorified rural life, associating it "with images of purity and productiveness," the source of national prosperity.[1]

Agriculture in Alberta was nonetheless beset with problems. Pioneer farmers faced a harsh physical environment, unstable wheat prices, high freight rates and tariffs, and a banking system that seemed remote and exploitive. Long cold winters, life-threatening blizzards, hailstorms, early frost, tornadoes, and in southern regions drought, were brutal realities. Faced with limited transportation and communication networks, isolation, a shortage of farm help, and lack of cash, pioneers had to be resourceful to survive. This meant adjusting to the climate and the conditions of a predominantly agricultural economy. Many did not succeed, and the years from 1896 to World War I were marked by disappointment as well as by high expectations and success.

Lured by the promise of wealth and a new society, newcomers from around the globe gradually developed a more jaundiced view of the new region than the one that had been conveyed by the romantics and the expansionists. The many grim realities of settlement gradually tempered the idea of a western agrarian utopia.

The Early Pioneer Years

If they lived in Europe, immigrants travelled by train to ocean ports and continued their voyage by ship. If they were from the U.S., they came by train or covered wagon. Those travelling to western Canada by train came on colonist cars. As they cooked for themselves and bedded down on hard wooden bunks in the crowded and noisy cars, they began to develop a feeling for the huge distances and isolation of their new home.

Immigrants who arrived during the settlement boom were mostly young and resourceful. In the Vulcan area of southern Alberta, for example, homesteaders averaged 31.7 years of age, and 80 per cent were under forty. But youth and determination were not enough to secure success. Estimates of the cost of starting a farm ranged from $300 to $1200, depending on how substantial the initial operation was. It would cost roughly $1000 for shelter, barn, stove, provisions, a well, implements, livestock, seed, and fencing. Yet some immigrants arrived almost destitute. Half of the Ukrainians who came before World War I had virtually no capital whatsoever, and an additional 42 per cent arrived with less than $500. In addition to capital, the settler's chances of success were also affected by previous agricultural experience, choice of land, climate and vegetation, proximity to friends and to a railway shipping point, family age and size, and not least important, luck. Of those who took out homesteads in Alberta from 1905 to 1930, 45 per cent failed to complete the government

Eager homesteaders line up at the Dominion Land Titles Office in Edmonton in 1909 during one of the many land rushes between 1896 and 1913. As the government threw open new townships of homestead land, settlers crowded and jostled to be first in line to get choice land. *(Glenbow Archives NA 1334-2)*

conditions (including three-year residency) that would give them title to their homesteads.

The newcomers who flooded into the region came to towns that were booming. Those who wanted to farm claimed their homesteads in government land offices or purchased them from land companies or the railways. Once they arrived at their new homesteads, they faced endless work. Feelings of loneliness, homesickness, and boundless optimism were all intertwined. One Barr colonist recalled the feeling of desolation when the land guide left him on his homestead.

> So there you are and the land guide says, "You are located on your land now"...No semblance of roads or anything else. "Now there you are boy...Get busy and build your house, put in your garden and look after your horses and you will do all right," and he went away. You are abandoned.[2]

The pioneers immediately made shelters—tents, shacks, sod huts, or in some cases even dugouts or caves. One winter along the North Saskatchewan River, eighteen Ukrainians were forced by circumstances to live in a ten- by twelve-foot cave in the riverbank. On the treeless southern prairies, the settlers often built sod huts, which were usually used for only a couple of years. If they chose land in the wooded parkbelt, they built log homes. Central and eastern European farmers placed roof beams on the logs, then added bundles of straw to

108

make a thatched roof. They coated their log homes with clay plaster and a whitewash that protected them from the rain and improved insulation.

On the southern prairies, limited availability of water was a serious problem. Few homesteaders had creeks or rivers nearby, so they had to dig wells. This task was difficult, frustrating, and dangerous because of cave-ins and gas. There were many headlines like the one in the *Lethbridge Herald* on September 12, 1912, "Overcome by Gas in a Well, Sad Fate of Young Homesteader East of Coutts," which told of the accidental death of a twenty-seven-year-old homesteader from Minnesota.

The land had to be turned over with a plow and broken up with a disc before the newcomers could begin farming. In the parkbelt, unless there were open patches of land, settlers also had to clear trees and brush with axes and grub hoes.

Most of the Americans and Ontarians had enough money and machinery to devote themselves full-time to farming, but many other new arrivals had to leave their families to look for work in order to buy food, livestock, and machinery. They set off for jobs on more established farms, with harvest crews, on the railway, in coal mines, in lumber mills, or in meat-packing plants.

While the men were gone, their wives cared for the children and often tackled the chores of pioneering. Many of the Ukrainian, Polish, and Romanian women enlarged their clearings, started gardens, gathered roots and berries, and helped to build log homes.

One way of providing for oneself was to be as self-sufficient in food as possible. This was essential in the earliest years of pioneering because of lack of cash and because some pioneers lived up to fifty miles (eighty kilometres) from the nearest settlement. Since pioneers could only make a few trips a year over these distances, they needed to grow and store their own food. Wild game, fish, farm animals, and gardens provided most food needs, but salt, sugar, baking powder, tea, and coffee had to be purchased. Farm families supplied their own milk, eggs, and meat, and made their own bread.

Pioneer women worked almost constantly, year-round. The family laundry was a major project since cauldrons of water had to be boiled and items scrubbed individually. Where money was scarce, as it usually was, women made their own soap, candles, and jams, and preserved food. Women and girls usually had the responsibility of milking the cows, making butter, looking after the poultry and the garden, and feeding the family. Homemade butter could be bartered for groceries at general stores in the local village or town, and selling butter and eggs was one of the few ways farm women could make extra money of their own. Mending, knitting, and making clothes for children was also time-consuming, especially when there were many children, as there often were. In addition to all this, it was sometimes necessary for pioneer women to work in the fields. They were also responsible for feeding the huge threshing crews at harvest time.

In rural areas, doctors were scarce and distant. Farm women usually nursed the sick or injured members of the family. Many pioneers depended on home remedies. Central and eastern Europeans had long experience with healing herbs and roots. Other settlers sometimes put their faith in patent medicines, bought in town or from travelling salesmen. Patent medicines, which claimed to cure almost every ailment imaginable, were often practically useless. Pregnant women usually relied on neighbour women or midwives to help with childbirth.

Working the Farm

The work of pioneer life seemed endless. The busiest time of year was during the harvest season. Cutting, binding, and stooking were followed by the season's climax of threshing. Until the late 1920s, when the combine came into general use, custom threshing was widespread and custom operators moved huge crews around rural areas at harvest time. With the great expansion in acreage devoted to wheat, the number of threshing outfits in Alberta increased from 325 in 1905 to 890 in 1908.[3] The number of men in a threshing crew varied from a dozen to thirty.

Because the province was developing so quickly and because it was relatively easy for young men with capital to homestead, securing farm labour was a serious problem. Large families usually had several sons to help with heavy farm work. Neighbouring young men could also be hired at peak season. During the fall, the government and the railways cooperated to bring in trainloads of young men from central Canada and the Maritimes.

Some attempts were made by radical labour groups, such as the American-based Industrial Workers of the World (IWW), to organize farm workers, but these efforts were unsuccessful. It was difficult to organize transient farm workers. The employer-employee relationship often had a paternal quality; farmhands usually saw their condition as temporary and identified with the farmer. It was also difficult to

Homesteading in the Beaverlodge area of the Peace River district, 1909. Pioneering was a hard, often lonely, struggle that required the effort of all family members. *(Glenbow Archives NA 488-8)*

organize labourers who were divided by ethnic, linguistic, and cultural differences. The federal government kept IWW organizers from coming into the country, and the police kept those who were here under surveillance. The provincial police bragged that they handled suspected IWW organizers "without gloves," and regularly arrested suspected IWW organizers on vagrancy charges.[4] Coal miners and urban workers would prove to be a much more fertile ground for organized labour.

The difficulties of securing farm labour and the dissatisfaction among overworked farm labourers contributed to a growing zeal for mechanization among some farmers. So too did the farm machinery companies themselves, through their continued experimentation with gasoline tractors and their fierce rivalry, which publicized and promoted tractors, particularly before World War I. The advantages of tractors were apparent. They could be used twenty-four hours a day and could plow deeper than horses. Nevertheless, many farmers were skeptical, making the displacement of horses a long and gradual process. Many were reluctant to acquire expensive and unreliable machines. Animal power was a known commodity and far cheaper. Nonetheless, in the last year of the war, the federal government supported a plan to provide tractors in order solve the labour shortage problem. After the war, however, tractors were still not universally adopted because of their cost, and because they contributed to soil erosion. In 1921, only 12 per cent of Alberta farms had tractors. It was not until World War II, when there had been many improvements in tractor design, and when cheap agricultural labour had disappeared, that the majority of Alberta's farmers used tractors.

Building the Rural Community

The hardships of pioneer life usually promoted both family unity and community cooperation. Churches and schools were usually the first organizations that brought rural settlers together and served as the main meeting places. The rural school district was the main unit of rural social organization. In the first years of settlement, church was often held in the one- or two-room schools. Dances and other social events were also held in the schools until the settlers built community halls.

Schools were usually a high priority for settlers who had come West hoping for a better life for their children, but building a one- or two-room schoolhouse and paying for a teacher required a financial sacrifice. Bachelors and immigrants with limited education were sometimes less enthusiastic about being taxed to support a new school. Gradually, however, schoolhouses began to dot the province. School districts were formed and school boards were set up. By 1910 there were 1501 school districts in the province.

Teaching was a difficult job in the small rural schools. Teachers were usually young, single, and inexperienced, with little training. Women outnumbered men by three to one in rural schools, but were paid less. Several grades were in one room. Pupils ranged from six years to sixteen, or even older. Schools were often poorly insulated, and on cold days everyone had to gather close to the stove to stay warm. To keep the attention and interest of such a variety of children, a successful teacher needed great imagination and patience. There was little money to buy books or equipment. Since all grades were together, there were often discipline problems. Many students spoke little or no English when they first arrived at school. Attendance was often irregular because of cold weather and the need for children to help with the harvest. Schools even closed temporarily for lack of funds, particularly in southeast Alberta during periods of drought or depression. Teachers occasionally faced children who were hungry, or inadequately clothed for the winter weather conditions.

Because the job was hard, the pay low, and living accommodations primitive, teachers moved frequently and were in short supply. Many schools averaged almost a new teacher every year. Some of the high turnover resulted from young women marrying and remaining in the community but stressful conditions were also an important factor. It was particularly difficult to get teachers in the Ukrainian bloc settlement because of loneliness and isolation. Settlers in this area usually spoke little or no English, accommodation for teachers was primitive, and better paying positions were available in towns and villages.

Many of the teachers came from eastern Canada (particularly Ontario), or Britain. Provincial educational authorities and the teachers patterned their schools on the Ontario model: they offered history, geography, and literature that emphasized Britain and the Empire. In 1897, during the Diamond Jubilee celebration of Queen Victoria's reign, teachers were instructed by educational officials to make "every effort to deepen the public's feeling of loyalty and respect for Her whose Beneficent reign, wisdom, and virtues Her grateful people are about to celebrate."[5]

In dealing with a multi-ethnic school population, school officials subscribed to the assimilationist tenets of Anglo-conformity. Not only politicians and educators, but Protestant clergymen, newspaper editors, patriotic organizations, and women's organizations saw the school as the major means of assimilating new immigrant groups. As one school inspector in northern Alberta argued in 1903, "The quickest and surest method of assimilating the foreign elements in our population is through our schools. Here is seen the ready adoption of dress, language, manners and customs."[6] The values to be inculcated by the schools were those of British Canadian nationalism, citizenship, individualism, and the work ethic.

The assumptions of Anglo-conformity were also evident in the strong resistance of the provincial department of education to attempts to introduce other languages, such as Ukrainian or German, into the school system. In 1913 a major confrontation developed between the Department of Education and Ukrainian teachers, parents, and community leaders in the Ukrainian bloc settlement in east-central Alberta. The government prevented thirteen uncertified Ukrainian Canadian teachers from teaching in Ukrainian district schools at a time when there were no teachers of Ukrainian background with Alberta teaching certificates. The Ukrainian parents in some school districts, who wanted teachers who could teach both English and Ukrainian, refused to pay taxes and temporarily set up their own schools. To many Ukrainians the teachers were "intellectuals and patriots, leading their own unfortunate people... before the deceptive enemy—the Anglicizers and assimilators..."[7] Only after much coercion (including the government forcibly seizing horses from dissident ratepayers) did the Ukrainian parents comply with the government's policies. Alberta's Minister of Education, J. R. Boyle, who represented the Sturgeon riding north of Edmonton, saw the conflict as one of both educational principle and politics, since he was afraid that the teachers were part of a movement that might undermine Ukrainian support for the ruling Liberals. He took a firm stand, arguing that he wanted no repetition of the Manitoba experience with bilingual schools: "This is an English-speaking province...and every Alberta boy and girl should receive a sound English education."[8]

School could be a traumatic experience for immigrant children, who were often punished by teachers for not speaking English. But despite the insensitivity to the problems of adjustment for immigrant children, and limitations in the quality of education, these schools provided a focus for rural families.

In the ethnic bloc settlements, the rural community halls, usually built soon after the schools and churches, were the focal points of an active community life. In 1903 Estonians began settling in a district that came to be known as Linda Hall (named after a legendary Estonian figure), ten miles (sixteen kilometres) south of Stettler. By 1905, once the railway reached Stettler, there were sixty Estonian households. In 1906 the settlers, mostly Lutherans, built a small chapel served by a visiting minister, John Sillak, who also served Estonian and other Baltic immigrants in a region ranging from California to Manitoba. In 1910 the settlers organized an agricultural club, and the following year built Linda Hall in the centre of the settlement. They used the hall for social and farm meetings, dances, Estonian plays, concerts, weddings, and other community gatherings. They also established their own library and a brass band. Initially activities were limited to Estonians, but as the first generation acquired greater fluency in English, members of the surrounding community began to participate in their Saturday night socials. In multi-ethnic regions, the halls helped integrate diverse peoples.

In the Ukrainian bloc in east central Alberta, settlers built over ninety community halls for meetings, lectures, choir rehearsals, dances, plays, and concerts. The halls were mostly named in honour of prominent figures from Ukrainian history. Hundreds of these community halls, built by Ukrainians and settlers of many other ethnic backgrounds, now mostly unused and in decay, dot the province.

114

Smalltown Life

Almost all of the hundreds of hamlets, villages, and towns that developed between 1896 and 1913 (with the exception of a few coal-mining towns) served the needs of farm families. These communities were all either on railway lines or in areas that expected to be served with railway lines. The railway company plotted town locations carefully, spacing them roughly thirteen to sixteen kilometres apart. This placement was based on the policy that grain elevators should be no more than one day's journey by horse-drawn transportation from the farms to be served.

As settlers arrived at the turn of the century, new towns appeared almost overnight. Newcomers put up tents, lived in train boxcars, and jammed new hotels. When new homesteading areas were opened to settlers, the land rushes led to real estate booms at the townsites, as the railways sold townsite land to merchants and land speculators.

The development of Nanton in southern Alberta provides a glimpse of the smalltown lifestyle that dominated Alberta for four decades. During the 1880s a number of large ranches were started in the area west of Nanton, including one owned by A. E. Cross of Calgary, patriarch of an influential southern Alberta family. During the 1890s, small ranchers dominated. In 1892 a railway from Calgary to Fort Macleod was built through the area. Nanton's first resident was a CPR section foreman who arrived in 1896.

Sifton's policy attracted a rush of settlers between 1900 and 1905. By 1905 most of the available homesteads were gone. The largest number of newcomers came from the U.S., although there were also Ontarians, English, and Scots, smaller numbers of Irish, Welsh, and Scandinavians, and a scattering of other Europeans.

The town boomed for a short time. The townsite was named after Augustus Nanton, whose financial firm of Osler, Hammond, and Nanton was banker, broker, and promoter for the railway. As such, the firm was responsible for selling railway land and for selecting town-sites. In 1901 and 1902, new settlers built a general store, hotel, and livery stable. Several business and professional people, mostly from Ontario, moved to the area in anticipation of an influx of settlers. In 1903 the CPR station opened, the town was incorporated, and the *Nanton News* made its appearance, edited by an American, J. M. Bender. Like much of the booster press of the day, the *News* tried to call into being the population it aimed to serve. On June 25, 1903, it declared Nanton to be "the Centre of the Meat Basket of the World,

Main street of Nanton. Like hundreds of other small towns and villages across the province, Nanton served the surrounding agricultural area. The town's active social, sports, and religious life knitted the community together. The lifestyle and economy of small towns and villages such as Nanton was one of the dominant forces in the province until after World War II. *(Glenbow Archives NA 1112-4)*

Where Wealth Comes Easy and Always," and an ideal spot for curing people of "catarrh, malaria, bronchial asthma and rheumatism." Soon the community boasted several doctors and other professionals, banks, farm machinery agencies, two hotels, boarding houses, and a Chinese restaurant and laundry. Eventually seven grain elevators stood out against the prairie sky. By 1911 the town had grown to 571, and by 1921 to 710.

The social and cultural life of Nanton reflected both the region's diversity and its dominant Anglo-Protestant nature. Social life in the community brought together townspeople, farmers, and ranchers, and revolved around churches, fraternal and women's organizations, and sporting events. The five churches in the community—Presbyterian, Methodist, Baptist, Anglican, and Roman Catholic—were local representatives of five of the six largest denominations in the province. (Only the Lutherans were missing.) The churches set up a network of men's, women's, and youth organizations and choirs. Money-making activities such as bazaars, bingos, and church suppers brought people together, and concerts provided opportunities for displaying local talent.

As elsewhere in much of the province, in Nanton the Presbyterian and Methodist churches were two of the largest Protestant denominations. They were also socially and politically the most powerful. But because numbers of either denomination were still relatively small, Presbyterians and Methodists eventually cooperated in 1911 to establish a common Protestant church, which lasted until 1918. The pragmatic reality of church cooperation and union in southern Alberta, and across the rest of the prairies, was crucial to the church union movement that eventually led to the formation in 1925 of the United Church of Canada.

The fraternal lodges, which provided sociability, insurance, and a degree of ethnic and religious solidarity for Protestants from Britain, Ontario, and the U.S., included an Orange Lodge, the Knights of Pythias, the Canadian Order of Foresters, and a Masonic Lodge. Women's organizations tended to be more concerned with social reform and education, and included the Woman's Christian Temperance Union (founded in 1904), the Imperial Order of the Daughters of the Empire (1914), and the United Farm Women of Alberta (1916). An early literary society and library had trouble surviving, but the young and sociability-starved community threw itself into sports, the most popular being baseball, curling, and hockey.

Farm issues dominated the community. Townspeople had to sell their services and products to the farmers, so they knew their prosperity depended on a strong farming economy. A local agricultural society (formed in 1906) organized annual fairs and stampedes, and the local United Farmers of Alberta (UFA) organized cooperative buying and promoted better grain marketing.

The rural district around Nanton became one of the hotbeds of agrarian protest in Alberta. In 1917 the area elected James Weir, an Ontario-born ex-newspaperman and farmer, as one of two Non-Partisan League candidates to the legislature. In 1921 the area elected an Ontario-born ex-banker and farmer, George Coote, as a UFA member of parliament. Coote pressed for banking reform in Canada, stressing the ways in which the Canadian banking system was not suited to supply the credit needs of western agriculture.

The early boosterism that energized the town did not survive the prairie-wide economic recession of 1913, which brought an end to town-lot speculation. Nanton's growth, like that of most small towns across the province, levelled off after 1913. By 1941 the population was practically unchanged from the prewar era. It did not top a thousand until the mid-1950s. In Nanton, as in so many other towns, the number and types of services changed little from 1913 until the late 1940s.

The social conditions of frontier life in Nanton and other small towns brought farmers and townspeople together, thereby minimizing social conflict. As Paul Voisey has noted in his study of the Vulcan area,[9] despite differences between farmers and ranchers and differences in wealth, ethnicity, and religion, open conflict seldom disturbed smalltown and rural life. Since the population base was small and institutions fragile, conflict could not be allowed to disrupt voluntary organizations, local politics, or commerce. Farmers and townspeople united instead against common enemies—banks, elevator companies, the CPR, eastern politicians, and rival towns. The price of unity was often intolerance of difference and dissent. Nonconformist personalities, and racial and religious minorities such as the Chinese and Hutterites, found themselves outside the circle.

Scientific Farming: Irrigation, Research, and Education

The period up to World War I was one of solid progress in agriculture. Farmers quickly became part of a larger commercial agricultural economy. The grain companies, farm machinery companies, and financial institutions, which the farmers came to dislike, nonetheless were part of a system that made Canada the world's leading wheat exporter, with a reputation as a reliable source of high-quality grain. Farm mechanization, irrigation, agricultural research, and education all helped give agriculture a solid institutional base.

Irrigation in southern Alberta had important economic and social consequences, and helped many farmers adjust to the relatively dry conditions of Palliser's Triangle. Because irrigation required expensive dams, reservoirs, elaborate canal systems, and an organized system of sharing water resources, it was essential that government, large private corporations, and local farmers cooperate.

Irrigation in Alberta began with small individual projects in the late 1870s and early 1880s near Calgary. However, it did not become large-scale until the turn of the century. William Pearce of the federal Department of the Interior was one of the first advocates of water conservation and irrigation. Despite concerns within his own department that talk of irrigation would discourage settlers, he convinced his superiors that irrigation was essential. Pearce was one of the key voices behind the passage of the North-West Irrigation Act of 1894. This act brought regulation, order, and federal government control to the water resources in the Northwest, though large-scale projects were slow to develop. When Sifton came to power in 1896, he wanted development to proceed quickly. He supported irrigation projects that had been on the drawing boards for years.

One of the largest and most successful of the irrigation schemes emerged from the partnership between the Galt coal mining interests in Lethbridge and the Mormon Church. This partnership in a massive irrigation project brought a new wave of Mormon immigration to southwest Alberta. The main promoter within the company was C. A. Magrath. He hoped irrigation would allow the company to sell its land and provide traffic for the railway and a local market for coal. Magrath formed a close partnership with Mormon leader C. O. Card, who also saw the potential for a major colonization scheme for land-hungry Mormon farmers in the American Great Basin. With the support of the federal government and British capital, in 1898 the Galt-owned North Western Coal and Navigation Company signed a contract with the Mormon Church to build an irrigation system. Subcontractors, labourers, and teamsters for the project were Mormon farmers who intended to settle in southern Alberta.

A new wave of Mormon settlers built both the irrigation system and several new Mormon towns, including Magrath and Stirling. The contractors completed 115 miles (184 kilometres) of canal in two years from Kimball on the St. Mary River to Lethbridge and beyond, opening up large tracts of land to irrigation. The whole canal was finished by 1900, and in September the Governor General, Lord Minto, officially opened the canal. By 1911 Mormons in southern Alberta had established eighteen new Mormon communities. Ten thousand Mormons, mostly farmers and their families, lived in the area. Irrigation, the village settlement pattern, cooperative economic enterprise, and an active cultural, social, and religious life were all transferred from the American Great Basin to southern Alberta by the Mormon settlers.

Irrigation made possible the development of a wide variety of crops. Sugar beets were among the first. With the encouragement of Galt interests and Mormon church leaders, in 1903 Jesse Knight, a wealthy Utah mine owner, established a sugar factory in the town of Raymond (named after his son). Sugar beets had been an important crop in irrigated areas of Mormon settlements in the U.S. Growing sugar beets was, over the long run, an ideal way of making intensive use of irrigation. Though dependent in part on tariffs because of ongoing competition from cheap foreign cane sugar, the industry has remained an important part of southern Alberta's economy.

Irrigation, sugar beets, and other vegetable crops had important

The Bassano Dam, shortly after its completion in 1914. The dam provided water for the Eastern Irrigation District centred at Brooks in southeast Alberta. Aided by the research work of agricultural scientists, irrigation helped many farmers adapt their land to farming in southern Alberta's dry conditions. There are now over 1.1 million acres of irrigated land in southern Alberta, accounting for 12 per cent of Alberta's agricultural production. *(Glenbow Archives ND8-490)*

economic and social consequences for southwestern Alberta. Since irrigated crops require more intensive farming than grain, farms were smaller and the rural population denser, allowing for an active social and economic life. The rural population and the towns in south-western Alberta grew much larger than those in the southeast. Lethbridge grew more quickly and remained larger than its rival, Medicine Hat, largely because of the impact of irrigation. By 1921, when the exodus from the southeast was well underway because of drought, the census area in southeast Alberta had a population of 31,000. This included 9,600 people in Medicine Hat, with only one other town over 1,000. The census area in southwest Alberta had 47,000 people. It included 11,100 in Lethbridge, and six other towns with a population of over 1,000.

The CPR also became interested in irrigation to promote coloniza-tion and traffic on the three million acres (1.2 million hectares) of land it owned between Brooks and Calgary. William Pearce encouraged William Cornelius Van Horne, the general manager of the CPR, to get involved in irrigation. After many delays, in 1903 the CPR pushed ahead with its Bow River irrigation scheme. The CPR had the land, capital, equipment, labour force, and engineers to tackle the project. Two of the major engineering feats during the construction of the project were the Bassano Dam and the Brooks Aquaduct. The dam was completed in 1914 on a horseshoe bend in the Bow River.

The CPR also used its extensive immigration and colonization network to bring immigrants to colonize an area that had over a million acres in the western bloc centred at Strathmore, and another million acres in the eastern bloc centred at Brooks. The CPR launched promotional campaigns in several countries, brought in landseekers' excursions, and hired priests and ministers to attract immigrants in Dutch, German, Polish, Danish, Mennonite, and Swedish settlements in the U.S.

From the beginning, there were problems in the relations between the CPR and the settlers. Although crop yields were greater than on dry land, the original plots of eighty acres (thirty-two hectares) were too small to make farming profitable. Land and water costs were relatively high. Farmers became discontented, and either left the land or formed their own associations to deal with the railway. The CPR claimed that it could not make money on the project, and in 1918 suggested that the farmers take it over themselves. After prolonged discussion, and active promotion by farm leaders such as Swedish American Carl Anderson, by 1934 a majority of the farmers in the eastern section had formed the Eastern Irrigation District. This organization took over ownership and control of the project. Despite the high cost, irrigation proved its value in dry years, when nearby parts of southern Alberta were too dry for farmers to survive.

The federal government not only gave strong support to irrigation, but also supported agricultural research and education. The Dominion Experimental Station at Lethbridge, which eventually grew to be the largest of the country's research stations operated by the Canadian Department of Agriculture, developed from the collaboration between the Galt interests and an American agricultural scientist, W. H. Fairfield, superintendent of the experimental station at the University of Wyoming. C. A. Magrath hired Fairfield to establish a model farm in Lethbridge in 1901 to experiment with grains, grasses, fruits, and shelter-belt trees. Fairfield successfully showed settlers how to grow alfalfa—a crop that previously grew poorly in the area because of lack of nitrogen-fixing bacteria. Leth-

Threshing crew in the Peace River district in 1916. Few farmers could afford their own threshing machines, so special crews travelled from farm to farm to harvest and thresh the grain. The threshing machine was powered by a steam engine and required crews of from ten to thirty men. *(Glenbow Archives NC-6-2786)*

bridge boosters then began campaigning for an agricultural research station. The newly completed irrigation system, the donation of a tract of land for the station by the Galts, and the political influence of a Liberal Senator from Lethbridge, Dr. George De Veber (a former NWMP staff surgeon) combined to secure the experimental station for Lethbridge in 1906. Fairfield remained as superintendent until 1945. One author briefly summarized the research efforts of the research station: "...research concentrated on improving farming productivity, helping farmers to resolve problems in soil drifting, irrigation, animal production, rangeland management, and control of wheat stem sawflies, cutworms and grasshoppers. Scientists developed higher yielding varieties and improved management of soils under irrigation and dryland farming."[10] The research scientists at Lethbridge played a particularly crucial role in the successful struggle against soil drifting during the dustbowl of the 1930s.

The federal government also established research stations at Lacombe in central Alberta in 1907 and at Beaverlodge in the Peace River district in 1919. The Lacombe station distributed seed and animal stocks, studied and developed new varieties of grains and breeds of swine and beef, and experimented with cropping practices on the soils of east-central Alberta. The station at Beaverlodge became responsible for research on the agricultural problems of northwestern Canada, with its wide range of soil and climate types. It began with the work of Donald Albright, a former agricultural journalist from Ontario who came to the Beaverlodge district in 1913. Albright, who had studied at the Ontario Agricultural College in Guelph, was anxious to know which varieties of grain were adaptable to the climate and soil of the region. In 1914 he began conducting experiments on his farm for the Dominion Experimental Farms. In 1919 he was appointed superintendent of the experimental sub-station at Beaverlodge, and not only began a long career of research, but spent countless hours writing for local newspapers and travelling to local country schoolhouses, where he lectured on agricultural techniques, the need for mixed farming, and the great potential of the north, including maxims from his own homespun philosophy. He dismissed doubters, and reassured settlers about the potential of the Peace River district. As he told his audiences in 1920, during a period of agricultural depression:

> The Peace River Country is naturally one of the choicest agricultural regions that lies out of doors. Picturesque and fertile, with long easy slopes, well drained yet well adapted to cultivation, it is capable of being developed. . . into a land of fine farms and happy homes.[11]

The station conducted a breeding program with cereals, forage crops, and eventually oilseeds, and focussed its research on the acidic soils of the North. Cliff Stacey, the first technical officer of the Beaverlodge substation (1924), and later superintendent, was a strong advocate of the use of legume crops to enhance crop production on newly-broken land, and the frequent use of forage crops to ensure proper soil structure and increase crop yields. Stacey was also active in the cultural and community life of Beaverlodge, and in promoting research and writing on the local history of the Peace River district.

The relationship between experts and farmers was sometimes strained, since so much of the scientists' work was experimental and depended on trial and error. In the area of dryland farming techniques in southern Alberta, some of their early advice was wrong and contributed to soil erosion. But gradually a close working relationship developed. This would prove crucial to solving problems of soil erosion caused by drought, wind, and unsuitable cultivation practices during the 1920s and 1930s.

In addition to a network of federal government agricultural research stations, substations, and demonstration farms, the provincial government (with federal support) set up agricultural colleges at Vermilion, Olds, Youngstown, Gleichen, Claresholm, and Raymond to bring scientific agriculture to farmers and their sons, and home economics training to farm girls. Agricultural research was also an important part of the mandate of the University of Alberta when the provincial government established it in 1908.

The research stations, colleges, and university were all very conscious of the need for extension work. The research stations held annual "field days" at demonstration farms across the province, where local farmers had been paid a small sum to try some of the techniques the experts had recommended. At a field day, a variety of agricultural experts demonstrated the latest techniques to farmers.

Farmers also established agricultural societies to help improve agriculture. These societies sponsored the annual agricultural fairs where farmers met, showed their livestock and produce, compared experiences, and listened to judges explain how livestock and farming could be improved. By 1913 there were eighty-two agricultural fairs. Though intended for educational purposes, the fairs, with their midways and entertainment, also became a highlight of rural social life. One of the first agricultural fairs in the region was in Calgary in 1886. The Calgary exhibition, run by "an amiable amalgam of town businessmen, farmers, and ranchers,"[12] would eventually be joined to a Stampede and promoted into a world-famous event.

The Decline of the Cattle Kingdom and the Rise of the Stampede

One casualty of immigration and settlement was open-range ranching in southern Alberta. The influence of the Conservative ranchers waned after the federal Liberals came to power in 1896. Frank Oliver, the feisty editor of the *Edmonton Bulletin* and a longtime champion of settlers' interests, became federal minister of the interior in 1905. One of his first acts was to sell off government-leased land (which had been used for ranching) to make it available for settlement.

Several other factors combined to make ranching less profitable, and to encourage a variety of new strategies. Poor markets adversely affected the industry; the railways were too busy making profits from bringing in settlers to worry about accommodating ranchers' needs in shipping cattle, and a series of adverse winters from 1905 to 1911 killed off thousands of cattle. For months during the winter of 1906-07 temperatures remained far below zero. By spring there were still

124

Aging Methodist missionary John McDougall leading hundreds of Indians in the first Stampede parade in Calgary in 1912. The Stampede would eventually become a central part of the national and international image not only of Calgary, but all of Alberta. (*Glenbow Archives NB 16-167*)

heavy snows, and feed supplies were exhausted. Some ranchers lost up to 80 per cent of their herds.

Many ranchers sold their land to farmers. The farm-oriented booster press did not spend much time lamenting the transition to farming. The *Medicine Hat News* in May 1906 claimed that the ranchers' "loss is the country's gain and they must retreat." Only the larger ranches along the foothills and in the Cypress Hills were able to survive by intensifying their operations. They benefitted from a sympathetic Conservative government in Ottawa after 1911. The remaining cattlemen were able to do well, but ranching was no longer king in southern Alberta.

It is ironic, but not surprising, that the Calgary Stampede, the symbol of the Alberta cattle industry, should have been born in 1912, when ranching had been replaced by farming as the major industry in southern Alberta. The Stampede was an exercise in nostalgia for a declining ranching industry, and for a frontier West that was being supplanted by settlers and cities.

The origins of the Calgary Stampede go back to the annual Calgary agricultural exhibition, and to touring American Wild West shows. One of the most famous was the Miller Brothers Wild West show, which made a one-day stand in Calgary in 1908 during a Dominion Exhibition. This agricultural and industrial exhibition was subsidized by the federal government and was intended to encourage farmers to improve the quality of their agricultural production. Guy Weadick, a New York-born cowboy, was a trick roping performer for the Miller Brothers. He was familiar with Alberta since he had previously worked on a southern Alberta ranch and had performed in a number of small rodeos. He was a natural showman with a knack for planning big events. Still in his early twenties, while in Calgary for the show he began promoting the idea of a week-long rodeo extravaganza in Calgary. H. C. McMullen, the CPR livestock agent, was finally persuaded.

In 1912 McMullen asked Weadick to return to Calgary and they convinced four wealthy Calgary cattlemen, George Lane, A. E. Cross, Pat Burns, and A. J. McLean, to back the venture (christened "The Stampede") up to a total of $100,000 for a six-day event. Weadick persuaded several hundred American cowboys and cowgirls and a troupe of Mexican rodeo performers to come to Calgary by offering large purses. Hundreds of Indians from across southern Alberta were brought in by the aging Rev. John McDougall, the Methodist missionary to the Indians, who pocketed a fee of $390 for his services. Not content with only southern Alberta Indians, Weadick brought in a hundred Indians from the U.S. to parade in their war paint.

The Stampede was a celebration of an era that had been shaped by two sharply contrasting ways of life: that of the self-sufficient Plains Indians and that of the ranching community. The Stampede combined these diverse elements with a third—a large measure of American show-biz hoopla.

The first Stampede parade was a strange synthesis of all the diverse elements of the frontier. It included two thousand Indians in war paint and feathers shepherded by McDougall, hundreds of cowboys, Red River carts, Métis, and Mounted Police. The Mounted Cowboy Band from Pendleton, Oregon, played "I Wish I Was in Dixie." The Stampede Committee had to pay $1500 to Calgary's labour unions to become part of the Stampede parade, which was being held on Labour Day, since the unions had traditionally held their own parade on that day.

The more experienced (at least as far as professional rodeo was concerned) American cowboys and cowgirls carried off most of the championships at the first Stampede, but an Indian cowboy from the Blood Indian reserve at Cardston, Tom Three Persons, delighted the Canadians by winning the world's bucking horse riding championship. Though a great spectacle attracting over a hundred thousand admissions, the first Stampede was not a financial success, and it was not until after World War I, when the Stampede merged with the annual Calgary agricultural fair and exhibition, that it finally became a yearly and financially successful event. The Calgary Stampede, by attracting competitors from across North America and promoting interest in rodeo, encouraged the sport across the province. The sport became an essential part of dozens of annual summer fairs across the province, one of the highlights of many Albertans' annual cycle of activities.

Though a reminder of a ranching past, the Stampede was in fact a product of a society that had shifted toward farming and urban life. The cowboys' skills were fast becoming relics of a bygone era. Calgary itself, with a population of 50,000 by 1912, had changed from a market centre for the surrounding farming and ranching community to the major commercial and industrial centre for the western prairies. Among the most impressive types of expertise displayed at the Stampede over the next few decades were the organizational and promotional skills used by the Stampede management to provide entertainment for a largely urban audience. The Stampede became such a successful event and tourist attraction that it became a key part of the image of Alberta in the rest of the world.

By 1913 the initial problems of the pioneer era were gradually being overcome. As farmers improved their land, and as villages and towns developed a wide range of amenities, whole regions evolved from isolated pioneer settlements to integrated agricultural communities, linked in a variety of ways to the outside metropolitan world. Farmers were organizing themselves to better their economic and social conditions, and their growing political power would be felt at all levels of the political system. But economic storm clouds and shifting international military alliances would ultimately change forever the rural society and agricultural economy of the prewar years.

CHAPTER SIX

The Boom Years (1896–1913): Politics, Cities, and Resource Development

The boom era was not only one of homesteading and massive agricultural expansion. It was also a time of rapid growth for towns and cities straining to service this agricultural expansion, and of brisk development of resources, especially coal. The CPR pushed a branch line into the Crow's Nest Pass in 1898, and by 1911 two new transcontinental railways, the Canadian Northern and the Grand Trunk Pacific, had been completed through Edmonton to the Rockies. These new railways, and other branch lines, opened up new agricultural areas such as the Peace River district. They also opened important new coal-mining areas that provided fuel for the railways and domestic heating. Coal-mining towns developed with a different ethnic, religious, and political composition than most rural areas. Oil and gas and hydro-electric power were also being developed during this formative era.

A broad range of new economic and social forces shaped Alberta's political system. Both the political institutions and political culture reflected the province's quasi-colonial relationship with Ottawa, its primarily agricultural economy, its diverse regions, and its character as an immigrant and ethnically diverse society. The heated public debates surrounding provincehood in 1905 reveal much about the status of the West within Confederation, and the balance of competing forces in Alberta.

Most of the political patterns that have recurred in Alberta throughout the twentieth century developed between 1896 and 1913. These included one-party dominance, western alienation, agrarian unrest and a strong farmers' protest movement, metropolitan rivalry between Calgary and Edmonton, and a preoccupation with the issues of transportation and resource development. A strong labour movement also developed during this period, with its greatest support in the coalfields. A four-fold division in political behaviour between cities, resource towns, rural northern Alberta, and rural southern Alberta emerged clearly. Economic development during this period demonstrated the province's reliance on outside capital from Europe, the United States, and central Canada, and brought early warnings of the boom-bust cycle that would plague the agriculture, oil and gas, and coal industries.

The Birth of a Province

The settlers who came in large numbers around the turn of the century began to demand that the North-West Territories be given greater political autonomy. Albertans were represented in the North-West Territories legislature when it was established in 1888, meeting in the territorial capital of Regina. The number of Albertans in the assembly gradually expanded in subsequent territorial elections in 1891 and 1894. This assembly, led by F. W. G. Haultain from Macleod, continually pressed the federal government for greater control over its own political affairs and less interference from the federally appointed Lieutenant Governor.

The new federal Liberal government finally granted responsible government in 1897, which temporarily eased some of the pressure for increased autonomy. However, since the legislative authority of the assembly was still restricted, the settlers soon revived their cries for autonomy. At a time when it needed money desperately to supply services to the massive numbers of newcomers, the territorial government was left without the per-capita grants that provinces received. It also lacked the authority to charter railways at a time when settlers were demanding more railways to market their grain.

At the turn of the century, Laurier and Sifton did not believe that the Territories were ready for provincial status. They initially argued that the area was too sparsely populated and that there was too much internal disagreement over whether there should be one or two provinces. Those who were impatient with the delay in granting provincial status wondered if the Liberals were afraid of a powerful political opponent, territorial premier F. W. G. Haultain, who increasingly identified himself with the federal Conservatives. As a champion of western interests and provincial status, Haultain badgered Laurier with demands for more money and more autonomy.

The Liberals eventually succumbed to the pressure, but not before settlers in the territories grew resentful. On March 21, 1904, the

Calgary Herald complained that "The conduct of the administration at Ottawa is quite sufficient to raise another rebellion in the North-West Territories." With the federal Conservatives also pressing the case for provincehood, Laurier finally agreed. He promised provincial status to the Territories if the Liberals were returned to power in the 1904 federal election. The Liberals were victorious, with seven of the ten seats in the Territories as a whole and two of four in Alberta.

Laurier's promise of provincial status had been vague, and there were a number of crucial questions still unresolved. Would there be one or two new provinces? Would the federal or provincial government maintain control over natural resources? What guarantees would be given for separate schools? Who would be chosen premier? Where would the capital(s) be located?

One other key issue was whether provincial politics, following the territorial model, would be non-partisan. Many believed that the West could achieve more if the assembly spoke with a single voice. Territorial Premier Haultain, believing that partisanship weakened the territorial government's hand in dealing with Ottawa, had been adamant about keeping partisan politics out of the territorial legislature, and he included both Liberals and Conservatives in his cabinets. Many Liberals and also many Conservatives, including Calgary lawyer R. B. Bennett, disagreed with Haultain and worked to bring partisan politics to Alberta. The ideal of political nonpartisanship, which had worked in the territorial legislature, did not survive the debate over the terms of entry for the new provinces.

Haultain disagreed with the federal government's position on almost all the major issues. On all these issues he lost. The final decisions on how many provinces and provincial ownership of resources were based almost exclusively on the interests of the Liberal party and the federal government.

Haultain wanted one big province that would have substantial clout in Ottawa. The opponents of this view, including both Laurier and R. B. Bennett, argued that one province would be too difficult to administer. Some also pointed to an incipient regional identity connected with the districts in the territory to justify creating two separate provinces. With two provinces, the federal government could neutralize the political power of Haultain, who obviously could not become premier of both, and also double the opportunities for federal patronage. The final choice of the boundary created two provinces, Alberta and Saskatchewan, of roughly comparable size and population.

The nature of the school system was also contentious since it reopened political sores that had festered for years. The issue went back to the question of the nature of Confederation—whether it was a pact between two founding peoples, English and French, Protestant and Catholic, and whether minority rights would be protected across Canada.

The conflict over separate schools had developed in the North-West Territories in the 1880s and 1890s in much the same way it had in Manitoba. In the 1870s the strong presence of French Canadians led to the establishment of school systems along denominational Catholic/Protestant lines. These schools were constitutionally guaranteed in the North-West Territories Act of 1875. However, during the 1870s and 1880s, new English-speaking settlers quickly outnumbered those who were French-speaking. In both Manitoba and the North-West Territories, the English-speaking settlers lobbied for a non-sectarian unilingual school system. They believed that if Western Canada were to develop as a unified society, all ethnic groups, including French Canadians, would have to be assimilated to an Anglo-Canadian norm through "national" (English-language) schools. In the tense debates over schools in Manitoba and the North-West Territories, the issues of French language rights, Roman Catholic schools, immigration, and the language rights of immigrant groups all became intermeshed.

During the 1880s, pressure had begun to build in the territorial legislature to eliminate separate schools. The territorial legislature throughout the 1880s and early 1890s gradually introduced changes that diminished the strict religious-based duality in the educational system, and in 1892, following an all-out offensive led by Haultain, brought Roman Catholic schools under strict state control. The still-powerful Roman Catholic hierarchy opposed the dilution of their school system, demanding that the federal government intervene to disallow these new measures. The federal government refused, unwilling to trample on what westerners felt were their territorial rights. At the same time, the federal government refused to give in to the demand of the territorial legislature that separate schools be abolished altogether, as had been done by the provincial government in Manitoba. Thus the continuing federal control in Alberta protected separate schools.

By 1905 neither Catholic nor Protestant politicians in the North-West Territories were happy with the existing educational system. Protestants such as Haultain feared that the Laurier administration would use its power to impose a Catholic school system on the new provinces. When the Laurier government revealed the school clauses of the autonomy bill in 1905, many concluded that it would bring back the church-controlled school system, which had been abolished in the North-West Territories in 1892. Critics of the government were not alone in fearing that this was the case; Clifford Sifton, who had been ill and absent when the clauses were drawn up, resigned from the federal cabinet to protest them. A substitute clause proposed by Sifton, which essentially preserved the educational status quo, was then adopted by the federal government. This meant that in each school district in Alberta and Saskatchewan, the first school had to be a public (majority) school with the minority thereafter free to establish a separate school. Although some Catholic clergy felt betrayed by this arrangement, and some Protestants were unhappy that separate schools had been allowed to remain, the compromise seemed to satisfy most people.

The educational provisions of the autonomy bills and the accompanying public debate reveal aspects of Alberta society and important differences between Manitoba and Alberta with regard to education. Maintaining separate schools in Alberta was more important to the French Catholic clergy and to the federal government than maintaining French language rights. Separate schools might indirectly make the maintenance of French possible in predominantly French Canadian communities, but the provision for allowing French instruction at the end of classes was hardly enough to provide adequate state support for the survival of the French language. In 1890 Manitoba did away with separate schools, and in 1897 compromised on minority rights by providing bilingual schools. But these survived only until 1916, when wartime nationalism and concern about cultural fragmentation led to their abolition. In contrast, Alberta provided separate schools and refused bilingualism; separate schools in Alberta were never seriously challenged after 1905.

The survival of separate schools in Alberta thus resulted from the federal control of the territorial period and the later arrival and more diverse nature of the people who settled there. By the time Alberta became a province in 1905, some of the intense anti-Catholicism that had wracked English-speaking Canada in the 1880s and 1890s had subsided. In Manitoba, vast numbers of Ontario migrants had flooded in during the 1880s and demanded that Manitoba society be reshaped on an Ontario Protestant model. Though the Ontario presence in Alberta was strong, it was more muted than in Manitoba, diluted by the large British, American, and European immigration. This led to a slightly more pluralistic view of society. Aside from perhaps a brief period during the early 1890s, Ontario's transplanted Protestant nationalism did not achieve the total dominance in Alberta that it achieved in Manitoba. Consequently, separate schools survived in Alberta.

The question of control of public lands did not attract nearly as much attention, though it would later become a volatile issue. Although the original provinces in Confederation in 1867 had retained ownership of their public lands, the federal government maintained control when Manitoba became a province in 1870, and continued this policy in 1905 when Alberta and Saskatchewan became provinces. Laurier argued that provincial control might produce a variety of different provincial policies for disposing of public lands, and thereby discourage immigration. This policy did not provoke widespread debate at the time, although ranchers chafed under federal control of water reserves, and by World War I oilmen were complaining about Ottawa's handling of oil development. Control of resources eventually emerged as a major source of contention between the federal and Alberta governments in the 1920s, and resurfaced in the energy and constitutional battles of the 1970s and early 1980s. The federal government's decision to maintain control of natural resources became one of the mainstays in the litany of grievances that fueled the fires of western alienation. However, in 1905 the federal government softened the blow by providing a generous financial grant to make up for lost revenue.

Party Politics and the Election of 1905

After the autonomy bills were passed in July 1905, plans were made to choose senior public officials and to inaugurate two new provinces in September. The Laurier government chose the lieutenant governors, who were then responsible for choosing the first premiers in advance of the election. Laurier chose George Bulyea, a Liberal, as Alberta's first Lieutenant Governor. Bulyea was from New Brunswick, and had come to the North-West Territories as a merchant in the 1880s, before entering politics and holding a succession of offices in the territorial government.

On September 1, Edmonton staged a huge show to celebrate Alberta's becoming a province. Thousands of visitors came to the city on a beautiful fall day to watch. An elaborate parade featured a cross

Alberta becomes a Province. Inauguration Day, Edmonton, September 1, 1905. Lieutenant Governor George Bulyea is sworn in by Canada's Governor General, Earl Grey. Platform party includes the Liberal Prime Minister, Sir Wilfrid Laurier, second from left, and Bulyea, signing. *(Glenbow Archives NA 1297-4)*

section of Alberta society—a French Canadian organization, Cree and Stoney Indians, Boer War veterans, an Old Timers' Association, and commercial floats. At noon, the Province of Alberta came into being as Governor General Earl Grey administered the oath of office to Bulyea. From an outdoor platform surrounded by throngs of people electrified by the feeling that they were witnessing the birth of a new society, Laurier talked of the immense changes that had occurred in Alberta, and spoke of a society of newcomers:

> We do not want nor wish that any individual should forget the land of his origin. Let them look to the past, but let them still more look to the future... Let them become Canadians, British subjects and give their heart, their soul, their energy and all their power to Canada, to its institutions, and to its King.[1]

Laurier's presence and the growing Liberal dominance of Alberta symbolized the political alliance between the West and Quebec that was emerging as the basis of Liberal rule in Canada.

The provincial Liberals decided upon a leader, whom Bulyea then selected as interim premier. The most prominent Alberta Liberal at the time was Frank Oliver, the editor of the *Edmonton Bulletin* and Member of Parliament for Edmonton. Oliver preferred the federal post of minister of the interior, replacing Sifton. With Oliver out of the running, the Liberals chose Alexander Rutherford, a lawyer from Strathcona.

Rutherford, the son of a Scots immigrant farmer, had grown up in rural Ontario before beginning a legal practice in a small Ontario town. He moved to South Edmonton (later renamed Strathcona) in 1895 and became active in local school politics, the Baptist Church, and several local business interests. He was first elected to the territorial legislature in 1902. Though he was neither dynamic nor innovative, he was viewed as someone with few enemies, a man who could unite the party.

The Conservatives were also building a provincial party and choosing a leader. Federally the Conservatives had done well in Alberta during the 1890s as long as the Conservatives were in power in Ottawa. The ranching community in southern Alberta was solidly Conservative and the CPR, powerful in Calgary, used its influence to build Conservative support. In 1905 the provincial Conservatives chose R. B. Bennett as their leader. Given the prosperity of the Laurier years and the changing ethnic and social composition of Alberta, whether or not the Conservatives could garner much support was debatable, particularly with CPR lawyer Bennett as leader. He provided an obvious target for criticism among farmers who disliked the CPR, which they saw as exploitive and monopolistic.

Bennett was an imposing figure who would become Canada's prime minister during the 1930s, but his start as provincial Conservative leader was not promising. James Lougheed, a wealthy lawyer and Conservative senator (appointed in 1889 when he was only thirty-five), persuaded Bennett to join his Calgary law firm in 1897. Lougheed had come to Calgary from Ontario in the 1880s and had grown wealthy through speculation in Calgary real estate. The twenty-seven-year-old Bennett arrived in Alberta from New Brunswick in 1897, and shared with Lougheed his ambition, partisan loyalties, and business acumen. Bennett, a rotund bachelor, was well-organized and disciplined, and possessed an exceptional memory. His three-fold ambition was to become a millionaire, prime minister, and a peer in the British Empire.

Bennett built up a political base in Calgary through his multiple business interests and community involvement in church and education. He had first run for the territorial legislature in 1898, making an immediate impression with his bombastic rhetoric and his demands for provincial status, more railways, and irrigation. His commitment to partisanship made him a thorn in Haultain's side. With his ambition and partisanship, Bennett was the natural choice for provincial leader. However, his personality, which as described by one historian was that of a "a cold, calculating, ruthless, thinking-machine," who in his private life "was a hide-bound Methodist who neither smoked nor drank"[2] limited his appeal.

By 1905, with the emergence of provincial Liberal and Conservative parties, the idea of a non-partisan government died. Haultain's own political career did not survive the autonomy debate. After being by-passed by the lieutenant governor in the selection of an interim premier for Saskatchewan, he led a short-lived and unsuccessful provincial rights party in Saskatchewan.

It gradually became evident nonetheless that the conditions that had fostered the non-partisan ideal had not entirely disappeared. The dislike of partisanship—of partisan loyalties, patronage, opportunism, and subservience to party machines dominated by central Canada—resurfaced repeatedly. The Non-Partisan League that emerged during World War I, the United Farmers of Alberta in the 1920s, Social Credit in the 1930s, and several small western protest parties of the 1980s all resurrected ideas of non-partisanship.

The 1905 provincial election was marked by intense partisan debate, yet there were few real ideological differences between the Liberals and Conservatives. Both were firm advocates of economic development and progress. The belief in the inevitability of growth and of economic expansion based on modern science and technology were articles of faith in frontier Alberta. The Conservatives attacked the terms of autonomy but they were no match for the Liberals, who won twenty-three of twenty-five seats and 58 per cent of the popular vote. Bennett himself went down to defeat. This first provincial election brought the first of many lop-sided victories in Alberta history.

From 1905 to 1917 the provincial Liberals won four successive elections, and until 1917 the Liberals also dominated among members elected from Alberta to Ottawa. How were the Liberals able to dominate in a new region with fragile partisan loyalties? First, the Liberals had been in power federally beginning in 1896, when an economic depression began to lift, and Liberals took credit for the rapid settlement of the West. Second, the Conservatives believed in the national policy and high tariffs, while Liberals believed in free trade. The farmers who displaced the ranchers found the Liberals, with their free trade views, more sympathetic to farmers. Third, the Liberals also had control of provincial and federal patronage, and decisions about government jobs and the location of various facilities affected how people voted. And the provincial Liberals seemed more responsive than the Conservatives to the reform ideas of women's rights, prohibition, and direct democracy (including the reforms of initiative, referendum, and recall) that were gaining popularity just before and during World War I.

The Conservatives were also tainted in the eyes of many new immigrants by their anti-immigrant nativist views. Conservative-oriented newspapers such as the *Macleod Gazette*, *Calgary Herald*, and *Edmonton Journal* attacked the Liberals for their open immigration policy, which, they believed, threatened "British" institutions. Once immigrants from central and eastern Europe could vote, the Conservatives were further disturbed by their overwhelming preference for Liberals. The Conservatives eventually followed the Liberal lead by establishing two German-language newspapers, but they had limited success. (The Liberals controlled one Ukrainian- and two German-language papers.) The either blatant or poorly concealed nativism of the Conservatives contributed to their successive defeats for decades.

Edmonton-Calgary Rivalry and Alberta's Urban Development

With the first election over, one crucial political decision remained: the choice of a capital. The capital controversy crystalized rivalry that was already growing between Calgary and Edmonton. Due largely to the political influence of Frank Oliver, and despite offers from Red Deer and Banff as neutral territory, the Alberta Act named Edmonton as the temporary capital.

Though Edmonton was the older of the two, Calgary's population had surged ahead with the completion of the CPR, while Edmonton's growth lagged until almost the turn of the century. Edmonton's population of just 1000 in 1897 felt the stirrings of change with the influx of goldseekers in 1897 and 1898. They used the head of steel in Edmonton as the jumping off point for an almost-impossible 1500-mile (2400-kilometre) overland route to the Klondike. While a handful made it, most of the roughly 1500 men who set off from Edmonton had to turn back. Most of the wealth from this rush came to Edmonton's merchants. The Klondike rush also publicized Edmonton, and many would-be goldseekers decided to stay and join the landrush.

As the agricultural centre for north-central Alberta, by 1905 Edmonton and Strathcona, with a combined population of 11,400, had almost caught up to Calgary, which had 12,000. Within the next five years, the populations of both Edmonton and Calgary would more than triple. They were shedding their images as frontier towns and yielding to urban patterns.

Edmonton gradually came to overshadow and dominate its earlier rival, Strathcona. By 1902, when the Low Level Bridge gave the CPR indirect access to Edmonton proper, it was clear that Edmonton had survived Strathcona's challenge. The businessmen of Strathcona, cut off by the North Saskatchewan River from a larger hinterland, were also out-promoted by Edmonton's boosters. The latter helped establish Edmonton as a railway hub; the Canadian Northern transcontinental was completed through the city in 1905, and the Grand Trunk Pacific in 1909. Edmonton absorbed Strathcona in 1912, and in 1913, the first CPR train crossed the newly completed High Level Bridge.

By 1905 Edmonton and Calgary had much in common. Strategically located on railways, they were primarily agricultural distribution centres, their economies based on meat packing, flour milling, brewing, and processing other agricultural products. Both were regional wholesale centres, and rivalled each other as regional headquarters for agricultural implement dealers, commercial travellers, and financial houses. Both were infected by a frontier boosterism that promoted frantic real estate speculation and glorified individualism, business success, and materialism.

The two cities were also dominated by an Anglo-Canadian professional and business elite that promoted these values and developed a similar social hierarchy. Both cities were affluent, and were at the beginning of booms that were producing massive new churches; large sandstone schools, banks, and office buildings; and spacious homes in prestigious suburbs such as Mount Royal in Calgary. The prosperous businessmen, professionals, and senior civil servants in Edmonton lived south of Jasper Avenue, and close to the North Saskatchewan River banks. Both cities experienced the negative effects of a boom economy, such as disparities in wealth, exploitation of labour, insensitivity to the plight of the poor, and ethnic prejudice. Clear differences between neighbourhoods emerged on class and ethnic lines.

Despite these similarities, there were social, political, and economic differences between the two cities. The economic and cultural presence of Anglo-Canadian and British ranchers and professionals and the CPR contributed to Calgary's remaining Conservative. Though the majority of the population in Edmonton was also of British origin (between 70 and 80 per cent in both cities), the proportion of Edmonton residents born in Britain was slightly smaller

Jasper Avenue, Edmonton, 1906. The choice of Edmonton as capital of the new province in 1905 assured its growth, but led to resentment from its rival, Calgary, which also lost out when the University of Alberta went to Strathcona (South Edmonton) in 1907. Both cities grew immensely in the immigration and economic boom that lasted until 1913. *(Glenbow Archives NA 303-20)*

than in Calgary. Edmonton had more Catholic French Canadians and other minorities, such as Ukrainians, who were more inclined to support the Liberals. Economically, Edmonton included in its hinterland the resource wealth of northern Alberta and the Mackenzie River basin. Calgary had Medicine Hat and Lethbridge as rivals for dominance of the agricultural hinterlands of southern Alberta, though these two cities were also part of Calgary's hinterland.

The crucial difference between the cities that determined the final outcome of the battle over the capital was not central location or size, but politics. Edmonton was Liberal. After the "temporary" choice of Edmonton as capital and the 1905 election, it was a foregone conclusion that Edmonton would remain the capital. The Liberals drew the 1905 provincial electoral map to ensure that a majority of seats would be in northern Alberta. For good measure, they drew the electoral boundaries so that six different constituencies radiated out from Edmonton like spokes on a hub. Not surprisingly, when the legislature first met in the spring of 1906, it confirmed Edmonton as capital. A year later, Calgarians were outraged when Premier Rutherford announced that the site of the provincial university would be in Strathcona.

The winning of the capital and the university kept Edmonton close to Calgary in size. By 1911, as the agricultural boom continued, Edmonton's population (including Strathcona) had jumped to

37,000. Calgary shot up to 43,700 by 1911. Given their locations, both cities had tremendous potential for growth, for encouraging provincial economic diversification, and for making possible the accumulation of wealth on a large scale.

The Edmonton-Calgary rivalry, which was heightened by the capital controversy, has for decades permeated almost all dimensions of the province's organizational life. Consequently, political parties, voluntary and professional organizations, and other groups organized on a provincial basis always have to carefully consider representation from the two cities. Each city remains smugly convinced of its own scenic, cultural, and business superiority, and there has been no sweeter satisfaction to sports fans in either city than to have their beloved team vanquish the archrivals from their sister city.

By the time of the capital controversy, the province's two other urban centres, Lethbridge and Medicine Hat, had already been far outdistanced by Calgary and Edmonton. Nonetheless, they shared many of the characteristics of boom-time Calgary and Edmonton, and they buzzed with construction and real estate speculation. An Anglo-Canadian business elite controlled each city government and board of trade, and did all it could to promote economic growth. Lethbridge, the irrigation capital of southern Alberta, grew from 2100 in 1901 to 9000 by 1911. Medicine Hat, which grew from 1600 in 1901 to 5600 in 1911, served as the centre for a region whose economic base was changing from ranching to dryland farming. In addition, the availability of ample natural gas and clay in Medicine Hat made possible the development of a small industrial sector based on the manufacturing of pottery, bricks, and tiles.

The Liberals in Power

The new government established the province's administrative structure and the basic organization of roads, bridges, ferries, telephones, railways, and schools. It also established Alberta's civil service around a core of territorial employees transferred from Regina. Administrative structures grew rapidly due to pressures generated by the large influx of settlers. Faced with a shortage of local capital and limited taxing powers, the government relied heavily on money markets in eastern Canada, Britain, and the U.S. in its plans for economic development.

Since Rutherford was not only premier, but also provincial treasurer and minister of education, his whole administration was marked

First Legislature of Alberta, 1906. Twenty-three of the first twenty-five MLAs were Liberals, and the Liberals remained in power until 1921. Premier A. C. Rutherford is in the centre on the top row. Seventeen of the first twenty-five MLAs were from Ontario, reflecting the strong influence of migrants from Ontario in the early political history of Alberta. *(Glenbow Archives NA-358-1)*

by his seriousness, caution, and determination. However, the Liberals under Rutherford initiated some bold projects: a government-owned telephone system, a provincial university, and an expansive railway policy.

In 1907 the Liberals took over the privately owned telephone system. They claimed that the Bell Telephone Company was profiteering and would not extend its services to sparsely settled rural districts. W. H. Cushing, the minister of public works and a wealthy Calgary businessman, attacked the Bell Telephone Company as "the most pernicious and iniquitous monopoly that had ever been foisted upon a people claiming to be free."[3] The government bought out Bell, established Alberta Government Telephones, and expanded lines to link a far-flung and sparse population. Though free enterprise views prevailed in the province, there was no ideological rigidity when it came to the province providing essential public services.

Rutherford moved quickly and carefully to establish a university.

The Alberta Legislative Building was completed in 1913 on the site of Fort Edmonton. Its architecture was based on the Late Victorian Beaux-Arts style. With its massive size, its columns, arches, and dome, it attempted to provide a sense of stateliness, stability, and tradition in a new, pioneer society made up of people from many lands. (*Glenbow Archives NC-6-2012*)

The bill to do so was one of the first legislative acts passed in Alberta. Since he wanted to avoid the interdenominational squabbling that marked the nineteenth-century history of Ontario universities, the new university was to be non-denominational. It was also to be co-educational. Rutherford's choice for president was Henry Marshall Tory, a man of broad vision and practical insight who became one of the giants in the history of higher education and scientific research in Canada.

Tory was born and educated in Nova Scotia before attending McGill University in Montreal. After two years as a Methodist minister, he returned to McGill to study and eventually teach mathematics and physics. While travelling through Alberta in 1906, he was caught up in the boom-time atmosphere of the province. He wrote to his wife, "This country fascinates me. There is wine in the air; a feeling of excitement; of expectancy. It is difficult to explain. Perhaps it is just that everything is new, the people young and the conviction grows that great things are bound to happen in this rich new country."[4]

Rutherford asked Tory's advice on educational policy, and Tory recommended the immediate establishment of a university. Rutherford then asked him to become president of the new university and director general of education in the province, and Tory agreed. They both wanted a non-denominational university with a strong emphasis on scientific research. They combined strong religious belief with a conviction that empirical methods and practical research were important for a modern university.

Tory recruited four promising young professors, and in 1908 they began classes in Strathcona Public School with forty-five students. Once he had established his arts and science faculty, Tory moved into the field of professional education, and successfully asserted university control over the education of professionals in the province. The university developed programs in agriculture and applied science in 1909, faculties of law and medicine in 1912, and gradually expanded into engineering, pharmacy, and commerce. Tory also worked towards establishing university control over teacher preparation. By the time he moved to Ottawa in 1928 to head the National Research Council, the University of Alberta had its own campus and a strong program in applied science. It boasted six buildings and over 1600 students.

Denominational colleges posed a threat to Tory's vision of a centralized post-secondary system. He countered this through a system of affiliations between denominational institutions and the University of Alberta. Religious colleges such as Alberta College (Methodist) and St. Joseph's (Catholic) eventually affiliated with the university.

Tory believed in the need to maintain one strong university rather than decentralize post-secondary institutions, so he opposed a Calgary rival. In September 1912, a group of prominent Calgarians launched a private university, Calgary College. Tory opposed the college, and the legislature supported his view. It closed in 1915 when the government would not grant it degree-conferring power.

The government decided instead to build an institute in Calgary that would support technical and vocational education. The Provincial Institute of Technology and Art (which became the Southern Alberta Institute of Technology in 1960) began classes in 1916, partly in response to federal support for vocational training of veterans. The institute gradually developed programs in art, aviation, and communications that brought it national recognition.

Calgary's educational and cultural growth was limited by the absence of a university. However, before World War I, Calgary became the site of a Normal School for teacher training (begun in 1906) and five private boarding high schools and first-year colleges, including the Methodist Mount Royal College. Calgary served as an educational centre for southern Alberta.

The Railways, the Alberta and Great Waterways Scandal, and the Development of the North

What the public demanded most was not universities but railways. Although the federal government subsidized two new national transcontinental lines, provincial politicians believed that Ottawa was not doing enough. The business interests of Edmonton wanted to expand their hinterland to the north, and they had a sympathetic ear in the Edmonton-dominated Rutherford administration. Rutherford was also responsive to the demands of farmers and entrepreneurs for railways to link new frontiers with transcontinental systems. His government's expansive railway policy created a legacy of debt, and eventually a scandal and a political crisis.

Edmonton commercial interests wanted a railway to Fort McMurray to circumvent the rapids on the Athabasca River, which greatly complicated transportation to the Arctic. They also wanted to develop the potential of the oil sands at Fort McMurray, a site largely forgotten since the days of Peter Pond and the North-West Company. While there had been four different fur-trade posts at the junction of the Clearwater and Athabasca rivers between 1786 and 1804, none had been viable, and after 1821 the last post had been abandoned. In 1870 Henry Moberly, a trader for the Hudson's Bay Company, was sent from the large post at Fort Chipewyan to the forks of the Athabasca and Clearwater rivers, where he built a new post, which he named Fort McMurray after the officer in charge at Fort Chipewyan. Moberly both traded with natives and worked on the transportation problems of the North, including studying the possibility of using steamboats on the Athabasca and Slave rivers. But from the time Moberly left the post in 1878 until the early 1920s, with the arrival of the Alberta and Great Waterways Railway (A. & G. W.), Fort McMurray made little progress. In 1899 one traveller described the site as consisting of "a tumble-down cabin and trading store."[5] The Hudson's Bay Company, discouraged by the post's lack of trading prospects, had moved north to Fort Mackay in 1898, but they had been replaced at Fort McMurray by a variety of other independent fur traders.

However, there were resources other than furs beginning to attract outsiders' attention. Both the federal government and private

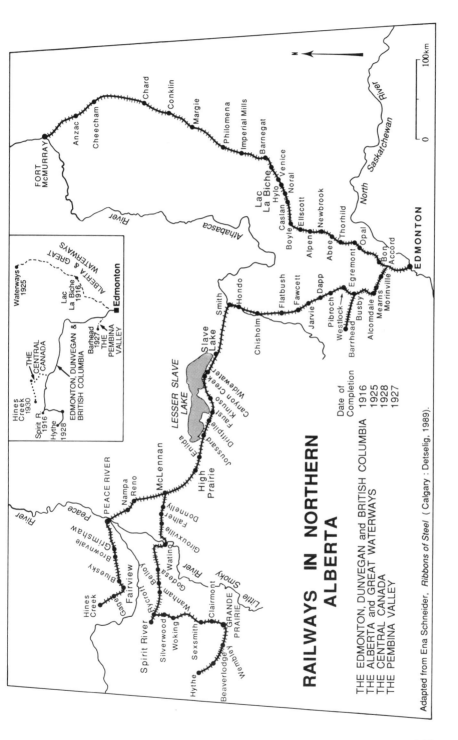

RAILWAYS IN NORTHERN ALBERTA

	Date of Completion
THE EDMONTON, DUNVEGAN and BRITISH COLUMBIA	1916
THE ALBERTA and GREAT WATERWAYS	1925
THE CENTRAL CANADA	1928
THE PEMBINA VALLEY	1927

Adapted from Ena Schneider, *Ribbons of Steel* (Calgary : Detselig, 1989).

investors were attracted to the potential of the oil sands. The black sticky mixture of sand, clay, water, and bitumen had first been noted by fur traders in the late 1700s. Both Indians and explorers had used it, along with resin, to seal their canoes. Government geologists and entrepreneurs saw great potential if some method could be invented to separate the oil from the sticky mixture. Federal geologists suggested that the sands had become saturated with oil that had seeped from huge pools beneath the ground. But after the government's Geological Survey failed in its repeated efforts to find these pools (which, it was later learned, did not exist), the federal government opened the district to private developers.

Among the many promoters who began drilling wells were J. K. "Peace River Jim" Cornwall, German immigrant A. Von Hammerstein, and R. C. Fitzsimmons, who would long be associated with oilsands development. Ontario-born James Cornwall had come to the Peace River district after travelling the world as a sailor and adventurer. He arrived in 1897, during the overland rush to the Klondike, and worked as a trapper, trader, and steamboat builder and operator on Lesser Slave Lake and along the Athabasca River. A great booster of the north and "a man of tremendous talents and a flare for salesmanship, he aroused mixed feelings in his contemporaries; many regarded him as a sham, but the majority fell under his spell and became his loyal supporters."[6] By 1905, he began promoting a railway from Edmonton to the Athabasca River, "at or near Fort McMurray." He also began drilling for oil in the region.

Cornwall saw the potential of a railway to open the oilsands, as well as provide access to the three thousand miles (4800 kilometres) of navigable waterways extending to the Arctic Ocean. A reported oil strike in 1909 heightened interest in the region, and Cornwall began subdividing the river flats at Fort McMurray as a townsite. He tried to interest Edmontonians in the oil sands by having a group of scowmen drag a batch of it upstream to Athabasca Landing. From there they took it to Edmonton, where it was used to pave a sidewalk on Jasper Avenue. The oil boom in Fort McMurray gradually faded before the formidable problem of extracting the bitumen, and the community barely eked out an existence based on furs, lumbering, and transportation. But the hope of an oil strike nonetheless affected government railway policy.

Boosterism, commercial development, railways, and politics were all intermeshed. Rutherford announced in early 1909 an expansive and expensive policy that provided bond guarantees for three northern railways—to Peace River country, to Athabasca Landing, and to Fort McMurray. Armed with this railway policy, the Rutherford government then called an election with the slogan "Rutherford, Reliability and Railways." The government won an overwhelming victory in thirty-six of forty-one seats. Cornwall was elected as the Liberal MLA for Peace River in 1909. He was to have a good deal of influence on the development of railway policy, along with the attorney general, Edmonton lawyer Charles Cross, and Premier Rutherford.

The victory soon soured for Rutherford. The extremely generous terms of the contract to the Alberta and Great Waterways Railway (A. & G. W.) to Fort McMurray eventually raised strong suspicions of either government graft or incompetence. In February 1910 backbenchers began raising embarrassing questions in the legislature. Extravagant government loan guarantees of $20,000 per mile for 350 miles (560 kilometres) appeared to have enabled promoters to profiteer. W. H. Cushing resigned as minister of public works, and a backbencher called for the expropriation of the A. & G. W. and the completion of the line by a government agency. Rutherford tried to hold the political factions together by appointing a royal commission to investigate, but growing party division and rising public outrage

Following a political scandal, Rutherford was replaced as premier in 1910 by Arthur Sifton, Alberta's chief justice. Sifton is shown here addressing a crowd at Wetaskiwin in 1910, when the town had a population of about 2400. (*Glenbow Archives NA 3592-8*)

147

The completion of the Edmonton, Dunvegan and B.C. Railway in 1916 opened up the Peace River district to large-scale settlement and led to the founding of many new towns. These passengers are headed to the Peace River district in 1917. *(Glenbow Archives NC-6-2738)*

forced him to resign. Although the Royal Commission eventually concluded that there was no dishonesty in the deal, Rutherford's political career was over.

The method of choosing Rutherford's successor was blatantly undemocratic. Following consultation with leading Alberta Liberals, the Liberal leadership in Ottawa, together with Lieutenant Governor Bulyea, decided that Arthur Sifton, chief justice of the province and elder brother of Clifford Sifton, was the one man who could pull the party together.

Arthur Sifton, like Rutherford, was a lawyer from Ontario and a member of a staunch Methodist and Liberal family. After attending university, Sifton went West and was called to the bar of the North-West Territories in 1883. After four years in the territorial legislature, he was named Chief Justice of the Supreme Court. Sifton became Alberta's first chief justice in 1905.

Despite his autocratic and aloof style, Sifton healed some of the rifts in his party and led it to victory in the 1913 and 1917 elections (though with much reduced majorities). Nonetheless, Sifton was never able to fully restore the public's confidence after the A. & G. W. scandal, and the party went into a decline, accelerated by the loss of his leadership in 1917, when he moved to federal politics.

As premier, Arthur Sifton continued the policy of government support for railways, particularly in the North. By 1912 most of central and southern Alberta had been settled. Branch lines had been built or were under construction, and these regions were evolving from pioneer settlements to developed ones. At the same time, excellent farmland was available in the Peace River district, although it was virtually inaccessible. Sifton turned to a Manitoba railway promoter, J. D. McArthur, to build a railway to the Peace River district (the Edmonton, Dunvegan and British Columbia Railway—E. D. & B. C.). Edmonton's business community supported the railway to Peace River, since they wanted to ensure that Edmonton, not Vancouver, gained commercial control of the region.

The Peace River district was sparsely populated and isolated. By 1912 there were only 5000 people, mostly native, in the whole northwest part of Alberta. Throughout the 1800s, the Peace River district had been a fur-trading region. Isolated agricultural settlement began in the 1880s around the church missions. Most of the first settlers, originally Klondike-bound, took up trading and cattle-raising in the Lake Saskatoon and Spirit River areas. Uneven quality of land and a short growing season made farming extremely risky. These factors, combined with transportation difficulties, delayed the rush to Peace River. Potential colonists struggled over the long Athabasca-Slave Lake Trail until 1911, when, with the completion of the Grand Trunk Pacific Railway to Edson, the government built the Edson Trail, 250 miles (400 kilometres) of "mud, muskeg and mosquitoes"[7] running north from the town of Edson.

This trail was used until 1915, when McArthur's company, working at breakneck speed over difficult terrain, completed the railway to the Peace River district. As it was built, the railway opened up new agricultural land north of Edmonton and brought into being agricultural towns such as Westlock. Then at Mirror Landing, where the mouth of the Lesser Slave River meets the Athabasca, the tracks turned west. The railway company surveyed a town on the south bank, opposite Mirror Landing, and the town of Smith, temporarily at the end of steel, became a short-lived haven for the gamblers, bootleggers, and prostitutes who invariably followed the railway construction crews across the West. As the railway pushed west, it opened up new towns at Slave Lake and Kinuso, among other communities. The railway also established High Prairie and by-passed Grouard, the old transportation centre and mission on the west end of Lesser Slave Lake, which then quickly faded. The new town of McLennan became the divisional point for the E. D. & B. C. One branch of the railway went north to the village of Peace River, which, strategically situated at the joining of rail and water transportation, became the transportation centre for northwestern Alberta. Trade goods for the north, which had previously been sent down the Athabasca River by scow past the almost unnavigable Grand Rapids, could now be sent by rail to Peace River, and then loaded on steamboats to be taken down the Peace River to the far-flung trading posts and missions of the North. Another railway branch went west to Spirit River, with another line looping south to Grande Prairie.

First begun as an HBC trading post in 1881, Grande Prairie had a population that scarcely increased at all until settlers began to trickle in after 1900. One of the early promoters was an Edmonton lawyer, W. A. Rae, who in 1909 selected a townsite, formed a company to promote the town, and divided it into lots. Stores, churches, a school, a land office, and a livery stable were soon built to accommodate newcomers, and in March 1913, when the town had a population of less than fifty, the first edition of the *Grande Prairie Herald* appeared. The pace of growth quickened when the railway was completed to Grande Prairie in March 1916, and by 1919, the town had reached the 1000 mark. With the new railway, the population of the Peace River district quadrupled between 1911 and 1921. Grande Prairie and the town of Peace River emerged as the region's major commercial centres and rivals.

From 1915 to 1930, Peace River country attracted Ontarians, Britons, Americans, French Canadians, Norwegians, Germans, and Ukrainians, as well as small pockets of Mennonites, Croats, Slovaks, Russians, Hungarians, and Poles. The Indians and Métis were isolated on the margins of settlement.

While the E. D. & B. C. railway was pushing its way to Peace River, Sifton in 1913 gave a contract to McArthur to complete the A. & G. W. railway to Fort McMurray. By 1915, the trains had reached Lac La Biche, where McArthur built an opulent railway hotel facing the lake. (Financial depression, war, and a tragic boat accident, which took the lives of seven guests, led to its closing by 1918.) Northwest of Lac La Biche, the builders moved into a world of sand hills, muskeg, and small trees, and construction bogged down in endless difficulties. By 1916, the railway reached Lynton on the edge of the descent into the valley of the Clearwater River, fifteen miles (24 kilometres) short of its destination at Waterways, the next town to Fort McMurray. But it did not reach Waterways until 1922. For the next fifty years,

Waterways served as the jumping off point for river transportation to the far north for traders, Mounted Police, missionaries, and oil explorers.

The coming of the railway was changing old patterns across the North. The arrival of the E. D. & B. C. marked the end of an era of isolation in Peace River history, and led to a new phase in agriculture. Northeastern Alberta had not yet come into its own, however. The railway to Waterways bypassed the exceedingly difficult journey by wagon road from Edmonton to Athabasca Landing and then by scow to Fort McMurray, thus making transportation to the north much easier. But the oil sands had not yet yielded their secrets, and while the railway made possible commercial fishing and the exploitation of salt deposits, it would be decades before the rich oil resources would yield to science and technology, and attract an influx of people.

Farmers Organize

Although the Liberals' ambitious railway policy had led to divisions within the party, they remained in power as long as farmers saw them as responsive to their needs. However, throughout the decade before the outbreak of World War I, the organized farm movement was becoming more powerful. As it grew in membership and influence, it had the potential to bring down the Liberals.

Until 1905 the organized farm movement in Alberta was limited to individual locals of the Territorial Grain Growers' Association. Then farmers around Edmonton organized a branch of an American farm organization, the Society of Equity. The Society, primarily concerned with profitable ways of marketing farm produce, set up a number of cooperative businesses. In 1906 other Edmonton-area farmers established a rival organization, specifically without American ties, the Alberta Farmers Association. In 1909 the two came together as the United Farmers of Alberta (UFA). By 1912 the organization had a membership of 7190. The UFA helped mould rural society, and ultimately altered the political future of Alberta and the rest of western Canada.

Newly arrived Alberta farmers were frustrated by high freight rates, boxcar shortages, unfair treatment by grain companies, high protective tariffs, and high interest rates. In 1898, responding to a public outcry against the CPR's monopolistic freight rates, the federal government negotiated the Crow's Nest Pass Agreement with the railway, providing lower rates on wheat and flour moving eastward and settlers' effects moving westward. (This negotiation of freight rates downward was necessary for the Laurier government to make politically palatable the subsidy given the CPR for the construction of the Crow's Nest Pass railway into the interior of B.C.) Many Alberta farmers remained convinced, however, that the rates were excessive. Farmers also pressured the Laurier government in 1900 to pass the Manitoba Grain Act (which partially regulated the grain trade through provisions for grading and inspection), and some farmers wanted to enter the elevator business on their own. Farmers were also dissatisfied with banks, which they saw as insensitive, remote, and rapacious.

The farmers' main grievance was the tariff. While they bought their goods in a protected national market, they sold on an open international market. After the federal Liberals came to power in 1896, they lowered the tariff. But their tariff revisions in 1899 and 1907 did not go far enough for western farmers. They saw the tariff as a form of economic imperialism, designed by central Canada to keep the West subservient. When Laurier made a western tour in 1910, he was forcefully reminded of the strength of free trade sentiment. In order to keep western support for the Liberals, he determined to press for freer trade with the United States.

When Laurier went to the polls in 1911 with freer trade the major election issue, Alberta returned six of seven Liberal seats, though the country as a whole rejected freer trade and the Liberals. Farmers began to consider the possibility of a new party that could not be dominated by central Canada.

One of the new Liberal MPs from Alberta was W. A. Buchanan, the Ontario-born owner and editor of the *Lethbridge Herald*, who was to become a major power broker for southern Alberta at the national level. As MP for Lethbridge from 1911 to 1921, and as a senator from Alberta from 1925 to 1954, Buchanan became the major link between southern Alberta and the federal Liberal party. Under Buchanan, the *Herald* developed as a paper with deep local roots and at the same time a cosmopolitan outlook, unusual for a small-city newspaper.

Despite their disenchantment with developments at the national level, the organized farmers found a sympathetic ear with the provincial Liberals. The Liberals often passed legislation based on ideas that had first appeared at UFA annual conventions. In 1913 the Alberta government, bowing to farm pressure, helped finance the Alberta Co-operative Elevator Company. This farmer-owned cooperative company, which would later become part of the United Grain

Growers, successfully competed with the private grain trade. The UFA also pressured the provincial Liberals into passing direct legislation. This democratic reform, based on American populist beliefs, enabled voters to initiate legislation and to vote on it in a referendum.

Farmers' discontent grew partly out of the conditions of prairie settlement. A wheat economy, dependent on radically fluctuating prices in an international market, was inherently unstable. Political discontent mounted in a debtor region, distant from centres of national power. The large proportion of immigrants, without strong ties to the major national parties, encouraged independent thought. Immigrants often brought with them radical ideas of a new, cooperative, and egalitarian society. Thousands of Alberta farmers began to feel a common sense of exploitation and grievance, and a common determination to change their status. The ideas of eastern Canadian agrarianism, American populism, and the British cooperative movement fused with frontier economic and social conditions to produce a politically uncontainable force that erupted dramatically during the latter years of the Great War.

King Coal: Industry Invades the Wilderness

Because the focus of Alberta's economy was agriculture, Alberta's farmers had a decisive say in the nature of the political system. However, other important sectors of the economy, particularly energy, also emerged during the prewar economic boom. Coal mining expanded enormously, attracting large-scale investment from the United States, central Canada, and Europe. Oil, gas, and hydro-electric power also began to develop, though on a much smaller scale than coal. While businessmen in Edmonton were pushing for railways to open up resources in northern Alberta, entrepreneurs in Calgary were eyeing the potential of oil, gas, and hydro-electric power. Calgary business people gradually dominated the early development of these resources.

Coal mining expanded enormously at the turn of the century, supplying fuel to prairie dwellers, the railways, and B.C. smelters. Coal production increased more than tenfold from 242,000 tons in 1897 to almost three million tons in 1910, and then to over four million tons in 1913. By 1911 coal mining employed 6 per cent of the non-agricultural workforce in Alberta. The major new coal-mining developments were in the Crow's Nest Pass area of southern Alberta between 1898 and 1912. After 1910 the focus shifted northward to the

153

Coal Branch and Jasper areas because of the building of the two new transcontinental railways that crossed the north-central prairies.

The close tie between railways and coal mining, evident in the development of the Lethbridge coalfields in the 1880s, was repeated on a larger scale in the late 1890s and the early years of the twentieth century. The railways determined the place and pace for the development of coal mining.

The Crow's Nest Pass, the largest of the new coalfields, had first been developed from the B.C. side. Gold rushes in the interior of B.C. in the 1860s had attracted adventurers to the region. During the 1870s and 1880s, Spokane, Washington, developed as a major commercial centre for mining and smelting operations. Spokane entrepreneurs opened up mines and smelters in Trail and Nelson, and built a railway to the interior of B.C. These developers also became interested in the coal deposits in the Crow's Nest Pass, which could provide fuel for their smelters.

The CPR looked warily at the growing ties between the interior of B.C. and American capital, and decided to push a railway from Lethbridge through the Crow's Nest Pass. In 1897, the CPR negotiated with the new Laurier government for a subsidy. The building of the Crow's Nest railway, completed in 1898, opened the area and brought an influx of capital and people.

The construction of the railway also led to growing public awareness of the intolerable working conditions of railway construction workers. Complaints by Welsh immigrant workers about deplorable conditions reached the British and Canadian press, eventually resulting in a federal Royal Commission. The Commission found that the mostly immigrant workforce of 4500 earned $1.75 per day, but they were poorly fed; they were not paid when poor weather prevented work, and deductions were made for food, lodging, mail delivery, and medical attention. Because of the high prices they had to pay for food and clothing, workers had to work two or three months before fares advanced by the railway company could be paid. Some had to live in the open, or in stoveless tents as late as January, and they lacked washing and sanitary facilities, which led to widespread illness. Workers who quit found themselves subject to arrest for breaking contracts. They were left to starve in the cold, as the company refused to transport them or allow them to obtain food as they trekked out from the workcamps. The government report demanded better treatment of labourers, but by then most of the work, and exploitation, had already occurred.

154

With the completion of the railway, miners poured into the Crow's Nest area from around the world to work for large coal companies financed by American, French, British, and central Canadian capital. On the Alberta side of the Crow's Nest Pass, entrepreneurs from Washington and Montana were especially important. H. L. Frank, who financed the mine in Frank, and C. P. Hill, founder of Hillcrest, were at the peak of their careers. Frank had worked in mining camps across the American West before arriving in Butte, Montana. Here he opened a liquor store, invested in hardrock mining, and became mayor and a state legislator. He saw the Crow's Nest Pass as a new district with tremendous potential. His plan, like that of many entrepreneurs, was to buy up as much land as possible and hold on while the value of his properties increased. As self-made men, they saw unions as an anathema. This attitude contributed to poor labour relations.

On the Alberta side of the Crow's Nest Pass, the short distances between outcrops led to a large number of mines and consequently of communities. By the outbreak of World War I in 1914, approximately 8000 people lived on the Alberta side. Of the nine communities on the Alberta side, Coleman and Blairmore eventually became the largest. Several mines manufactured coke for B.C. smelters.

As in other mining areas of the province, the Crow's Nest Pass attracted immigrants from across Europe. Ethnic diversity and ethnic stratification were both pronounced. By 1919, when a royal commission studied the coal industry, 90 per cent of the workers in the Pass were immigrants: 34 per cent were British, 23 per cent Slovak, 14.5 per cent Italian, 7 per cent French and Belgian, 2 per cent Russian, 8.5 per cent "other European," and 1 per cent American. The ethnic composition of each town differed, but all were highly diverse. The American, Anglo-Canadian, and French management lived in areas separate from the workers and usually frequented different clubs and churches. The Slavs and Italians in Coleman and Blairmore each had their own ethnic neighbourhoods and ethnic organizations. The mine managers were mostly Protestant and the miners Catholic, although organized religion in the coal camps was mainly the domain of women and children.

The Crow's Nest Pass area was plagued by a series of disasters. At 4:00 A.M. on April 29, 1903, tragedy struck Frank, a town of 600 people huddled near the coal mine at the foot of Turtle Mountain. Ninety million tons of limestone crashed down from the mountain, burying the mine, railway, and part of the village, taking seventy

Frank, Alberta, April 30, 1903, the day after part of Turtle Mountain crashed down, burying part of the town and killing seventy people. (*Glenbow Archives NA 411-9*)

lives. Although the mouth of the mine was buried, the entombed miners dug their way out through another tunnel. Strangely, the slide did not deter the company, which was soon back in business with a new mine, and Frank continued to grow. However, after several geological studies concluded that there was danger of further slides, in 1911 the government ordered that the townsite be moved.

Alberta's coal mines were among the most dangerous in the world. Fierce competition encouraged operators to take chances with the lives of their employees. Ever-present coal dust and gas also made the Crow's Nest Pass mines highly dangerous. Operators, inspectors, and workers were each partially to blame for the high number of deaths. At Bellevue, an explosion on December 9, 1910, caused in part by the negligence of the coal company, killed thirty-one men. The Hillcrest mine disaster of June 1914, Canada's worst, claimed 189 lives. Methane gas had ignited and touched off an explosion of coal dust.

From 1905 to 1945, more than a thousand miners lost their lives in Alberta mines. Other major disasters in Alberta included Coleman, 1926, ten fatalities; Coalhurst, 1935, sixteen fatalities; and Nordegg, 1941, twenty-nine fatalities. These horrific disasters contributed to uniting the labour community in the coalfields. A miner's safety depended on his co-workers, and a supportive community was essential to help cope with constant danger.

The Crow's Nest Pass was the largest of the coalfields, but coal mining was spread across many regions of the province. In the Lethbridge district, forty-two shafts opened before 1920, including those in the small communities of Hardieville, Diamond City, Coalhurst, and Taber, where farm life and mining were closely intertwined. In the Banff area, the Anthracite mine, first opened in 1886, closed in 1904 because of unstable markets, labour unrest, and technical problems. The CPR looked for another supply to supplement the Canmore mine. They developed the townsite of Bankhead just north of Banff on Cascade Mountain, and began mining operations in 1903. The CPR built a model company town at Bankhead, with individual houses with indoor plumbing, boarding houses, offices with a mess hall, and a power plant. The community also included a Roman Catholic Church, a four-room school, and a hall for concerts and community events for the population of 900. For a brief time village life bustled, but in 1922 the CPR closed the plant because of

Coal mining expanded enormously at the turn of the century to serve the railways and the new settlers. Earl Cass, a native of North Dakota who had homesteaded at Strome, was one of the many homesteaders who braved the danger of the mines to supplement his income during the winter months. This photo was taken in Edmonton in 1908. (*Glenbow Archives NA 2991-12*)

competition from other mines, labour disputes, and the difficulty of mining the twisted coal seams on Cascade Mountain.

As the railways pushed out branch lines across the prairies, they took care to pass over farming lands underlain with coal. Mines developed in the wheat fields at Big Valley, Sheerness, and Alix in central Alberta. In 1911 the Canadian Northern built a branch line to the Drumheller Valley in central Alberta. This led to the opening of a number of new coal mines at Wayne, Rosedale, Newcastle, Nacmine, and Midlandvale. Drumheller was transformed from a ranching backwater to a transportation, commercial, and coal-mining centre. By the 1920s, the Drumheller Valley had a population of 10,000, including approximately 2000 miners who worked in twenty-nine different mines producing coal for domestic use. Drumheller itself had a population of 2500 by 1921. Some of the coal miners supplemented their wages with agricultural labour, or homesteaded and gradually turned to farming.

The building of the transcontinental Grand Trunk Pacific (GTP) through the Yellowhead Pass opened up another rich new coal area, the Coal Branch. The GTP consumed much of the coal from this area. From 1911 to 1913, the GTP laid one hundred miles (160 kilometres) of track to connect the isolated mining camps of the Coal Branch with the outside world through the GTP mainline. Collieries were opened at Cadomin, Luscar, Robb, Mercoal, Sterco, Coal Valley, Foothills, and Lovett. By 1929, when the Coal Branch reached its peak, it produced 22 per cent of Alberta's coal. From 1912 to 1914, German entrepreneur Martin Nordegg also developed a coal-mining community in west-central Alberta in partnership with the Canadian Northern Railway. By 1914 Nordegg had established a model townsite, coal mine, and railway.

Given the difficult living conditions, large number of single men, and ethnic differences, it is little wonder that coal-mining towns gained a reputation as places where drinking, crime, prostitution, and labour radicalism flourished. So much was spent on liquor in the Crow's Nest Pass that merchants complained about miners being unable to pay their bills.

Despite these conditions, coal-mining camps often developed an active community life, with a strong sense of community pride and solidarity. Bowling, pool, boxing matches, and horse-racing were popular pastimes. The Europeans played soccer while the native-born preferred hockey. In the Crow's Nest Pass and other areas, "opera" houses accommodated travelling theatre companies. Fraternal lodges and ethnic organizations also provided many social activities.

The working conditions of the mines contributed to unrest and solidarity among the workers, and helped turn the coal miners into the vanguard of the fight for organized labour in Alberta. Coal mining not only diversified the Alberta economy, but also led to a much more politically varied and class-conscious society. More than 60 per cent of all strike activity in Alberta from the early 1900s until the demise of the industry in the 1950s was in the coal mines.

Miners' discontent had many causes. In addition to the dangers in the mines, pay was also a problem. Most of the miners did not work for wages, but on a piece-rate or contract system whereby the worker was paid based on the amount of coal he dug. This often gave rise to disputes between management and miners. Management also deducted money for a number of items; in "closed" or company towns (owned and controlled by coal companies), miners were charged high rents for their homes. Food prices in isolated coal towns such as in the Coal Branch were 25 per cent higher than in urban areas. The camaraderie spawned by this exploitation, and by the alien and dangerous underground, eventually overrode differences among miners. Not surprisingly, they turned to unions to protect themselves.

Unions and Left-Wing Politics

While the growth of organized labour in Alberta was closely tied to the struggles of the miners, other workers were also involved. The earliest labour disputes occurred among railway construction workers in 1883, and the earliest unions in Alberta developed among engineers, firemen, and conductors on the railroad. The first Alberta local of the Brotherhood of Locomotive Engineers was formed in 1886. Railway employees and the construction trades in the cities developed craft unions as one of the two main centres of unionism in Alberta. The other centre of union activity was among the coal miners. These miners were more militant than workers in the cities, and they favoured industrial unions, which brought all the workers in one industry into one union. The miners' orientation inevitably strained the relationship between them and the urban craft unions.

The Alberta miners first turned to the Western Federation of Miners (WFM) to represent them. This tough, militant organization, born in the metal mines in Montana, came to the Galt mines in Lethbridge in 1897 and led the first coal miners' strike to oppose wage cuts. Miners concluded that by themselves, they could not withstand the power of the company. However, under pressure from management, the Canadian government, and the NWMP, and wanting to focus its attention on its major constituency, American metal miners, the WFM withdrew from the Canadian coalfields.

In 1903 the seemingly more moderate United Mine Workers of America (UMWA) replaced the WFM. The struggle by the UMWA for recognition in the Alberta coalfields precipitated stark ethnic and class conflict. Their strike in Lethbridge in 1906 also led to important new national labour legislation. Miners in Lethbridge decided to strike unless the Galt interests recognized the UMWA as their union. The mine management, which had maintained a paternalistic relationship with the miners, refused, and on March 9, the largest mine in the province came to a halt. Augustus Nanton, the managing director of the company, refused to negotiate with the union, and the Mounted Police were quickly drawn into the dispute.

Nanton was the Winnipeg-based partner in the Toronto financial firm of Osler, Hammond and Nanton. He had built up a prosperous portfolio in railways, insurance, mortgages, and real estate. In 1904 his firm began to buy up shares in the Galt-owned Alberta Railway and Irrigation Company (AR&I), which ran the coal mines. In 1905 Nanton became managing director of the AR&I, and the conduit for Winnipeg and Toronto capital in the development of southern Alberta. Nanton took a determined stand during the strike, demanding that the NWMP maintain a strong contingent because, as he told the police, "if they are withdrawn before the strike is settled. . .there will be both riot and bloodshed, as there is a large and ignorant foreign element."[8]

The company began firing employees who were union members. In late May, management reopened the mine with non-union workers. Supposedly to prevent violence, the police made a strong show of force and escorted strikebreakers back and forth to the mine. In response, militant miners blew up two homes and burned a third house of strikebreakers. They openly confronted police with rocks, fists, and clubs.

By the fall of 1906, railway bottlenecks helped precipitate a fuel crisis on the prairies, and the public demanded government action to end the strike. The federal government sent in Mackenzie King, then Canada's deputy minister of labour, to mediate the strike. Finally, in November 1906, the union agreed to a settlement. While they did not achieve most of their demands, the workers won a wage increase, and the agreement recognized a limited number of workers' rights.

Based on his experience in this strike, King returned to Ottawa and drafted the Industrial Disputes Investigation Act, which forbade strikes or lock-outs in coal mines or public utilities until a board had investigated the dispute and recommended a settlement. This act was important in Canadian labour history as the major piece of labour legislation for two decades, though it did little to stop the unrest in the Alberta coalfields. District-wide strikes occurred in 1907, 1909, and 1911.

Coal miners also led in the fight to represent workers in the legislature. The first labour member of the legislature was Donald McNabb, a Lethbridge miner and socialist who won a by-election in 1909. Charles O'Brien, another miner and socialist, won a seat in the provincial election in 1909. O'Brien was an Ontario-born radical who had come west as a labourer on the Crow's Nest Pass Railway. Described by one historian as the "evangelist" of Alberta socialism, O'Brien belonged to the Socialist Party of Canada (SPC). It had its strongest base of support in British Columbia, though it also won support in the coal towns in Alberta. Like many other SPC activists, O'Brien was a Marxist who believed that strong collective action was necessary to obtain even moderate concessions. The flamboyant O'Brien was not averse to making waves in the legislature; he always wore a red necktie in the House. In 1910, when a resolution of sympathy for Edward VII's widow was introduced in the legislature, O'Brien moved an amendment that extended condolences to the wives of British miners killed in a recent disaster. O'Brien's colleagues were so upset that they threw inkwells and books at him when he refused to withdraw the amendment.

While socialists generally moved unions to the left, they were particularly influential with the miners. In 1914 the United Mine Workers of District 18, which included the Alberta coalfields, voted to endorse the SPC as its political arm. Urban unions, surrounded by conservative influences, including churches, newspapers, and mass popular culture, were usually not as radical.

In 1912 Alberta workers adopted a new strategy to influence the political process. McNabb chaired a meeting in Lethbridge of forty delegates, who met to establish a provincial Alberta Federation of Labour. The founders originally hoped to work closely with farmers, and the organizers of the meeting invited representatives of the United Farmers of Alberta. Despite these overtures, the interests of the two groups were too diverse, and labour-farmer cooperation was never as successful as McNabb and others had hoped. Temporary alliances developed during the war, and later in the 1920s and 1930s, but the relationship was always strained.

161

Energy and Conservation: The Early Years

While coal was rapidly reaching its peak, another energy source, which would only gradually come into its own, went through a pioneer stage of development. Like the coal industry, the oil and gas industry faced boom-bust economic conditions.

The story of the development Alberta's oil and gas resources begins with the "seeps" noted by travellers and settlers as early as the eighteenth century. In 1883 CPR drillers seeking water accidentally found natural gas at Langevin (near Medicine Hat). The gas ignited almost immediately and destroyed the drilling rig. In 1890 drillers again struck gas near Medicine Hat, and by 1900 the town began using the gas to light the streets. Gas also provided cheap fuel for the development of manufacturing in Medicine Hat.

Calgary businessmen saw the potential of natural gas as a cheap and clean fuel. Archibald Dingman, who was from Ontario and had some experience in the Pennsylvania oilfields, began drilling several natural gas wells in southern Alberta. Dingman hit gas in east Calgary in 1908, and Dingman's company supplied gas to the city, serving the brewery and lighting streets. Eugene Coste, a successful Calgary geologist and promoter, turned his attention to the area around Bow Island in southeast Alberta. In 1909 Coste brought in several gas wells and built a pipeline to Calgary. Coste then bought out Dingman and, through his Canadian Western Natural Gas Heat and Power Company Ltd., claimed the exclusive right to distribute gas in Calgary. The natural gas era arrived in north-central Alberta in 1914, when a major gas field blew in at Viking, southeast of Edmonton.

Western Canada's first producing oil well was in Oil City, in the area that eventually became Waterton Lakes National Park. The Indians were aware of the black sticky substance oozing from the banks of a stream, and "Kootenai" Brown and other early settlers used the oil as a lubricant for their wagons and a medicine for their cattle. One nearby Mormon settler, William Aldridge, soaked up the crude petroleum with gunny sacks, squeezed it into barrels, and sold it in neighbouring communities as a fuel, lubricant, and medicine. In 1901 the Rocky Mountain Development Company was formed by Calgary and Okotoks businessmen John Leeson and John Lineham, and surveyor A. P. Patrick, to drill for oil. The company struck oil in September 1902, and a mini-boom began with the development of a townsite and the formation of several rival oil companies. Transportation from the mountains was difficult, and when geological reports

By 1916 Calgary had grown to 57,000 people, and served as the commercial, small-scale manufacturing, financial, and educational centre for a wide agricultural area in central and southern Alberta. This view of 8th Avenue shows the streetcars that carried people to their homes in new suburbs, and also the cars that were beginning to displace horse-drawn vehicles. (*Glenbow Archives NA 3522-14*)

were discouraging and successive drilling attempts found nothing, Oil City was abandoned. The development of major oil discoveries in Alberta would prove long, difficult, and expensive.

Western Canada's first major oil boom was created by the discovery of oil at Turner Valley, southwest of Calgary, on May 14, 1914. This field was also developed by Calgary businessmen. William Herron, a tough and enterprising Ontario-born rancher, became interested in the seepages along Sheep Creek and put together the company that made the find. He had been a logging contractor in Ontario, and had developed a consuming interest in petroleum geology before coming to the Calgary area in 1903. He purchased the farm where seepages were evident and in 1912 recruited A. W. Dingman, who helped organize the Calgary Petroleum Products Company, backed by Calgary's leading real estate men and investors.

Drilling finally paid off in May 1914. The well blew in with a daily flow of four million cubic feet of wet gas saturated with a straw-coloured light oil or condensate. Hundreds of excited Calgarians rushed out to see the first successful well. The gasoline was so pure that it could be used as car fuel on the spot. The city went wild. Money was exchanged for oil company shares as fast as the shares could be printed.

More than five hundred companies were formed within a few months as real estate promoters, whose business had soured in the recession of 1913, became oil stock promoters. The boom attracted money not only from major investors but from labourers, clerks, housewives, and small businessmen. Most of them lost it all. Of the five hundred companies, only about fifty built derricks and fewer actually drilled for oil.

The boom faded quickly as few of the companies found oil. Although there was oil in Turner Valley, it was not in the gushing volumes anticipated. By September, when Canada entered the Great War, public attention and investment capital faded, just as it had farther north in the Athabasca oilsands. As exploration ceased, small companies desperately hung on. By 1920 only nine wells were producing. Though the yield of oil at Turner Valley was modest, it was enough to establish Calgary as an oil and gas centre, a position cemented by further strikes at Turner Valley in the 1920s and 1930s.

Hydro power was never a major source of energy in the province, though its early development showed the same combination of urban commercial ambitions coupled with political influence that marked Edmonton's northward ambitions. In 1907 two Calgary contractors set up the Calgary Power and Transmission Company (CPTCO). Further organizational changes and the need for capital brought onto the scene a young Montreal millionaire named Max Aitken. (He would later become Lord Beaverbrook, an important politician and publisher in Britain.) Aitken recognized Calgary's need for power for utilities (particularly street railways), as well as the power needs of cement companies at the edge of the Rockies. He put together Calgary Power and bought out the older CPTCO. He appointed an old New Brunswick friend, Calgary lawyer R. B. Bennett, as director and solicitor for the company. By 1910 construction on Horseshoe Falls on the Bow River was underway, and Bennett used his influence to negotiate an extended power contract with the city. Calgary Power discovered it needed additional power to meet its contract with the city, and pushed the federal government to allow it to proceed with another power station at Kananaskis Falls, which would give Calgary Power an effective monopoly on hydro development in southern Alberta. Other companies contended for the project. But Calgary Power picked Bennett as president in June 1911 and after September,

Bennett sat on the government side of the House of Commons as MP for Calgary. With this type of political influence, Calgary Power was able to get approval for the second power station and largely ignore concerns about the company's interference with land in the Rocky Mountains (later Banff) National Park and on the Stoney Indian reservation.

The Horseshoe Falls plant, completed in 1911, was the first major hydro installation in the province. The capacity of the system developed rapidly with the addition of plants at Kananaskis Falls in 1911 and the Ghost River in 1929, and Calgary Power dominated the power field in much of southern Alberta. Elsewhere in the province, coal and gas were used to fire steam plants to produce electricity.

One of the side effects of the extensive resource development was, partially in reaction, a growing public awareness of the need to conserve Alberta's wilderness. A strong conservation movement developed in the U.S. and spread into Canada. The Alpine Club of Canada, established in 1906, spread information on the Rockies, and its members published accounts of the beauty and challenge of the mountains. Partly in response to this conservation movement, the federal government developed new national parks at Jasper, Waterton, Elk Island, and Wainwright, and appointed a new Dominion Parks Branch Commissioner in 1911. The Department of the Interior also established large forest reserves along the foothills and mountains to the Peace River district to protect forests from fires caused by railway construction and clearing operations by homesteaders.

The Jasper Forest Park, established in 1907, was named after fur trader Jasper Hawes, who ran a post called Jasper's House in 1817. The park bordered the route of the two projected transcontinental railways along the Athabasca River and the Yellowhead Pass. The major impetus behind the formation of the park was the desire to conserve natural resources from abuse, and to protect the scenery for the projected tourist trade that the railways hoped to exploit. In 1910, the Grand Trunk Pacific chose the present townsite of Jasper as its station and divisional point. In the same year, the park superintendent authorized three stores, three blacksmith shops, and one veterinary office at the same location, and railway and park employees began moving into the townsite. By 1914 there were 125 people in the town of Jasper, living in hastily constructed homes, rooming houses, and tents. Though there was little development in the town during World War I, tourism would develop strongly during the 1920s.

Waterton had first been established as a forest reserve in 1895.

This move resulted from the federal government's concern about water management along the Rocky Mountain watershed, and in particular William Pearce's and the Department of the Interior's plans for irrigation in southern Alberta. With continuing oil and lumber development in the region, a number of groups pressed for government action to create a national park. Sportsmen and guides such as "Kootenai" Brown complained of the growing scarcity of wildlife. In June 1911 the government finally acted, and Waterton became Waterton Lakes Dominion Park. Though small-scale mining and drilling was still permitted, game was now protected by law, and commercial fishing and lumbering halted. At seventy-one years of age, the legendary Brown became the park's first superintendent.

Elk Island National Park, founded east of Edmonton in 1904, and Buffalo National Park, started near Wainwright in 1907, grew out of efforts to save dwindling wildlife. Elk Island was set aside to preserve a threatened herd of elk from destruction by hunters. Howard Douglas, the second Superintendent at Banff, also determined to save one of the last remaining buffalo herds, which was located in Montana. In 1907 he convinced his superiors to buy the herd from under the noses of the Americans, and the buffalo were finally rounded up and moved to Wainwright in 1912. Widespread disease eventually led to the decision to remove the remaining buffalo to Wood Buffalo National Park, established in northern Alberta.

Alberta's formative period of institution-building came to an end in 1914 with the outbreak of World War I. Hints that an era was ending first came in 1912 and 1913, with the onset of an agricultural depression as wheat prices dipped. The western land boom crested in 1912, and cautious businessmen began selling off their urban land-holdings. As warclouds gathered in Europe, European capital began to dry up. The most optimistic boosters across the province held on, but the value of their land plummeted. The completion of the two transcontinental railways threw large numbers of labourers out of work, and the unemployed poured into Edmonton. By February 1914, there were 4000 unemployed in a city of 72,000, straining civic relief facilities and contributing to labour unrest and strife.

The prosperity of the boom years was gradually revealed to be precarious, as it gave way to over two decades of alternating stagnation and crisis. The outbreak of war in 1914 led to important social, economic, and political changes that challenged the Liberals' ascendancy, brought ethnic and class strife to a head, and irrevocably altered the mood and shape of Alberta.

CHAPTER SEVEN

The Great War and After: The Fervent Years, 1914–1921

In the long summer days of 1914, Alberta seemed very remote from events in Europe. But when war broke out in August, Albertans felt the shock waves almost immediately. The war's effects, both direct and indirect, would continue to be felt long after the armistice of 1918. Wartime conditions precipitated irreversible social, economic, and political change. Not only were the families of those overseas affected; the war changed ethnic and labour relations, altered the agricultural economy, hastened movements for women's suffrage and prohibition, and contributed to farm protest.

In the summer of 1914, Albertans were neither a military people nor greatly interested in international affairs. They were preoccupied with pioneering, farming, and ranching, and with real estate and oil and gas promotion. Four thousand men belonged to volunteer militia units, but these were ill-equipped and poorly trained. Farm, labour, and women's groups were peace-oriented. No one was prepared for the cataclysmic events and slaughter of the Great War.

Nevertheless, Albertans did not hesitate to join the war effort; the province had one of the highest enlistment rates in the country and eventually the highest casualty rate. By the end of the war in 1918, one-third of the eligible men between eighteen and forty-five had enlisted. A total of 45,136 Albertans served overseas and 6,140 did not return. In the shadow of war, the exhilaration, optimism, and boosterism that had characterized the heady days of the settlement boom faded.

Answering the Call

The initial response to the war was enthusiastic. On the nights of August 4 and 5, 1914, large crowds in the cities sang patriotic songs and paraded with bands and flags. In Edmonton, scores of British, French, and Russian immigrants and one thousand Alberta volunteers marched shoulder to shoulder, singing the national anthems of their native lands.

Respected community leaders who had previously been prominent in the militia were crucial to the recruitment drive. They included, among others, W. A. Griesbach, an ambitious and military-minded Edmonton lawyer; English-born W. C. G. Armstrong, a Calgary real estate developer; F. O. Sissons, a Medicine Hat rancher; John Stewart, a Lethbridge dentist; Hugh B. Brown, a Cardston businessman; and "Peace River Jim" Cornwall, businessman and politician. With the outbreak of war, Cornwall formed a Peace River regiment known as the "Irish Guards." Typical of Alberta's heterogeneity, the Guards included Indians as well as recruits who, among them, spoke sixteen different European languages. Stewart and Griesbach had served previously in the Boer War, and both became brigadier generals. Both eventually translated their status as war heroes into political success as Conservative MPs.

The first to join the military ranks were recently arrived British immigrants and the unemployed. In 1911, 26 per cent of the population of military age was British-born. Large numbers of young men in British enclaves such as Banff, the foothills ranching community, the rural communities of Macleod, Gleichen, Pine Lake, Alix, and Lloydminster, and in the cities, joined up to "do their bit" for the Empire. Between 1914 and 1917 approximately four hundred men from the Lloydminster area enlisted, and one hundred died in the fighting. The decline in railway building and the collapse of the urban construction boom in 1913 had also left many men in the cities out of work. For them, the army's offer seemed preferable to urban unemployment, or to the hardships of homesteading.

John Kerr, for example, was homesteading in the Peace River district when the war broke out. He and his brother immediately set out for Edmonton, leaving a note tacked to the door of their homestead shack: "War is hell, but what is homesteading?"[1] Kerr won a medal for bravery at the Battle of the Somme in September 1916, but was killed the next year.

Some members of minority religious and ethnic groups hoped to prove their loyalty by joining the armed forces. Before the war, in order to offset criticisms about their patriotism, Mormon leaders had asked several young men to take officer training. As a consequence, by 1915 over two hundred young Mormons from the Cardston area had been recruited. Not all those with American roots were as enthusiastic. Initially, many Americans and Scandinavian Americans imitated the policy of their homelands and, skeptical of milita-

In 1916, in the midst of wartime fervour, Canada's Governor General, the Duke of Connaught, visited Alberta. Here he inspects a guard of honour, accompanied by R. B. Bennett, Calgary's Conservative Member of Parliament (and later prime minister) [in front on the left], and Lieutenant Governor R. G. Brett [behind on right]. (*Glenbow Archives NB 16-90*)

rism, favoured a peace policy. With time, wartime emotionalism gradually convinced some to join up. Eventually military authorities recruited both a Scandinavian and an American battalion.

For some minorities, wartime alliances meant that ethnic loyalties and commitment to Canada coincided. French and Belgian miners from the Crow's Nest Pass and French ranchers from Trochu returned to their home countries to fight. Many Alberta Italians left to fight for the allied cause once Italy joined the war in 1915. The war also enabled the Italians to allay some prejudices against them and to express some of their own. In June 1915, Italian miners in the Crow's Nest Pass joined with Britons to strike in protest against the employment of "enemy aliens" from central and eastern Europe. Jews looked with skepticism on anti-Semitic Russia as an Allied power, but some young Jews enlisted and the Jewish community mobilized assistance for European Jewish relief efforts.

Twenty-nine young Indians also went overseas. Indian Affairs officials who had spent years trying to eradicate the warrior ethic of the Plains Indians suddenly began to promote it. Some Indians joined the military to escape reserve life and residential schools. On the Blood Reserve, the Rev. S. H. Middleton had established a cadet corps to encourage discipline and physical activity for young Bloods, and he urged them to enlist. Authorities even recruited in isolated Indian districts in northern Alberta. Recruits were shipped by scows to Peace River and then to Edmonton before being sent to fight for "civilization." Those who signed up were usually considered good soldiers. They were easily disciplined, anxious to do their share, and performed well in combat.

Despite the occasional dissenting voices of socialists such as Stephan Stephansson and William Irvine, the public overwhelmingly supported the war. Newspapers were the vital source of world news and influenced perceptions of the war. Newspaper editors, who were almost all either Ontario- or British-born, supported the war. When it broke out, the *Calgary Herald* of August 5, 1914, gave its readers the following assurance: "That success will crown our banners no Britisher doubts, for God is with the right. The star of Britain's empire, which has lit the path of civilization for a thousand years, will shine all the more brightly once these clouds are past." Protestant clergymen also saw the war as a righteous crusade to vanquish evil and they urged their members to enlist. Some prominent clergymen, such as Methodist George Kerby in Calgary, founder of Mount Royal College, became recruiting officers.

The tragic Allied losses in the war's early years brought home its grim reality. Churches and other social institutions helped the anxious and bereaved. Patriotic and women's organizations, such as the Red Cross, Imperial Order of the Daughters of the Empire, and the Women's Canadian Clubs, provided clothes and parcels for soldiers and raised funds for overseas relief. The university, schools, businesses, and other institutions had to cope with a shortage of workers.

The economic impact of war was wide-ranging. Wheat production increased as the price of wheat soared; wheat acreage in Alberta doubled from 1914 to 1916. Though many farmers tasted prosperity, they also faced higher costs for labour, land, and machinery. Most of their profits were used to finance further expansion.

In the coalfields, wartime conditions increased markets. Labour shortages also led to economic change. Companies with the capital to expand did extremely well. Other mines that were heavily in debt, such as the Leitch Collieries at Passburg, collapsed. With war demands pushing the mines to peak production, rapid inflation, and labour shortages, workers had enough leverage to push for increased wages and improved working conditions. Consequently, miners generated most of the strike activity in Alberta during the war. In 1917, when 7500 miners were on strike, the federal government stepped in, appointing a director of coal operations to run the mines. Under the resulting hybrid of free enterprise and state regulation, prices and profits rose. Due to the strength of popular patriotism, left-wing organizations in the coal-mining communities lay largely dormant until the end of the war.

The war's economic impact was less dramatic in the urban areas. Towns and cities benefited from agricultural prosperity but experienced little new growth. The federal government concentrated almost all its war contracts in central Canada, and no wartime industry developed in Alberta. Due to the waning of the boom and the departure of men for the front, Edmonton's population declined precipitously from 73,000 in 1914 to 54,000 in 1916.

The "Enemy Alien"

Growing wartime nationalism had serious consequences for the thousands of immigrants of German and eastern European background. The frustration, deprivation, and bitterness of war found a convenient scapegoat in the "enemy alien." The Germans, formerly desirable immigrants, were now considered undesirable. Wartime propaganda portrayed them as barbarous "Huns." Immigrants from the Austro-Hungarian Empire, including Austrians, Croats, Poles, Hungarians, Czechs, Slovaks, and by far the largest group, Ukrainians, were under intense suspicion, even though many had been oppressed people within Austria-Hungary and had come to Canada to escape military service.

"Enemy aliens" faced a barrage of official and unofficial restrictions. Many were dismissed from their jobs and placed under police surveillance. Their language schools and many of their churches were closed. At first the federal government censored their newspapers, then suppressed many of them. German clubs in Calgary and Edmonton disbanded because they feared reprisals.

Martin Nordegg, the German Jewish entrepreneur who had developed a coal-mining community in west-central Alberta, found that none of his political or business connections could shield him from prejudice or government restrictions on German nationals. The government seized his property, and he avoided internment by leaving for New York. This turn of events left him disappointed and resentful. Nordegg returned to Canada after the war and advised the Canadian government on coal policy, but his plans to develop Nordegg as a model community were cut short by the wartime anti-alien hysteria.

Anti-German hysteria reached a climax in Calgary in February 1916. At 5 per cent of the population, the German community in Calgary was the largest of any city in the province. On February 10, a mob of five hundred soldiers and civilians attacked and tore apart a restaurant that allegedly had discharged returned veterans and hired Germans. The following night a mob of fifteen hundred wrecked the Riverside Hotel in the predominantly German-speaking district of Riverside-Bridgeland.

Other "enemy aliens" suffered similar treatment. During the course of the war, hundreds of innocent immigrants were rounded up and put behind barbed wire in internment camps. Some urban relief authorities reduced their case loads by having unemployed immigrants interned. Ukrainians from the Russian Empire joined the Canadian army, while Ukrainians from the Austrian Empire were not only rejected but actually interned when they tried to enlist.

Ukrainian and other "Austro-Hungarian enemy aliens" in an internment camp at Castle Mountain, near Banff, during World War I. Their bitterness over the injustice of this internment would remain for many years. (*Glenbow Archives NA-1870-6*)

The federal government established several internment camps in Alberta, including one at Banff. The government put immigrants who had not yet been granted citizenship to work clearing land for an exclusive residential subdivision and building a highway to Lake Louise. Unemployed young men during the Depression, and religious conscientious objectors and Japanese-Canadians during World War II, continued the roadbuilding by virtual forced labour.

Although many internees were released in 1916 to fill a manpower shortage, pressure again mounted at the end of the war from veterans' and patriotic groups to have "enemy aliens" fired from their jobs to make way for the returning veterans. The immigrants' resentment over their treatment resurfaced at the end of the war in their support for radical political organizations. Despite hopes of greater national unity during wartime, the reality was an increase in ethnic tensions toward the 20 per cent of Albertans who were of German or central and eastern European origin.

Reformers, War, and the Liberals

During the war, several interrelated reform movements—the social gospel, prohibition, and the women's and farmers' movements—reached a new peak of influence. Each was part of a broader progressive movement sweeping the English-speaking world. In Alberta, these movements brought together a mixture of newcomers from central Canada, Britain, and the United States. They expressed the hopes and fears of the dominant Anglo-Protestant majority.

Prohibition came to the province as a result of the efforts of a coalition of church groups, women's organizations, and farm groups. The underlying religious ideology of the social gospel was that through strenuous moral reform and government legislation, social ills could be eradicated and a truly Christian society established. Protestant clergymen saw it as their duty to try to bring "civilizing" and Canadianizing influences to the pluralistic and male-dominated frontier. The main Protestant churches, principally the Presbyterians, Methodists, and Baptists (who together made up roughly 40 per cent of the total Alberta population), devoted a great deal of time and effort to imposing their vision of the ideal society on the new frontier. Among their principal reform causes were instituting prohibition, eliminating prostitution, and bolstering their missions to immigrants in order to promote "Canadianization." The social gospel and the churches provided both the intellectual base and the institutional

173

support system that ultimately convinced a majority of Alberta men to vote themselves dry in the 1915 prohibition referendum.

The prohibition campaign was led at first by the Woman's Christian Temperance Union, which was closely connected to the large Protestant churches. Although it had difficulty getting fully organized in Alberta in the 1890s, the WCTU began to expand rapidly after 1903 with the arrival in Olds of Mrs. S. J. Craig, a former member of the national WCTU executive. She launched a grass-roots drive under the organization's motto, "For God, and Home, and Canada," and by late 1904 "had visited 22 towns, . . . held fifty-one meetings in the interest of moral reform, traveled 2,368 miles, written 509 letters and post cards, and distributed 5,000 pages of literature."[2] The WCTU was convinced that liquor lay at the root of most of society's social problems and that prohibition would solve most social ills. Gradually the WCTU and the church-based Alberta Temperance and Moral Reform League (begun in 1907) built a broad base of support among church, women's, and farm groups.

By 1913, one of the most difficult reform issues facing the provincial Liberal government was prohibition. Partially to get around this political minefield, the Sifton administration passed direct legislation in 1913 that enabled groups to demand binding referendums. Seizing this opportunity, the prohibitionists organized, held huge rallies, and began a petition campaign. The campaign played on rural fears about the city and wartime Anglo-Canadian fears about the lifestyles and loyalties of immigrants. Its supporters argued that prohibition would solve virtually all social problems and improve economic efficiency. In 1913 this campaign gained the support of the UFA.

The outbreak of war provided the final impetus for prohibition, its proponents arguing that it was needed to protect the moral and physical health of young westerners in the army, and to increase economic efficiency at home. Wartime necessity also accustomed the public to increased governmental intervention in their lives.

The UFA, the WCTU, and the Temperance League, with the support of most of the province's newspapers, cooperated in a petition campaign to force a prohibition referendum. By contrast, organized labour, the liquor interests, and the *Calgary Herald* and the *Edmonton Journal* opposed prohibition. The prohibitionists, however, conducted a well-organized campaign. Their efforts culminated in Edmonton in a giant parade, which included an estimated ten to twelve thousand participants and stretched for two miles.

During the prohibition campaign, Methodist, Presbyterian, and Baptist ministers gave repeated sermons to their own and each other's congregations. The Catholic clergy remained silent on the issue and the Anglican clergy preferred temperance to complete prohibition. Nonetheless, the Protestant churches built up support for legislation partially designed to control the behaviour of new immigrants and the working class, who were regarded as the main abusers of alcohol.

The Protestant clergy's participation foreshadowed a pattern in Alberta of clergymen's and lay preachers' participation in public life. The involvement of Unitarian clergyman William Irvine and Methodist Norman Priestley in the UFA and socialist CCF movements, and Baptists William Aberhart and Ernest Manning in the Social Credit movement in the 1930s, were only a few examples of the close tie between religion and politics. Given the strongly religious orientation of many Albertans, almost any political movement that hoped to be successful in Alberta had to appeal to widely shared religious perspectives. The organizational and communication skills of clergymen and lay preachers were also crucial to the success of any new political movement.

At least in part due to the efforts of committed clergymen and

Prohibition was a major social and political issue during the war and into the early 1920s. This prohibition rally in Edmonton featured children spelling out their message. With strong support from the farm and women's movements and the Protestant churches, prohibition came into effect in 1916 and remained until 1923. *(Glenbow Archives ND 3-2151)*

church-related organizations, on July 21, 1915, 61 per cent of the all-male electorate voted for prohibition. The vote revealed the province's ethnic, class, and regional cleavages. The constituencies that voted "no" were in the coal-mining, working-class, and immigrant-dominated areas of Lethbridge and along the Rockies. In the frontier constituencies of northern Alberta, French Canadians, central and eastern Europeans, and frontiersmen also resented the attempt by an Anglo majority to impose on them its values.

Prohibition, which came into effect on July 1, 1916, proved unenforceable. Calgary's irrepressible journalist, the Scots immigrant Bob Edwards, captured the spirit of the skeptics in his satirical *Calgary Eye Opener* on February 18, 1919:

> The Moral and Social League of Alberta, alias the Drys, meet...next week for their annual celebration of victory. No, that's wrong. We take it back. The Drys may win a victory but they cannot celebrate it. Their kind of victory destroys the means of celebration.

The prohibition legislation provided for liquor for medicinal, scientific, and sacramental purposes, and for two percent "temperance" beer, and each of these exceptions to the ban was subject to abuse. The act also did not regulate the manufacture, import, or export of liquor. The Liberals left a few loopholes in the legislation, since many of their strongest supporters, including northern Albertans, French Canadians, and central and eastern European immigrants, were firmly opposed to prohibition. The divided and conflicting jurisdiction on the issue between provincial and federal governments also complicated matters.

The NWMP had attempted to enforce prohibition from 1875 to 1891 during the territorial period, and had primarily been rewarded by public hostility. In order to avoid having to enforce prohibition again, Mounted Police officials recommended cancelling their policing contract with the provincial government, which was then forced to establish its own police force. In March 1916, Sifton's Liberal government established the Alberta Provincial Police (APP). Given limited manpower (125 men), poor organization, and the willingness of poorly paid police to accept bribes, the provincial force could do little. Business flourished for rumrunners and bootleggers, who supplied drinkers in Alberta, as well as in Montana once the U.S. went dry in 1919.

Was prohibition in any respect successful? According to historian

James Gray, its positive social impact could be seen in decreased crime, more harmonious and less impoverished family life, and greater efficiency among industrial and farm workers. In Calgary, arrests for drunkenness dropped from 1743 in 1914 to 183 in 1917.[3] Another plebiscite, over the shipping of liquor to provinces such as Alberta, which had prohibition, was held in 1920. This time women voted. The result reaffirmed a dry majority and closed a loophole in the law, which had permitted citizens to order supplies from adjoining provinces. However, the majority in this plebiscite was much reduced, and the issue would continue to bedevil social and political debate throughout the early 1920s.

Women and the Reform Movement

The Liberals also responded during World War I to the growing power of the women's movement. While there had been stirrings over women's rights during the territorial period concerning voting rights at the municipal level and property rights for wives of homesteaders, the movement for women's suffrage began about 1910. In its early stages, the suffragist movement was an urban cause led in the towns by the WCTUs, who supported suffrage as a means of achieving prohibition, and in the cities by the local councils of women, which were coalitions of various women's groups.

The struggle to obtain the vote for women in Alberta was neither long nor arduous. The crucial role that women played in pioneering, and the consistency of the suffragists' social vision with that of other reform movements, garnered widespread public support. On April 19, 1916, with the passage of provincial legislation, Alberta women joined those in Manitoba and Saskatchewan in having the right to vote and hold provincial office. At the federal level, in 1918, with the passage of the Women's Franchise Act, women over the age of twenty-one who were British subjects were given the vote and the following year became eligible to be elected to the House of Commons.

Both the prohibition and suffragist movements grew out of the optimism of the settlement period, but they also had a brooding, conservative side that feared social change, particularly the impact of non-British immigrants. They were strongly utopian and puritanical, and were energized by the social gospel commitment to reforming society. Both were basically middle-class Anglo-Protestant causes. The proponents of equal suffrage feared the social impact of central and eastern European immigrants. Louise McKinney, one of the leaders in the WCTU in Alberta and the first woman legislator in Canada, told a WCTU convention that "immigrants must be educated to high standards or our whole national life will be lowered by their presence among us." She regretted that the planned enfranchisement of women was not accompanied by "plans to reduce our illiterate vote."[4]

The first women's clubs in Alberta were apolitical, beginning as adjuncts to religious denominations. They raised money for church charities and hospital aid societies. Urban, educated women realized that their goals in charity, health, cultural affairs, and morality could only be achieved if they had the vote. These women gradually transformed the "ladies' aids" into groups working on social problems, and then into organizations fighting for political equality.

Farm groups supported women's suffrage. This was partly because, as the influential *Grain Growers' Guide* argued on November 19, 1913, farm wives as "fellow partners...in the arduous work of making homes on the prairies" deserved political equality with men. Farm groups also believed women could purify a corrupt political system because of their presumed non-partisanship, moral superiority, and non-materialistic approach to life. The UFA supported women's suffrage, and in 1915 helped form a women's organization, the United Farm Women of Alberta (UFWA). The support of the UFA movement proved crucial to the suffragists' success; Premier Sifton first announced government plans to give women the vote in a letter to the president of the UFA.

Dynamic women, including several who would later become known as the "famous five," led the suffrage campaign. Nellie McClung was the pre-eminent feminist in Alberta and in western Canada. Born in Ontario in 1873 and raised in Manitoba, she became a teacher and a writer, and married a young pharmacist. McClung came to Alberta in 1914 following an active role in the prohibition and suffrage campaigns in Manitoba. As a persuasive and witty public speaker, she campaigned for women's rights across western Canada and the United States.

McClung became one of Canada's best known and most popular writers. Her first novel, *Sowing Seeds in Danny*, portrayed life in a small prairie town. In her sixteen earthy and humorous novels set in the rural west, McClung idealized pioneer women and western farm society and crusaded for a variety of causes—feminism, prohibition, and penal reform. She later recalled the reform thrust of the women's movement: "We were in sight of the promised land, a land of richer sunshine and brighter fruitage, and our heads and hearts were

Three leaders of the women's suffrage movement in Alberta. Nellie McClung, the leading suffragist in western Canada [on the left], Calgary judge Alice Jamieson, and Edmonton magistrate and writer Emily Murphy. (*Provincial Archives of B.C. HP39854*) Other leading figures in the women's rights movement in Alberta were [on the left] Louise McKinney, [below left] Irene Parlby, and Henrietta Muir Edwards. (*Glenbow Archives NA825-1, NA2204-12, NA 2607-1*) The latter three, together with McClung and Murphy, would, during the 1920s, lead the fight for women to be legally considered "persons."

light. . . . We were in deadly earnest and our one desire was to bring about a better world for everyone. . . . Ours was not a rage; it was a passion."[5] McClung pursued her views into politics after being elected a Liberal MLA in 1921.

Henrietta Muir Edwards, another of the "famous five," came from a wealthy Montreal family. She helped working girls in Montreal, became an authority on the legal status of Canadian women, and was an accomplished painter. She helped found the National Council of Women, the leading women's organization in Canada, before moving to Macleod in 1903 with her husband. She joined the WCTU when she came to Alberta and helped interest the Alberta WCTU in the franchise issue.

In her own life, Louise McKinney combined all the reform movements—the social gospel, prohibition, feminism, and the farmers' movement. Born in rural Ontario in 1868, she had moved to North Dakota, where she became a schoolteacher and later married. She fought for prohibition before moving to Alberta in 1903. As president of the Alberta WCTU, she crusaded against the "evils" of alcohol and non-Anglo-Saxon immigration, and advocated moral education. She entered politics, and in 1917, running for the agrarian Non-Partisan League in Claresholm, became one of the first two women in Canada to be elected to a legislature. (In the same election, a nursing sister serving in the armed forces, Roberta MacAdams, was elected by Alberta service voters stationed overseas.) As a staunch proponent of the church union movement, McKinney was the only woman to sign the "Basis of Union" that created the United Church of Canada in 1925.

Another member of the "famous five," Emily Murphy, was also a popular author on western themes. Born in Ontario in 1868, she was the granddaughter of the founder of the Orange Order of Canada. She married an Anglican clergyman and businessman, and moved to Edmonton in 1907. Her work for the Equal Franchise League of Edmonton made the female suffrage movement socially respectable for many of Edmonton's prominent clubwomen. She led the campaign for the passage of a Dower Act, which safeguarded the interests of the wife in the event of the husband attempting to sell or dispose of their home or homestead. Shortly after women received the vote, Premier Sifton appointed Murphy as the first woman police magistrate in the British Empire.

Irene Parlby, although from a genteel British background, became the voice of Alberta farm women. Born in London in 1868 to a prominent family, well-educated and widely travelled, she came to central Alberta in 1896. She met and married Walter Parlby, one of several British ranchers in the small community of Alix. In 1913 she helped start a country women's club that became the first women's local of the United Farmers of Alberta. Though not a key participant in the suffrage campaign, she became a leader in the women's movement during the World War I. In 1921 she ran for the UFA and became minister without portfolio in the first UFA government, the first woman cabinet minister in Alberta and the second in the British Empire. Once in office, she devoted herself to improving rural health, education, and the legal status of women and children.

Strong leadership, the economic importance of women on the agricultural frontier, and the ideology of maternal feminism (which emphasized the moral necessity of women's involvement in politics) all contributed to women getting the vote. Paradoxically, since the prewar suffrage movement had been pacifistic, the war also contributed to its success. This was partly due to the contribution women made to the war effort. Women's groups flourished, cooperating in Red Cross and Patriotic Fund campaigns. The Patriotic Fund provided volunteer contributions to support the families of servicemen. As they knitted and sewed together for the troops, the women were exposed to the ideas of suffragists. The rhetoric of the war effort strengthened the arguments for female suffrage. Shouldn't a war for democracy and liberty extend to democracy for women?

With the wartime achievement of prohibition and suffrage, the women's movement began to decline. Mainly urban, Protestant, and middle-class, the suffragists had strong religious, ethnic, and class prejudices that stifled a broader vision of equality. The use of arguments based on the moral superiority of women, the focus on prohibition, and the exploitation of anti-immigrant sentiments helped the cause of suffrage in the short run, but weakened the long-term ideal of equality for women.

Alberta farm women's need for social ties and their economic role in the pioneer farm enterprise gave them a strong agrarian identity; their interest in women's rights was secondary. The United Farm Women of Alberta (UFWA) began in 1915 to provide social contact, and improve rural health services and education. The UFWA partially supplanted the Women's Institutes among rural Alberta women.

The Women's Institutes had first been started in Ontario to teach homemaking skills to rural women, and were brought by Ontario migrants to Alberta, beginning at Lea Park in 1909. The Institutes had provincial Liberal government backing through organizers and grants to individual locals. They tried to improve rural schools, encouraged preventive health measures for children, and set up cultural programs (including travelling libraries) for rural areas. While the UFWA gained considerable strength among farm women, the Women's Institutes provided a comparable range of social, cultural, and educational activities for women living in hamlets, villages, and towns.

Ethnic and religious barriers among women were strong. Urban women's organizations seldom tried to bridge the language, cultural, and class barriers between British and non-British women. The WCTU and the Imperial Order of the Daughters of the Empire appeared more concerned with how they could secure cheap immigrant domestic help. Protective legislation did not cover domestic service, one of the most common jobs for immigrant women. Women's organizations resisted efforts to increase the low monthly wages of $15 for domestics or to control the hours of work. The main Anglo-Protestant women's organizations were also preoccupied with notions of the "regeneration" of the "Anglo-Saxon race." Some leaders of women's groups were caught up in the pseudo-scientific eugenics movement, which demanded immigration restriction and the compulsory sterilization of the "feeble-minded."

Despite these limitations, the women's movement made enduring contributions to social services, public health, and improving the status of women. When Alberta became a province in 1905, there was no system of child or public welfare, then considered the responsibility of local governments. Women's organizations were crucial in the fight against inadequate housing and poverty, and for better public health and child welfare. Largely in response to pressure from women's organizations, the Liberal government created a public health portfolio in 1918. In 1919 the UFWA helped convince the government to support municipal hospitals. The Victorian Order of Nurses, Red Cross, Women's Institutes, and UFWA led the movement to establish health facilities.

Farm Protest and the War

The prohibition and suffrage crusades reflected a growing commitment to reform. By responding, the Liberals kept these powerful groups as allies. However, the Liberals had more difficulty in dealing with the growing farm movement. The farmers had first channelled their grievances through the Liberal government, but in the atmosphere of wartime reform, they became disenchanted with "old line" parties.

Above: A United Farmers of Alberta picnic. The UFA, first formed in 1909, was a potent social and political force in a predominantly agrarian province for almost three decades. By the end of the war, once the UFA decided to enter politics, its political and moral crusade was unstoppable. In 1921 it swept aside the once-powerful Liberals. *(Glenbow Archives NA 2142-3)*

Henry Wise Wood, an American immigrant who farmed in the Carstairs area, was the dominant force in the Alberta farmers' movement. He was president of the United Farmers of Alberta from 1916 to 1931, and chairman of the Alberta Wheat Pool Board from 1923 to 1937. His views of "group government" had a strong impact on the farmers' movement. *(Glenbow Archives NA 2715-4)*

During World War I, the UFA had common economic goals. They were divided, however, on the means of achieving them. A radical wing wanted direct political action to give the farmers political power. A more conservative wing, led by Henry Wise Wood, wanted reform through existing political parties.

Wood, "tall, loose-jointed, weather-beaten. . . bearing some suggestion of Lincoln in manner and mien,"[6] dominated the farmers' movement. Born to a prosperous Missouri farm family in 1860, Wood belonged to the Disciples of Christ, a denomination that emphasized the need for Christian ethics in economic affairs. After coming to

Carstairs in 1905, he became vice-president of the UFA in 1915. At that time the organization had 11,000 members in 704 locals. He became president the next year and was re-elected yearly until his retirement in 1931. Under Wood's leadership, the UFA first shunned direct political action, preferring to lobby the provincial Liberal government. The Non-Partisan League (NPL), which established branch organizations in Alberta in 1916, directly challenged this stand. The rise of the NPL finally convinced the UFA that it would have to enter politics.

The NPL originated in North Dakota, where it condemned the mainline parties and advocated a socialist platform. Agrarian activists soon spread it to Saskatchewan and then to Alberta. Five people, including the Scots-born social gospeller William Irvine, Calgary's radical Unitarian minister and political journalist, met to establish an Alberta Non-Partisan League in December 1916. Irvine became its main spokesman, and launched a political career that had national significance.

Irvine had been born in the Shetland Islands in Scotland in 1885, the son of a fisherman. He believed that Christianity and socialism were inseparable. As a young man, he learned to be a boat builder and carpenter, worked as a lay minister, and became an accomplished fiddler, singer, and mimic. In 1902, when he was sixteen, Irvine emigrated to North America. He was educated in the U.S. and Manitoba, and served briefly as a Presbyterian minister in Ontario. His unorthodox liberal religious views and his social activism led to a heresy trial in Ontario and his departure from the Presbyterian Church, and in 1916 Irvine came to Calgary as minister of the liberal Unitarian Church.

Irvine believed that the only way Christian churches could justify their existence was to respond to the social concerns of the day. He established a Sunday school, began writing a weekly column for the daily *Albertan*, and became actively involved in Calgary's political life. Irvine organized a weekly "Peoples Forum," held Sunday afternoons in the Empress Theatre. These were lively sessions where speakers debated controversial issues of the day. Irvine established the forum "for the intelligent discussion of subjects of public interest, for enlightenment and information."[7] The meetings aroused a good deal of controversy because of the number of socialist and anti-war speakers and because those attending, emphasizing their belief in equality, joined in singing "When Wilt Thou Save Thy People?" instead of "God Save the King." In May 1917, with wartime hyper-patriotism beginning to reach a crescendo, the theatre cancelled the lease on the grounds that the forum was unpatriotic, and it had to move elsewhere.

To gain a wider audience for his reform views, in November 1916 Irvine started a hard-hitting and controversial newspaper, the *Nutcracker*. In October 1917, the *Nutcracker* became the *Alberta Non-Partisan*, the official mouthpiece of the NPL. Bringing a wide variety of radical religious, social, and political views to the province, Irvine helped to galvanize organized farmers and labour through his involvement in both the NPL and labour politics in Calgary.

The reluctance of the UFA under Wood to go into politics, along with wartime economic conditions, created fertile ground for a new farmers' movement. Problems peculiar to the wartime economy further radicalized farmers, who faced higher costs for labour, land, and machinery. Though grain prices were high and some farmers prospered, most of their profits went to finance further expansion. Given the high wartime interest rates, many farmers were in trouble. The NPL responded to the farmers' grievances, offering a platform that demanded the regulation of wheat prices, the end of land speculation, state control of public utilities, an end to tariffs, and prohibition.

In the provincial election of June 1917, the NPL contested four seats and won two, both in southern Alberta. While the Liberals won thirty-four of fifty-eight seats, these NPL victories warned both the Liberals and the UFA that farmers were restless.

Conscription and the Crisis of Liberalism

Despite growing political ferment, political revolt was postponed by preoccupation with the war and the emotion-charged federal election of 1917. Wartime nationalism, fanned by the election, temporarily overshadowed growing regional dissatisfaction.

The backdrop to the election was the worsening condition of the Allied forces in Europe. In 1916 victory was nowhere in sight. In the horrific conditions of trench warfare, tens of thousands of Canadians were blasted to bits in France. The storming of Vimy Ridge in April 1917, though a great victory for Canadian soldiers, cost over 10,000 dead and wounded. Prime Minister Borden called for a force of 500,000 men, but enlistments did not mount fast enough. Some nationalists in English Canada raised the cry for compulsory military service.

When Conservative Prime Minister Borden asked the Liberals to join a coalition to bring in conscription, the issue divided the Liberals throughout English Canada. Some followed the anti-conscription policy of Laurier, who refused to support a coalition. However, Liberals who supported conscription joined the Conservative party to form a "win the war" Union government, announced in October 1917. The Conservatives ensured their victory on the prairies by introducing the Wartime Elections Act, which disfranchised Germans and central and eastern Europeans, depriving some of the Liberals' staunchest supporters of the vote. It also extended the franchise to women in the armed forces and to female relatives of soldiers.

While Frank Oliver's *Edmonton Bulletin* denounced Union government, most of the major newspapers and most Liberals in Alberta supported it and conscription. Among the supporters was Premier Sifton. Partly through the urging of his brother Clifford, one of the architects of Union Government, Arthur Sifton resigned as premier to join the federal cabinet.

Unionist candidates in the December 1917 federal election wrapped themselves in patriotic fervour and claimed that the election issue was whether Canadians would unite to defeat the Germans. Huge billboards demanded to know "How Would the Kaiser Vote?" The *Calgary Herald* devoted massive space to "Horrible Hun Atrocities" and on December 10, 1917, warned that a vote against the Union government was a vote for the Germans. Promised an exemption for their sons from military service by the Union government, and influenced by Wood's hope that Union government would mark an end to partisanship, many farmers supported it. The Unionists received 61 per cent of the Alberta vote and eleven of twelve seats. The only seat the Liberals kept was in east-central Alberta. There Scandinavian American Liberals, who were isolationists, outnumbered eastern Canadian and British-born Unionists.

Residual Conservatism, patriotism, and hostility toward immigrants and French Canadians produced a massive Unionist win in Alberta. Although working-class leaders opposed conscription, the urban working class voted predominantly Unionist. Female relatives of soldiers added to the size of the victory.

The 1917 election marked the beginning of the Alberta Liberals' collapse. Deeply divided over conscription and threatened by a growing farm revolt, the Liberals floundered. The new premier, Charles Stewart, had been a member of the cabinet since 1912 and was chosen because it was felt that as a farmer, he might be able to handle the rising unrest. However, Stewart did not have the status of Premier Sifton. Ontario-born, Stewart had come with his family to east-central Alberta to homestead in 1906. A practical man with limited education, he had worked as a stonemason, in real estate, and as a farm machinery salesman as well as a farmer. He became active in local politics in Killam and was elected to the legislature in 1909.

The jovial, robust farmer rose rapidly, serving as minister of municipal affairs and minister of public works. As premier, he had a divided party. After his government fell in 1921, Stewart moved to federal politics. Mackenzie King put his political talents to great use, naming Stewart his minister of the interior, one of the West's important cabinet posts. As a strong champion of Alberta, Stewart remained an important national figure until the 1940s.

The Aftershocks of War

Following a long and costly war, Alberta welcomed the armistice of November 1918. The *Lethbridge Herald* of November 12, 1918, described the celebrations in Cardston: "The Kaiser was hung, burned and buried. All morning, whistles, bells, cans, trumpets, drums and improvised band horns, and shouts of hurrah created pandemonium. Every car available paraded the streets, filled with cheering crowds." Across the province, there were religious services, torchlight parades, fireworks, and dancing in the streets. In parts of the province with a high percentage of people of British birth, large numbers of young men had been killed. In the Gleichen area, 250 young men marched off to war and fifty died. Many of those who did return came back considerably less idealistic than before the war.

The veterans became a social problem and a political force. In response, the federal government established soldier resettlement schemes, whereby a Soldier Settlement board could provide 320 acres (128 hectares) of land and a loan of up to $1500 for stock, equipment, and buildings. Much of the land still available had already been bypassed by homesteaders and was covered with forest, dense scrub, or swamp. Consequently, most of the schemes were unsuccessful, and many veterans left for the towns and cities. The veterans heightened social unrest. Many were bitterly anti-"enemy alien" and demanded that they be given jobs held by immigrant workers. Many served as strikebreakers for capital in its confrontation with radical labour in 1918 and 1919.

Some returning veterans also brought with them the influenza epidemic that had struck soldiers in Europe. Before it had run its course, 38,000 in Alberta contracted the disease and over 4000 died. The highly contagious disease easily led to pneumonia, still frequently fatal before the introduction of antibiotics during World War II. The only effective preventative was to avoid contact with the disease. The government ordered all citizens to wear masks outside the home, and the whole urban population went to work wearing them. Cities closed all public places. Several small towns imposed a quarantine to prevent anyone from entering, but these efforts proved fruitless.

Influenza struck swiftly. Some families lost both parents, and the children were put up for adoption. Dozens of widely advertised patent medicines proved ineffective. Nurses and doctors, with the help of volunteers, performed heroic feats caring for the sick, often at the cost of their own health and even their lives. One positive legacy of the epidemic was a greater awareness of the need for public health programs and more hospitals.

Another consequence of World War I was the boost it gave to aviation. The skills garnered by young Albertans who served in the Royal Air Force sparked their interest in aviation and they developed the province's first commercial air operations. Edmonton's W. R. "Wop" May and C. H. "Punch" Dickins, Calgary's F. R. "Freddy" McCall, and Lethbridge's J. E. "Jock" Palmer were wartime flying aces who began barnstorming, or performing daredevil stunts, throughout the region shortly after the war. These operations built on the tremendous public interest in the novelty of flying, but they were economically marginal since aviation technology was not sufficiently developed to make commercial aviation economically viable. As noted by one author, the barnstormers "lived a hand-to-mouth existence, occasionally doing very well, more often scrambling for every dollar available, earning fees teaching others to fly, accepting short charter trips and stunt commerical assignments such as air mail delivery of newspapers to a neighbouring community, [or] touring the fairs..."[8]

May was particularly important in opening up northern bush flying. A Manitoba-born and Alberta-educated World War I flying ace, he began his first shoestring flying enterprise in 1919, on the basis of a rented plane, "The City of Edmonton." In 1920 he convinced Imperial Oil to use aircraft for their new oil fields at Fort Norman in the Northwest Territories, and ferried the company's first aircraft from New York to Edmonton. But lack of suitable aircraft for both passenger and freight transportation eventually took its toll, and May went out of business in 1921. By 1928, however, improved aviation technology enabled him to develop a viable commercial operation.

The profound impact of the war can also be seen in the commemorative fervour that developed in its aftermath. Mountains were named and others renamed for famous battles, generals, and war heroes and heroines, from Mount Vimy at Waterton to Mount Edith Cavell at Jasper. The cenotaphs erected after the war in town squares became hallowed ground, and solemn rituals were conducted annually on November 11. The Great War Veterans Association and its successor, the Canadian Legion, provided a focus of male camaraderie for veterans and emerged as a political force. They lobbied for veterans' benefits, demanded government action against immigrant radicals, and opposed pacifist religious minorities.

Paradoxically, the war both heightened Canadian nationalism and reaffirmed a British tie. Albertans, along with other Canadians, justly pointed to the role they had played in the allied victories, and remembered with bitterness the incompetence of British generals. At the same time, the allied victory and the popularity of the monarchy reaffirmed British ties. Edward, Prince of Wales was lionized when he came to Calgary and Banff in 1919. The future king cemented his tie to the area through the purchase of the EP Ranch at Pekisko, south of Calgary. Most Alberta opinion leaders also continued to regard British immigrants as the most desirable.

Labour Radicalism and the 1919 Strikes

The veterans' return led to job competition in the urban and coal-mining areas, adding to economic and social unrest. Dramatic new developments were changing organized labour. During the war, many workers began to see unions as the only way to increase their control over their own lives. Inflation ran rampant; resentment grew over wartime conscription and business profiteering; and there was a growing hope, fanned by the example of successful working class revolutions in Europe, that change for the working class was possible. These factors combined to arouse discontent among organized labour.

This unrest reached its peak in western Canada in 1918 and 1919. By 1918 western labour was dissatisfied with the conservative, eastern-dominated Trades and Labour Congress. At a western labour conference in Calgary in March 1919, many western labour leaders decided to develop their own solutions. B.C. members of the radical Socialist Party of Canada quickly took control of the labour conference. They advocated the establishment of a single union, or One Big Union (OBU), whose aim was to place industry in the hands of labour and escape the domination of international unions centred in the United States. Rejecting political action through the parliamentary system, supporters of the OBU advocated a general strike of all organized labour to enforce their demands.

Many of the Alberta labour leaders at the conference were opposed to the OBU, since they supported electoral action. Despite this opposition, the conference passed resolutions supporting the OBU. The meeting also proclaimed its support for various European revolutionary movements, including Lenin's Bolshevik regime in Russia. The OBU rift with craft unionism was one more instance of the growing dissaffection of the West from central Canada. It also highlighted working-class radicalism and class and ethnic tensions.

Much of the support for the OBU in Alberta came from railway workers and coal miners. The Alberta coal industry had emerged as a vital part of the economy. By 1920 the nearly seven million tons of coal mined annually made up 41 per cent of Canada's coal production, and Alberta rivalled Nova Scotia as the number one Canadian coal producer.

The danger in the mines and the stratified social conditions of the mining towns contributed to political radicalism. The mining camps generally had poor housing, with families living in small, often uninsulated, frame shacks. Bachelors either shared these modest shacks as boarders, or lived in overcrowded, unventilated, lice-infested bunkhouses. Good sanitation and clean water were usually in short supply, and educational facilities for miners' children were often overcrowded. Tight budgets or the death of a father in an accident forced males as young as twelve into the mines. Compensation for injury or death was also poor; it was usually paid only if a worker were killed, the maximum payment being $1500.

The high percentage of immigrants in the work force also contributed to radicalism. Ninety per cent of Alberta's 12,000 coal miners were immigrants. They had arrived with high expectations for the future and were attracted by the promise of a new political and social order. For them, the ethnic and labour halls were usually a more important part of their lives than the conservative-minded Catholic or Orthodox churches. Where ethnic and class loyalties overlapped and fused, immigrants proved willing to challenge the system. Ethnic groups differed, however, in their inclination towards radicalism. Ukrainians, Russians, and Finns were among the strongest supporters of the left.

Activism in the mining camps combined British, American, and European labour radicalism. The labour movement was divided, though, over the OBU. Moderate leaders urged action through the existing system rather than the extremes of a general strike. However, events quickly rendered this internal debate within the labour movement irrelevant. In 1919 the OBU tested its strength in a series of strikes and was crushed by capital and the state.

The Winnipeg General Strike began in May 1919, when 35,000 workers struck in support of the demands of the building and metal trades for collective bargaining. It had repercussions in Alberta. In both Edmonton and Calgary, nearly 2000 workers went out in support of the Winnipeg strikers. In Edmonton, strikers cut off power to industries and stopped streetcar service for five days. While Conservative papers such as the *Calgary Herald* saw the strikes as Bolshevik-sponsored and a dangerous portent of a planned revolution, many Alberta labour leaders saw the Winnipeg General Strike as just and part of the common people's struggle for a better life. As William Irvine put it in the *Alberta Non-Partisan* of June 5, 1919:

We are witnessing today perhaps the greatest uprising of the common people in Canadian history. . . . The cause of this group organization negatively expressed may be said to be self-protection. But positively stated it is the urge toward a more abundant life. . . . Not only will the plutocratic government of this country be overthrown, but the economic system upon which our government is based must also go.

Although the Winnipeg General Strike had only a tenuous connection with the OBU, management and government saw the organization as part of a revolutionary plot. Consequently, in the summer of 1919, when coal miners in Alberta called a strike in support of the OBU, management, the federal government, the police, and the conservative United Mine Workers of America (UMWA) cooperated to crush it.

Labour unrest reached its high point in the Drumheller valley, where labour-management relations had been strained for years. Violence erupted in August 1919. The largely immigrant work force had attempted to prevent strikebreakers, mostly veterans, from going to work. The veterans armed themselves, attacking the miners and their makeshift homes. Mine owners and leaders of the veterans told

Immigrant miners on strike in Drumheller in 1919. Here they demonstrate their support for the One Big Union, and their determination not to be intimidated by management, police, and returning veterans. Labour unrest reached its peak in the coal mines in 1919, but coal miners would remain a radical political force in the province for two more decades. (*Glenbow Archives NA 2513-1*)

the strikers to either return to work or leave the valley. Veterans seized the OBU leaders, brought them to a kangaroo court-martial at Drumheller, and ran them out of town. With this vigilante pressure operating while the police stood by, striking miners had little choice but to return to work. One of those "tried" and expelled was Phil Christophers, a blunt and outspoken English radical who had helped swing UMWA members over to supporting the OBU. He was elected to the Alberta legislature from the Crow's Nest Pass two years later. By the time he was elected, however, the OBU was in decline.

Though clashes between veterans and striking miners were less violent elsewhere, the combined pressure from management, police, the conservative UMWA, and poverty were just as effective in getting the men back to work. Eventually 12,000 miners in Alberta returned to work as members of the American-dominated UMWA.

Although the OBU died quickly, labour began to gain credibility and power as a force in Alberta politics in the 1920s. Some labour leaders saw the general strike as the main vehicle to change the existing system, but the majority saw electoral politics, and a socialist party, as the best hope for the future. William Irvine in Calgary, and British-born printer Elmer Roper in Edmonton, had in 1917 organized Labour Representation Leagues (LRL) to oppose conscription and draw trade unionists into politics. These leagues were modelled on the socialist program of the British Labour Party. In early 1919 urban trade unionists organized the Dominion Labour Party (later to become part of the Canadian Labour Party) and in 1921 ran Labour candidates in both provincial and federal elections. They advocated the socialization of industry, changes in national finance, and guaranteed minimum incomes for all citizens. Organized labour and socialism became virtually synonymous.

Labour electoral success peaked in Alberta during the 1920s. In 1921 one Labour MP was elected from Calgary (William Irvine), and another MP from Calgary (J. T. Shaw) had close ties to organized labour. Four Labour members from Alberta were elected to the legislature. There were many successes of Labour aldermen and members of school boards in Edmonton, Calgary, and Lethbridge. These all indicated the growing strength of socialism. During the 1919 General Strike, Edmonton's mayor, Joe Clarke, whom labour had helped to elect, supported the strikers. In 1923, at the peak of labour's strength, half of the twelve aldermen in Calgary supported labour, and in 1929 six of Edmonton's ten aldermen were labour supporters.

Although organized farmers were launching a protest of their own, there were ideological and social differences between the farm and labour movements. While the farmers eventually swept into power, the miners in particular remained relatively powerless and marginalized. They were often stigmatized as alien revolutionaries, or simply viewed as undesirable aliens.

The Farmers Enter Politics

During 1918 and 1919, Alberta farmers debated whether they should enter politics. They had quickly become disenchanted with the Union Government, which reneged on its promise not to draft farmers' sons. Farmers were also hurt by the recession following the war. The disbanding in 1920 of the Wheat Board, established by the wartime government to provide minimum wheat prices, led to further unrest.

In southeastern Alberta, a succession of dry years after bumper crops in 1915 and 1916 created hardship. When wheat yields fell from an average of 35 bushels per acre in 1915 to 1.4 bushels per acre in 1919, farmers could either abandon the land or seek political solutions. Farmers' land was heavily mortgaged, their credit overextended, their money exhausted. Bankers began to pressure them. In December 1920, sensing the impending natural and financial calamities in eastern Alberta, one farmer observed that "Western Canada is rushing heedlessly, unknowingly into the very jaws of the most crushing debacle recorded in the history of the West."[9]

Drawing on the atmosphere created by natural calamity, economic distress, and the wartime reform spirit, the NPL grew dramatically, while the Liberals fell apart. Henry Wise Wood found it impossible to stem the increasing pressure for the UFA to enter politics directly. The NPL's growing popularity ultimately forced the UFA to choose between going into politics itself, or being overtaken by the League.

The struggle between the NPL and the UFA ended in compromise. Following intense debate, the 1919 UFA convention gave UFA locals the right to take political action. But as part of the compromise, the UFA absorbed the NPL. Henry Wise Wood's ideas of group government, which demanded that farmers enter politics on their own without the support of other radical groups, triumphed over William Irvine's vision of a more broadly based reform movement. Consequently, between May and July 1919, after extensive debate at the local level, the Non-Partisan League merged with the UFA.

Despite tactical differences, Irvine and Wood, the two key leaders of the farm movement, shared a utopian belief in progress, the triumph of democracy, and cooperation over the forces of plutocracy and competition. They shared the same vision of a cooperative world, rooted in the social gospel. As reported in the *Lethbridge Herald* of July 8, 1916, Wood claimed that the legislators of the world worshipped "Mammon" rather than God, and put their faith in money rather than in love of their fellow men, and that "until this is remedied and love of God and humankind actuates the hearts of the ruling powers, there can be no true Christian civilization."

Although Wood compromised his view that farmers should not enter politics, he shaped their involvement in a way that had a lasting impact. He proposed that farmers enter politics as an organized economic group rather than as a party. He developed a theory of "group government," in which occupational groupings would be the basis for a new cooperative political order.

By the end of the summer of 1919, the UFA had committed itself to political action. With this debate resolved, UFA membership increased from 18,000 members in 1918 to 30,000 in 1920 (in 1200 locals), while the United Farm Women of Alberta nearly tripled in size from 1450 to 4005. At UFA picnics, which attracted large crowds, horseracing and baseball games were followed with speeches by

Gardiner, Wood, and other farm leaders. One of their campaign songs went:

Fighting for democracy with ballots in our guns,
Tyrants and plutocrats—we'll beat them as the Hun;
All the hordes of privilege will soon be on the run,
For we're marching to victory.[10]

In October 1919, a UFA candidate won a provincial by-election in the Cochrane riding. The federal by-election victory of UFA candidate and Scots immigrant Robert Gardiner in Medicine Hat in June 1921 was another sign that political loyalties were changing.

Fearing the farmers' growing power, the provincial and federal governments called elections, hoping to win before the farm movements grew further. But Liberal Premier Stewart was too late. The UFA had launched a moral crusade to usher in a new era of democracy based on the Christian ethic. Reformers' fear was that unless a new society were created, the incredible sacrifices of the wartime era would have been in vain, and that the old system with its alleged corruption, exploitation, and dominance by a greedy few would return. Times had changed and better roads, the spread of automobiles and telephones, improved mail delivery, and the radical farm press quickly spread the new ideas.

The UFA demanded an end to "partyism," endorsed direct legislation, and denounced the parliamentary system of caucus secrecy and cabinet domination. The farmers recommended that politicians vote independently, free of party constraints. Capitalizing on the ever-expanding reform climate, the UFA seemed poised to soundly defeat the Liberals and begin a new era of political experimentation.

In the July 1921 provincial election, the UFA won thirty-eight seats, nearly two-thirds of the sixty-one seats, taking virtually all the rural constituencies in central and southern Alberta. The Liberals were reduced to fourteen seats and the Conservatives were wiped out. The UFA did less well in northern Alberta, where French Canadians and Ukrainians still had Liberal loyalties, but the size of their victory surprised even the UFA. One of the four Labour candidates who was victorious, Alex Ross, a Scottish stonemason and Calgary labour leader, became labour minister in the new UFA government.

It was generally assumed Wood would become premier. He was reluctant, however, because he felt his American background could be used by opponents to discredit the UFA. Wood's preference for premier was John Brownlee, the legal adviser for the UFA. The caucus baulked at the choice of an urban lawyer and selected Herbert Greenfield, a Wood loyalist and a successful farmer in his late fifties from Westlock. Greenfield was born in England in 1865, came to Ontario in 1892, and homesteaded in Alberta in 1906. He had been active in the English cooperative movement, had considerable experience in municipal politics, and had long been active in the UFA.

In the federal election of December 1921, Albertans returned ten UFA MPs out of twelve members from Alberta. The other two members were both from Calgary, and they were elected on a labour platform with the support of the UFA. The contingent of UFA and labour members included some of the ablest and most radical politicians ever sent to Ottawa from Alberta. These articulate community leaders expressed eloquently the frustrations and aspirations of Alberta's farmers, and defended the downtrodden across Canada. They included Edward Garland, an Irish-born orator and farmer from Rumsey; Donald Kennedy, a farmer who had come to Waterhole in the Peace River district from Scotland; Ontario-born George Coote from Nanton, the UFA's economic expert; and Irvine and Gardiner. Only one of the twelve Alberta MPs was American-born, undermining the argument that the Alberta farm revolt was primarily an American import.

By the election of 1921, the province's broad patterns of social and political geography were clearly established. The predominantly Anglo-Canadian and Scandinavian Protestant areas of southern and central Alberta voted heavily for the UFA. The northern frontier communities, with large numbers of French Canadians and central and eastern Europeans, were not as enthusiastic about the UFA, which was dominated by Anglo-Protestants. Resource communities voted labour, and the cities supported either the old line or labour parties. The 1921 election marked a shift in political power from the Liberals' stronghold in the north to the south, which emerged as the UFA's bastion.

By 1921 the mainline parties had been tried and found wanting. Albertans, deeply affected by the reform ethos of the war era, as well as by its socially and economically disruptive effects, were ready to experiment with new movements that might reform Alberta and the nation. Alberta had become the most politically radical province in Canada. Miners and farmers were in revolt, and a strong labour movement had emerged in the cities. The strength of farm protest in Alberta even made it difficult for the emerging national Progressive Party to hold together.

Why greater radicalism in Alberta than in the other prairie provinces? Transportation costs were higher than elsewhere, and Alberta was a more recent frontier with a debtor economy. As well, there were fewer Ontario people who might provide links with the main Canadian political traditions. The farmers' political revolt was partly an assertion by newcomers from Britain and the United States that they were no longer willing to be led by others. The presence of strong personalities such as Wood and Irvine also shaped the distinctive nature of Alberta's farmers' revolt, and the drybelt disaster radicalized many farmers in the southeast.

Immigrant radicalism combined with the difficult economic conditions of the agricultural and mining frontiers to forge a new tradition of political radicalism. Unlike in Saskatchewan, where the ruling Liberals were able to contain the farm revolt and remain in power throughout the 1920s, in Alberta the overlapping political thrust of the NPL, theories about group government, and the radicalism of farmers led to the rise of a third party.

The Liberals were swept aside in 1921 by an electorate determined to achieve reform. Those observers who were distanced from the euphoria of victory might well have wondered whether the UFA could meet the high expectations it had raised in its crusade. They might also have wondered whether its ideas of democratic reform, drawn in part from the American populist tradition, were workable in a parliamentary system, and whether a farmers' government would be able to deal effectively with the problems of the cities, organized labour, and class and ethnic conflict.

CHAPTER EIGHT

The Transitional Twenties: Struggling with Change

Economic recession cast a shadow over the early twenties. Rather than renewed economic growth, Albertans experienced hardship, and either consolidation or relocation. Wheat prices dropped alarmingly, plummetting from $2.31 per bushel in 1919 to $0.77 per bushel in 1922. Drought compounded the economic distress. In 1922 average wheat yields were only eleven bushels per acre. Farmers in the drought-stricken southeast abandoned their homesteads, pleaded with governments for help, or demanded radical political change. Conditions in the southeastern drybelt during the early 1920s proved to be a grim foreshadowing of the devastating events of the 1930s. Deeply worried, the province's business community met the dramatic slowing of growth with a return to the old nostrums of boosterism and immigration promotion. Despite the hardships of the early 1920s, by mid-decade wheat yields and prices were recovering, ushering in a brief era of prosperity.

The recession of the early 1920s discouraged new settlers, as did the fact that most of the best land in central and southern Alberta had already been taken. Negligible growth from 588,000 in 1921 to 608,000 in 1926 caused considerable concern. However, a new wave of immigrants came to the province in the latter part of the decade. They opened up new agricultural areas, and added further to the province's ethnic diversity. The growth in population to 732,000 in 1931 was an increase of 24 per cent over the 1921 population. This was a far cry from the visions of huge influxes of people that had energized real estate promoters and other Albertans during the prewar boom.

The 1920s are remembered as a time of social change across North America. Alberta was no exception. These changes resulted from new technologies and from the impact of American popular culture. With the returning prosperity of the late 1920s, more Albertans could afford to buy cars, radios, telephones, and farm machinery, and attend movies. Modern technology changed the nature of work both in the workplace and in the home. Better transportation and communication broke down isolation and social barriers, bringing farm families closer to town and city. These changes in transportation and communication also encouraged the development of organized sport and the growth of tourism. Ultimately they lessened the power of families and ethnic groups, creating a more homogeneous society.

Common experiences and social trends encouraged by new technology hastened the merging of British, central Canadian, American, and European traditions into a new prairie culture. The combination of these trends began to move Alberta away from the British-Ontario cultural model that had been dominant. Although ethnic and religious differences remained strong, deeply rooted in the bloc settlement pattern, a new Alberta identity slowly emerged.

Under the UFA the political system became more representative. British and American immigrants began to play a greater part in provincial politics, which had previously been dominated by the Ontario-born. The UFA attempted to unite all farmers, regardless of ethnic origin. Nonetheless, non-British ethnic groups remained under-represented in the UFA. The UFA victories in 1921 illustrated the development of a province-wide agrarian identification that embodied and stimulated a strong provincial and regional consciousness.

This farmers' protest, which reached its peak in the early 1920s, was a regional reaction to central Canadian domination and a class objection to the abuses of capitalism. Their views also included an implicit critique of an urban life they considered parasitic and immoral. Since the farmers' political victory in 1921 meant that urban Albertans were largely shut out of political power, it had the potential to aggravate rural-urban conflict.

Immigration, Settlement, and Ethnic Relations

During the early 1920s, the prolonged drought in southeast and east-central Alberta led to a mass exodus. When farmers by the thousands pulled up stakes and either returned to the U.S. or moved to irrigated areas or to the Peace River district, the social and economic life of the southeast collapsed. The region could support only a few small centres. Some, such as Foremost and Manyberries, survived; many others did not. Towns such as Alderson, Winnifred, Retlaw, and Travers, which once had grain elevators, several stores, a school, and churches, gradually disappeared; others, such as Orion and Dorothy, barely clung to life. A handful of farmers and ranchers gradually took over land that once supported dozens of families. This drybelt disaster was the first and most difficult problem facing the UFA government.

Despite these economic difficulties, in the late 1920s over a hundred thousand immigrants came to Alberta. Their numbers were small, however, compared to the main settlement boom prior to World War I. Many came to Alberta because of the restrictive quota system the U.S. introduced in 1924. Almost as many Albertans were leaving for the U.S. Most of those leaving were disappointed homesteaders. Others were the Alberta-born generation, who were coming to maturity in the 1920s and had decided that there were more opportunities in the U.S. Among those who left were Fay Wray, a young actress born in Cardston who achieved fame in the movie *King Kong*, and Johnny Longden, who became one of horse-racing's most successful jockeys.

The new immigrants strengthened existing patterns of ethnic settlement, made the province more ethnically diverse, and confirmed its predominantly rural character. The majority of newcomers headed to farms, where they often joined friends, relatives, or fellow countrymen. They usually worked as agricultural labourers before setting up their own farms or leaving for the cities. The immigrants depended on pioneers who, still struggling themselves, often took advantage of newcomers as cheap labour.

Some of the immigrants moved to newly irrigated land in southern Alberta, where they helped to develop a sugar beet industry. The Lethbridge Northern Irrigation District opened in 1921 and farmers, including many new settlers from Europe, took up land near Picture Butte and Iron Springs. The Raymond sugar factory had closed in 1914 because of low beet prices, high grain prices, technical problems with beet raising, and lack of cheap labour. But Mormon entrepreneurs and farmers re-established a sugar beet industry in 1925, when they convinced the Utah-Idaho Sugar Company (largely owned by the Mormon Church) to reopen a sugar factory in Raymond. The CPR, the newly formed Alberta Sugar Beet Grower's Association, and several ethnic organizations cooperated to bring immigrants as workers for this labour-intensive industry.

Many immigrants joined the rush into the Peace River district during the 1920s. New railway lines opened up the towns of Wembley, Beaverlodge, Grimshaw, and Fairview. With the completion of the railway, the old settlement at Lake Saskatoon moved en masse to the railway at Wembley. Land-hungry and dried-out farm families from central and southern Alberta and other parts of the prairies also moved into the region. Clyde Campbell, a former pharmacist from Ohio, who came to farm on the frontier hoping to improve his physical and emotional health, captured the mood:

> Now it is a chance of a life-time and I am thankful that we are here on the ground. Why, it's just like a gold rush here; the Land Office is jammed packed every time the train comes up, and this inter-esting event occurs twice a week. . . . Out here, with a limitless horizon, the sun shining so brightly, the smell of the prairie in my nose and a future in the making, who wouldn't feel like a made-over man?[1]

Some farmers who had arrived earlier deserted the Peace River district during the early 1920s because of low prices for wheat and cattle. Poor roads and limited schools, hospitals, churches, and other facilities created hardship. But the overall pattern was one of expansion. Between 1921 and 1931, the population of the area more than doubled, from 21,000 to 44,000.

The ordeals facing wheat king Herman Trelle of Wembley reveal the opportunities and challenges of the Peace River district during the 1920s. Trelle followed his parents to Peace River to farm during World War I. He experimented with crossbreeding strains of grain and in 1926 won his first World Wheat Championship at Chicago. Trelle subsequently won three more championships, bringing publicity to Alberta, but the prize money was minimal. Only through UFA government assistance could he escape living in abject poverty in a made-over grain bin while letters and telegrams of congratulations poured in from all over the world.

Newcomers had a difficult time establishing farms in the 1920s. Many who began as farm labourers in the growing season then drifted through seasonal jobs in resource areas or jammed urban boarding houses, becoming part of an underemployed working class.

Since the government made special provisions to attract domestic workers, many of the female immigrants going to urban areas were domestics. Domestic work for British, Scandinavian, and central and eastern European women usually meant living with middle-class families, where they had relatively good food and accommodation and learned Canadian customs and behaviour. However, they were often socially isolated, lacked privacy, and worked long hours at low pay in a job with little social status.

More immigrants came from Britain during the 1920s than from any other country. Since British immigrants continued to be at the top of the list of "preferred" settlers, a category that also included Americans and northern Europeans, the Canadian and Alberta governments were anxious to entice them to Canada. Consequently, both cooperated with the British government in a variety of subsidized emigration schemes. But British immigrants often had problems adjusting to rural life, and many of them soon left for the cities to find work. Some, destitute and disillusioned, demanded deportation back to Britain. Local CPR officials were caught by the great gulf between the immigrants' high expectations about the conditions they would find, and the desire of the farm employers for cheap labour.

In 1925 the federal government entered into a Railways Agreement with the CPR and CNR to attract more central and eastern Europeans. If the "preferred" Britons, Americans, and northern Europeans would not come in sufficient numbers, then other immigrants would be persuaded to help settle the West. After the Railways Agreement, the number of immigrants coming to Alberta increased dramatically. Under this agreement, the railways brought 165,000 central and eastern Europeans and 20,000 Mennonites to Canada. Between 1926 and 1930, over 72,000 immigrants arrived in Alberta, almost half of them from central and eastern Europe.

Postwar Europe experienced tremendous political upheavals: the collapse of the Austro-Hungarian Empire, the emergence of new states, the dramatic shifting of borders, rising nationalism, and economic crisis. These factors encouraged a new wave of emigration. The Mennonites in Russia, for example, in the aftermath of the Russian revolution, fled civil war, famine, disease, and murder. A cultural crisis also arose when the communist state assumed control of Mennonite education, and nationalized church property. The Mennonites were desperate to find a new home.

Many of the Hungarians, Croatians, Czechs, Slovaks, and Mennonites went to the sugar beet fields of southern Alberta, where they faced tedious and seasonal work, low wages, isolation, and inadequate housing. They were poor, ineligible for government relief, and lacked English language skills. They survived primarily by depending on each other. The Mennonites in Coaldale, for example, developed a network of institutions that eventually included cooperative health and life insurance schemes, a hospital, an agricultural society, a German Saturday school, a library, a high school, and a cheese factory. Hard work, frugality, cooperation, and in some cases credit from the CPR, eventually made it possible for many of the new immigrants, after years of grinding labour, to own their own farms.

Despite government regulations favouring farmers and domestics, newcomers from central and eastern Europe also included unskilled workers, artisans, tradespeople, and merchants. At times the contact between the older wave of immigrants and the newcomers was fraught with tension because of political and class differences.

While European immigration continued throughout the 1920s, Asian immigration virtually halted. Because of growing anti-Asian sentiment across Canada, the federal government barred all Chinese in 1923, including family members of those already in Canada, and restricted Japanese immigration. The small Chinese community in Alberta (about 3600 people) remained throughout the interwar years as basically a bachelor society with a wide variety of political, clan, and district organizations that substituted for the families they had left behind. They remained highly concentrated in the laundry and restaurant trades. Socially and residentially they were segregated from whites. This was particularly painful in small towns where there were few other Chinese with whom they could socialize. Most of the Chinese focussed their life goals and political activities on China.

The Japanese, however, were still able to bring over their families and consequently their community life developed differently from that of the Chinese. During the 1920s, the few hundred Japanese in Raymond and Hardieville joined together to build institutions that eased their adjustment to the new society and at the same time maintained important cultural and religious traditions. In 1929 they founded a Buddhist temple in Raymond. There they started a Japanese language school and began a martial arts society. Class and regional differences that had been important in Japan gradually faded. While the Japanese maintained a tightly knit and distinctive community, they were able to integrate into the larger society to a greater extent than the Chinese, since most Japanese had families and their children drew them into the larger society through school, sports, and other community activities.

By the late 1920s, the new influx of immigrants from central and eastern Europe faced growing religious and ethnic prejudice. Organized labour and UFA members of parliament opposed immigration on economic grounds. But even more vocal and emotional were nativist groups such as the National Association of Canada (headed by an Anglican bishop, George Exton Lloyd, who had led the Barr colonists), the ultra-Protestant Orange Order, and even a short-lived Ku

Klux Klan. These self-appointed "patriots" claimed that the newcomers from central and eastern Europe were allies in a French Catholic plot to undermine the Anglo-Protestant character of English-speaking Canada. The rhetoric of the Orange Order and the Klan harkened back to the anti-Catholicism of nineteenth century rural Ontario and the American Midwest. Both Orangemen and Klansmen warned about Roman Catholic authoritarianism, political plots, and the moral degeneracy of the Roman Catholic clergy. Though explicitly racist, these organizations directed little attention to Asians or blacks in Alberta; white supremacy was not a priority of the Alberta Klan because the number of non-whites in the province was so small.

During the late 1920s and early 1930s, under the leadership of an anti-Catholic agitator from Ontario, J. J. Maloney, the Klan attracted between five and seven thousand members in fifty communities in the province—mostly in the Anglo-Protestant heartland of rural southern and central Alberta. Maloney came to Alberta after the Conservative victory in the Saskatchewan provincial election of June 1929, in which the Klan had helped to topple the Liberal regime. Headquartered in Edmonton, which he called the "Rome of the West" because of its concentration of Roman Catholic ecclesiastical institutions, Maloney attempted to instigate boycotts of Catholic businessmen, prevent religious intermarriage, intimidate politicians who "catered to Rome," combat the use of the French language, and stop continental European immigration. The Klan was also solidly opposed to the Liberals, whom it viewed as subservient to French Canadians and the Roman Catholic Church. After the 1930 federal election, the Edmonton Klan burned a fiery cross to celebrate the victory of Conservative A. U. G. Bury, a former Edmonton mayor whom they regarded as sympathetic to their prejudices.

The Klan did not survive the Great Depression. By 1933 it had collapsed, partly due to economic difficulties, but also because of the scandals surrounding Klan leader Maloney's involvement in separate fraud, theft, vandalism, and slander cases, which led to his serving a prison term.

Though fortunately the Klan's ignominious career was short, it nevertheless revealed the anxieties in predominantly Protestant Alberta during the late 1920s. The Klan's twisted appeal to patriotism, moralism, and law and order undoubtedly reflected a desire for security amidst the rapid social changes of the postwar period.

Oil and Coal: Symbols of Boom and Bust

While the new immigration was helping to develop the province's main industry of agriculture, there were also important changes in its resource industries, petroleum and coal. During the 1920s, the Turner Valley field passed out of the hands of British and Canadian investors and came under American control. In 1921 Imperial Oil took over the assets of the Calgary Petroleum Products Company, which had made the original Turner Valley discovery in 1914. Imperial became the key player in the field, and in 1922 opened a refinery in Calgary to handle the high-quality naphtha gas (which, after processing, could be used for both heating and motor fuel). Imperial also established a Canadian subsidiary known as Royalite, which in October 1924 drilled a new well at Turner Valley. This discovery led to another boom and opened up vast reserves of naphtha or wet gas.

Drilling in the 1920s was so capital-intensive that only the big companies survived. Capital-starved and without access to other refining or pipeline facilities, many of the existing Canadian independents sold out to Royalite, which soon controlled production, refining, and distribution. In the Turner Valley field, the capital, technology, and about a third of the labour was American. One of the few Canadian companies to survive was Home Oil, established in 1925. It prospered due to a combination of good luck and Vancouver capital.

Turner Valley oilfield, 1924. The plant in the foreground is the Royalite refinery. The Turner Valley field was Alberta's, and Canada's, largest oilfield until the major discoveries at Leduc after World War II. *(Glenbow Archives ND-8-436)*

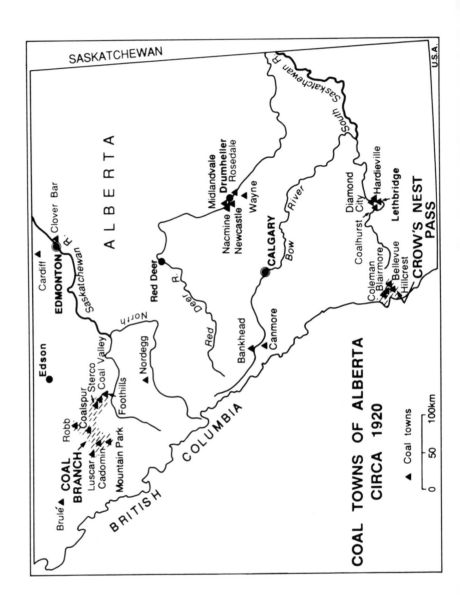

COAL TOWNS OF ALBERTA
CIRCA 1920

▲ Coal towns

0   50   100km

Rapid exploitation and foreign domination of the resource were the costs of diversifying the economy into petroleum. Oil and gas conservation measures were neglected. Independent producers of naphtha, who lacked a market for natural gas, simply flared their gas. Between 1924 and 1930, one-third to one-half of the recoverable gas was wastefully flared. Once it took over control of natural resources from the federal government in 1930, the UFA government passed conservation legislation. However, the Supreme Court of Canada ruled the Oil and Gas Conservation Act of 1932 outside provincial jurisdiction, thus delaying necessary conservation legislation.

The Turner Valley field, though small by later Alberta standards, in its day was nationally significant. By 1930, 92 per cent of all Canadian petroleum came from Alberta. Discoveries of crude oil in 1936 led to further expansion of the field, which remained Canada's largest until 1947. Although a minor part of the Alberta economy at the time, the Turner Valley field established the pattern for later developments in the oil industry, including the dominance of American capital and the role of Calgary as the industry's management centre.

The Turner Valley oilfield communities that developed during the 1920s and 1930s at Black Diamond, Turner Valley, and smaller communities with ironic names like "Little Chicago" (Royalties) and "Little New York" (Longview) were in many ways similar to the coalfield communities. All were closely linked to fluctuations in international markets, and they relied on imported capital, expertise, and equipment. Socially the communities were originally transient and predominantly male, notable for drinking, gambling, and organized sport. Housing for the workers was makeshift, sanitation and medical care primitive, and air pollution ongoing. There was also a clear residential and social division between management and workers. In the oilfields, like the coalfields, danger was constant. Drilling accidents and explosions were frequent.

In contrast to the coalfields, however, in the oilfields continental European immigrants were virtually absent and labour unions weak or non-existent. The proximity of a large labour pool in Calgary and the free-enterprise ideology prevalent in the oilfields hindered the growth of unions.

While the oilfields were developing during the 1920s, the coalfields were steadily declining. Problems included depression and deflation in the postwar economy, over-staffing of mines, and high wages. Among the mines to close were those at Bankhead, near Banff, and at Pocahontas, along the railine near Jasper. A mine and town had sprung into being at Pocahontas in 1910, and eventually attracted over a thousand people. After a brief period of prosperity, the mine closed in August 1921, partly because of the inferior quality of the coal. In 1925 an Alberta government Royal Commission on Coal, finding that there were too many mines producing too much coal for too few markets, recommended that the number of mines be restricted. The provincial government subsequently conducted a publicity campaign in Ontario for Alberta coal. The Canadian government under Liberal Prime Minister Mackenzie King also finally agreed to pay a freight subsidy. The Alberta argument was that since Albertans subsidized Ontario industries through the tariff, other Canadians should help subsidize Alberta coal.

Despite these efforts, profits in the industry fell. In the early 1920s, Alberta mine operators cut wages between 35 and 50 per cent, locking out those who would not accept wage reductions. The result was another bitter period of labour conflict. The miners had emerged from the One Big Union (OBU) experience in 1919 determined not to yield ground. When the leaders of the United Mine Worker's (UMWA) union failed to protect the workers in this round of wage cuts, the UMWA union collapsed. By 1925 it had been replaced by the new Mine Workers Union of Canada (MWUC), a curious amalgam of moderates and communists. After the OBU's defeat in 1919, the communists gained increasing strength in the Alberta coalfields, and during the 1920s Alberta was second only to Ontario in numbers of communist supporters.

The coalfields of the Drumheller valley continued to be a centre of radicalism and class conflict. In 1925 a violent strike pitted left-wing miners, supported by the communists, against the companies, provincial police, and more moderate miners, who were willing to accept the proposed wage cuts. The strike led to small riots, dozens of arrests, and jail sentences. Provincial police used tear gas to disperse picketers, and shot one striking miner. Although this strike ended in defeat for the miners, it was a barometer of continuing class conflict and class solidarity in the coalfields.

Most historians regard the 1920s as a quiet period in labour solidarity and working class militancy throughout Canada. However, although radicalism declined from the high point of 1919–20, many sectors of Alberta's working class, particularly coal miners, refused to march to the company tune.

Urban Development

Modest economic growth during the 1920s led to only minor growth in urban areas. Between 1921 and 1931, Calgary grew from 63,000 to 84,000, partly because of the new oil boom at Turner Valley. This boom strengthened the prominent role of Calgary's entrepreneurs and lawyers as supporting actors in the oil industry, and contributed to the stock market frenzy that gripped urban Alberta in the late 1920s.

The Calgary Exhibition and Stampede became an annual event during the 1920s. In 1919 Guy Weadick, the owner of a combined cattle and dude ranch near High River, returned to Calgary to stage a Victory Stampede that had many economic spinoffs for the city. By 1923, the directors of the agricultural exhibition could see attendance dwindling, partly because of the agricultural recession. On Weadick's suggestion, they decided to revive the rodeo to go along with the exhibition. With the addition of chuckwagon races, a wild cow milking contest, outdoor dances, the closing of Calgary's main street so that cowboys and Indians could ride down it on horses, fancy store fronts in imitation of a frontier town, and the opportunity for townspeople and visitors to "dress western," the event became an enormous success. Showman Weadick's energetic promotion of the Stampede across North America included his backing of a commercial film, *His Destiny* (1928), which shamelessly plugged the Stampede.

Other Alberta cities also grew, but not with the explosive energy of the prewar boom years. Edmonton grew from 59,000 in 1921 to 79,000 in 1931 with the further development of agriculture in north-central Alberta and the Peace River district, and with Edmonton's further development through railways and aviation as the gateway to the North. Railroad extensions in several directions—into new areas of the Peace River district, the Pembina Valley Railway to Barrhead (1927), the Alberta and Great Waterways Railway (A. & G. W.) to Fort McMurray (1924), a new railway to St. Paul (1920), and through what became Willingdon and Hairy Hill in the heart of the Ukrainian bloc (1927)—confirmed Edmonton as the transportation hub and metropolis of the North. Because of the railway, St. Paul developed as the main town in the northeast region, the centre of a large French Canadian settlement.

In southern Alberta, Lethbridge and Medicine Hat grew slightly despite problems in agriculture. Coal mining was still important, but Lethbridge benefitted from the further development of irrigation and the allied sugar beet and vegetable canning industries. Lethbridge's population of 13,500 was divided between a multi-ethnic working class (mostly Slavic miners) in the city's north end and an Anglo-Saxon middle class in the south.

Despite the severe drought in the dry belt, Medicine Hat, with a population of 10,300 in 1931, held its own because of flour mills, brick plants, clay works, and potteries fueled by cheap natural gas. Alberta Clay Products, Medicine Hat Potteries, and Medalta Potteries made Medicine Hat a busy industrial centre not totally dependent on its shrinking agricultural hinterland.

Though there was some growth in the largest cities and in newly opened regions during the 1920s, most towns and villages in central and southern Alberta either stagnated or declined. Having carved out a hinterland in the prewar era, they had already peaked. Those in the southeast declined precipitously.

Farmers in Power

The new UFA government confronted a major farm crisis in the southeast. Nearly one-quarter—20,000—of Alberta's farmers lived in the drought area. Some had not had a single crop since 1916. Many departed, and those who remained were desperate. In the spring of 1921, some farmers in the Medicine Hat area brought in an American rainmaker to work his magic, but the summer was dry. As described in one local newspaper, "The harvest work is so slim that it is hardly worth speaking of; to mention it only makes all feel badly."[2] A Red Cross survey conducted in September in southeast Alberta schools revealed that nearly two-thirds of 638 pupils were suffering from malnutrition.

Farmers pleaded for relief in the form of seed grain and animal feed. The UFA government appointed a Survey Board for Southern Alberta. It recommended relief payments. The government agreed for 1922, but in 1923 it discontinued the program. Premier Greenfield worried that the plan was leading farmers deeper into debt and making them dependent on the government.

Despite radical UFA rhetoric, the provincial UFA government was cautious and pragmatic. The provincial cabinet included Calgary lawyer John Brownlee (attorney general) and former Conservative party leader George Hoadley (minister of agriculture). While sympathetic to the farmers' plight, they and their cabinet colleagues were unwilling to challenge the country's financial and political establishment. The conflict between the movement's conservative leadership and the more radical grass roots became apparent at the 1922 UFA convention, where delegates debated a resolution proposing a moratorium on debts. Attorney General Brownlee had to use all his persuasive powers to convince delegates to temporarily shelve the resolution.

Farmers bombarded the government with other demands for monetary reform, including a provincial bank that would operate on a service rather than a profit basis. Scottish engineer Major C. H. Douglas (the founder of Social Credit theory) and other monetary reformers gained followers in the UFA. In fact the organization's central office stocked copies of their writing. American-born George Bevington of Winterburn was one of the founders of the UFA. Bevington, MP William Irvine, and former Kansas governor John W. Leedy were particularly strong UFA advocates of monetary reform. Demands for debt moratoriums, monetary reform, and a provincial bank resurfaced dramatically during the 1930s and periodically in the years that followed.

The conservative leadership of the UFA government rejected most of these radical measures. However, their Drought Area Relief Act of 1922 enabled farmers in dried-out areas to renegotiate their loans through a government-appointed commissioner. The 1923 Debt Adjustment Act made all Alberta farmers eligible to renegotiate their loans. Both acts included provisions of partial debt moratoria.

Farmers also wanted reform in the grain marketing system. During World War I, the government controlled wheat prices through a Wheat Board, but the board closed after 1919. By 1922 Alberta farmers were divided between those who wanted another wheat board and those who wanted cooperative wheat pools. Many farmers were fascinated by the co-ops developed by Aaron Sapiro and the California Fruit Growers. When unresolved conflicts among farmers and the opposition of the Manitoba government prevented the re-establishment of the Wheat Board, Alberta farmers turned to the concept of the cooperative wheat pool. Pools, it was hoped, could reduce wild fluctuation in prices and the power of middlemen.

Henry Wise Wood supported the wheat pool and helped swing the UFA behind it. First caught up in the idea in 1923, Wood originally decided to postpone the drive for pool contract signatures until 1924. However, the *Calgary Herald*, which was both critical of Wood's theories of group government, and willing to drive a wedge between Wood and his supporters by making Wood look overly cautious, invited Sapiro to Alberta. Sapiro arrived in August 1923. Through his dynamic oratory, he convinced farmers to sign up for the pool immediately. The UFA government and Wood moved quickly to support the movement, which signed up farmers controlling 45 per cent of the province's total wheat acreage.

The Alberta Wheat Pool was a major achievement for Alberta's farmers. In October 1923, the pool opened for business, with Wood as its president. Throughout the 1920s, it handled over half of the annual wheat crop. The pool built a modern elevator and terminal system, and by 1928 was Alberta's largest grain company. It inspired the dedication of thousands of farmers, the backing of the UFA government, and the cooperation of businessmen, banks, and even other grain companies. Because of UFA support, the pool movement was more successful in Alberta than in Saskatchewan or Manitoba.

While relief and grain marketing occupied farmers in central and southern Alberta, railways continued to preoccupy northern farmers. One of the major fiscal problems the provincial government faced was the high cost of railways. The collapse of subsidized syndicates left the province supporting four incomplete and unprofitable railways. Believing that the lines were potentially profitable as branches of the two transcontinental systems, the UFA government began negotiating for their sale. Negotiations were long and complex and continued throughout the 1920s.

The Politics of Booze

Prohibition was one of the most difficult problems facing the new UFA government. Loopholes in the law that made enforcing it difficult gradually brought prohibition into disrepute. The UFA government was caught in a political crossfire propelled by rural-urban, class, and ethnic differences. While their rural supporters continued to favour it, people in the cities became increasingly disenchanted with prohibition.

The illegal liquor trade was lucrative. Rumrunners and bootleggers were resourceful, and were regarded by some as folk heroes. Consequently the provincial police spent much time and energy in fruitless pursuit. Prohibitionists felt the police were not determined enough, and it was rumoured that police tacitly condoned the trade, or were bribed to ignore violations.

Professional rumrunners, such as Emilio Picariello in the Crow's Nest Pass, became wealthy and notorious. The crime and violence associated with prohibition was highlighted in the Picariello case in 1922. It involved a clash between immigrant cultures and Anglo-Saxon law enforcement, gunbattles, the killing of a policeman, and two hangings, and attracted sensational press attention across the country.

Emilio Picariello was born in Sicily in 1875. He immigrated to Canada at the turn of the century, and in 1911 moved his family to the Crow's Nest Pass, where he developed businesses catering to a large Italian community. Prohibition opened new opportunities. Picariello made large profits running liquor from British Columbia into Alberta and Montana. He used his hotel as a front for his operations. He also acquired a fleet of elegant McLaughlin-Buicks with special features for handling extra cargo, and reinforced concrete bumpers for breaking through police barricades. Though he had plenty of competition, he developed the largest rumrunning operation in southern Alberta. Because of his charitable donations to the poor, the local immigrant community thought of him as a benefactor. They elected him an alderman for Blairmore.

On September 21, 1922, Picariello and his son, Steve, in separate cars, were stopped by a police roadblock. As Steve sped off, pursuing police shot and wounded him. When false rumours reached Emilio that his son had been killed, he left with Mrs. Florence Lassandro (reportedly Steve's girlfriend), both armed with revolvers. They confronted an unarmed constable, Steve Lawson, at the Alberta Provincial Police barracks. During a scuffle between Lawson and Picariello, Lawson was shot and killed, probably by Lassandro.

Shortly thereafter, the police charged both Picariello and Lassandro with murder. After a sensational trial, both were found guilty. Their appeals were turned down and they were hanged at Fort Saskatchewan in May 1923.

The trial provided a focus for much of the emotion-charged debate in Alberta on the issues of prohibition and immigration. Attorney General Brownlee's attendance throughout the trial gave strong evidence of the government's resolve to crush rumrunning. Outside the Pass, public opinion ran against Picariello. When Brownlee announced in the legislature that the Supreme Court had turned down his appeal, several MLAs applauded.

Ironically, the Picariello case contributed to the demise of prohibition. Growing fears of violence reinforced the drive of "moderates" to end prohibition. With strong support from veterans and funding from breweries, moderation leagues advocated government-run liquor stores that would ensure quality and bring money from liquor sales to the state rather than to criminals. In early 1923, the Moderation League and the Alberta Hotelkeepers presented the government with petitions demanding a referendum on whether to allow government control of liquor. The Greenfield cabinet decided to allow a referendum offering four alternatives. In November 1923, Albertans voted to end their eight-year experiment with prohibition. The alternative providing for government sale of beer and liquor was the overwhelming favourite. As reform zeal waned along with the war-induced willingness to "do without," Albertans turned to a system that promised to control crime and raise money for government programs.

In May 1924, the government established the Alberta Liquor Control Board. The board was the only legal importer of liquor, and it maintained strict licensing regulations reflecting a strait-laced attitude toward alcohol. No food could be served in bars. Women were not allowed into bars without escorts, and men unaccompanied by women were served in separate rooms. No singing or dancing was allowed. Many of these restrictions remained in Alberta law until the 1960s and 1970s. The legislation also reflected disillusionment with prohibition. Prohibition had become so unpopular that even the staunchly dry UFA had to bow to majority opinion.

The Rise of John Brownlee

By 1925 discontent was brewing over the leadership of Premier Greenfield, since he was seen as administratively inexperienced and ineffective. There were also recurring ideological disagreements within the UFA cabinet and caucus over issues such as government ownership of railways. Greenfield had become extremely dependent on John Brownlee. In addition to his own responsibilities as attorney general, Brownlee had been receiving a steady stream of correspondence from the premier's office with a simple memo attached: "Kindly let Mr. Greenfield know what to reply to this."[3] Rumblings within UFA ranks over Greenfield's leadership were temporarily suspended when Brownlee threatened to resign if there were more calls for Greenfield's resignation. Nonetheless, opposition to Greenfield continued to grow. The UFA members pressed Brownlee to become premier. Brownlee, as an urban lawyer, was hesitant about becoming the premier of a farmers' government. In November 1925, Greenfield resigned. Under pressure from Henry Wise Wood,

214

Calgary lawyer John Brownlee, Premier of Alberta from 1925 until his political career ended in a sex scandal in 1934. Brownlee's political caution and pragmatism contrasted sharply with the radicalism of many other leaders in the UFA movement. *(Glenbow Archives NA 1451-11)*

Brownlee agreed, with seeming reluctance, to become premier. Brownlee insisted that he be asked by Greenfield himself in order to be assured that Greenfield did not hold a grudge.

Born in rural Ontario in 1884, Brownlee was the fourth Alberta premier to come from that province. By selling encyclopedias, he had financed his education at the University of Toronto, where he studied history and political science. After graduation, he moved to Calgary and took a position with the law firm of Lougheed and Bennett, where he was closely tutored by Bennett. In 1912 the twenty-nine-year-old Brownlee married and was admitted to the bar.

Brownlee had first become involved with the UFA as their legal advisor. His social connections, however, were with Calgary's business and professional elite. He taught a Methodist Sunday School class and joined the local Masons. Though Wood and Brownlee had very different backgrounds, they grew to respect each other.

By 1921 Brownlee thought of himself as a westerner. He was supportive of the farmers. Although he did not run in the 1921 election, he was acclaimed Ponoka's MLA shortly thereafter, following the death of the incumbent, and was appointed to the cabinet as attorney general. The inexperience of the other UFA members contributed to his dominance of the cabinet and the legislature. Only one of the UFA members had ever sat in the legislature, and none represented urban ridings. Thus, almost every issue before the government drew on Brownlee's legal expertise. Brownlee, at six foot four, was an impressive figure. His "rimless glasses, high tight winged collar, and dark, bulky suit made him look very much the part of a bookish corporate lawyer."[4] But he was always so well prepared, and spoke so deliberately and carefully, that he awed and impressed the less experienced UFA members.

Brownlee's social and legal background predisposed him to caution, and he was one of the major forces tempering the UFA's radicalism. His approach to the crisis of farm debt typified his style. He opposed the radical ideas of the banking reformers, and attempted instead to get the banks to be flexible in individual cases. When he became premier, Brownlee felt the major tasks facing the province were to balance the budget, dispose of the provincial railways, and secure from Ottawa provincial control of natural resources.

Though UFA membership declined from its high in 1921, Alberta farmers still believed in cooperative government and continued to support the UFA government. In addition, an economic upswing in the mid-1920s contributed to their continued support. The 40.5 per cent of the popular vote that the UFA received in the provincial election of 1926 gave it forty-three seats out of sixty-one, including all rural seats but four.

The victory obscured problems within the movement. UFA locals were steadily disintegrating as reform zeal waned and local UFA leaders became involved in federal and provincial politics and wheat pool organizations. Cooperation between farmers and labour was also declining. Although five Labour members were returned in 1926, Brownlee did not appoint a Labour member as a cabinet minister as had occurred after the 1921 election. Organized labour began to see Brownlee as a foe because he used the provincial police to support management in labour disputes in the coalfields.

Following further intense negotiations, Brownlee succeeded in 1928 in selling the government-run northern railways to the major transcontinental railways for $25 million. The deal reflected well on Brownlee's skill as a negotiator, although it also revealed the conservatism of a cost-conscious government that did not see railways as a public utility.

Brownlee also pressed the federal government for control of natural resources. In 1929, after eight years of negotiations complicated by renewed disputes over the constitutional status of separate schools, the federal government surrendered control over natural resources. The agreement included an annual financial payment to compensate the province for previous lost revenues. The federal

216

government was amenable to a generous settlement as a way for the federal Liberals to demonstrate their belief in equality for the West and to accommodate the western Progressive revolt. Albertans regarded this achievement as a triumph for Brownlee and for Alberta. When Brownlee returned from Ottawa, over two thousand people met him at the railway station in Edmonton in freezing weather. Organizers lit a large bonfire, a band played, and fireworks exploded in the night.

Brownlee's success with the railways and with securing provincial ownership of natural resources contributed to his victory in the 1930 provincial election with thirty-nine of sixty-three seats. The Liberals, Conservatives, and Labour divided the urban seats, while the UFA swept rural Alberta (with the exception of the predominantly French Canadian ridings, which went Liberal). Nonetheless, radical UFA members chafed at Brownlee's conservatism, particularly his unwillingness to give more than lip service to public ownership of hydro resources, and his reluctance to expand social services. Brownlee initially even opposed a national old-age pension scheme supported by the federal UFA members, since he regarded it as unnecessary and expensive. He finally gave in to public pressure and passed an old-age pension act, but Alberta was the last western province to join the program, which was jointly funded by the different levels of government.

While the federal UFA members continued throughout the 1920s as the country's most outspoken force for political and economic change, the provincial UFA quickly put reins on any radicalism. A rift consequently developed between the radicalism of the federal UFA and the more conservative views of the provincial UFA. The attempts by doctrinaire UFA members in their first provincial legislative session in 1922 to bring down "partyism" by voting against the government on a bill to amend the Dairyman's Act had almost led to the downfall of the UFA government. These backbenchers opposed the act, but had not expressed their dissent in caucus. They believed it was a member's duty to express the views of constituents on the floor of the assembly, and they refused to be muzzled by caucus discipline. Only the support of the Labour group saved the government from defeat by its own backbenchers. Rather than bringing an end to "partyism," the backbenchers almost brought an end to the first UFA government. However, the backbenchers' experimentalism was soon brought into line by Brownlee and the other members of the cabinet.

The conservatism of the provincial UFA had many causes: inexperience of the new members, the underlying conservatism of Wood and Brownlee, concern about fiscal solvency, and limits of provincial jurisdiction. The government also wanted to answer charges of class favouritism by showing that they could govern for non-farmers as well. In addition, as reform zeal in the UFA declined because of the prosperity of the late 1920s, Alberta's farmers themselves became less radical. Because of their ambivalent position within the class structure, farmers in the province have historically vacillated between radicalism and conservatism. Many saw themselves as independent entrepreneurs with much in common with capitalists. Their sense of themselves as independent commodity producers limited their radicalism.

During the early 1920s, the urban press and politicians continually denounced "class" government by the farmers, but the cautious, pragmatic policies of the UFA did little to antagonize urban interests. The presence of Brownlee reassured the urban business community. Edmonton reconciled itself to the government in 1926 by returning Edmonton lawyer J. F. Lymburn as the UFA MLA with the largest electoral majority, and the *Edmonton Journal*, a Conservative-oriented paper, on June 29, 1926, characterized Brownlee as "a man of first-rate ability, [with] a very sincere devotion to the public good."

There were too many interests linking rural and urban Alberta for rural-urban conflict to become a dominant theme: family, religious, ethnic, and various other organizational ties cut across rural-urban differences. Alberta's cities were too economically dependent on agriculture to remove themselves from rural life and too small and conservative to seem to pose much of a moral threat to rural people. The wide-open boozing, gambling, and prostitution that had marked the prewar boom period in urban areas waned as the population became older and less mobile, the male-female ratio more equal, and stable family life the norm. The drybelt disaster in the southeast also fed growing doubts about country life as the ideal. The potential for rural-urban conflict subsided, symbolized in the amiable relationship between farm leader Henry Wise Wood and shrewd urban lawyer John Brownlee.

The UFA in Ottawa: the Ginger Group Arrives

The UFA MPs returned to Ottawa in the 1921 federal election faced a very different situation from that of the provincial UFA. The sixty-five Progressive members (including the ten UFA members from Alberta)

These are the new United Farmer of Alberta MLAs, in Edmonton shortly after the stunning UFA victory in the 1921 provincial election. In the back row, second from left, is Richard G. Reid, a farmer from the Mannville area, who would in 1934 become Premier of Alberta. Mrs. Irene Parlby, minister without portfolio, is in the centre of the front row. The UFA was a populist reform movement, determined to change Alberta's and Canada's economic and political system. *(Glenbow Archives NA 2204-4)*

who were returned to the 1921 minority parliament formed the second largest group, but they were not united. True to their non-party origins, they had not campaigned as a national party. Those who went to Ottawa were deeply divided between the "Manitoba wing," who wanted to make the Progressive movement a reform party that would "recapture the historic Liberal party of rural democracy and low tariffs from the protectionist elements of Quebec and Ontario,"[5] and the "Alberta wing," who believed in group government and wanted to replace the party system with representation by occupational groups. While the Manitoba wing was willing to consider a coalition with the Liberals, the Alberta wing was totally opposed. Without party discipline, the farmers could not hope to force their program on the ruling Liberals.

However, the Progressives were able to claim some achievements. Anxious to attract the Progressives back into the Liberal fold, in 1922 Liberal Prime Minister Mackenzie King restored the Crow's Nest Pass freight rates, suspended during the war. The federal government also proceeded with a project long advocated by the farmers—a railway from the prairies to Hudson Bay to cut transportation costs. In addition, the Progressives helped to modify parliamentary rules to make way for third parties and kept the Liberals inclined toward free trade. The UFA members popularized the idea that credit could be controlled by national banking policy and that the existing Canadian banking system was unsuited to the credit needs of western agriculture. On William Irvine's initiative, the House of Commons Standing Committee on Banking and Commerce invited Social Credit theorist Major C. H. Douglas to testify before them on monetary reform.

Despite these achievements, the differences among the Progressives led to their rapid disintegration. In June 1924, six Progressive members (four from Alberta) who believed in a state-regulated economy and constituency control of MPs split off to form what the press dubbed the "Ginger Group" (because of the pep it injected into Parliament). Though hysterically attacked by the *Financial Post* as being part of an "International Communist Conspiracy," they were soon joined by other UFA members. Working in close cooperation with Labour members, the Ginger Group became one of Canada's most important voices for radical change during the 1920s and early 1930s.

The Progressive Party collapsed in the 1925 federal election, returning only twenty-four MPs, including nine from Alberta. The federal UFA vote in Alberta declined dramatically from 52 per cent in 1921 to 31 per cent in 1925. In 1925, 1926, and 1930, there were only a few percentage points separating the votes received federally by the UFA, the Liberals, and the Conservatives. In both 1925 and 1930, the federal Conservatives in Alberta actually outpolled the UFA, but because they were concentrated in urban areas, these votes translated into few seats.

One noteworthy event of the 1926 federal election was that Michael Luchkovich, the UFA member from Vegreville, became the first Ukrainian Canadian member of parliament. The bilingual, American-born, college-educated Luchkovich served as spokesman for Ukrainian Canadians, defending them against attacks by bigots and bringing to Canadian attention the violation of Ukrainian rights in eastern Europe.

Although most central and eastern European farmers saw the UFA as more democratic than the old-line parties, they did not fully embrace the movement, whose leadership was Anglo-Saxon and Protestant. There were disagreements on issues such as prohibition and immigration policy. When the more radical Farmers Unity League, which was linked to the Communist Party, began organizing among Ukrainian farmers in the early 1930s, it made rapid headway partly because Ukrainian farmers had not been fully integrated into the UFA.

In contrast, minorities such as Mormon and Scandinavian-American farmers were fully integrated into the Anglo-Protestant-dominated UFA. Southern Alberta Mormon community leaders such as John Johansen, George Stringam, and Lawrence Peterson (all American born), and Norwegian Lutheran leaders such as Chester Ronning, felt at home in the UFA and influenced its development. (Ronning served as a UFA MLA, later becoming Alberta leader of the socialist Cooperative Commonwealth Federation, before developing a distinguished career as one of Canada's foremost international diplomats after World War II.)

The Conservatives took advantage of divisions within UFA ranks to stage a minor revival during the late 1920s. While it was of little long-term consequence specifically for Alberta, the revival had broader implications for Canada as a whole because it was led by Calgary lawyer R. B. Bennett, who became Prime Minister in 1930. Bennett had run in Calgary in the 1921 election, but had been defeated. After a bitter quarrel with his law partner, James Lougheed, who attempted to dissolve their partnership without Bennett's agreement, Bennett established his own law firm and renewed his political activity. He was successful in the 1925 and 1926 federal elections. His ability to get elected on the prairies, and his wealth (which he was willing to devote at least in part to the Conservative party), were major factors in his being chosen national Conservative leader in 1927. By combining economic nationalism, British Canadian patriotism, and mild anti-immigrant sentiment with a bombastic campaign style, Bennett helped the Conservatives capture four seats in urban Alberta in the 1930 federal election, alongside the UFA majority of nine seats.

Shaping a New Identity: Technology and Social Change

Social change during the 1920s contributed to the emergence of a new Alberta identity. While ethnic, religious, class, and urban-rural differences remained, the widespread use of new forms of transportation and communication and a school system dedicated to democracy, mass education, and cultural assimilation generally eroded social differences. A new Alberta-born generation emerged, educated in that school system and open to new influences.

The decade of the twenties was the heyday of the small town in

Alberta. Cars, roads, and the telephone broke down rural isolation. Amateur sport, music, drama, school fairs, picnics, and rodeos reached their zenith. The end of pioneering in most regions and growing farm mechanization gave farmers more time for social activities. Farm families rode many miles over poor roads in uncertain weather to attend concerts and political meetings.

The popular summer Chautauquas embodied much of the ethos of rural Alberta during the 1920s. Chautauquas, which were first brought to Alberta from the U.S. in 1917, were four- to six-day travelling ventures aimed at educating, uplifting, and entertaining rural, smalltown, and even city audiences. They included music, singing, drama, oratory, "wholesome" entertainment, and lectures on a wide variety of subjects from religion, citizenship, labour, and prohibition to curing the common cold. The entire Canadian enterprise, which eventually extended to four hundred communities, was organized out of Calgary by American immigrants John and Nola Erickson. In 1927 Chautauqua visited fifty-eight Alberta towns. Communities as small as Kirriemuir, Alberta, with only twenty-seven adult residents, put on Chautauquas. The characteristic brown tents became a symbol of magic and the exotic, as well as adult education and moral uprightness, that would be remembered long after the Chautauquas died out during the Depression of the 1930s.

A crowd emerges in Vulcan from the characteristic brown tent of the popular summer Chautauqua. From the late teens until the early 1930s, the Chautauquas brought four to six days of entertainment and education, and were long remembered in small-town Alberta. Note that cars had replaced horses as the main form of individual transportation. (*Glenbow Archives NA 2685-87*)

The Chautauqua was one of the many organizations linking farm families and smalltown business people. Although economic interests, UFA politics, and ethnic differences sometimes separated townspeople from farmers, the business and professional people of smalltown Alberta were often similar to the farmers in cultural background, age, and optimism about the West. Given low population densities, if volunteer organizations such as churches, and women's, fraternal, cultural, and sports organizations, were to survive, farmers and townspeople had to join together to make them work. This growing cooperation between town and farm during the 1920s paved the way for joint political action in the 1930s.

The new technologies brought Albertans closer together, but they also contributed to growing Americanization. This influence could be seen in radio, movies, magazines, and social and educational movements such as the Chautauqua, and in voluntary organizations as diverse as the evangelical churches, the Rotary Club, the Odd Fellows, and the Ku Klux Klan. Moving pictures, which first came to the province in 1909, expanded rapidly in the 1920s, particularly with the introduction of "talkies." Movie-going was most common in the cities, but by 1930, eighty-five movie theatres took the images of the movie stars and an array of new models of dress, personality, and behaviour into almost every corner of the province.

Cars and trucks also provided a powerful impetus for social change. The first car arrived in Alberta in 1901. The number of vehicles remained small until World War I, when prosperity made it possible for more people to buy them. Most Albertans adopted cars as soon as they could afford to, and family portraits often recorded a family proudly displaying a new vehicle. By 1931, 42 per cent of farm families owned a car or truck. The number of motor vehicles jumped from forty thousand in 1921 to over a hundred thousand by 1930. The growing adoption during the late 1920s of gasoline tractors and combine harvesters (which combined reaping and threshing) also led to changes in work patterns and in the demand for farm labour.

Aviation also expanded dramatically in the late 1920s, particularly in northern Alberta. Most of the commercial aviation efforts immediately after the war had gone out of business. "Lack of adequate financial backing, lack of any clear understanding of where the future of Canadian aviation lay, and above all, the lack of an efficient aircraft designed to take passengers and cargo had severely disabled them; and their inability to generate any consistent public interest in their operations killed them."[6] But growing interest in the north, and better aircraft, eventually revived aviation in northern Alberta. The national Department of Defence encouraged the training of qualified pilots by donating aircraft to qualified flying clubs. With the promotion of Kenneth Blatchford, Edmonton's mayor and from 1926 to 1930 its Member of Parliament, Edmonton started a flying club and built an airfield (subsequently named Blatchford Field). In 1927 W. R. "Wop" May became the first president of the flying club. In 1928 he helped start Commercial Airways and became its chief pilot, carrying mail to the Mackenzie River district, and mail and passengers into the Peace River district.

May's heroic "mercy flight" in January 1929 to Fort Vermilion, to take a desperately-needed antitoxin to fight a diphtheria outbreak, heightened public appreciation of the advantages of airplanes. Department of Health officials asked Commercial Airways for assistance, and May and Vic Horner set off in desperately cold weather, in a plane with an open cockpit, to help. They reached the community safely and delivered the antitoxin, which stemmed the epidemic. They returned frostbitten to Edmonton, where they received a heroes' welcome from ten thousand Edmontonians, who had received ongoing news of their flight from reports sent by farmers and trappers to an Edmonton radio station.

C. H. (Punch) Dickins rivalled May as a pioneer in developing northern bush flying. He had been awarded the Distinguished Flying Cross for his persistence in aerial assignments under fire during the war. Upon returning to Canada, he joined the short-lived Canadian Air Force, then became one of the original officers of the Royal Canadian Air Force when it was formed in 1924. His work included high altitude experiments, forest patrol duties, and photographic surveys. In 1927, Dickins left the RCAF to join the Winnipeg-based Western Canada Airways, which established operations in Alberta. In 1929 he began flights from Fort McMurray to Fort Chipewyan and points farther north in the Northwest Territories and went on to a distinguished career in commercial aviation, particularly in the development and expansion of flying routes in northern Canada. Though the impact of aviation in the 1920s and 1930s was still limited, it was nonetheless helping to break down the isolation of northern regions.

Cars, Roads, and Tourism

Automobiles promoted the development of tourism and resorts, as well as closer social and economic ties among different parts of

Alberta. During the 1920s, urban business people launched a campaign to promote good roads. They saw the need for improved roads to widen their market area, and eyed the tantalizing economic potential of American tourism. They were particularly concerned about better roads to the national parks, partly for tourism and partly because the parks were becoming their own summer playgrounds. City automobile clubs, first started in Calgary in 1908, came together briefly during World War I as the Alberta Motor League and in 1926 as the Alberta Motor Association. The automobile clubs also banded together with Montana boosters to promote the "Sunshine Trail," supposedly running from Mexico to Alaska, to encourage tourism.

The UFA government was initially unsympathetic to the auto clubs' equation of good roads with prosperity, and focussed its priorities on market roads for farmers. Gradually, however, road-building became a critical item in the provincial budget, and roads came second only to education in provincial expenditures during the 1920s.

During the 1920s, the federal government developed a road system in the mountain parks that brought in more tourists and led to the development of more facilities. Pressure from Calgary motorists had convinced the federal government in 1914 to lift a previous ban on automobiles in Banff. The government-built Banff-Windermere highway through the Rockies into the interior of B.C. was completed in 1923.

Located on the major transcontinental railway, and close to

A group of motorists headed to the mountains at Banff. Cars promoted tourism in the mountains, and democratized access to the parks. (*Glenbow Archives NC-6-2568*)

Alberta's largest urban centre, Banff National Park was the country's premier national park. (Until 1930, when it was finally renamed, the park was officially called Rocky Mountains Park, but Banff was the popular name of the park as well as the town.) Banff was heavily promoted by the CPR, which invited wealthy travellers to "See this World Before the Next." The CPR brought talented photographers and artists west to portray and promote the mountains. However, the new road-building program gradually shifted the balance from train to car traffic, and from wealthy tourists to a much broader cross section of society.

Roads brought in more tourists, and enabled more Albertans to take advantage of mountain wilderness. The national parks, particularly Banff, still provided exclusive facilities for wealthy Europeans, Americans, and central Canadians. Alberta's urban professional and business elites also built numerous summer homes and promoted new park facilities. But improved roads ultimately democratized the parks. The government and private business developed a whole new range of tourist facilities such as campgrounds and bungalow camps (the forerunners of motels) to appeal to a broader spectrum of society. The mountains ceased to be simply a backdrop; travelling to them for recreation became part of the seasonal routine for many Albertans.

The outfitters and guides, who had been the pioneers in the parks, gradually adjusted to the new regime. In 1904 in Banff the CPR had chosen as its "official" outfitters and guides two young men, Bill and Jim Brewster, owners of a small outfitting and guiding concern. By 1915 they had gained control of horse-drawn transportation at the mountain hotels, and during the 1920s they turned to motorized touring cars and buses. This operation provided the basis for Brewster Transport Company, which became North America's largest private sightseeing business.

Local boosters also promoted winter sports and began to turn Banff into a year-round resort. Skis had first been sent to Banff in 1894 by a Norwegian American visitor. The sport did not develop significantly, however, until the Banff Winter Carnival was established in 1917. Promoted by Norwegian immigrants, ski jumping and cross-country skiing preceded alpine (or downhill) skiing. In 1921 Banff was given a place on the American Professional Ski Jumping Circuit. In 1930 the Banff Ski Club began promoting alpine skiing. With CPR support, Banff attracted the Dominion Ski Championships in 1937 and CPR ski trains began bringing ski enthusiasts every year. Ski lodges at Norquay, Skoki, and Sunshine, built during the interwar years, provided the foundation for the development of skiing as a mass sport.

In response to pressure from conservationists, and from boosters promoting tourism, park policy gradually moved away from allowing mining, forestry, and hydro-electric development within park boundaries. J. B. Harkin, first Dominion Parks Branch Commissioner (1911), saw the wilderness as the ultimate expression of God's creation, and worked to create a National Parks Act to protect the parks from industrial exploitation. The act that he helped to draft, finally passed in 1930, ensured there would be no future industrial development. At Banff National Park, the cost to the Parks Branch of this policy was the loss of lands at Canmore, Exshaw, and the Upper Spray Lakes, where substantial economic development had already occurred. The Alberta government regarded the coal, limestone, and hydro power in these locations as essential to provincial economic development, and insisted that the park boundaries be reduced to allow commercial ventures to continue. At Jasper, coal mining, lime quarrying, and lumbering had developed between 1910 and 1930, but was halted with the new Parks Act.

Limited accessibility by road was one of the major reasons Jasper's development lagged behind that of Banff. Tourists continued to come to Jasper by rail, and several new hotels were built during the 1920s to accommodate them. One famous hotel began when two younger members of Banff's Brewster family, Jack and Fred, helped start a tent camp at Lac Beauvert in 1915. Though it closed during the war, they reopened and expanded the camp in 1919, adding a large cabin as the kitchen and dining room. This camp was then taken over by the newly amalgamated Canadian National Railway, which opened Jasper Park Lodge in 1922. The railway then began an elaborate development, with a large central building and bungalows (which eventually housed 650 people), a boathouse, and a golf course, which became very popular with the rich and famous.

Boosters in Edmonton also saw the potential for a highway on the discarded roadbeds of the Canadian Northern and Grand Trunk Pacific railways (which had been combined when they were nationalized in 1917), and they began a campaign during the 1920s to promote the Yellowhead Highway route. The provincial and federal governments cooperated to complete the Edmonton-Jasper road by 1928. Throughout the 1930s relief camp workers improved this road, but as late as 1946, it was nearly impassable in places. The Banff-Jasper highway was begun as a relief camp project by the federal government

Waterton Lakes National Park, the major resort in southern Alberta, developed significantly during the 1920s. The Prince of Wales Hotel, in the centre of the picture, was built in 1927 by the American Great Northern Railway company. New roads were developed to link Waterton with the lucrative American tourist trade. *(Glenbow Archives NB-32-12)*

in 1931, and was completed as a regular labour project in 1939. The highway made accessible a range of spectacular scenery, including the Columbia Ice Fields.

During the 1920s, improved roads into Waterton Lakes promoted the development of the area, and the final jewel in Alberta's crown of railway hotels was not built on a railway at all. In 1927 the American-based Great Northern Railway built the Prince of Wales Hotel in Waterton on one of the most scenic spots in the province. Like Alberta's other railway hotels, its European architecture and British interior combined a rustic character with an old-world gentility designed to attract American tourists.

The Waterton area had been changed from a forest reserve to a national park in 1911, but the war impeded its development. However, throughout the 1920s, government facilities, hotels, garages, stores, a playground, a tennis court, a golf course, motor launches, a dance hall, churches, a swimming pool, auto bungalow camps, a movie theatre, a school, and new cottages transformed what had formerly been an area limited to timber and oil extraction and wilderness hunting and fishing into a full-fledged mountain resort.

The evolution of Waterton as a resort during the 1920s and 1930s illustrates how economic self-interest, local pride, and a belief in conservation fostered Alberta's parks. Rotarians in southern Alberta and Montana, led by Cardston Anglican clergyman Canon Middleton, joined to promote an International Peace Park that received the support of the Canadian Parliament and the American Congress. Including both Glacier and Waterton, it was dedicated by American President Herbert Hoover in 1932. In 1936 the Chief Mountain Highway from Glacier to Waterton (built by Depression relief workers) directly connected the two parks, and Waterton developed as a vital link with the lucrative tourist traffic in American national parks.

Better roads, more cars, and the prosperity of the late 1920s helped develop other Alberta resort towns. The many lakes west and south of Edmonton served as recreation and cottage country for Edmontonians, while Rochon Sands (on Buffalo Lake) and Sylvan Lake attracted people from central Alberta. By the late 1920s, almost everyone in the province had access to a lake resort. The provincial government, short of money, was reluctant to spend on recreation. However, it recognized the growing demand for recreational facilities and in 1929 established a provincial parks system.

Picnics, regattas, sports days, and evening dances became part of summer life in the resort towns. A generation of Albertans grew up dancing to the sounds of orchestras such as Mart Kenney and His Western Gentlemen. During the 1930s, the Canadian Radio Broadcasting Commission (CRBC) broadcast his music nationally from the dance pavilion on the shore of Waterton Lakes.

The Impact of Radio

Like the automobile, radio helped end the isolation of farm life, expanded urban economic and cultural dominance over rural areas, enhanced amateur sport, drama, and music, and bolstered American cultural influence. It also provided a new vehicle for religious and political propaganda.

By 1922 both Edmonton and Calgary had radio stations. The first stations were owned by newspapers, which saw radio as a means of boosting their circulation. The newspapers also wanted to neutralize the danger radio posed as an advertising rival. The inaugural broadcast on Edmonton's CJCA on May 1, 1922, featured Edmonton's mayor, who signed off with "Edmonton leads the way in all Alberta. Calgary and others follow. That is all. Goodnight."[7] Calgary retaliated the next day when the president of Calgary's board of trade opened CFAC radio, owned by the *Calgary Herald*. By 1923 the federal government had issued six private licences in Alberta, and by 1927 there were ten private commercial stations.

Alberta's major radio entrepreneur was W. W. Grant. A wartime radio technician and inventor, Grant was hired after the war by the federal government as director for an experimental radio station at High River, geared to assisting aviation. By 1922 Grant was manufacturing and retailing radio equipment in Calgary. Partly to boost sales, he began his own station, CFCN. With the help of the managerial skill of an Ontario-born businessman, H. Gordon Love, CFCN became the most powerful station on the prairies.

Other Albertans, recognizing tremendous social and educational potential for radio, helped develop national broadcasting and the experimental use of educational radio. They included agricultural journalist E. Austin Weir, and H. P. Brown and E. A. (Ned) Corbett, directors of the Faculty of Extension at the University of Alberta. In 1927 the latter began "taking the university to the people" through CKUA radio. The amiable and witty Corbett, a leader in adult education and the first director of the Canadian Association for Adult Education, worked closely with Norman Smith, editor of the UFA newspaper and the Canadian Radio League. They helped gain the support of R. B. Bennett, prairie farm organizations, the Alberta government, boards of trade, and leading Alberta newspapers for a national publicly owned radio system, which was finally begun in the early 1930s with the Canadian Radio Broadcasting Commission (CRBC). In 1936, the Canadian Broadcasting Corporation (CBC) replaced the CRBC.

Radio's early emphasis on local talent enabled, among others, the Calgary-based country and western singer Wilf Carter to gain a national and eventually a continental audience. Carter became known on local radio, worked summers for the CPR singing on trail rides in the mountains, and during the 1930s moved to New York to pursue a musical career.

The Golden Age of Sport

Like cars and radio, organized sport forged regional and provincial links and promoted social integration. Before World War I there was considerable sporting activity, but it was usually local and relatively unorganized.

During the 1920s, sport became more formalized, commercialized, and spectator-oriented. Professional sports developed, including hockey and rodeo. The intense sports rivalries that emerged between neighbouring towns and cities cemented home-town loyalties. Provincial championships were developed in several sports.

Sports participation by the 1920s cut across class, ethnic, and rural-urban lines. Baseball, hockey, curling, and golf, each previously identified with one ethnic group or class, began to be played by a wide cross section. Whereas up to thirty different sports had been played prior to World War I, the 1920s saw a growing focus on a few sports that seemed most fitted to the new prairie culture.

The churches, YMCA and YWCA, schools, and community leagues in Calgary and Edmonton all encouraged sports. Community leagues were first developed to lobby for municipal and educational services. Later they were expanded to provide recreation. In Edmonton, the number of community leagues increased from one in 1917 to twenty by 1924. The generally sports-oriented community leagues still provide a sense of community in a mobile and pluralistic society.

The social trend in the 1920s of cultural integration within the province, and the growing influence of American popular culture, were reflected in the overwhelming popularity of two sports—hockey and baseball. Recreational skaters dominated ice rinks until the turn of the century, when hockey, which was brought to the province by Ontarians, gained popularity. In 1907 the Alberta Amateur Hockey Association was formed. By the early 1920s, the largest cities could support professional hockey teams. In 1923 and 1924, the Edmonton Eskimos and the Calgary Tigers, both part of the professional Western Canada Hockey League, played for the Stanley Cup. For second-generation children of European immigrants, hockey promised social acceptance as well as competition and fun.

Baseball was Alberta's dominant summer sport throughout the 1920s, while British sports such as cricket and polo declined. Nor could soccer compete with the glamour of commercialized American baseball. Brought to Alberta by Americans and central Canadians, baseball was an ideal summer activity requiring little equipment. It was strongest in southern Alberta, the domain of American immigrants. A short-lived professional league was started in 1907, but it was disbanded because of World War I. The growing influence of American popular culture helped revive interest after the war. At World Series time, huge crowds gathered outside urban newspaper offices to watch play-by-play results of the games displayed on giant scoreboards. Baseball also swept up the second generation of many ethnic communities, providing both a focus for ethnic community pride and a symbol of integration into Canadian society.

Curling had originally been brought by Scots immigrants. By 1906 an Alberta Curling Association formalized inter-community play. Because of the opportunities it offered for sociability, curling rivalled hockey as Alberta's favourite winter sport. By the 1920s curling had spread beyond the city and town elites to rural Alberta, where it brought farmers and townspeople together.

Basketball also surged in popularity during the 1920s, particularly in southern Alberta and among women. The dominant forces in men's basketball were several small Mormon communities in southern Alberta where the churches were active social and recreational centres. The recreation halls, often part of the churches, were multi-purpose centres used for dances, plays, concerts, and basketball games. The churches and schools in these towns served as training grounds for several provincial and even national basketball championship teams. During the 1920s and 1930s, the Raymond Union Jacks dominated Alberta senior men's basketball (winning fifteen provincial titles between 1921 and 1941), and in 1923 they won the national men's championship.

The Alberta sports sensation of the 1920s was in women's basketball with the world-champion Edmonton Commercial Grads. Their story embodies a number of developments of the 1920s—the emancipation of women in sports, civic boosterism, sports promotion, and the development of spectator sports. From their beginnings in 1915 until they disbanded in 1940, the Grads played 522 games and won 502. At four Olympics, the team won twenty-seven consecutive games. From 1922 to 1939, they won every Canadian title except one.

Teacher Percy Page organized the team, made up of students and graduates of Edmonton's McDougall Commercial High School, in 1915. The popularity of the Grads increased dramatically in 1923, when Edmonton sports promoter W. F. "Deacon" White brought in an American team to compete with them. With the support of local service clubs and the media, the Grads began drawing crowds of up to 6500.

When the Grads were victorious at the 1924 Paris Olympics, they returned to a tumultuous celebration with almost 20,000 fans at Market Square. Percy Page was eventually able to translate his fame into a political career, first as an Edmonton MLA (beginning in 1940), then as house leader for the provincial Progressive Conservative party, and from 1959 to 1965 as lieutenant governor of Alberta.

Alberta Women: Politics and Change

The 1920s was a period of transition for women. Women experimented in areas such as sports, fought for better legal status, and participated more in politics at the provincial, municipal, and school board levels. Nellie McClung served as a Liberal MLA and Irene Parlby as a UFA cabinet minister. As minister without portfolio in the UFA government, Parlby was outspoken on issues of importance to women, especially those in the United Farm Women of Alberta. These issues included a minimum wage for women, mothers' allowances, homesteads for women, married women's property rights, and children's welfare. In Calgary, several women in the labour movement served on the school board and city council. Marion Carson, Amelia Turner, and Edith Patterson all ran successfully as labour candidates. Turner, who served for twelve years on the school board, ran unsuccessfully as the first CCF candidate in Canada in a 1933 provincial by-election in Calgary.

Some working- and middle-class urban women decided to support labour parties, which they saw as vehicles in the fight for economic and legal justice. The radical Women's Labour League, established in 1919 to support the Winnipeg General Strike, had small locals in Alberta throughout the 1920s in urban areas and mining towns. They advocated prison reform, old age pensions, and civil rights. Their demands for equal pay and birth control information were out of step with the more sizable and powerful conservative women's groups such as the Imperial Order of the Daughters of the Empire (IODE) and the WCTU. When they affiliated with the Communist Party, they also collided with women in the socialist Canadian Labour Party, which was strongly anti-communist.

Despite these divisions, one political issue that united most women's groups during the 1920s was peace. The Women's International League for Peace and Freedom (WILPF) came to western Canada in the early 1920s. It attacked cadet training in schools and militarism in school textbooks. In 1927, at the height of its strength, WILPF was joined by seventeen United Farm Women of Alberta locals and the Alberta WCTU. During the 1930s, the movement was closely allied with the left wing of the United Church and the socialist CCF before it declined during World War II. From the 1920s to the present, Alberta women have provided the backbone for a small yet articulate peace movement.

Although during the 1920s women were able to make some advances in the political realm, the vast majority of married women remained in the roles of wife and mother. Women's work outside the home was carefully circumscribed. It was assumed that only single women would work at careers, and would only be in the work force during the time between graduating from school and getting married. Only 3 per cent of married women worked outside the home. When women teachers married, they were expected to resign their positions, and the civil service did not employ married women.

Women were channelled into jobs consistent with their presumed interests—domestic work, nursing, teaching, and office work. Almost 90 per cent of Alberta professional women were teachers or nurses. Of the teachers in the public school system, 85 per cent were women, but they were paid less than men, and there were few female principals. Nor were there many women in business. Boards of trade and the exclusive clubs of the urban business and professional class did not accept women. New fields were opening up for women, however, in library work, social work, and home economics.

Those who worked in the home found their lives changed by new

The Edmonton Grads basketball team in 1926. The 1920s was Alberta's golden age of sport, and the Grads were one of the most successful and best known teams in the history of the province. The 1920s was a period of change for women in many areas, including sports. *(Glenbow Archives NA 3878-3)*

technology. As the distribution of electricity widened, new and improved appliances such as washing machines, electric irons, stoves, and vacuum cleaners became much more widely available. Magazines and newspapers provided an avalanche of advice for women on consumerism and how to apply scientific management principles to the household.

Although the economic status of women did not change significantly during the 1920s, their social status did. The social revolution affecting women in other parts of North America—new fashions, dance crazes, hair styles, make-up, and courtship patterns—all had an impact in Alberta. Experimentation was aided by magazines, movies, and cars. For young women, university education was possible, if rare. For most rural women, there were many opportunities for exposure to new trends, even as they pursued traditional careers. Farm girls who left home to study nursing, home economics, teaching, dressmaking, or stenography encountered a new set of urban values. They developed new interests in drama, public speaking, music, and sports, and freed themselves from some of the courtship restraints of home. Many stayed in the cities.

Frontier practicality occasionally opened new opportunities for women. The UFA government was having difficulties getting doctors to practice in the isolated Peace River district, which had a high infant mortality rate. When Dr. Emma Mary Johnstone, a visiting physician from England, offered to serve in the North, it responded to the offer for her services. Johnstone had been born to an English family in India in 1879. She returned to England to medical school, where she studied psychiatry. She had heard about the Peace River country from the Anglican Fellowship of the Maple Leaf, which wanted to aid settlers in remote pioneer areas, and Johnstone subsequently came to Canada and offered her services to the UFA health minister, George Hoadley. Health officials were glad to get women doctors for the Peace River district, since it was felt they could care for women and children, and in the opinion of some, were less likely to succumb to alcohol. She was sent to Wanham, a small community populated mainly by English war veterans, Norwegians, Swedes, and Scots-Canadian families. She was provided with a small cabin where homesteads were just being carved out of the brush. For transportation she depended on walking or hitching a ride with a passing horse and wagon. Johnstone was impressed by the capacity of pioneer women to work hard and make a success of their farms, as they gardened, cared for their children, and created a close-knit pioneer community.

Johnstone then returned to England to recruit other women doctors. One who came in 1929 was Mary Percy (later Jackson), who became a legend in the North because of her willingness to cover vast distances to serve her patients. In her first year, she was responsible for covering 350 square miles (906 square kilometres) from her fourteen-by twenty-foot shack near Peace River. She served not only as doctor, but as nurse, druggist, social worker, veterinarian, and dentist. After her marriage in 1931, she moved farther north with her husband to Keg River, where she first practiced out of her husband's trading post. Her largely native patients paid her in moosemeat, berries, and moccasins. As the only doctor between Manning and Fort Vermilion, Dr. Jackson fought an uphill battle against the ravages of tuberculosis among the natives.

Although the momentum of the suffragist movement was largely lost during the 1920s, a few activists continued the struggle for full legal equality. The case that brought women's rights activists in Alberta to national attention during this time was the "Persons Case." A landmark event, one that would have enormous and continuing symbolic significance for women throughout the country, this case hinged on the constitutional question of whether or not women were, in the legal sense, "persons," and hence, under the terms of the British North America Act, eligible for appointment to the Senate. This bizarre legal issue first emerged after the appointment of Alice Jamieson as a judge of the juvenile court in Calgary in 1914. Male lawyers challenged her presence on the bench on the grounds that she was not a "person" and therefore not eligible to hold office. In 1918 the Alberta Supreme Court ruled against this challenge.

This did not settle the legal issue. In 1919 women's organizations across Canada began pressing the federal government to appoint women to the Senate; their candidate was Edmonton's Emily Murphy. The federal government refused because of uncertainty over the constitutional interpretation of the word "persons."

In 1927 Murphy became aware of a legal provision that enabled five people to petition the government for a constitutional ruling. She turned to the other leading women's rights activists to be her co-appellants—Henrietta Muir Edwards, Nellie McClung, Louise McKinney, and Irene Parlby. The Supreme Court decided in 1928 that women were not legally persons. The women appealed the case to the Judicial Committee of the Privy Council (JCPC) in Britain, then

Canada's ultimate court of appeal. In October 1929, the JCPC reversed the Supreme Court's decision, ruling that women were "persons" and hence prospective senators.

This significant decision influenced the full legal status of women in Canada, and was the high point of the struggle for women's rights in Alberta. Mackenzie King did appoint a woman to the Senate; however, because of partisan considerations, his choice was not Emily Murphy, a Conservative. It was not until 1979 that an Alberta woman, farm women's leader Martha Bielish, a Conservative, was appointed to the Senate.

The Arts in the Interwar Years

During the interwar years, Alberta's small population base, closeness to frontier conditions, and economic difficulties all impeded development of the arts. Writers and artists could hardly make a living.

Robert Stead and Nellie McClung were Alberta's best known novelists. Stead came to Calgary from his native Manitoba to work for the *Albertan* in 1912, and in 1913 became chief publicist for the CPR. During the war, his prairie adventure novels *The Bail Jumper* (1914), *The Homesteaders* (1916), and *The Cowpuncher* (1918) expressed the view that the West was a breeding ground for a superior race, a democratic frontier of freedom and independence. Stead idealized the pioneer farmer as the soul of the nation. Despite his popularity, Stead could not support himself with his writing. In 1919 he left Calgary to become publicity director for the Department of Immigration and Colonization in Ottawa. Nellie McClung was another major fiction writer living in Alberta. Defeated as a Liberal candidate in the 1926 provincial election, McClung continued to publish collections of short stories and newspaper collections. In 1925 she published her last novel, *Painted Fires*. In this melodramatic novel, McClung used the story of a young Finnish immigrant, who finds herself at a disadvantage in Canada because she is both an immigrant and a woman, to crusade for a potpourri of causes—feminism, prohibition, and penal reform.

Interest and activity in drama flourished during the interwar years, though theatre in Alberta was not professional. From the 1890s to World War I, touring vaudeville road shows and dramatic companies had visited the cities, presenting comedies, farces, and romantic dramas, and featuring entertainers such as the Marx brothers, Jimmy Durante, and Stan Laurel, who would later star in movies. These touring companies were largely replaced during the 1920s and 1930s by a lively amateur "Little Theatre" movement. It had the support of the University of Alberta's Faculty of Extension, which gave training and advice to amateur groups and maintained a lending library of scripts: in 1924, the department provided scripts to over two hundred communities. Radio also promoted amateur drama, since the university's CKUA broadcast numerous plays.

English-born and Ontario-educated Elizabeth Sterling Haynes, who lived in Edmonton, was one of the key forces in the development of drama; in 1928 she helped establish the Alberta Drama League, which sponsored annual drama festivals. In 1933 she was appointed provincial drama director for the University of Alberta's Faculty of Extension. The university and the provincial Department of Education jointly sponsored drama classes that led to the establishment in the mid-1930s of the Banff School of Theatre.

The Banff School was the depression-born brainchild of E. A. (Ned) Corbett of the University of Alberta. It began in 1933 as a summer program, with Elizabeth Sterling Haynes as instructor for the first 130 students. By the mid-1930s the Banff Theatre School had become the Banff School of Fine Arts. In 1935 Corbett was succeeded by Donald Cameron. The son of Scots immigrants who came to Alberta in 1906, Cameron gained a strong sense of the needs of small communities from his rural roots, and from the example of his father, who was for many years a UFA member of the legislature. This background, combined with his executive ability and his education, both at the University of Alberta and in Europe, admirably equipped Cameron to direct the Banff school. He devoted himself to this task until his retirement in 1969. The school was attended by many painters and writers including, among others, Alberta playwright Gwen Pharis Ringwood, who grew up in Magrath.

English emigré painters A. C. Leighton, Walter Phillips, and H. G. Glyde attracted an impressive group of faculty and students to the Banff school from the 1930s through the post-World War II period. In 1933 Leighton, an intense, hardworking, and talented perfectionist, started the summer school that became the painting department of the Banff School. He came to Calgary in 1929 from England to become head of the art program at the Provincial Institute of Technology and Art. He took over following the unexpected death in 1929 of Norwegian Impressionist Lars Haukness, who had first introduced commercial art classes at the institute in 1926. Leighton made a broad-ranging contribution to Alberta art by stimulating other artists, partly through the Alberta Society of Artists, which he helped establish in 1931. Englishmen H. G. Glyde, known for his figure painting and historical allegories, and Walter Phillips, known for both his landscape watercolours and his colour woodcuts, also taught at the Provincial Institute and at the Banff Centre during the summers. There were joined by many other famous North American landscape painters, including Group of Seven notable A. Y. Jackson. Collectively, they helped establish the landscape tradition that has continued to dominate Alberta art to the present.

Two other artists who began their careers in the 1920s and 1930s were Maxwell Bates and W. L. Stevenson, both trained at the Provincial Institute in Calgary. They experimented with the ideas of French modernism. Given conservative art tastes in a relatively small provincial city, their work was not immediately appreciated. In 1928 the two were forbidden from exhibiting with the Calgary Art Club because of their unorthodox styles. Despite their talent, both had to earn a living at other occupations until the 1960s.

Music, like drama, combined a strong amateur movement and growing provincial organization with a fledgling professional base. While most group music in the interwar years consisted of brass and dance bands and choral music, classical music also gained a broader audience. International booking companies brought in light and grand operas to the two largest cities. Musical clubs sponsored lectures and recitals, and an annual Alberta music festival promoted new talent and encouraged music appreciation. The Calgary Symphony, which was inaugurated in 1913 only to collapse during the war, was revived in 1928 with amateur musicians. Edmonton also established a Symphony Orchestra. In 1935 the Edmonton Civic Opera Society began regular performances with local amateur talent. The university supported music through its extension program, and eventually, in 1946, the provincial government established the Alberta Music Board, which promoted music in a number of ways, including sponsoring concerts by Alberta artists.

The interwar years were not ones of immense creativity in the arts due in part to both economic problems and psychological factors inherent in a frontier society. Nonetheless, particularly in urban areas, an amateur base had been created in writing, drama, painting, and music. A small core of dedicated professionals, with limited government support, had also nurtured the seeds that would flower after the war.

Church Union and the Growth of Fundamentalism

The impact of radio and the growing uneasiness over social change were evident in the growth during the interwar years of a wide variety of competing fundamentalist Protestant sectarian groups. Though their numbers remained proportionately small (roughly 10 per cent of the population), the fundamentalist sects that grew and developed in rural Alberta, and to a lesser extent among the urban working and lower middle class, ultimately had a strong social and even political impact on the province.

Fundamentalist advances during the 1920s and 1930s owed much to radio evangelists. The significance of fundamentalism and of radio evangelism would become apparent during the Depression of the 1930s, when William Aberhart, founder of a Calgary-based fundamentalist Baptist sect and a Bible college, as well as a radio evangelist, developed Social Credit into the most powerful social and political movement in Alberta's history.

A variety of factors during the 1920s eroded the moral authority of the mainline Protestant denominations, whose political and social power had first become evident during the war in their successful prohibition drive. During the 1920s, their missions to new immigrants faltered, their efforts to protect prohibition ended in failure, and they faced growing challenges from both secularism and smaller Protestant sects. Asserting their authority as guardians of Canadian public morality became increasingly difficult. Many veterans resented church sanction of the killing they had witnessed in the trenches in Europe. In addition, prohibition did not turn out to be the panacea that many people had expected. The struggle to retain prohibition in the early 1920s drained the churches' energies.

The drive to achieve church union during the early 1920s also focussed the energy of the two largest Protestant churches, the Methodists and Presbyterians, on their internal group dynamics. Alberta Methodists were overwhelmingly in favour of church union, but the debate in the Presbyterian Church proved to be a bitter one, in Alberta as elsewhere. Two of the leading opponents of church union in the country were the Rev. David McQueen, the highly respected minister of First Presbyterian Church in Edmonton and longtime civic leader, and the Rev. W. G. Brown of Red Deer.

When the churches finally merged in 1925 as the United Church of Canada, several of the largest and wealthiest Presbyterian churches in the cities and 75 per cent of the Presbyterian churches in the Red Deer presbytery decided against the union. In Alberta, 550 Methodist, 572 Presbyterian, and 24 Congregational churches joined, while 40 Presbyterian churches voted to stay out. The struggles and conflict within churches, families, and individual consciences over the issue of church union focussed the churches' attention away from broader social concerns of the 1920s.

A number of other factors also contributed to the problems that the mainline Protestant denominations, and the Catholic and Orthodox churches, had in responding to the needs of rural and working-class Albertans, thus contributing to a religious vacuum that was partially filled by Protestant sects. Institutional inflexibility and central control in the larger churches opened the way for smaller churches. These sects were usually organized and controlled on a local congregational basis and could thus adapt quickly to local needs. They also depended on local lay leadership rather than a professional clergy and were, therefore, not dependent on the availability of outside clergy, or on the ability of the congregation to pay a minister's salary.

In contrast, the more centralized larger churches with their headquarters in eastern Canada or the U.S. "were...separated from the Alberta scene both by distance and by differences in social and cultural outlook."[8] Since their educational requirements for clergy were much more stringent than the fundamentalist sects, the major churches also found it harder to secure local clergy who were sensitive to the needs of rural communities and working-class neighbourhoods in the cities. It should be noted, however, that despite the difficulties the main Protestant churches experienced during this period, for decades the Alberta membership of the new United Church of Canada outnumbered the combined membership of all the province's approximately forty fundamentalist Protestant sects.

Most of the fundamentalist sects were brought by immigrants from the rural American Midwest. They proved to be sufficiently flexible to meet the needs of people of many different backgrounds, particularly those of lower economic or social status such as poverty-stricken farmers and people of non-Anglo-Saxon and/or working-class backgrounds. They grew through natural increase, through appeals to the unchurched, and by attracting nominal members of larger Protestant, Catholic, and Orthodox bodies. The strong degree of lay participation and informality, and the close social bonds in the sects, harmonized with the social ideals and needs of frontier society. Prayer meetings, revival meetings, and summer camp meetings that included all family members provided a full round of emotionally stimulating and satisfying activities.

While the growth of sects during the early stages of pioneering prior to World War I was slow, by the 1920s they were beginning to make some major advances. New Bible schools and radio evangelism contributed greatly to their success. The aim of Bible schools was both to provide a Christian education for prairie youth, and to produce pastors for local fundamentalist churches and missionaries to "foreign lands." Four new Bible schools opened in Alberta in each decade of the 1920s, 1930s, and 1940s. The largest was the Prairie Bible Institute (PBI), founded at Three Hills in 1922. A local family, the Kirks, who had come west from Ontario, hired a twenty-six-year-old Kansas Bible student, Leslie Maxwell, to start a school in order to teach their children and their neighbours' children more about the Bible. Maxwell was energetic and forceful, and by the 1940s he had built the PBI into one of the largest Bible schools in North America. Maxwell remained the dominant force until his retirement in 1982. In the post-World War II era, he became known across North America in evangelical circles for his bestselling religious books including *World Missions: Total War* and *Born Crucified*, which emphasized an introspective, puritanical, mystical, and fundamentalist Christianity.

The students from PBI and other Bible schools provided religious leadership in rural and urban Alberta and also worked in foreign missions. Many people in the Third World first heard of Alberta, and often of Canada, either through contact with evangelical missionaries trained in the province's Bible schools or from the hundreds of Mormon missionaries from southern Alberta.

One of the smaller Bible schools in the province, the Calgary Prophetic Bible Institute, established by William Aberhart in 1927, had the greatest political impact on Alberta. Aberhart's radio broadcasts, begun on CFCN, a Calgary radio station, in 1925, eventually reached an audience of three hundred thousand. Aberhart built up this audience through his "flair for making religious instruction simple and entertaining,"[9] his strident attacks on religious modernists, and his detailed exposition of future world events, based on biblical prophecy.

Although Aberhart was the most successful radio evangelist, other evangelists and sects also saw the potential of radio. In 1927, the Christian and Missionary Alliance bought radio station CHMA in Edmonton and sold air time to other denominations. The growth of the Pentecostal Assemblies, Nazarenes, Swedish Baptists, Seventh Day Adventists, and Jehovah's Witnesses was often closely related to their success in radio. The fastest-growing sects and Bible schools were usually those that pioneered in radio evangelism. These religions provided a sense of security in a society in transition, one in which traditional religious values and doctrines were being questioned on many fronts.

Many of the major developments in Alberta during the 1920s reflected broader trends in the prairie region and in Canada. The mass media made Albertans aware of their isolation and of broader social trends. Paradoxically, as elsewhere in Canada, the influence of both Canadian nationalism and American popular culture grew.

Developments in Alberta paralleled those in the other prairie provinces in a number of ways. During the 1920s Albertans, like other prairie dwellers, saw the collapse of the OBU and other setbacks to organized labour. They struggled over prohibition, and watched the rise of the nativist Ku Klux Klan and the rise and gradual decline of the Progressive Party. They participated in the struggle to develop the wheat pools. Religious debates over the new United Church and the clash between fundamentalism and modernism rocked church halls across the prairies. Municipal governments faced serious problems related to over-expansion and indebtedness, legacies of the prewar boom. Albertans also speculated wildly in the stock market during the late 1920s.

Despite these similarities, other developments made Alberta unique. Southeast Alberta felt most acutely the effects of drought, massive depopulation, and the disintegration of social institutions. Political alienation and agrarian radicalism on the prairies found fullest formal expression in the Ginger Group, and Albertans were more interested than other Canadians in monetary and banking reform. Irrigated farming, coal mining (and its radical political subculture), oil, and tourism also set Alberta apart. Though fundamentalist sects grew elsewhere on the prairies, in Alberta they built a stronger network of Bible schools and used radio in more innovative ways to broadcast their message.

The 1920s was a period of transition. Despite boom-bust economic cycles, sizable movements of people, and continuing ethnic, religious, and class tensions, the passage of time, the shared effort involved in building the institutions of a new society, and modern technology contributed to a growing sense of community. New professional, business, sports, political, and cultural clubs and institutions provided a net of organizations operating within a provincial context. A new regional and provincial identity had emerged out of the experiences of pioneering, war, and regional protest.

CHAPTER NINE

The Crisis Years and the Rise of Social Credit

The 1930s was a period of crisis. Albertans experienced the most intense economic depression, the greatest class and political conflict, and the most labour and social violence, along with the slowest population growth and the greatest challenges in agriculture in the province's history. Protectionist economic policies and economic depression in Europe cut off food imports from Canada and wheat prices plunged—from $1.24 per bushel for #1 wheat in 1929–30 to $0.64 per bushel in 1930–31. Because of this price collapse and low yields, net farm income slid from $102 million in 1928 to only $5 million in 1933, the low point of the Depression. Average per capita income in the province declined from $548 in 1928–29, third highest in the country, to $212 in 1933, well below the national average.

This drop in prices for agricultural goods precipitated a vicious cycle. Farmers stopped buying. Railways and coal mines cut back on their operations, and shops laid off their employees. The collapse of prices, coupled with prolonged drought and soil drifting in southern and east-central Alberta, brought many farmers to the brink of disaster. They were seen lining up at the railway sidings with teams and wagons, waiting to get their dole of hay and grain for their stock, and food for their families. In winter, rural children often had to miss school because they lacked adequate clothing.

In the cities, bread lines, soup kitchens, make-work relief projects, protest marches, and confrontations between police and unemployed workers became routine. Desperate young men rode the rails in search of work, panhandled for food, and found "shelter" in urban hobo "jungles." An increase in domestic strife, divorce, and suicide reflected the growing stress caused by economic hardship.

Many turned to political panaceas to help them understand and change their circumstances. The UFA, once the bright hope for the future, came to be seen as just another old-line party. Some of the

The Great Depression brought many farmers to the brink of disaster. Here, farmers are lined up at the railway siding at Lomond in the southern Alberta dry belt, waiting to get their dole of hay and grain for the stock and food for their families. Their poverty and continual struggle made many rural Albertans desperate for some ray of hope. *(Glenbow Archives NA 1308-13)*

working class flirted with the Communist Party of Canada, while radical farm leaders tried to take the remains of the UFA into the socialist CCF. The political sensation of the 1930s, attracting attention throughout the English-speaking world, was Social Credit, a new and dynamic movement offering to cure a sick economy. Its charismatic leader, William Aberhart, met the needs of a people hungry for authoritative guidance.

Many questions about Social Credit continue to intrigue. Why was Alberta the only province during the 1930s to turn to Social Credit? How radical was Social Credit in its early years? Who were its main supporters? Why did Alberta embrace Social Credit and remain loyal for over three decades while neighbouring Saskatchewan, with a similar economic and social base, largely shunned radicalism during the 1930s, and then turned to the socialist CCF? A complex interaction among economic, social, and political forces shaped life in Alberta during the 1930s.

The Impact of the Depression

Because of the Depression, Alberta's population remained stagnant during the 1930s. The increase from 730,000 in 1931 to 796,000 in 1941 was smaller than in any other decade in the twentieth century.

The birth rate declined as the marriage rate dropped and people postponed having families. Discouraged people left, hoping for brighter economic prospects in British Columbia or Ontario, and Alberta's growth did not even keep pace with natural increase. The federal government virtually halted immigration. It was responding to the changing economic climate and to pressure from various groups; in Alberta these included veterans, labour, and the provincial UFA government. New federal regulations limited immigrants to close family members, farmers with substantial amounts of capital, and British subjects and American citizens with financial means. From 1931 to 1939, only 12,500 immigrants arrived in the province.

In the the dry belt of eastern Alberta, which endured year after year of drought, more farmers abandoned their land. Family after family fled down the province's roads with their household effects and machinery piled high on horse-drawn hayracks or old trucks, headed for wetter areas. In southeastern and eastern Alberta, entire rural communities were abandoned and lands were taken for taxes, completing the process of depopulation that had begun after 1910. Farm families relocated to irrigated areas in southwestern Alberta, to the parkbelt of north-central Alberta, to the Peace River district, or to the cities. Six out of nine census divisions in central and southern Alberta lost population. Schools and churches closed.

Cities grew only minimally. Despite the first sizable discovery of crude oil in nearby Turner Valley in 1936, Calgary grew only slightly, from 84,000 in 1931 to 89,000 in 1941. Crude oil was discovered by Turner Valley Royalties, owned by George Bell, publisher of the Calgary *Albertan*, and R. A. "Bob" Brown, superintendent of the City of Calgary electric light department. The discovery revolutionized financing in the oil industry. Instead of selling common stock, they committed 70 per cent of the production of their wells to royalty payments. Their strike led to the third and last boom in Turner Valley.

During this period, Edmonton grew more than Calgary, from 80,000 in 1931 to 94,000 by 1941. This growth partly reflected agricultural development in the wetter areas of northern Alberta, and farm people moving into the city. Edmonton was also developing further as the air service centre to the north, supplying goldmining enterprises in the Northwest Territories. By 1937, forty-two planes operated out of Edmonton. One of the many daring bush pilots was Grant McConachie, who began Yukon Southern Transport Ltd. and pioneered in building airstrips throughout the north. During the 1940s, Canadian Pacific Airlines bought out his firm, and he subsequently became president of CP Air.

In southern Alberta, Lethbridge and Medicine Hat scarcely grew at all. Lethbridge itself didn't suffer as badly as Medicine Hat from drought, since extensive irrigation projects nearby guaranteed crops. However, it was hard hit by the slump in coal mining. Medicine Hat's diverse industrial base protected it from the massive depopulation that occurred in the surrounding rural areas.

Unemployment and relief were among the most troubling problems facing the urban centres. Always a seasonal problem in the 1920s, unemployment began to rise dramatically; roughly 20 to 25 per cent of the labour force was unemployed throughout the early 1930s. By 1932, 12 per cent of Calgary's population, 13 per cent of Edmonton's, 8 per cent of Medicine Hat's, and 20 per cent of Lethbridge's received relief. The financial burden on the municipalities and the province brought both to the brink of bankruptcy.

Having to go on relief was usually profoundly humiliating. Inexperienced and unsuitable staff in relief agencies were often harsh and uncaring. Unemployed workers began staging protests in the cities in the winter of 1929–30, becoming more and more vocal in subsequent years. The unemployed paraded through the streets and department stores, and these demonstrations often ended in violence with the police.

Urban mayors such as Andy Davison in Calgary and Dan Knott in Edmonton, both originally elected with substantial labour support, became unsympathetic to the unemployed. In 1931 Edmonton officials issued orders prohibiting transients from coming to the city. Calgary city council fought an ongoing battle with the unemployed over relief policy. Hard-pressed municipal governments, facing financial crisis and fearing immigrant radicalism, turned over immigrants who had not yet been granted citizenship to federal authorities for deportation as a way of keeping down relief costs. From 1930 to 1934, the federal government deported over 2500 immigrants from the province. Cities, towns, and villages cut expenditures on public works, recreation, and transportation.

The Working Class Rebels

The economic collapse and the upsurge of discrimination against new immigrants created conditions ripe for the spread of radical political movements. In the early 1930s, the Communist Party made inroads in organizing the urban unemployed and immigrants. Some middle-class Albertans became concerned about the possibility of a communist revolt.

While the Communist Party had attracted some support in the 1920s, primarily among immigrant miners, it expanded its following throughout the 1930s. Most of the strikes and marches in the early 1930s were organized by affiliates of the Communist Party such as the Farmers' Unity League (FUL), the Workers' Unity League (WUL), unemployed workers' associations, and the Young Communist League. The FUL gained particular strength among some Ukrainian farmers in northeast Alberta and led a series of grain strikes, where farmers refused to deliver grain because of low prices and dishonest grading practices by the grain companies. Although the Communist Party itself was banned by the federal government in 1931 and its leaders arrested, it continued to function through these related organizations.

During the 1930s, many of the immigrants who had arrived in the 1920s and earlier had to cope simultaneously with the traumas of economic crisis, culture shock, and family separation. These difficulties were compounded by hostile public opinion, and civic officials who discriminated against them in relief payments or attempted to deport them. Unemployed Chinese immigrants, most of whom had been in Canada since before World War I, received a relief allowance of only $1.12 per week compared to $2.50 per week for single non-Chinese. Government officials used their own stereotypes about the "low standard of living" of the Chinese to justify giving them smaller payments. A Calgary alderwoman stated bluntly: "White people...should be looked after before the Chinese."[1] Officials decided in May 1936 to cut some off relief altogether, and in December 1936 three single unemployed Chinese in Calgary died of malnutrition. Although Chinese immigrants were not a particularly fertile ground for communist organizers, the callousness of officials toward them was typical of the attitudes that turned many immigrants to support the left.

The ethnic left provided a counterculture for many European immigrants, although only among Hungarians and Finns did the communists numerically rival the non-communists. Communist-dominated organizations such as the FUL and WUL were led mostly by Britons experienced in the British labour movement, but 95 per cent of the communists during the 1930s were central and eastern European immigrants. Determined Communist organizers such as Jan Lakeman in Edmonton, Harvey Murphy in the Crow's Nest Pass, and Irishman Patrick Lenihan in Calgary (who organized the Calgary unemployed and was elected a Calgary alderman in 1938) challenged government callousness. They advocated working-class solidarity and condemned ethnic discrimination. Strong "foreign" language affiliates to the Communist Party, such as the Ukrainian Labour Farmer Temple Association (ULFTA), the Hungarian Mutual Benefit Federation, and the Finnish Organization of Canada, combined radical ideology with insurance benefits, sports, and cultural activities. Thirty-nine of 101 ULFTA labour temples in Canada were in Alberta, more than in any other province. The immigrants were joined by young, idealistic Canadians who felt the left had, as one supporter put it:

> an explanation for the troubles plaguing our society...Most important of all, they had a program of action, based on unity of labour and farmers to compel government to take immediate remedial action...it was the communists who led most struggles for jobs, for relief, against wage cuts.[2]

There was, however, a price for supporting the left: police surveillance, harassment, and arrests. Many immigrants were denied citizenship papers or deported because of their political activity.

The most intense class conflict occurred in the mining camps. The Depression led to a dramatic cut in the use of coal. Alberta's production decreased by a third. Coal miners were seriously underemployed; one or two days of work a week was the most any miner could expect. The miners' resentment over this situation was intensified by what many saw as blatant job discrimination and favouritism by pit-bosses.

The Workers' Unity League, formed in 1930, led the workers' struggles in the coalfields. Radicals within the Mine Workers Union of Canada (MWUC), an amalgam of moderates and communists that had replaced the UMWA in the coalfields in the mid-1920s, subsequently attempted to convince the union to join the Workers' Unity League. This effort led to violent strikes in the Coal Branch and the Crow's Nest Pass in 1930 and 1932. In July 1930 the MWUC called a strike at Mercoal in the Coal Branch and tried to prevent other miners from strikebreaking. Violence between strikers and supporters of the UMWA (who opposed the MWUC) evoked a forceful response from the government, which sent 120 provincial police constables equipped with a machine gun to end the strike.

A similar strike in the Crow's Nest Pass in 1932 led to a bitter struggle, renewing class and ethnic tensions. Early in 1932 a rumour predicted wage cuts. In late February, 1400 miners went on strike.

Wives and children joined in mass demonstrations and picketing. In early May, seventy-five RCMP and a handful of strikebreakers faced 1200 pickets at the Bellevue mine. In the ensuing riot, the police used batons against the strikers, who retaliated with rocks and threw pepper in the policemen's eyes. Mine owners, Protestant clergy, businessmen, and newspapers demanded government action to rid the country of dangerous "foreign reds." Strikers at Coleman returned to work in May after a narrow vote won by workers distressed by immigrant radicalism. Strikers in the other mines, living off game and contributions from sympathizers elsewhere, continued their strike until Labour Day, when Premier Brownlee personally intervened.

While the strike brought little in the way of concrete advances, it did leave a legacy of radicalism. In February 1933, Blairmore elected a workers' slate to the town council and school board. The council then proclaimed May Day a civic holiday and renamed the town's main street Tim Buck Boulevard, after the national communist leader.

Growing class and ethnic tension, and the inability of the UFA government to respond effectively, was symbolized by the communist-led hunger march on Edmonton in December 1932. On December 20, several thousand farmers, miners, and unemployed workers converged on the city, demanding unemployment insurance, cash relief, cancellation of interest on debts, and abolition of seizures by creditors. Brownlee worried about the possibility of riots and, together with Edmonton city officials, refused a parade permit. The protesters, however, were determined, having been stung by statements similar to those of the editor of the *Vegreville Observer* on December 21, 1932: "Most of these people brought their trouble on themselves, by poor management, by improvident living, by reckless expenditure in good times, by sheer, downright laziness." Brownlee asked for special assistance from the RCMP, who obliged with hundreds of heavily armed reinforcements. When the police raided the marchers' headquarters, they failed to discover any firearms, though they did find a group of Ukrainian women cooking turkey for the marchers.

Several thousand demonstrators converged on Market Square, planning to march to the legislature. The police intervened. The *Edmonton Bulletin* of December 21 described the ensuing battle: "Police batons rose and fell, skulls were cracked, men and women were trampled underfoot and the hoarse roars of angry men echoed for two hours in downtown streets." Police jailed several strike leaders. The government's response confirmed cynicism about those in power, including the UFA. In Edmonton, disenchantment among unemployed workers with their Canadian Labour Party mayor, Dan Knott, was fed by Knott's decision to allow troops to break up the hunger march.

The "On to Ottawa Trek" by striking relief camp workers and the unemployed in the spring of 1935 highlighted the growing political and social unrest and the efforts of the left to organize these forgotten men to challenge the government. The mountain relief camps, which both the federal and provincial government organized in the early 1930s, generated considerable resentment because of low pay (the federal camps paid twenty cents per day), menial work, military discipline, and restrictions on how workers could spend their free time. Conditions in the camps were primitive and the men often lacked adequate clothing. Labour unrest and strikes in the relief camps were endemic, even though authorities made strong efforts to keep labour organizers out. For the workers, the camps became a symbol of all that was hated in the Bennett regime.

In the spring of 1935, relief camp workers in B.C. went on strike, determined to trek to Ottawa to present their demands. They were led by communist Arthur "Slim" Evans, who had previously worked in Alberta as a carpenter, farm hand, and miner. He had been a leading figure in the miners' section of the OBU and in the UMWA in Drumheller in the early 1920s, and spent time in jail for allegedly misappropriating union funds. The trek began in Vancouver on June 3, 1935. By the time it reached Calgary there were 1500 "trekkers," who arrived by clinging in the open to the tops of boxcars, fighting off cold, rain, coal dust, and cinders. Three hundred more men joined in Calgary, and they surrounded the local relief office until the provincial government agreed to supply them with two meals a day for two days while they regrouped. Although the trekkers garnered a good deal of public sympathy, government officials saw them as dangerous revolutionaries, and Bennett stopped them cold in Regina.

Some of these angry, disappointed, and radical men became part of the 1250 volunteers who joined the Mackenzie-Papineau Batallion to fight for the Spanish republic against Franco's fascists in the late 1930s. They included dozens of Ukrainians, Hungarians, and other immigrant radicals from the urban areas and mining camps, who had become part of the left-wing immigrant counter-culture. At least twenty-three men from Alberta lost their lives in the fight against fascism in Spain.

Many of the immigrant and native-born radicals were not dedicated communists, but were willing to follow those who would stand up for them. When Social Credit provided an alternative, most of them deserted the communists.

The Crisis in Agriculture

The combination of low grain prices, drought, and soil erosion made the 1930s a period of great change and challenge in the history of agriculture in Alberta. Between 1930 and 1937, southern Alberta experienced a severe drought. It brought dust storms, soil erosion, and serious grasshopper infestation. The combination of drought and inappropriate cultivation practices caused millions of acres to blow out of control. Dry and dusty as 1930 was, 1931 was worse. On October 9, clouds of dust blanketed all of southern Alberta. City traffic virtually halted, and daytime streetlights had little effect. Over time, on the farms, soil drifted to the tops of fences. By the mid-1930s, the CPR had to use snowplows to clear the tracks of soil drifts up to ten feet high.

The psychological impact of unrelenting wind, a film of dust covering everything, no crops, and the disappearance of the topsoil was devastating. Many farmers, and even some farm scientists, began to conclude that Palliser's Triangle really was a desert that could not be cultivated.

The struggle against soil drifting was won in the chinook belt of southwestern Alberta by collaboration between experts at the government-sponsored experimental farms and the farmers themselves. Their solutions included strip farming, the Noble blade, and the promotion of plowless fallow or "trash cover."

Before 1920, soil drifting in the windswept Nobleford and Monarch areas became so severe that two Dutch American settlers, Leonard and Arie Koole, experimented with the ideas of alternating long, narrow strips of crop and summer fallow running north and south to counter the effects of prevailing westerly winds. When soil drifting became severe in the 1930s, farm experts encouraged other farmers to try this method. It gradually became apparent, however, that strip farming solved only part of the problem. The recognition of the significance of "trash cover" came through the work of Utah-born soil scientist Asael E. Palmer, assistant superintendent of the Lethbridge experimental station. A former homesteader and a leader in the Mormon community, Palmer observed that summer fallowed fields that weren't ploughed, and where the stubble and other plant residue was left on the surface, were protected against wind action.

He became an ardent promoter of the idea of leaving a "trash cover" on the surface, and he was able to convince farmers to try a technique that offended their earlier ideas of good farming.

For trash cover to work effectively, a blade cultivator was needed to go under the stubble and kill the weeds. Farmers experimented with a wide variety of cultivators. C. S. Noble came up with the blade that changed cultivation techniques in prairie agriculture. Noble had come to Alberta from North Dakota in 1903, settling first in Claresholm, where he sold real estate and farmed, and then in Nobleford (named after him). By 1917, he operated a huge "bonanza" farm of 30,000 acres (12,000 hectares), requiring three hundred men at harvest time. By 1922, a series of crop failures and low wheat prices had forced him to give up his land to mortgage companies. Undeterred, he rented back part of the farm and by 1930 was again farming 8000 acres (3200 hectares).

In 1936, working in close contact with the Lethbridge research scientists, Noble devised a new blade cultivator that made the "trash cover" method workable. The V-shaped blade could slice through unplowed ground, kill weeds without burying the stubble, and operate in heavy stubble without clogging. Through the enthusiastic promotion of the Lethbridge researchers, the Noble blade attracted the attention of other farmers. Noble then transformed his farm machine shop into a factory. The Noble blade, strip farming, and trash cover attracted the attention of American soil conservationists, and their use spread steadily across the continent and eventually even to the Soviet Union.

Ultimately these new techniques of dryland agriculture helped save the southern part of the prairies. Through the Prairie Farm Rehabilitation Administration (PFRA), first established by the Bennett government in 1935, federal and provincial agricultural departments cooperated to publicize the effectiveness of the new soil conservation practices. The PFRA established demonstration substations across the dry belt. They were too late to prevent the evacuation of large parts of Palliser's Triangle, but the new techniques restored much of the damaged land. This made it possible for those who remained to farm or ranch successfully. The PFRA regrassed land that could not be cultivated and turned it into community pastures.

The province took over much of the abandoned land and turned it into "Special Areas." The Special Areas Act (1934) established a provincial board to administer regions with acute settlement problems. It provided hundreds of thousands of acres for private and community grazing, and helped in the transition to economically viable ranching/farming operations.

The UFA and the Agricultural Crisis

The UFA government's political dominance had been renewed in the June 1930 election, based on its record of successful northern railway development and the transfer of control of natural resources to the province. However, as the full force of the Depression was felt, support for the UFA eroded steadily.

In 1930 the developing crisis in the wheat markets absorbed the attention of the provincial government. Wheat pools were among the early victims as prices plummetted. They had expanded rapidly during the late 1920s, but in 1929 they were caught short. Their guaranteed initial payment of $1.00 per bushel of wheat was substantially too high. The prairie pools were forced to borrow extensively, on the basis of loan guarantees from the provincial governments. Late in 1930, as the pools' financial crises worsened, they turned for help to the newly elected Conservative government of R. B. Bennett in Ottawa.

These economic conditions led to the strident revival of all the traditional western grievances, along with outspoken demands for reform. The Brownlee government responded to the crisis with increased frugality, severely cutting back the civil service, shutting down agricultural colleges, shortening the school year, and reducing teachers' salaries. The provincial government initially rejected farmers' demands for seed and feed relief and a moratorium on debt. Premier Brownlee was convinced that, as he privately put it, "every concession made by the Government and every measure of relief given simply [served] to multiply the demands."[3] He felt that the problems of the Depression could only be solved on a national or international scale. Most Albertans, increasingly desperate, were unwilling to accept Brownlee's determination to cut costs and balance the budget, or his cautious explanations as to why others' solutions were unworkable.

In contrast the UFA organization, associated with the federal Ginger Group, was further radicalized by the Depression. The drift to the left in the UFA was apparent in 1931 when the aging Henry Wise Wood stepped down as president and was replaced by left-winger Robert Gardiner, a member of the Ginger Group. Norman Priestley, a former United Church minister and another socialist, became secre-

254

tary. Partly under their influence, the UFA convention passed resolutions urging public ownership of land, radio, and hydro-electric power, nationalization of the monetary system, drastic reduction of debts, and postponement of interest payments. The UFA executive called for a "Cooperative Commonwealth," which would transfer economic power from "entrenched private interests" to "bodies responsible solely to the people's representatives."[4]

In 1932 the Ginger Group helped form a new radical party, the socialist Cooperative Commonwealth Federation (CCF). They held their key organizational meeting in May 1932 in William Irvine's office in Ottawa. Six of the nine MPs who attended were UFA members. The CCF held their founding convention in July 1932 in Calgary, bringing together farm and labour groups from across Canada. Albertans such as Irvine and Priestley were crucial leaders in its national development.

The UFA's decision in 1932 to embrace socialism and join the CCF helped split the UFA and contributed to its inability to respond effectively to the Social Credit challenge. As the federal UFA turned leftward and the provincial government retreated into fiscal conservatism, Albertans were faced with the confusing spectacle of a UFA divided against itself, particularly since Brownlee's government studiously ignored the radical resolutions of UFA conventions.

Some historians have argued that the radicalism of the CCF alienated Albertans, who then turned to Social Credit as a less radical and more concrete means of dealing with the Depression. Others have suggested that the inability of the UFA organization to influence the conservative policies of the provincial UFA government caused its dramatic decline. Either way, in the depths of the Depression, Alberta's farmers had given the UFA a chance, and they decided to opt for a new political movement.

Scandal

The Depression and internal political conflict were devastating to the UFA government. Worse, two widely publicized scandals shook the government to its foundations. The Minister of Public Works was involved in a divorce trial in 1933 in which there was evidence of wife-swapping. Worse still, in November 1933 Edson mayor A. D. MacMillan and his daughter Vivian filed a statement of claim against Premier Brownlee. Vivian MacMillan, a young government stenographer, alleged that Brownlee had arranged a job for her, seduced her, and had sexual relations with her against her will. Brownlee was immediately immersed in the fight of his life, not only for his reputation and personal career, but for the survival of his government.

The trial, held in June 1934, received front-page coverage throughout the province and substantial coverage across North America. These stories highlighted the image of an immoral urban politician taking advantage of an innocent country girl. MacMillan claimed to have had a lengthy affair with a sex-crazed premier. Brownlee admitted only that she had become a close family friend. In a counter-suit (eventually dropped), Brownlee claimed that MacMillan and her boyfriend had conspired against him to obtain money and, with the help of the Liberals, were attempting to discredit his government. Although there were no witnesses, the all-male jury believed MacMillan's story and awarded damages to her and her father. The trial judge overruled the damage award. The legal appeals subsequently ground on until 1940, when the Privy Council in Britain upheld the original jury decision.

The scandal ended Brownlee's political career. In July 1934 he resigned as premier. One of his cabinet ministers, R. G. Reid, replaced him. In retrospect, it is unlikely that Brownlee's political opponents set up MacMillan to entrap him, but the Liberal lawyers who represented the MacMillans used the case to discredit him. They did little for the Liberal cause, however, succeeding only in paving the way for a morally untainted Social Credit movement.

When Social Credit eventually ran for office in 1935, it carried all the utopian promise once embodied in the UFA. Aberhart had a religious aura and the ability to attract religious and community leaders. Together these helped establish the trust necessary to motivate rural people to desert the UFA. Even without the scandals, it is unlikely the UFA could have survived the Social Credit groundswell.

"Bible Bill" and the Birth of Social Credit

William Aberhart, leader of the Social Credit movement, was a dynamic and complex personality. An educator and lay preacher, he had almost no interest in politics until he was in his fifties, shortly before he became premier of Alberta. Born in Ontario in 1878, Aberhart had been influenced by the dispensational theology of American fundamentalism, which emphasized biblical prophecy and the Second Coming of Christ. He began preaching as a Presbyterian layman in Brantford, Ontario (where he was also principal of a public

Calgary high school principal and fundamentalist lay preacher William Aberhart was converted to the Social Credit economic theories of British economic theorist Major C. H. Douglas in 1932. Through his organizational genius and his popular radio broadcasts on Calgary's CFCN radio, which after 1932 mixed religion and politics, Aberhart developed Social Credit into the most powerful social and political movement in Alberta's history. It swept to power in 1935, obliterating the UFA government. (*Glenbow Archives NA 2771-2*)

school), but decided against entering the ministry. After coming to Calgary in 1910, he plunged into the city's religious life and established Bible classes at various Presbyterian, Methodist, and Baptist churches between 1910 and 1916. In 1916 he began concentrating his activities at Westbourne Baptist Church and became the unofficial minister. Partly through donations from his CFCN radio audience, in 1927 Aberhart established the autonomous Calgary Prophetic Bible Institute, which eventually became the birthplace of the Social Credit movement. Though Aberhart was principal of Calgary's largest high school, Crescent Heights, his passion was the Bible Institute, and it absorbed all his spare time.

Carrying both high school and Bible school responsibilities, Aberhart often worked from 6 A.M. until the early hours of the following morning. He possessed unbounded self-confidence and exceptional powers of concentration and retention. In the groups with which he was involved, he characteristically assumed that he had the right answers and that those who disagreed with him were his enemies. This generated numerous conflicts. To his intensely loyal supporters, he was a man of conviction, willing to fight for others; to his critics, he was either a charlatan or a fool, misleading people in potentially destructive ways.

The first graduate of the Bible school was Ernest Manning, a farm boy from Saskatchewan who had heard Aberhart on the radio and determined to study under him. Manning, who was born in 1908, boarded with the Aberhart family. Aberhart was impressed with Manning's keen mind, resilient character, energy, and willingness, ultimately, to defer to Aberhart's authority. Aberhart had two daughters, but Manning became the son he lacked. After his graduation in 1930, Manning joined the Prophetic Bible Institute staff as a teacher. Throughout the rise of Social Credit, Manning was constantly at Aberhart's side. He would later become, at age thirty-four, a cabinet minister in Aberhart's first government. Eventually, as successor to Aberhart, Manning was Canada's longest-serving provincial premier.

The Depression was responsible for arousing Aberhart's interest in politics. In the summer of 1932, he was marking exams in Edmonton. Bewildered by the Depression, which demoralized his colleagues and his students, he needed something more hopeful than his earlier explanation that Alberta's climatic disturbances were attacks from the devil. Charles Scarborough, an Edmonton high school teacher, introduced Aberhart to Social Credit, an economic doctrine based on the ideas of a British engineer, Major C. H. Douglas. Aberhart was converted overnight.

Social Credit principles included a monetary theory that explained the inner workings of capitalism and offered a remedy for its unsatisfactory functioning in periods of economic depression. According to Douglas and his famous A plus B theorem, the paradox of "poverty in the midst of plenty" could be ended by printing and distributing "social dividends." This would keep purchasing power and productive capacity in balance. He believed that the power to issue or withhold credit was the power to control the commerce of the world. This power was in the hands of a small band of bankers and international financiers and had to be recaptured by "the people."

Beginning in August 1932, Aberhart introduced the new subject cautiously into his radio broadcasts. He claimed Social Credit was compatible with Christian beliefs. He deliberately mixed Social

Credit and prophecy, hoping to convert his audience to both. The response was positive. His goal was to educate the public, who would then demand that the UFA government investigate and implement Social Credit. Aberhart's new message of good and evil, hope and salvation, soon attracted followers who accepted him as a political leader as well as a religious one. He soon dropped the apolitical focus of the Bible Institute and, while continuing its religious education, turned it into a training centre for Social Credit.

Social Credit, as an alternative to both socialism and capitalism, could appeal to almost all sectors of the population. Douglas's theories did not advocate overthrowing capitalism, but rather controlling the financial interests who had usurped power. These views enabled Douglas (and Aberhart) to uphold private ownership and enterprise while denouncing those aspects of capitalism—such as the concentration of economic power—that were widely disliked by farmers and the urban middle and working classes.

Aberhart expounded the main principles of Douglas's political and economic theory, but modified and supplemented them. A rival faction of Alberta Social Crediters, who had been interested long before Aberhart's conversion, publicly claimed that he did not understand Social Credit. Even this did not deter him.

Aberhart forged ahead with what he did best—organization and propaganda. He organized Social Credit study groups at the Bible Institute, turning his students into speakers and organizers of other study groups. In the summer of 1933, he and Manning made a speaking tour of southern Alberta. He conducted lectures for UFA locals, arguing that Social Credit had the advantages of socialism, but went further in destroying the existing financial system. Soon there were sixty-three study groups in Calgary alone, and eventually 1600 across the province.

In 1934, under growing pressure from Social Credit supporters, the UFA government established a legislative committee to consider the Douglas proposals. By inviting both Aberhart and Douglas to the committee hearings, the UFA government hoped to show the differences between the two and discredit Aberhart. At the hearings Douglas suggested that constitutional difficulties would make it impossible to apply Social Credit to Alberta, yet Aberhart insisted that it could be done.

A rival faction of the Social Credit movement hosted Douglas while he was in Alberta. This faction wanted to break Aberhart's growing dominance over the Alberta movement. Like Douglas himself, these "Douglasites" resented Aberhart's mixing of biblical prophecy with Social Credit theory. At a huge meeting at the Mewata Armories in Calgary in April 1934, the differences between the rival factions became public theatre when Douglas spoke to an audience composed primarily of people who had been attracted to Social Credit by Aberhart. The audience was incensed when Aberhart was slighted by not even being asked to speak. Only careful stage management at the end of the meeting prevented a riot.

The first face-to-face meeting between Douglas and Aberhart ended in rancour. The urban newspapers, hostile to Social Credit, made much of the breach between the two, but this only served to cement the loyalty of Aberhart's followers. The strained relationship between Aberhart and Douglas would have important consequences once Aberhart became premier.

Until the spring of 1934, the Social Credit movement was mainly an educational enterprise. The inconclusiveness of the legislative hearings led to a crucial stage in the transformation of Social Credit

The rise of the Social Credit movement led to intense debates between its supporters and opponents. As it tried to spread its message to rural and urban Alberta, and to people of all social classes, religions, and ethnic backgrounds, the movement used every educational device possible. The Alberta Social Credit League float in the 1935 Calgary Stampede parade, during the run up to a provincial election, portrayed a new dawn of hope, equality, and justice for all if Albertans would give Social Credit a chance. (*Glenbow Archives NA 2590-1*)

to a political movement. When the report of the legislative committee concluded that the evidence did not offer any practical plan for the adoption of Social Credit, Aberhart gave up on the UFA and began looking for other political alternatives. Aberhart's search coincided with widespread discontent with the UFA, heightened first by the hostile report of the legislative committee, and then deepened in July 1934 by the Brownlee sex scandal.

Aberhart and Manning spent the summer of 1934 on speaking tours. Their efficiently arranged itinerary included two meetings a day, five days a week. Thousands of Albertans, on the brink of hopelessness, flocked to hear them. Aberhart also began a newspaper, the *Alberta Social Credit Chronicle*, which, in a lively, unpolished, and amusing fashion, promoted the Social Credit cause when no other newspapers did so. But the most effective means of propaganda were the radio broadcasts with their mixture of religion and politics, their clever use of dramatization, and their shrewd involvement of the listeners as people who could make a difference. Schoolteacher Aberhart reduced Social Credit theories to a few simple and easily understood equations. Parades, picnics, and special appeals to the working class also helped build support.

Something for Almost Everyone: The Basis of Social Credit Support

The appeal of Social Credit cut across class, gender, rural-urban, religious, and ethnic lines. It appealed to debt-laden farmers who faced bank foreclosures. Many farmers had been barely able to keep up interest payments on their land and machinery before the Depression. The collapse of prices and the drought left them desperate.

Social Credit also had strong appeal to Alberta's workers. The labour movement was divided and partially discredited. It had split during the 1920s over how closely it should work with a non-Labour (UFA) government. The division was between socialist moderates in the Canadian Labour Party (CLP), who favoured cooperation with the UFA, and radicals, some of them communists, who denounced cooperation. The CLP expelled communists from the party in 1928, and its fear of being associated with communists limited its ability to reach out to the needy in the early 1930s. Thus, during the 1930s, it was the communists rather than the CLP who led the movements of the unemployed. In addition, the UFA-Labour alliance, which had largely benefited organized labour during the 1920s, now served to discredit

Labour along with the UFA. Social Credit thus stepped into a political vacuum in the urban working class. Urban workers who were disturbed by the callous treatment of the unemployed by the "labour" mayors in Edmonton and Calgary, and by the reluctance of labour's political leaders to criticize the UFA government, now had a political alternative.

Working class support for Social Credit effectively destroyed the strong base that had developed in the 1920s for both the Canadian Labour Party and the Communist Party. Social Credit's ideas and organization eroded this earlier type of working-class consciousness. The rituals and institutions that had become an important feature of workers' lives—Labour Day parades, solidarity strikes, mass rallies, and Labour churches—gradually withered. Strong working-class support for Social Credit continued for decades, despite periodic strains between Social Credit and organized labour and the arguably anti-union views of Aberhart's successor, Ernest Manning.

Although Social Credit would later become increasingly right-wing, in its early stages it was genuinely radical, which enabled it to attract working-class support. Besides monetary reform and the redistribution of income, it espoused price controls, medicare, and some state control over industry. When Aberhart denounced the "fifty big shots" who ruled the country, he struck a responsive chord among workers. In Calgary, some of the strongest Social Credit supporters were the CPR workers in the Ogden shops. In the 1935 elections, in the working-class area of north Lethbridge, 60 per cent voted Social Credit in a four-way race in the federal election, and over 70 per cent voted Social Credit in the provincial election in another four-way race.

Social Credit offered a new force for social integration. It provided the people of villages, towns, and cities an opportunity to re-enter the province's political life, from which they had been partially excluded during the UFA era.

Social Credit reached out to a cross section of religious and ethnic groups. The early Social Credit movement undoubtedly had a definite Anglo-Canadian caste and bore the strong imprint of Protestant fundamentalism. This was reflected in Aberhart's insistence that political meetings begin with the hymn, "O God Our Help in Ages Past," his refusal to accept donations raised by raffles or dances, and his early attempt to get supporters to sign a temperance pledge before they could become leaders. As the movement grew, however, Aberhart became more flexible in his religious views. Groups he had previously publicly denounced from the pulpit—members of the United Church of Canada, Catholics, and Mormons—were welcomed, and the movement attracted leaders from all three groups. Particularly drawn by the way Aberhart put Social Credit within a Christian context were religious groups such as Mennonites, most fundamentalists, and ethnic groups closely tied to organized religion such as Dutch, Danes, and Germans.

In the Mormon communities, the majority supported Social Credit despite church leaders' warnings against unsound economic doctrines. Mormon schoolteachers N. E. Tanner, Solon Low, and John Blackmore used their teaching skills and community influence to spread Social Credit ideas, and all three eventually became prominent in the movement: Blackmore and Low as leaders of the national Social Credit party, and Tanner as a key cabinet minister in both the Aberhart and Manning administrations.

Despite strong support among many fundamentalist groups, Aberhart did not carry the whole fundamentalist camp with him. Many fundamentalists criticized Aberhart for political activism. L. E. Maxwell, principal of the Prairie Bible Institute, counselled other fundamentalists that while Christians should vote, they had no business trying to bring about social reform. J. Fergus Kirk, president of PBI, warned that Aberhart was preaching materialism and communism.

Social Credit appealed to minorities who encountered discrimination. The movement was more willing than the traditional parties to nominate non-Anglo-Saxon candidates, and attacked those powerful sectors of society that minorities perceived as sources of discrimination. Focussing on economic issues, Social Credit minimized the importance of ethnicity and offered to accept almost all groups on an equal footing. In the French Canadian settlements in northeast Alberta, a young bilingual St. Paul lawyer and graduate of the University of Alberta, Lucien Maynard, helped convince French Canadians that Social Credit offered a solution to the Depression and was consistent with Catholic theology. After hearing about Social Credit from fellow delegates at a school trustees' convention in Edmonton in February 1935, Maynard organized study groups in both English and French throughout the constituencies of Beaver River and St. Paul, which had large numbers of French Canadians. Maynard's political meetings, like Social Credit meetings elsewhere in the province, had a strong recreational component. They often included a baseball tournament in the afternoon, a supper, a talk on

Social Credit, and a dance. When the new Social Credit government was elected, Maynard became a cabinet minister.

Despite these successes, Social Credit never dominated the Ukrainian and French communities in northern Alberta in the same way it swept rural central and southern Alberta. The Liberals in the French Canadian communities and communists in the Ukrainian bloc mounted strong challenges. Nonetheless, Social Credit won seats in both Ukrainian and French Canadian areas.

Women from many different backgrounds were also attracted to Social Credit. The labour and farm movements had provided new opportunities for women in politics during the years between World War I and 1930. Because specifically women's issues were neglected, it could be argued that women's rights took a step backward with the advent of Social Credit. However, its promise of quick action to deal with economic hardship and its openness to their participation heightened its appeal to women. Calgarians Edith Gostick and Edith Rogers were two of Social Credit's earliest promoters. Both were elected in the 1935 provincial election. Rogers, who had come to Alberta from Nova Scotia in 1912 to teach school, became chief "women's organizer." She used the model of women's study groups, already a part of many middle-class urban women's lives, as a key base for promoting Social Credit. From May to December 1934, she spoke in 190 different locations and helped spread Social Credit to northern Alberta. Although these two were the only women elected as MLAs in 1935, many more were elected as Social Credit candidates for school boards and town councils. In urban areas particularly, women were valuable organizers.

The sweep of Social Credit was not, of course, total; its appeal was limited by cultural, class, ideological, and technological factors. The spread of radio had a direct effect on Social Credit fortunes. By the mid-1930s, Social Credit had penetrated least in northern Alberta, where the signal of CFCN was weakest and where less than 10 per cent of the population owned radios. In the 1935 elections, Social Credit was most successful in the southern and central part of the province, where at least a quarter of the farmers owned radios and many more had easy access to those of their neighbours. The central and eastern Europeans and French Canadians were seldom attracted to English language broadcasts, particularly of the Protestant fundamentalist variety. Thus technology, language, and culture restricted the Social Credit sweep into northern Alberta.

Ideology and class also influenced reaction to Social Credit.

Dedicated CCF and Communist supporters remained unsure whether to denounce Social Credit as quasi-fascist or to cooperate with it as a genuine reform movement. Business interests had no such ambivalence. Although some small retailers supported Social Credit, most larger business people strongly opposed it. In 1935 the Drumheller Board of Trade organized the Economic Safety League, which gathered the support of other boards and began a massive propaganda campaign against Aberhart's "indefinite and contradictory" plans, which would bring "a major disaster to the province."[5]

The Social Credit Victory

By Christmas 1934, since the UFA refused to implement any Social Credit measures, Aberhart realized that a political career lay ahead of him. In January 1935 the UFA annual convention in Calgary heard Aberhart outline his plans, but voted overwhelmingly against his brand of Social Credit. Following this rejection, Aberhart took direct political action. Local enthusiasts rapidly formed constituency organizations and nominated candidates. Under Aberhart's plan, each constituency submitted three or four nominees. After interviewing the nominees, a provincial committee (including Aberhart) would choose one. Aberhart wanted to avoid having opportunists represent the movement. This led to charges that the Social Credit leadership was undemocratic.

None of the other parties could cope with the unrest. Reid's task as UFA premier following the Brownlee scandal was unenviable. A teetotal Scots immigrant, Boer war veteran, one-time lumberjack, farmhand, and amateur dentist, Reid had homesteaded in the Mannville area in 1904. A strong believer in the cooperative movement, he had become an MLA and cabinet member in 1921 and had served in several cabinet portfolios, including minister of lands and mines once Alberta gained control of its natural resources in 1930. Calm, determined, and conservative, Reid could do little more than delay an impending election, hoping that the taint of the scandals and the Social Credit momentum would gradually fade. But defections from the UFA to Social Credit accelerated, and many UFA locals simply became Social Credit locals. The UFA, which in 1921 had over 37,000 members, had by 1935 declined to under 10,000.

The UFA government tried in the spring of 1935 to drive a wedge between Douglas and Aberhart by hiring Douglas to prepare a Social Credit plan. The government, desperate to expose Aberhart, also

265

offered to hire him to prepare a plan, but he sensed a trap and refused. The UFA's efforts to stem the tide of Social Credit by using Brownlee as a critic also backfired. Brownlee's defence of his efforts to protect the province's credit, and his claim that Social Credit could not be introduced provincially, simply reminded the public of the sins of the UFA government.

Amidst the abundance of reform parties—Social Credit, CCF, Communists—the two traditional parties, dependent on the most economically secure sectors of the population, seemed almost lost. The Liberals directed their attack on the UFA and adopted a conciliatory attitude toward Social Credit, while the Conservatives opposed Aberhart outright.

These efforts were futile. The appeal of the new movement, with its charismatic leadership, positive philosophy, and effective organization and promotion, was overwhelming. Aberhart's promise of $25 a month to increase people's purchasing power was irresistible.

By the summer of 1935, the personal loyalty of many of Aberhart's supporters was so great that they refused to discuss the validity of Social Credit proposals with opponents. On Aberhart's suggestion, they also boycotted the newspapers, which were becoming increasingly hostile to Social Credit. Fanatical Social Credit devotees sometimes broke up meetings of their political opponents by surrounding meeting halls with their cars and blowing their horns, or by pounding on the walls and doors. Members of the once-proud Ginger Group, who could legitimately claim that they had originally introduced Major Douglas's ideas to Canada, found they could scarcely get a hearing. Some left public meetings to find the tires on their cars slashed.

The sixty-three Social Credit candidates in the August 1935 provincial election represented a broad cross section of Alberta. Two-thirds of them were drawn from four groups: eighteen small-town merchants, agents, and salesmen, twelve farmers, eight school-teachers, and four preachers. The rest ranged from the high end to the low end of the socio-economic spectrum, including several professionals (four lawyers, two doctors, two dentists) but also three railway workers, two clerks, and two butchers. None had held elected office previously at the provincial or federal levels, though many were community leaders.

If the Liberal era was marked by the dominance of lawyers and the UFA era by the ascendancy of farmers, the Socred era was noteworthy for the leadership of schoolteachers, perhaps because Social Credit was based on a complex theory that potential supporters had to be "taught." Like the clergy, schoolteachers often had public speaking skills, an interest in ideas, and a close personal knowledge of the whole community. They ultimately formed a disproportionately large share of Social Credit legislators and cabinet ministers.

The Social Credit candidates were also representative of an Alberta-born generation. While none of the MLAs during either the Liberal or the UFA periods had been native Albertans, a sizable minority of the Social Credit legislators were, and many more had been raised in Alberta.

On August 22, 1935, Social Credit swept into power with fifty-six of sixty-three seats and 54 per cent of the popular vote. Both Labour and the UFA were totally eliminated from the legislature. The Liberals with five seats and Conservatives with two continued the lonely vigil of urban lawyers huddled on the opposition benches. Aberhart accepted the premiership, and the seat of Okotoks-High River was opened for him.

By October 1935 the Social Credit sweep was complete. In the federal election, campaigning on the proposition that "Social Credit absolutely demands that the power of the banker and the financier be broken,"[6] Social Credit returned fifteen members out of seventeen, with one Liberal and one Conservative. The Ginger Group members, now running as CCF candidates, were wiped out.

William Irvine, for example, was overwhelmingly defeated by Norman Jaques in the Wetaskiwin riding. Jaques was an Englishman who came from a well-off and well-educated family. He had immigrated to Canada in 1901 at age twenty-one. He purchased a large parcel of land in the Castor area, where he built a two-storey English country house. Following his marriage in 1918 to the daughter of other English immigrants, he and his wife experienced a series of misfortunes. Their crops were hailed out several years in a row. The land blew away in the drought of the early 1930s. The Jaques family finally left their land (which was repossessed by the CPR) and ended up living in a shack in the town of Mirror, where they survived on relief and food from a brother's farm. Jaques was one of the scattered network of ardent Douglasites who had been attracted to Major Douglas's ideas before the Aberhart movement developed. Jaques walked barefoot to meetings to save his only pair of shoes, and put on the shoes before entering the hall. To save money, he used brown paper to write speeches and letters. Many others in his riding were in similarly desperate circumstances, and turned to Social Credit in

1935 as their last, best hope.[7] After his defeat, Irvine, once a popular and respected MP, became increasingly isolated politically in Alberta. He spent the rest of his career fighting a losing battle for the CCF in the West. The only time he returned to Parliament was in 1945, when he ran successfully for the CCF in British Columbia.

Social Credit Takes Power

The Social Credit victory attracted puzzled attention across the English-speaking world. A Boston newspaper was headlined, "Alberta Goes Crazy." Alberta business leaders were appalled. R. B. Bennett wrote to a Conservative supporter in Alberta, "I fear our people are getting to a point where they are sacrificing their judgment to their emotions on the terrible experiences through which they have passed."[8] But great enthusiasm reigned among Social Credit supporters. The morning after the election, some of them lined up at city hall in Calgary, confidently expecting to receive their first instalment of the promised $25 per month dividend.

Aberhart immediately cabled Major Douglas, then under contract with the Alberta government as an economic advisor: "Victorious: when could you come?" While Douglas pondered this request, Aberhart learned from Premier Reid of Alberta's serious financial position, made worse by the flight of capital in the wake of Social Credit's victory. Responding to this economic emergency, which made it difficult even to pay civil servants, Aberhart hired an orthodox Canadian economic advisor. Robert Magor was a Montrealer who had experience in reorganizing financially troubled governments and corporations. Aberhart also turned to the Bennett government for an $18-million loan, and received $2.25 million.

When Douglas learned of these developments, he refused to come to Alberta. A government that had stated explicitly that it needed Douglasite advisers before it could proceed was left without its expert. Douglas, it would appear, didn't have the courage to try his ideas in the face of reality. Perhaps he feared that Aberhart's incompetence might irrevocably doom the Social Credit movement elsewhere. He didn't want to risk his reputation in a province led by a headstrong, incompatible premier.

Douglas did, however, send his advice by cable. His counsel was too general to translate into concrete action, and he sent it with a dictatorial tone that Aberhart resented; after all he, not Douglas, had to answer to the Alberta electorate. After six months of cables and letters back and forth, in which Douglas demanded that steps be taken before he left for Alberta and Aberhart insisted that he come before anything dramatic was initiated, Douglas resigned. Aberhart was left to proceed on his own.

Even from the beginning, Aberhart must have realized the difficulties he would face in implementing his promises. Just one week after the election, he stated that 75 per cent of those who voted for him did not expect a dividend but hoped for a just and honest government. He argued that he needed to "set the province's financial house in order" before he could deliver the dividends. He promised, though, that Social Credit dividends would be introduced within eighteen months of the election. His first budget, in the spring of 1936, was an exercise in orthodox economics, attempting to balance the budget through tax increases, which went primarily to meet the high costs of unemployment relief.

Through the 108 acts passed in the first session of the legislature, Aberhart began laying the framework for a social welfare state. Social Credit introduced legislation providing for minimum wages and free treatment for TB patients. Manning, as minister of trade and industry, introduced minimum and maximum prices. The government also provided for the recall of MLAs if they lost the confidence of their constituents.

Aberhart initiated educational reforms that reflected his own background and the strong contingent of teachers in the government. Over the opposition of rural school board trustees, who had close links with the UFA movement, Aberhart consolidated rural school districts to save money and extend educational opportunities for rural children. He also gave Alberta teachers professional status by making it compulsory that they belong to the Alberta Teachers' Association.

The government showed its radical leanings by refusing to pay the interest on maturing government bonds. This refusal was based partly on Social Credit beliefs, but also on the fact that Alberta simply did not have the money. The province had a massive public debt the interest from which, from 1930 to 1935, was absorbing anywhere from one-third to more than half of the government's annual revenue. In April 1936, the province defaulted on its bond payments after the federal government refused a loan unless it was supervised by a federal loan council. Aberhart rejected this condition because he wanted to protect provincial rights and feared (along with Douglas) a bankers' plot to destroy Social Credit. The bond default shocked financial circles but delighted Social Credit supporters.

In the summer of 1936 Aberhart used another experimental measure to placate his supporters. A committee of MLAs developed a scheme to relieve the shortage of purchasing power by issuing government scrip, known as "prosperity certificates." The first to receive these certificates were workmen on government relief road-building projects. The plan was a flop. Orthodox Douglasites denounced the plan as having nothing to do with Social Credit. Boards of trade refused to accept the certificates, and the province itself refused to accept them in payment of taxes. The scheme died within months.

Throughout 1936 and 1937, Alberta's politics were highly volatile. The legislature convened six times, passing reams of controversial legislation, while the Social Credit movement and the province were kept in a perpetual state of agitation. Aberhart faced a constant refrain: Where was the $25 per month? His reply was virtually the same as the one used by his critics to ridicule his proposals before the 1935 election: Where would the money come from? By late 1937, four of his original seven cabinet ministers had resigned or been fired when they disagreed with Aberhart, or found their health shattered by constant cabinet meetings that lasted late into the night.

As opposition mounted from the press and from business, and as his own supporters began to waver, Aberhart forged ahead with a series of measures that tantalized with the promise of implementing Social Credit. The Alberta Credit House Act and the Social Credit Measures Act in August 1936 appeared to put teeth into the fight with bankers and financial interests. One of the acts cancelled interest payments on all debts contracted before July 1932, and established a Debt Adjustment Board to rule on repayments and property seizures. Aberhart also asked Albertans to register for the proposed (although still elusive) dividends. They had to sign covenants in which they agreed to "cooperate most heartily" with the government. The covenants were signed by 360,000 people, representing about 70 per cent of the province's adult population. Those who signed often waited in line for hours. However, this was simply enabling legislation, and no action was taken on the dividend. Socred workers rather than civil servants did the registration, and opponents of Social Credit saw these covenants as fascistic. As opposition to his legislation mounted, Aberhart blamed the press, banks, and business for his inability to make good on his promises.

The Backbenchers' Revolt and the Challenge to Ottawa

Aberhart also came under increasing pressure from within the movement. The issue came to a head with the arrival in December 1936 of British writer and Social Credit organizer John Hargrave. Hargrave had founded his own anti-war outdoor alternative to the Boy Scouts in 1920 under the name of Kibbo Kift. As the Wa-Whaw-Goosh, leader of the Kibbo Kift, he introduced Social Credit ideas to his British followers and adopted Green Shirts as the marching uniform of the urban unemployed. While in Alberta, Hargrave met with Social Credit backbenchers and, on his abrupt departure in late January following strong disagreements with Aberhart, sharply condemned the government for not implementing Social Credit.

By early 1937, almost eighteen months had passed and the promised dividend was nowhere in sight. Aberhart and his government were wrestling with debt defaults and struggling to find enough money to meet relief payments. Several Socred MLAs began publicly doubting the courage and sincerity of the government. They faced constant pressure from their constituents over unkept promises. When the budget introduced in the spring session of 1937 was again an orthodox one that increased personal income tax and for the first time introduced a sales tax, twenty-two Social Credit backbenchers joined local Socred groups in demanding Aberhart's resignation.

The strategy of the insurgents was to refuse to support the budget until the government introduced Social Credit measures. Some of them hoped Aberhart would resign and one of their own would take over. They moved adjournment of the legislature and their motion carried. Aberhart, on a technicality, refused to consider this a vote of confidence.

After several gruelling meetings with the insurgents, Aberhart reached a compromise. He proposed that, with the assistance of Douglasite experts, the insurgents take over responsibility for introducing Social Credit through a Social Credit Board, while the cabinet would continue running the rest of the government. Aberhart believed the insurgents would find out for themselves the obstacles that the government faced.

On April 8, the cabinet introduced the Alberta Social Credit Act, which established the Social Credit Board. Staffed by the insurgents, the board served as a miniature cabinet to develop Social Credit legislation. By in effect disassociating themselves from the Act, Aberhart and his cabinet hoped to avoid responsibility if the board failed. The chairman of the board then headed to England to bring back Douglas. Douglas still refused to come but sent instead two Social Credit "experts," G. F. Powell and L. D. Byrne. They soon met with insurgents and Aberhart loyalists and, through a heady dose of Social Credit indoctrination, helped heal the rifts. The board began planning legislation that they hoped would either fully implement

Social Credit, or expose those powerful forces that were thwarting the people's will.

The insurgency was a trying period for Aberhart. He was deeply hurt and it shook his confidence that people he had worked with, placed confidence in, and urged to become members had turned against him. Ernest Manning was ill at the time of the insurgency, so he was not directly part of the intense factionalism.

As a result of the work of the new board, the August 1937 session of the legislature was momentous. The government, energized by the insurgency and the "experts," introduced radical legislation to control the banks. It included the Credit of Alberta Regulation Act, which regulated banks and required annual licences; the Bank Employees Civil Rights Act, whereby bank employees had to be licensed and could not take the government to court; and an Amendment to the Judicature Act, which prohibited attacks in court on the validity of provincial statutes. This drastic legislation, modelled on earlier recommendations by Douglas, put the banks under provincial control. Describing the atmosphere of the legislature when the acts were introduced as "electric with anticipation and almost prostrate with suspense," the Social Credit newspaper declared that the legislation ushered in the "dawn of true democracy."[9]

This legislation brought to a head the conflict between Social Credit on one side and the business community and federal government on the other. Attorney General John Hugill, a Calgary lawyer who had been recruited during the election by Aberhart even though he had doubts about Social Credit, was forced to resign because he advised Aberhart that the legislation was unconstitutional. Mackenzie King's government had originally promised "hands off Alberta," hoping that Social Credit would simply undermine itself. Now it intervened directly, quickly disallowing all three acts. It had the support of the banks and almost all the weekly and daily newspapers in Alberta, which were growing increasingly hostile to Social Credit.

This revival of the power of disallowance, which had not been used by the federal government since 1924, caused deep resentment among Social Crediters. They saw in it both discrimination against the West and contempt for the will of the people on the part of an insensitive government, subservient to financial interests. When Aberhart announced the disallowance to his followers, some began calling for separation from Canada. Aberhart counselled moderation and rejected talk of secession.

Whether or not he actually believed the federal government would allow the legislation to stand is difficult to say, yet this direct assault on the banks helped heal the rifts in the Social Credit movement. On the second anniversary of the Social Credit victory, at a rally of an estimated 22,000 people on St. George's Island in Calgary, Aberhart promised to proceed with "as great haste as we can to bring into existence...what you have demanded."[10]

In September the Alberta government met to re-enact the disallowed bills. The session also repealed the recall act, which the government had enacted with such fanfare in 1936, since Aberhart's constituents in the High River-Okotoks district, spurred on by the opposition, had initiated recall proceedings against him. On a petition demanding his recall, his opponents had gathered the signatures of the necessary two-thirds of the voters in the riding. To the opposition, this repeal was the height of hypocrisy. Aberhart accused the oil companies in the riding of intimidating workers into signing the recall petition.

The government also caused an uproar with its new Accurate News and Information Act, which restricted the freedom of the press. The act required the press to be "fairer" in their coverage of Social Credit by forcing them to print government-supplied articles equal in length to those attacking the government, and to divulge their sources. For Social Crediters, this legislation was necessary because a major change in the province's economy and financial structure could only be successful with a strong measure of public support, and the media's hostile coverage threatened to erode that support.

The almost unanimous opposition by the Alberta press had frustrated and enraged Aberhart and his supporters. Through stock sales to Social Credit supporters, Aberhart had gained virtual control of the Calgary *Albertan* in January 1936 as an outlet for Socred views, but he faced a constant barrage of criticism from the rest of the urban daily press. The most vociferous of his opponents, the *Calgary Herald*, even hired a political cartoonist, Stewart Cameron, to lampoon Aberhart. He did this in a series of brilliant cartoons that pictured Aberhart as an egotistical puppet of Douglas, with traits distressingly similar to Hitler and Mussolini.

The Accurate News and Information Act led to a new stage of conflict within the province and with the federal government. Lieutenant Governor John C. Bowen reserved the major Social Credit acts and referred them to the Supreme Court, which eventually found them unconstitutional. The People's League, begun in

1936 by business interests, mainly Conservatives, to unite Social Credit opponents, organized huge rallies calling for Aberhart's resignation. The press, led by John Imrie of the *Edmonton Journal*, also strenuously opposed the bill. Along with five urban dailies and ninety weeklies, the *Journal* received the 1938 Pulitzer Prize for its opposition to the legislation.

The tension between Social Credit and its opponents was heightened by the arrest of two Social Credit leaders. On September 29, 1937, a one-page leaflet entitled "Bankers' Toadies" appeared on members' desks in the legislature. It was a wild bit of political propaganda that suggested the "Bankers' Toadies" should be exterminated! The pamphlet listed nine of Edmonton's prominent Liberal and Conservative politicians and lawyers as the "toadies." After one of them laid charges, police raided the offices of the Alberta Social Credit League and seized thousands of the leaflets. J. H. Unwin, government whip and member for Edson, appeared in court, followed by Social Credit "expert" George Powell. The "Bankers' Toadies Two" were charged with criminal libel and counselling murder; both were sentenced to jail with hard labour. They became instant martyrs to the Social Credit cause.

Responding to financial interests, corporations, and investors' groups, the federal government disallowed eleven Alberta statutes between 1937 and 1941. Nonetheless, the provincial government forged ahead with measures to increase taxation on corporations and banks, and to protect debtors. Most of the debt adjustment legislation was declared unconstitutional, but in the interim, as these measures wound their way through various court challenges, farmers and urban homeowners were protected from foreclosure.

Despite these reversals, Aberhart did not give up the attempt to change the financial system. The Socreds encouraged credit unions. In 1938 they reintroduced a plan to establish State Credit Houses to replace the banks. These Treasury Branches had some unusual features, including a system of non-negotiable transfer vouchers instead of cheques, which encouraged a "Buy Alberta" campaign. Though the Treasury Branches captured only a small share of the banking business, they acted as a prod to better banking and provided services in areas banks had vacated. The Treasury Branches are today one of Alberta's few visible legacies from the Aberhart era.

The reformist character of the Aberhart government, reflected in its social welfare measures and attempts to change the economic order, was mildly evident in its dealings with the Métis. Under the

274

leadership of Métis school teacher Joe Dion, the Alberta Métis Association had been organized in the early 1930s to fight the terrible health conditions they faced, the lack of schools and jobs, and the refusal of municipal governments to grant relief to many Métis families. They put enough pressure on the UFA government to convince it to appoint the Ewing Commission to examine their grievances. The commission recommended that some of the Métis demands for land, education, and health services be met. In 1938 the Aberhart government passed the Métis Population Betterment Act, whereby associations of Métis could apply to have land set aside as reserves. In the late 1930s, the government set aside nine settlements or colonies in northern Alberta, comprising approximately two thousand square miles (5180 square kilometres). In doing so, the Aberhart government "proved more willing than its predecessor or any other government in western Canada to provide land for the dispossessed and desperate Métis."[11]

Convincing the Nation and Staying in Power

When federal disallowance stopped the provincial Social Credit scheme, Aberhart began to see no alternative except to expand into other provinces and build a strong federal party. In the 1938 Saskatchewan provincial election, Aberhart and other Albertans made a determined drive to gain support. Aberhart made barnstorming tours of western Saskatchewan, reminiscent of the 1935 Alberta campaign. Social Crediters argued that a victory in Saskatchewan would increase pressure on the federal government to enact reform. In some areas, the CCF and Social Credit cooperated as reform movements, although leaders in both organizations were wary of an alliance. Racked by internal conflict, including resentment over Aberhart's dictatorial control, and faced with the failure of Social Credit to deliver on its promises in Alberta, the Saskatchewan Social Credit movement failed. It won only two seats, compared to ten for the CCF. The defeat in 1938 left the field open to the CCF as the main reform movement in Saskatchewan.

The exhausting battles internally and with the federal government had taken their toll on the Aberhart government, and it was almost defeated in the 1940 provincial election. The 1940 election campaign was the third attempt since 1935 to form a united opposition. Bringing together Conservatives, Liberals, and some UFA supporters, the opposition Independents were a strange blend of reactionary conservatism and populism. Their election promise of a sound business-like administration ran up against the fact that they had no leader, and the only thing they could agree on was the necessity of ousting Aberhart. In spite of their factionalism, petty rivalries, and negative approach, the Unity Movement almost succeeded. They reminded voters of Aberhart's failure to fulfill his promises, and painted him in Hitlerian hues. Aberhart's campaign was also hampered by the federal government's vindictive wartime regulations, aimed at him, that religious broadcasts could no longer have political content or personal greetings, and had to be made from a studio rather than from before a live audience.

The Independents and Social Credit each received 43 per cent of the popular vote. Social Credit won thirty-six seats, compared to the Independents' nineteen, because of the preponderance of rural seats. Aberhart's victory in 1940, despite the overwhelming efforts of Alberta's socio-economic elite, was a testament to the depth of Social Credit's appeal among Alberta's farmers, smalltown dwellers, and the urban working- and lower-middle classes. In opposition, the unstable Independent alliance quickly fell apart, virtually disappearing by the 1944 election.

Social Credit's efforts to break out of its Alberta stronghold were intense though futile. The decision to organize a nation-wide Social Credit party, with the seventeen Social Credit members in the House of Commons as its nucleus, was taken as early as 1938. While there was strong interest in parts of rural Quebec in Social Credit, linguistic, religious, and regional differences (to say nothing of the ethnic prejudices and insensitivities of the Alberta MPs) made it very difficult for the Alberta members to build a unified national party. In an attempt to broaden the party's appeal, in the 1940 federal election Aberhart and the federal Social Crediters merged forces with W. D. Herridge, former Canadian ambassador to Washington and renegade Conservative, who wanted to reform the country's economic system. Aberhart placed high hopes in a leader of national reputation and a new name (New Democracy). However, Herridge and Aberhart disagreed on conscription, since Aberhart wanted conscription of wealth before there was any conscription of manpower. Herridge's stand alienated French Canadian Social Crediters, who were largely anti-conscription. New Democracy went nowhere outside Alberta, and even in the province won only 34 per cent of the popular vote. With a majority of Albertans wanting to show their loyalty to the war effort, the Liberals outpolled New Democracy. The urban seats went Liberal, and in 1940 seven Liberals from Alberta joined ten Social

Crediters (the latter sitting temporarily under the name of New Democracy) in Ottawa.

Social Credit and the CCF: A Comparison

Why Social Credit was successful in Alberta and the CCF in neighbouring Saskatchewan has long baffled political observers. Some analysts argue that in Alberta, the influence of individualistic-oriented Americans operating in a "Bible Belt" atmosphere made socialism unattractive, while perhaps a stronger presence of British and continental Europeans in Saskatchewan, more versed in European socialism, made socialism more acceptable. It is doubtful whether these social factors can explain the divergence as the differences between the British-born and American-born in the two provinces in the 1930s were minor. In 1931 Alberta had 15 per cent British-born compared to 11 per cent in Saskatchewan, and 11 per cent American-born compared to 8 per cent in Saskatchewan. Census figures also suggest only about 10 per cent of the population in each province was associated with fundamentalist or unorthodox sects, although these figures obviously give no indication of the social or political influence of fundamentalists.

Ethnic and religious factors are significant in explaining prairie politics. However, perhaps a more fruitful approach in explaining the differences between Social Credit and CCF in the two provinces is to look at the two movements as alternatives to much the same set of economic and political circumstances. Both movements represented a populist protest against capitalism and central Canadian political dominance. Both wanted to use provincial powers to defend farmers, the lower-middle class, and the working class. During their drive to power, both supported organized labour and focussed on issues of debt, credit, and security of tenure for farmers. In power, both tried to deliver social, economic, and health security. Farmers in both movements vacillated in their attitudes toward organized labour between radical and reactionary stances. Both movements supported the modernization of the educational and transportation systems as a way of diversifying the economy and attracting outside capital. Although under Manning Social Credit became increasingly conservative, originally it had much in common with the CCF. Alberta's shift to the right during World War II and the postwar era needs explanation, but it cannot be assumed that because Social Credit became a right-wing movement that it began as one.

The explanation of the differences in the two provinces in the

1930s and 1940s lies more in the common populist origins of the two movements, along with the sequence of historical events leading to their victories. Social Credit came to power in Alberta because the CCF, with its tangled roots in the UFA and the Canadian Labour Party, was discredited before it began. Alberta's decision to eventually go Social Credit dates in part from the 1920s, when the UFA overturned the Liberals in Alberta while the Liberals remained in power in Saskatchewan. During the Depression, when looking for a new alternative, Albertans turned to Social Credit. Following the Depression, when people in Saskatchewan decided to support a radical movement, the CCF was new and untainted, unlike its counterpart in Alberta. The Alberta CCF carried the legacy of the UFA and Labour parties, which had been tried and found wanting.

Once in power in each province, Social Credit and the CCF effectively blocked each other's growth because they appealed to the same sectors of society. In addition, the association of each movement with provincial identity hindered its spread into the neighbouring province. As rivals for the same segments of society, they became bitter enemies. Nonetheless, the gradual intensification of this rivalry and the growing divergence of their ideas and policies should not obscure the original similarities between the two.

Social Credit and the UFA: A Comparison

Social Credit, like the UFA, was a populist attack on the national policy. In its origins, ideology, rise to power, leadership, and locus of rural support, it was strikingly similar to the UFA. Social Credit built on the non-partisan political tradition, hostility to the East, and inflationary monetary theory already present in the UFA. The ethical and political theories of the two movements, with their Christian base, stress on the rights of the individual, and concern with collective economic security, had much in common. Religious leaders also served as a bridge between different social classes in both movements. Social Credit's organizational structure, based on local study groups with charismatic leadership at the top, also in many ways replicated the UFA. Both came to power quickly, though both Wood and Aberhart had been reluctant to turn their movements into political organizations. Social Credit's major rural strongholds, like those of the UFA, were in the wheat-growing areas of central and southern Alberta that had been largely settled by Anglo-Saxons and Scandinavian Americans. The strong rural base of both ensured a stranglehold on the legislature, and they were usually returned with overwhelming majorities to face weak and divided oppositions.

Once in power, they encountered many of the same difficulties. Neither movement was able to do much to reverse the forces against which they protested. They came to power so quickly that their provincial legislators were inexperienced and cautious. The limits of provincial jurisdiction severely circumscribed their ability to put their ideas into practice: in both cases, the remedies they proposed fell primarily within federal jurisdiction. Once in power, their leaders began to see some of the practical limits to their ability to solve Alberta's fundamental economic and political problems. Subsequently fissures developed between the grass roots and the provincial government: the former wanted more than the latter could deliver. The federal wing of both movements was consistently more radical than the provincial, since the most radical proponents were attracted to the federal scene, and their isolated and minority position in Parliament placed few constraints on their ideological purity. Just as the late 1920s saw a decline in reform zeal among UFA supporters, the 1940s would bring a similar decline in the reform zeal of Social Crediters faced with new political and economic conditions. The utopian enthusiasm of 1921 and then of 1935 faded in a remarkably short time, to be institutionalized in the bureaucratic machinery of party and government.

Despite all these similarities, Social Credit was not simply the UFA in disguise. Unlike the UFA, which began as a farmers' democratic movement, Social Credit owed much more to the work of one man, William Aberhart. Religion was more central in Social Credit. The UFA was rooted in the liberal theology of the social gospel, while Social Credit was nourished in Alberta fundamentalism, though it broadened to reach a much wider audience. The UFA's key doctrines of group government were tied to a radical analysis of the political system, while Social Credit's analysis focussed on the economic system.

Social Credit's political theory was not as democratic as the UFA's. Social Credit placed much greater confidence in experts and argued that people and their representatives didn't need to understand the economic system, but should simply demand results. Thus the UFA, one of the most democratic movements in the history of North America, was replaced by one that looked to outside experts. Social Credit continued the challenge to the national policy begun by the UFA, yet it partially destroyed the UFA's legacy of grass roots democracy.

The economic crisis of the 1930s precipitated Albertans' second major attempt to change the national economic and political order. This second revolt also arose out of the conditions of a frontier economy, dependent on and dominated by the metropolitan East. Motivated by both despair and utopian hope, Social Crediters set out to convert the nation. This second effort of Albertans to change the national economic and political order again had national implications. For a time, Social Crediters changed provincial politics across the West. Working with Social Crediters from Quebec, for three decades they also had a significant impact on national politics.

By the end of the 1930s, weather and economic conditions in the province had begun to improve slightly. Yet the legacy of crisis lingered, with many Albertans still experiencing deprivation and bitterly divided by political, class, and ethnic differences. Despite all the sound and fury of Alberta's internal political and economic debate during the 1930s, it was not Social Credit but ultimately World War II that pulled Albertans out of their seemingly interminable economic crisis.

CHAPTER TEN

World War II and the Beginnings of Transformation: 1940–1947

Wartime Alberta was a different place from Alberta of the Depression, and few people remained untouched by the war's effects. The war brought economic growth, nationalism, and general social solidarity, but also social change and dislocation. It altered Alberta's agricultural and resource-based economy, its rural-urban demography, and its politics, as well as modifying ethnic relations and the role of women.

Politically Social Credit remained in power during the 1940s, but the political and economic conditions that nourished it had changed. Provincial politics were much less important to Albertans than they had been just a few years before. Political innovation ceased and the rhetoric of monetary reform became almost quaint in the transformation to a wartime economy. Political actors also changed. Aberhart's death in 1943 and his replacement by Ernest Manning ended one phase in Alberta's political life and ushered in a new one that lasted for twenty-five years; Manning's premiership was the longest in Canadian history. Social Credit also underwent a fundamental ideological shift to the right, which partially changed its base of support and began the process of a reconciliation between Social Credit and Alberta's economic and social elites.

The Home Front

As they had done in World War I, Albertans joined the armed forces in large numbers. However, lingering memories of the Great War restrained the enthusiasm of the new recruits. Albertans' response was one of grim determination rather than jingoist elation. This time the heavy enlistments did not come from the British-born, who were now aging and fewer in number. The high enlistment rates reflected depressed economic conditions, the growth of Canadian nationalism,

Aberhart, following seven stormy years as premier, died in 1943. He was replaced by thirty-four-year-old Ernest Manning, shown here at the time he became premier. Manning, who grew up on a farm in Saskatchewan, had been a student at Aberhart's bible school. He was Aberhart's closest associate during Social Credit's rise to power, and during Aberhart's years in office. Manning remained premier for twenty-five years and presided over a remarkable transformation in Alberta's economy and society. *(Glenbow Archives NA 2922-14)*

and youthful desire for adventure. By 1940 almost 70 per cent of the population was Canadian-born and over half was Alberta-born. For many minorities, joining the armed forces was proof positive of full participation in Canadian society. Eventually 78,000 men, making up 43 per cent of the eligible adult male population, and 4,500 women entered the forces.

World War II was fought differently than World War I. Modern warfare made it possible for Albertans, despite their limited military training, to contribute in important ways. Prairie boys, experienced with machinery, guns, and great distances, were at least minimally prepared for the technical and mobile nature of modern warfare. Albertans' particular fascination with aviation, nurtured in part by the saga of the opening of the north by World War I flying aces, attracted them to the air force. For a small minority, the engineering skills derived from experience in mining and construction were also useful.

Although Alberta was far from the arena of combat, those at home were deeply affected. The Battle of Britain, the disaster at Dieppe, and the North African and Italian campaigns were all-absorbing. Those left in Alberta had to cope with fear and loneliness, and in many cases, with supporting families. Daughters and sisters of servicemen often departed for war-related work, or to enlist in the women's divisions of the armed forces. Businesses had to cope with the gap left by the departure of so many. Civilians found their lives complicated by such wartime measures as the rationing of food, housing, and fuel, and by wage and price controls. There were endless "victory bond" campaigns and community drives to collect scrap metal, paper, and rubber. Women's groups formed auxiliaries to provide articles for hospitals, European bomb victims, and the armed forces. Cities also "adopted" RCAF squadrons in Britain.

The war brought a large military presence to Alberta. This included Canadian army bases, personnel from the British Commonwealth Air Training Plan (BCATP), and a large American presence. Most Americans in Alberta were involved in reinforcing Alaska after Japan attacked Pearl Harbor in Hawaii in December 1941. The Mackenzie King government realized that Canada could contribute significantly to the war effort through its expertise and facilities in aviation. The BCATP was instituted in 1939, and by 1945 over 130,000 flyers from Canada, New Zealand, Australia, Britain, and other countries had been trained. Taking advantage of the prairies' secure airspace, vast distances, and sunny skies, the government established seventeen of the country's 105 flight training schools in Alberta. There was an observer school in Edmonton and six separate facilities in Calgary, including one of four national training command headquarters. There were training schools in towns scattered along the major highway from Penhold to Lethbridge and Medicine Hat.

The military and BCATP bases brought rapid economic growth and social change. New military bases at Cold Lake and Wainwright, for example, came to play important roles in local economies. The sudden need for modern buildings, large hangers, and runways for the BCATP revitalized the province's construction industry. Hundreds of airforce personnel strained existing facilities but gave a needed economic boost to local communities. Calgary, a stagnant small city in the heart of a depressed farming area, boomed for the first time since before World War I. In addition to construction, service industries in many towns and cities received a boost. "Bus and taxi firms, drug stores, shoe repair shops, restaurants, beer parlors, movie houses, hotels, dance halls, clothing stores, laundries, barber shops, and even churches" benefited from the coming of the Air Training Schools.[1] Close relationships often developed between newcomers and townspeople. Many families adopted members of the armed forces as surrogate sons, and townspeople followed the careers of airmen after they left. Nor was it uncommon for the airmen to marry local women.

The other major military contribution Alberta made was through its strategic position in U.S. defence plans to protect Alaska. Edmonton became an important air terminal and supply centre in the Northwest Staging Route, which formed a link with Alaska through a series of airfields. Though military authorities doubted the strategic value of a highway to Alaska, civilian leaders were anxious to demonstrate the government's commitment to the war effort. In 1942, 1400 American troops came north and built 1500 miles (2400 kilometres) of pioneer road within eight months, linking the airfields and completing the Alaska Highway.

The highway confirmed Edmonton's role as gateway to the North. While construction began in British Columbia, Edmonton was a staging centre, and the Edmonton, Dunvegan and British Columbia Railway (now renamed the Northern Alberta Railway) proved valuable. The influx of Americans had a significant social and economic impact on Edmonton as they jammed all possible accommodation and competed with the local population for consumer goods.

The Northwest Staging Route expanded Edmonton's role as the air and staging centre for the North. This included air traffic to Alaska and the American shipment of planes to their wartime ally, the Soviet Union. Edmonton's airport became, for a time, the busiest on the continent: on one day in September 1943, the planes passing through numbered 860. Grande Prairie's airport also expanded and the American DC-3 became a familiar sight, heading out for the defence of Alaska. Five hundred Canadian and American Air Force personnel were stationed at the airfield.

Edmonton was also the engineering headquarters and supply centre for the Canol Pipeline, built by the U. S. War Department from Norman Wells in the Northwest Territories to a refinery at Whitehorse in the Yukon to supply fuel for planes. Huge amounts of equipment were shipped by train to Waterways, where they were loaded on tugs, steamers, and barges for shipment down the Athabasca River. One steamer, the Athabasca River, on one voyage north in July 1942, hauled or pushed six hundred tons of freight. By 1946, this route was also the jumping off point for uranium exploration and development in the north, thus keeping alive Fort McMurray's role as a trans-shipment point.

Albertans received a sobering reminder of the nature of modern warfare in 1941 when a station for chemical warfare experimentation was established at Suffield. By the end of the war, the Suffield station employed six hundred people in research on toxic chemicals, flame warfare, and ballistics. Research and training at Suffield still involves joint British and Canadian projects.

Five prisoner-of-war camps for captured German soldiers also brought the war close to home. Lethbridge and Medicine Hat had Canada's two largest camps, each with a capacity of 12,000 prisoners. Despite complaints that the camps received better food than local people, they contributed to local economies as markets, and the POWs eased the critical farm labour shortage. Several POWs developed close ties with local farmers, and some returned to Canada after the war. Although POWs posed little danger to local citizens, because of divisions in their attitude toward Hitler and the Nazis, the POWs occasionally were dangerous to each other; the camps witnessed some grisly murders.

Although the armed forces generated economic activity and mobility, the size of Alberta's population was relatively stable, increasing from 769,000 in 1941 to 803,000 in 1946. From 1941 to 1946, there was a net emigration of 72,000, including those who left to serve in the armed forces and for war-industry jobs elsewhere. A trend toward urbanization developed as rural people moved to work in urban wartime industries and military bases. Although agriculture generally prospered during the war, the number of people living on farms declined.

The Economic Impact of War

War lifted Alberta out of its economic depression. Improved prices for farm products and wartime industries generated overall economic growth. Many farmers diversified into livestock and feed grain production. Economic activity kindled by the Turner Valley oilfield further stimulated growth. Nearly all economic indicators doubled during the war years. By the end of the war, the province's annual per capita income of $829 equalled the national average.

Agriculture remained the mainstay of the economy with over half of the net value of production, although there were some important changes. Total farm income rose from $118 million in 1939 to $347 million in 1944. At the war's onset, many farmers expected large increases in wheat prices, but Hitler's European victories cut off Canada's traditional markets, and wheat prices remained stable. The Canadian government encouraged farmers to diversify to supply British markets. Consequently, wheat acreages declined, while barley and other grains and vegetable crops increased. The sugar beet industry was revitalized since imports of sugar were cut off. More farmers raised cattle and pigs, and the meatpacking industry flourished.

Higher farm incomes, a shortage of farm labour, and better and cheaper farm machinery spurred mechanization. The shift to tractors, which had stalled and even reversed itself during the 1930s, surged ahead. By 1946 there was one tractor for every two farms in Alberta and over 10 per cent of the 84,350 farms had combines. Mechanization, which accelerated rapidly after the war, changed prairie agriculture and rural prairie society. Larger farms were required to make economical use of machinery, while much less hand labour was needed. This meant the land could support fewer farmers and small towns. By the end of the war, marginal farmers on small acreages, with large overheads, found they could not compete with larger, more mechanized farms, and many were forced to sell out. By 1951 over half of Alberta's population was urban.

Alberta made few strides in industrialization during the war. This was a source of frustration and resentment to the provincial Social Credit government, concerned about encouraging secondary industry that would provide jobs after the war. The federal government concentrated its industrial war contracts in central Canada; only 2.6 per cent were placed in Alberta, including munitions plants in Calgary and Medicine Hat and an ammonium plant in Calgary. The ammonium was used in explosives, although by 1943 some of the output was converted to nitrogen fertilizer. The lack of industrial war contracts led to some public outcry, but in general Albertans placed perceived national interest before regional considerations, and stifled regional complaints.

The war created a new national interest in Alberta's energy supplies—coal, conventional oil, and the oil sands. It also lifted coal out of its ten-year slump. Because of its importance, the coal industry was highly regulated and production reached peak levels. Because of lingering idealization of Russia among left-wing miners, military recruitment picked up in the mining camps after Russia entered the war in 1941. This precipitated a critical labour shortage, so after May 1943 the armed forces no longer accepted miners.

There was some discontent in the coalfields over the cost of living, particularly in the "closed" company towns. Miners also objected to food and alcohol rationing. Workers had considerable bargaining power because of fuel and labour shortages, and used this leverage to improve working conditions. A district-wide strike in 1943 in defiance of a government ban led to important concessions.

A national royal commission examined the coal industry in 1945. The unions proposed that government, coal owners, railways, and unions cooperate in the "orderly marketing" of coal. Calls were again heard for the establishment of a national fuels policy, including subsidies on the transportation of coal to central Canadian markets, to make western coal competitive with American imports. These ideas quickly faded in the late 1940s as oil discoveries led to dramatic changes in fuel supplies.

The war period was the final boom for Alberta's coalfields. During the late 1940s and 1950s, conversion to natural gas for home heating led to disaster in the Drumheller and Lethbridge coalfields, while the railways' conversion from coal to diesel fuel devastated Nordegg and the Coal Branch. During peak wartime production, 350 mines employed eight thousand men; by the early 1960s, less than one hundred mines employed one thousand men. Many coal miners, who had been the backbone of radical political activity, retired. During the 1950s, the "proletariat in wild rose country" disappeared as a political force. Some coal towns in the Crow's Nest Pass lingered on in the 1960s and 1970s, and Grande Cache developed in 1966 to provide coking coal for Japan, but the coal industry had lost its substantial role in Alberta's economy and society.

The war also promoted federal intervention in the oil industry. Goaded by the American government's desire for maximum oil production and concerned about Canada's reliance on foreign imports, the Canadian government became interested in the Turner Valley field. It overrode provincial conservation legislation and encouraged maximum production. A federal crown corporation, Wartime Oils, provided lowcost loans for drilling. Principal and interest had to be repaid only if the well struck oil. This policy encouraged a flurry of drilling.

The federal government also took an active interest in the oil sands. Its Mines Branch had been interested prior to World War I, but decided in the early 1920s that oil sands production was too expensive. The Mines Branch was replaced during the 1920s by the provincial government, through its Scientific and Industrial Research Council (SIRCA), later the Alberta Research Council, a joint University of Alberta/Alberta government project and the brainchild of University of Alberta president H. M. Tory. The Research Council and its main oil sands researcher, chemical engineer Karl Clark (working closely with his talented assistant Sidney Blair), utilized the technique of water flotation extraction. This process mixed oil-bearing sand with hot water, then skimmed the bitumen tar from the surface. This was followed by further refining. Despite frustrating reverses, the Research Council's successful experimentation led during the late 1930s to commercial development.

During the 1930s, American oil engineer Max Ball established Abasand Oils and took over the Research Council plant. It produced synthetic crude in 1940–41; in 1943 the federal government took it over. However, the enterprise was not successful, and when the plant burned down for a second time in 1945, the federal government lost interest. This shifting pattern of interest among federal, provincial, and private actors in developing the oil sands continued. In 1946 the provincial government, annoyed with federal inaction, built a plant at Bitumount, where they experimented from 1946 to 1949. The long gestation of oil sands development was not yet complete, though the war promoted some progress.

The Metamorphosis of Social Credit

Social Credit remained in power during the 1940s, 1950s, and 1960s. However, the war contributed to the gradual erosion of Alberta's strongly regional outlook and led to other changes in the province's political culture. In the late 1930s, the Alberta government had refused to cooperate with the Rowell-Sirois Royal Commission on Dominion Provincial Relations, which had been appointed to study dominion-provincial relations and finances. Aberhart argued that the terms of reference and personnel of the commission predetermined its failure to understand the country's financial crisis. Instead of making a representation to the commission, in 1938 Alberta published *The Case for Alberta*, a detailed survey of economic conditions together with ideas for economic and constitutional reform. In 1941, when the King government called a dominion-provincial conference to discuss the commission's report, Aberhart joined premiers Hepburn of Ontario and Pattullo of British Columbia in sabotaging the conference. Aberhart's experience with the federal government had left him extremely wary of federal initiatives.

However, Aberhart was not opposed to all centralization, and during the war there was growing evidence of cooperation with the federal government. Late in 1941 he came to an agreement with federal officials on tax rental, whereby the federal government collected all income and corporation taxes for the duration of the war. Aberhart also responded to federal appeals for cooperation in economic planning, recruitment, war savings, and Victory Loan drives. Though suspicious that King was using the wartime emergency as a pretext for expanding federal authority, Aberhart did not want to give any hint of seeming disloyal. He argued that Canada needed a total war effort, which included mobilization of the country's financial institutions as well as men and resources.

In May 1943, at age sixty-four, Aberhart died suddenly of cirrhosis of the liver—often associated with overwork, lack of sleep, and stress. He had destroyed his health in his struggle to better the lot of Albertans and change the country's economic system. The press was kinder to him in death than in life. The *Edmonton Bulletin* of May 24 praised his social legislation and concluded "whatever one may think of his politics...he was the champion of the oppressed" and "he loved his fellow man."

As Aberhart's closest political and religious associate and acting premier, thirty-four-year-old Ernest Manning was the logical successor. The Social Credit caucus chose him almost unanimously.

The rightward shift that had become apparent in Aberhart's thinking during the early 1940s was accentuated under Manning. With disarray in the ranks of the opposition Independents, who were split between their rural and urban wings and lacked viable policies, and with the growing national popularity of the CCF, Manning came to see the socialists as his chief opposition. He began to define the major enemy of the people not as big finance, but as socialism. Like Major Douglas, Manning made a rather improbable link between financiers and socialists, arguing that financiers controlled socialists in their joint drive to full state control.

In the 1944 provincial election campaign, the Social Credit government opposed many forms of government intervention it once had favoured. This anti-socialist stance, coupled with a record of expanding education and health services, adjusting debt, promoting Alberta-made products, and aiding farmers, gave Manning a decisive win. The Alberta CCF under Edmonton printer Elmer Roper, a veteran in the labour movement, garnered 25 per cent of the vote, but this translated into only two seats. The Independents' vote collapsed to 17 per cent and three seats, while the 52 per cent of the vote captured by Social Credit represented a massive majority of fifty-one seats. Social Credit maintained this majority virtually unchanged until the mid-1950s.

Manning's crusade against socialism gradually reconciled Alberta's middle class to Social Credit. While the middle class certainly didn't embrace Social Credit fully, it was preferred over socialism. In fact, as later happened in British Columbia in the 1950s, some Alberta business people quietly deserted the Conservatives and Liberals to support Social Credit in order to keep the CCF out of power. Investors were also reassured by Manning's promise to refund the public debt, on which it had defaulted during the Depression. He was able to fulfill this promise by 1945. His fiscal policy of avoiding debt reassured the business community that Social Credit was becoming financially sound.

As leader, Manning was more pragmatic and less dogmatic than Aberhart. Consequently, despite the perceived drawbacks of his youth and inexperience, many saw him as a welcome relief from Aberhart. Unlike Aberhart, Manning did not judge everything in terms of black and white; nor did he assume that those who disagreed were his enemies. He was more patient and less demanding than Aberhart, and this made for more harmony within his cabinet, caucus, and party. The Alberta media, which had attacked Aberhart ferociously, gradually came to respect Manning.

The test of Manning's pragmatism came at the end of World War II. The staunch Douglasites within Social Credit once again became restive over the failure of the government to implement Social Credit. Manning's response to their activities was considerably different than Aberhart's had been.

During the 1940s Douglas, who had been anti-Semitic before the war, became increasingly so. He argued that international financiers were using the war to gain world power. For Douglas, at the centre of the plot were the leaders of World Jewry, who controlled both international finance and communism.

In the context of the war effort against Hitler, Manning and the Douglasites were on a collision course. Manning still paid lip service to Social Credit ideas. In 1946 he introduced an Alberta Bill of Rights, which included a philosophical statement of the need for monetary reform. (It was declared unconstitutional by the courts.) But Manning was unwilling to tolerate the growing Douglasite extremism.

The Douglasites included the old Social Credit Board; some Social Credit Members of Parliament, including Norman Jaques, MP for Wetaskiwin; and the editors of the *Canadian Social Crediter*, the newspaper organ of the national Social Credit movement. Jaques gave regular speeches in the House of Commons denouncing the alleged Jewish conspiracy, and identifying Jews as the common link in the plot of international finance, socialism, and international organizations to dominate the world.

The Douglasite conspiratorial frame of mind was part of a recurring phenomenon in a province with a strong populist tradition. Alberta populism, partly a legacy of American rural influence, had a positive side that stressed equality and democratic practices. But it often had another side: a rhetoric of exaggeration drawn from a susceptibility to conspiratorial fantasy. This tendency was fed by geographic and political isolation, which lent plausibility to various alleged conspiracies against the will of the common people. The conspirators might be Hutterites bent on dominating rural Alberta, French Canadians trying to dominate Canada, or Jews trying to dominate the world. The Douglasite notions of the Jewish world conspiracy (later recycled in the late 1970s and early 1980s by Eckville school teacher and mayor James Keegstra) provided a scapegoat to explain broad social changes.

Manning's showdown with the Douglasites came in 1947 after the Social Credit Board released its Annual Report. The anti-Semitism of the document, produced at public expense, precipitated an uproar. Partly under pressure from national Jewish organizations, Manning denied that Social Credit was anti-Semitic, condemned anti-Semitism as unchristian, and purged the Douglasites. He abolished the Social Credit Board, banned anti-Semitic articles in the *Canadian Social Crediter*, and forced the editors to resign. Manning saw the possible political consequences of Social Credit's being identified with anti-Semitism. His religious views also made anti-Semitism repugnant to him. Douglasite opposition to Zionism was incompatible with the world view of many Alberta Protestants, who saw the return of the Jews to Palestine as a fulfillment of prophecy. This purge of the Douglasites symbolized Manning's pragmatism, conservatism, and his effort to make Social Credit more acceptable to a broader public.

Wartime Nationalism and Ethnic Minorities

Although anti-Semitism intensified during the war among a small group of political extremists, overall the wartime economic boom eliminated many of the economic grievances that had kindled prejudice during the Depression. Wartime prosperity also blunted ethnic political radicalism, which had previously poisoned public attitudes toward central and eastern Europeans. The federal government's heavy-handed proscription of several left-wing ethnic organizations, and internment of some left-wing ethnic leaders early in the war, also stifled ethnic radicalism.

291

The sense of nationalism that the war fostered generally blurred political and class divisions and encouraged the greater acceptance of some previously stigmatized minorities. However, the negative side of wartime solidarity was hostility to minorities associated with "enemy powers," or those thought to be insufficiently loyal.

World War II aroused new issues for people of German and Japanese background in Alberta. Though anti-German sentiment was muted compared to World War I, there were brief outbursts of it led by "patriotic" groups. In the anxious climate created by the thrust of German troops into western Europe in the late spring of 1940, considerable publicity was given to "fifth column" activity—aid furnished to the German army by sympathizers. In May and June 1940, urban service clubs sponsored mass meetings demanding that the government take "vigorous action" against "enemy aliens." The federal government at the same time moved to outlaw several ethnic organizations. This, combined with improving war fortunes, failure to uncover any evidence of "fifth-columnist" activities, and the large numbers of German Canadians who enlisted in the Canadian Armed Forces, gradually calmed public fears.

Anti-Japanese feeling peaked after the bombing of the American base at Pearl Harbor in December 1941. In February 1942 the federal government ordered the evacuation of all 22,000 Japanese from coastal British Columbia, though half of them were Canadian-born and three-quarters were Canadian citizens. Subsequently, in the spring and summer of 1942, 2600 Japanese were brought to Alberta's labour-short sugar beet fields. The new arrivals multiplied by five the number of Japanese in the province.

Many Albertans opposed the Japanese when they first arrived, reasoning that if they were too dangerous to keep in B.C., they would also be dangerous in Alberta. Large and stormy protest meetings in southern Alberta opposed their entry. Premier Aberhart demanded that the federal government shoulder any costs and remove the B.C. Japanese after the war. City councils banned Japanese Canadians from living within city boundaries—even if they only wanted to attend school or work. Because of wartime regulations, no Japanese could travel more than twelve miles (nineteen kilometres) without a permit. Nor could they buy property, sell their homes, or move without government permission. The government also censored their mail and telephone calls, which were among their few means of expressing to each other their sense of bitterness and betrayal.

At the end of the war, these gross injustices were compounded by the Manning government's demand that the Japanese who had come from B.C. be removed from the province. Church groups and the press, however, felt that the federal government's attempts to deport Japanese Canadians and the provincial government's refusal to allow them to remain in the province were unjust. Sugar beet growers were desperate for their labour. In 1948, three years after the war was over, the evacuees were finally given official permission to remain. Some discriminatory hiring practices continued into the 1950s. However since that time, Japanese Canadians have broken through most social and economic barriers and have made outstanding contributions in agriculture, the professions, visual arts, and literature. The moving semi-autobiographical novel *Obasan* (1981) by Joy Kogawa, who came from B.C. to Coaldale with her family as a girl during the war, tells of the uprooting and its varying impact on three generations of Japanese Canadians, from the viewpoint of a young woman.

Hostility also mounted during the war toward members of three small pacifist sects, Hutterites, Mennonites, and Doukhobors, because of their pacifism and isolation. Resentment against Mennonites and Hutterites was particularly intense because they were German-speaking. Ironically Mennonites, who had argued during the 1920s that they were among the "preferred" category of German immigrants, now had to disassociate themselves from Germans. Under pressure from patriotic groups, Mennonites closed their German-language Bible and Saturday schools and German libraries. In Vauxhall, opposition to the use of German in church services swelled to such proportions during June 1940 that two Mennonite churches were burned.

In response to these intense pressures, nearly half of the eligible Mennonite young men joined the armed forces, partly to prove their loyalty. This inevitably led to considerable soul-searching and generational conflict within Mennonite communities. Mennonites also participated in war bond drives and established their own war relief programs. Those who registered as conscientious objectors were sent to work in government-supervised camps, national parks, forest experiment stations, or after 1943 were placed by the government's alternative service system on farms and in factories.

The Hutterites, in addition to being pacifists and German-speaking, were very visible with their distinctive dress and concentrated communal settlements. By the early 1940s, the original ten colonies in the province had grown to thirty-four and the number of Hutterites to approximately 4000, or about 120 in each colony, with the average colony occupying 5000 acres of land. Many groups, particularly in southern Alberta where the Hutterites were concentrated, objected to the Hutterites' being allowed alternative service. They felt that these exemptions from military service freed the Hutterites to buy more land while other Canadians were overseas fighting. Threatened violence against the Hutterites led in 1942 to a provincial government ban on all land sales to them for the duration of the war.

Hostility continued after the war. In 1947, after public hearings in which various farm, municipal, and patriotic groups repeatedly denounced the Hutterites, the Manning government restricted the amount of land Hutterites could own and designated where they could expand. This led to the dispersal of new Hutterite colonies. The Communal Property Act remained in force until 1972, when a new Conservative government repealed it.

Despite the growth of prejudice toward many peoples during the war, some groups such as the Chinese, Poles, and to some extent Ukrainians, achieved a new legitimacy as full-fledged Canadians through their support for the war. Some concerns lingered among Anglo-Canadians about the loyalty of Ukrainians, by far the largest of the three groups. Efforts were made by the Canadian government, a government-initiated umbrella organization of various Ukrainian organizations called the Ukrainian Canadian Committee, Ukrainian members of parliament such as Vegreville's Anthony Hlynka, and the Ukrainian Canadian press to gain support for conscription. However, a few Ukrainian nationalists remained lukewarm toward the war effort, since Poland and the Soviet Union were uncomfortable allies. Some Ukrainian communists also opposed fighting what they considered a capitalist war. In the 1942 national plebiscite on conscription, the whole province voted 70 per cent in favour. The predominantly No vote (57 per cent) in the largely Ukrainian Vegreville constituency partly reflected a long-standing opposition to conscription, a widespread feeling that enough young Ukrainian Canadians had already enlisted, and a protest vote against federal policies in a number of areas. Ukrainian nationalist and communist leaders blamed each other for the No vote.

Nevertheless, the war was a turning point in public acceptance of Ukrainians. Large numbers of young Ukrainian Canadians enlisted, support for the left amongst Ukrainians was waning, and the socio-economic status of Ukrainians was improving. They were led increasingly by an educated Canadian-born generation. Alberta-born

Ukrainian Canadian lawyer John Decore, elected as a Liberal in Vegreville in the 1949 federal election, personified this trend of upward mobility, integration, and the growing acceptance of Ukrainians.

Despite the anti-Hutterite, anti-Japanese, and anti-Semitic sentiment, several developments during the war undermined prejudice, laying the basis for a new pattern of ethnic relations. The channels for mobility provided by the armed forces, wartime industries, and urbanization undermined many social barriers. Economic development laid the basis for the postwar prosperity that helped ease ethnic tensions through reduced job competition and rising educational levels.

As more of the population was Canadian-born, social tension stemming from ethnic diversity declined. The wartime revulsion against Hitler and Nazism also gradually led to a growing rejection of explicit racist ideologies.

Alberta Natives Organize

The war period also saw new organizational strength among Alberta Indians with the successful building during the mid-1940s of the Indian Association of Alberta (IAA). This organization was the successor of an earlier League of Indians of Canada that had emerged during the 1920s, demanding better schools, extra rations for the old people, an end to surrenders of tribal land for white settlers, the preservation of Indian hunting, trapping, and fishing rights, and an end to government cutbacks in healthcare. In 1939 the League became the IAA. This new Indian organization continued to challenge the arbitrary power of the Indian Affairs Branch (IAB), which administered Treaty Indians. As noted by one author, "because the Indian was a ward of the state and did not have the franchise, there was little political input into Branch affairs. The IAB, run by ex-military men, was virtually immune from political monitoring and was in practice, accountable to no one."[2] The forced isolation of the reserves created common grievances against the IAB and the Indian Act. Yet this isolation, and tribal differences, made it difficult for Indians to unite. Their lack of political influence, and white indifference or racism, meant they had few outside allies to champion their cause.

A remarkable group of three men, Malcolm Norris, John Callihoo, and John Laurie, came together in the 1940s to build a solid base for the IAA. Norris had, during the 1930s, been one of the organizers of the Alberta Métis Association. Born into a well-to-do Métis family in 1900, he had traded and trapped in northern Alberta. As a strong socialist, he devoted his life to bettering the native peoples' position. While stationed in Calgary in the Canadian army during the war, Norris took up the cause of Treaty Indians. His friend John Callihoo was an educated Cree and a former freighter. He eventually became a farmer and had been active in radical farm organizations before becoming involved in Indian politics. Norris and Callihoo worked closely together to build the IAA. Norris recruited John Laurie, a white high school English teacher in Calgary whom he met through his CCF socialist ties. Laurie was anxious to help natives and had built close ties with Stoney, Sarcee, and Blood Indians. He encouraged young natives to pursue their education. For example, young Blood artist Gerald Tailfeathers lived with Laurie while studying art in Calgary. Laurie tirelessly lobbied for the native cause among whites, and also served as executive secretary of the association. Working together, the three men were able to gradually draw Indian support for the IAA from across the province.

Spearheaded by these three devoted and tireless activists, beginning in 1944 the association pressed the government to guarantee Indian and Métis veterans' grants, and to hire Indians in the IAB. The association also urged that the reserves be expanded to serve a growing population. The return of Indian and Métis veterans at the end of the war encouraged more contact and better relations with whites, and led to more white concern with native issues. Throughout the late 1940s and early 1950s, as the Canadian government's social welfare system expanded, social, health, and economic conditions on reserves gradually began to improve. The numbers of natives in the province, which had been in decline during the 1930s because of disease, began to increase rapidly. The federal government began to encourage Indian students to complete high school and enter technical colleges and universities. After 1951, under a revised Indian Act, the Department of Indian Affairs gradually gave band councils increased powers.

Women, the War, and Returning Veterans

While the war led to permanent changes in other areas of Alberta's economic and social life, the role of women was more resistant to change. Although women played a more direct part in this war than

Women played a more direct role in the war effort during World War II than during World War I. Women served in the armed forces in the Royal Canadian Air Force (Women's Division), the Canadian Women's Army Corps (CWAC), and the Women's Royal Canadian Naval Service (WRCNS). They were used on ground crews and in office work to release men for combat duty. These women of the CWAC are training at Coronation, Alberta. *(Glenbow Archives NA 3960-20)*

previously, taking them out of the home to an unprecedented degree, these changes proved transitory.

In addition to their volunteer effort in selling savings stamps and victory bonds, and monitoring rationing, women were directly involved in the war effort. They responded not only as nurses, but for the first time the three armed forces were open to women. Many educated Alberta women served as officers in the women's divisions of the armed forces. Calgary's Mary Dover reached the rank of lieutenant colonel in the Canadian Women's Army Corps and headed the country's largest training centre. Women who became officers had usually been teachers or professionals, and many had served in the volunteer Alberta Women's Service Corps, established at the onset of the war to train women in military discipline.

Perhaps more Alberta women would have enlisted in the ranks if the government had not assigned them almost exclusively to routine and menial tasks and paid them only two-thirds of the amount paid to men. The women were used to free men for combat, and only a small minority served overseas. Most spent the war as clerks, hospital assistants, storeroom workers, drivers, and cooks.

Alberta women also entered the paid labour force in greater numbers than ever before. By mid-1941, the reserve pool of male civilian workers had been exhausted, and the federal government began to encourage women to join the labour force. Women responded, driven by patriotism, the desire to work outside the home, and the need to augment low family incomes. Many worked in new areas of the civil service and in the aircraft, meat packing, and textile industries. Edmonton's GWG was Canada's largest garment manufacturer during the war, and it employed primarily women.

These opportunities in the services and labour force did not mean a real change in status. Women were regarded as a convenient source of labour, and there was considerable anxiety that this work not compromise traditional notions of femininity. With the end of the war, the government cut back its programs to help working women and pressured them to make way for returning men. At the end of the war, most women returned home. The proportion of women in the workforce plummetted, and did not return to 1945 levels until the mid-1960s.

After the war in Europe ended on May 7, 1945, Albertans welcomed home their service men and women. Economic, social, and personal adjustments had to be made on all sides. Wives and husbands, long separated by the war, had to reacquaint themselves. Many servicemen and their wives, who had married hurriedly during the war, faced the reality of building relationships with people they scarcely knew.

The returning veterans (mostly male) accelerated economic and social change. They came back changed. No longer did they see themselves as insignificant smalltown and farm boys. They were war heroes who had seen the world and fought in the world's greatest struggle. But their education was usually limited and the skills they had learned in the army seldom had much relevance to the economy of the postwar world. Some came back bitter against those who had not joined the services, and many were temporarily frustrated over difficulties in finding jobs and accommodation. Their adjustment problems often paled compared to those of their war brides. For British or Dutch girls, fantasies of rural life on the prairie seldom matched the reality of hard work in remote rural areas, in primitive accommodation and a different culture, building a relationship with someone they often scarcely knew.

Government programs helped ease the veterans' economic transition. The Veterans' Land Act provided land for those who wanted to farm. Life on farms in remote cabins in the Peace River district, where land was still available, proved difficult. Governments provided roads and equipment, but the economics of agriculture and the lack of schools and hospitals meant few succeeded as farmers. Most sold their land and moved to the cities, or went to work on the oil rigs in the post-Leduc era.

The biggest difficulty facing the veterans who returned to the cities was a housing shortage. The federal government eased the problem by establishing a program to build homes for veterans, and entire subdivisions for veterans were developed. The postwar housing shortage was also eased by the thousands of Dutch, German, Austrian, Italian, and other European immigrants who arrived in the early 1950s and immediately went to work building the new suburbs.

The government also paid tuition fees and subsistence allowances to veterans who wanted to attend university, and veterans jammed the University of Alberta, preparing themselves for a new postwar world. The generation of Albertans who emerged from university in the late 1940s and early 1950s graduated to a world of economic opportunity created by an oil boom. They experienced unprecedented prosperity, and would be influential in shaping Alberta's economic, social, and political institutions over the next twenty years.

After their often horrific wartime experiences, the veterans wanted normalcy, which for many meant a return to the security of family life and religion. In a social milieu that romanticized motherhood, marriages increased and the birthrate skyrocketed. Churches were revitalized by high levels of attendance. Paradoxically, this return to what were perceived as traditional values occurred alongside unprecedented economic growth and technological development, both of which would ultimately change profoundly both Albertans' values and their ways of life, heralding the age of consumerism and a revolution in social patterns.

While women who had worked during the war returned home, a new group of women—the displaced persons—were brought in to fill menial jobs in hospitals, in restaurants, and as domestics. They helped the urban middle-class cope with the care of the many new young Albertans—the "baby boomers"—who would have a momentous demographic and social impact.

World War II changed Alberta economically, socially, and politically. The postwar world was one neither of economic recession, as it had been after World War I, nor of stability. Massive oil discoveries in 1947 were about to thoroughly transform the Alberta economy and society, and usher in a prolonged period of economic growth.

CHAPTER ELEVEN

Oil and the Birth of Modern Alberta: 1947–1971

While World War II had brought social and economic changes to Alberta, immense oil and gas discoveries after the war totally transformed the province's economy, hastening political and social change. These discoveries began in 1947 at Leduc, south of Edmonton, and continued throughout the 1950s and into the 1960s. Prosperity brought immigration, urbanization, and a more consumer-oriented society, permeated by American popular culture. In the decade after the Leduc discoveries, Alberta changed from a predominantly rural, agricultural society into an urban one, dominated by the oil and gas industry. In 1951 just over half of the population lived in larger towns and cities. By 1961 almost 70 per cent was urban. Fed in part on the wealth generated by the petroleum industry, northern Alberta developed rapidly. The province's educational and cultural institutions burgeoned, and a sizable moneyed class emerged in the largest cities.

Although a Social Credit government presided over this transformation and under Manning won huge electoral majorities, these large-scale social and economic changes gradually undermined support for Social Credit. In 1958 Albertans deserted Social Credit at the federal level. In 1971 a revived provincial Conservative party under Peter Lougheed finally defeated the seemingly invincible Social Credit administration, ending a thirty-six-year dynasty.

The Leduc Discoveries and the Postwar Oil Boom

On February 13, 1947, five hundred reporters, businessmen, and government officials gathered in the cold in a farmer's field near Leduc to witness an historic event. Gushing surges of oil, water, and drilling mud spewed into a flare pit. There the flame was lit on the Leduc No. 1 well. Imperial Oil, which had drilled 133 dry holes and spent $20 million with little to show, finally had a major discovery.

MINING **OIL** FINANCE

Western Examiner

Vol. XXI No. 42   THE WESTERN EXAMINER, CALGARY, SATURDAY, FEB. 22, 1947   Price 10 Cents

At Birth of New Alberta Oil Field

IMPERIAL LEDUC No. 1 WELL—Discovery for a second major Alberta oil field, blowing out its huge billow of burning oil and heavy smoke when the well was completed as a big producer last week.

The oil discoveries at Leduc in 1947 ushered in a new era in Alberta's history. Oil-based wealth brought new people and ideas, transforming Alberta from a predominantly rural to a highly urban and consumer-oriented society. *(Glenbow Archives NA 789.80)*

Alberta's Social Credit minister of mines, former Cardston school principal and Mormon bishop N. Eldon Tanner, turned a valve to divert the flow into a storage tank—and ushered in the modern age of the Canadian petroleum industry.

Following the initial Leduc find, further drilling proved the existence of a large oil field. The spectacular Atlantic No. 3 well, which came in as a gusher in March 1948, blew wild for six months, spilling over a million barrels of oil over the surrounding fields. The spectacle was shown on newsreels and newspapers around the world. The Leduc oilfield was a 200-million-barrel discovery, ten times the size of the Turner Valley field, but it would soon be overshadowed by other Alberta oilfields.

In the late 1940s and early 1950s, scores of companies joined the search for oil. World petroleum reserves were low and exploration was frenetic, particularly by American oil companies. Oilfields were discovered in Redwater (1948), Golden Spike (1949), Fenn-Big Valley (1950), Wizard Lake (1951), Acheson, Bonnie Glen, and Westerose (1952), Pembina (1953), Swan Hills (1959), and Rainbow Lake (1965). Pembina, Canada's largest oilfield, was discovered by Arne Nielsen, a young geologist who grew up on a farm in the Danish-American settlement of Standard, Alberta. Nielsen would later play a key management role in the industry, becoming the first Canadian president of Mobil Oil Canada in 1967.

Oil production rose dramatically, from 7.7 million barrels in 1946 (mostly from the declining Turner Valley field) to 143.7 million barrels in 1956. Major pipeline systems were built from Edmonton to carry Alberta oil to Ontario, Vancouver, and the U.S. The pipeline to the American northwest was considered strategic by American politicians because of their need for oil supplies during the Korean War. These oil pipelines, which were soon accompanied by transcontinental gas pipelines, were the megaprojects of the 1950s.

The determined search for petroleum also yielded major natural gas discoveries at Pincher Creek and Cessford (1947), Jumping Pound (1948), and Waterton (1957). In the late 1950s, significant gas reserves were also found near Calgary at Crossfield, Harmatton, and Elkton.

Oilfield development brought growth and change to many small towns, such as Leduc, Calmar, and Fort Saskatchewan, and created new ones. The area around Fort Saskatchewan gradually developed into the largest industrial complex in the province, based on petroleum and petrochemical refining. The oil companies and provincial government jointly created towns, such as Devon, Redwater, Drayton Valley, Swan Hills, High Level, and Rainbow Lake. Natural gas plants in many small communities transformed local economies and social structures.

National debates over gas marketing and pipelines were heated and complex because they combined a variety of overlapping issues concerning economic viability, financing, differing estimates of reserves, self-sufficiency in fuels, American investment and control, and Canadian sovereignty. Advocates of "all-Canadian" routes revived the nineteenth-century nationalistic arguments that had justified government support for the transcontinental railway.

Beginning in 1949, Ottawa's economic czar, Liberal cabinet minister C. D. Howe, tried to persuade the Alberta government to supply natural gas to energy-short central Canada. Manning resisted at first, since the estimates of gas reserves indicated that there was barely enough for a thirty-year supply for Albertans, who considered natural gas an important God-given legacy, one that might provide the basis for industrialization. Both opposition parties, the Liberals and the CCF, opposed gas exports on these grounds. Pressure on the Alberta government from Howe and the petroleum companies gradually increased, and this pressure coupled with increasing gas reserves finally led the Manning government to relent. In 1951 Parliament granted a charter to Trans-Canada Pipe Lines, the subsidiary of an American company, to construct a pipeline from Alberta to

Montreal. Fearful that the federal government might use the pipeline project to encroach on Alberta's jurisdiction over natural gas, the Alberta government set up the Alberta Gas Trunk Line in 1954 as a joint business/government company to gather and transmit gas, as well as to keep jurisdiction over gas-gathering within Alberta.

The negotiations leading to the start-up of the transcontinental pipeline were long, arduous, and politically sensitive. In 1954, C. D. Howe forced two rival companies, Western Pipelines and Trans-Canada Pipe Lines, into a shotgun marriage, using the name of the latter company. To cement the union, Manning and Howe recommended that N. Eldon Tanner, who had left the Alberta cabinet in 1952 to head a Calgary-based oil company, should become president. Canadian financial houses shied away from the huge project, and the federal cabinet split over whether to help finance it. Howe finally convinced the federal cabinet to advance 90 per cent of the cost of the western section of the pipeline and to agree that the Canadian and Ontario governments would build the costly portion through Northern Ontario. Of the seventeen Alberta MPs, eleven Social Crediters, four Liberals, and one of the two Alberta Conservatives strongly supported the proposal.

Many Canadians objected to leaving control of the pipeline in private hands or those of Americans (since Trans-Canada Pipe Lines was still regarded as an American company). However, the issue that most aroused public opinion was the government's heavy-handed use of closure to ram a bill through Parliament and get the pipeline underway by the summer of 1956. Howe, Manning, and Trans-Canada temporarily had their way and the pipeline quickly moved forward, an engineering feat that generated economic activity across Canada.

But the Liberals' handling of the scheme was a major factor in their loss to the Conservatives in the 1957 federal election. They received little political credit for the project in Alberta, losing three of their four Alberta seats.

Postwar Immigration: Diversity and Change

After the Leduc discoveries, the province's population surged. From 803,000 in 1946, it rose to 939,000 in 1951, and to 1,332,000 in 1961. The rise of more than 40 per cent between 1951 and 1961 was in large part due to natural increase, though 13 per cent of the growth came from net migration. This reflected an influx of American and European immigrants, and of former Saskatchewan residents.

The postwar wave of immigrants promoted economic growth and urbanization, and contributed to the rightward shift in Alberta's political culture. This wave of European immigrants was smaller than the major wave before World War I; nonetheless, it had an important impact. It included political refugees ("displaced persons" in the language of the day) from central and eastern Europe, and thousands of German, Dutch, Scandinavian, and British immigrants who sought better economic opportunities. Some of the refugees served a period of enforced apprenticeship as farm workers because of immigration regulations that assumed that farm labour was most needed; but most of the immigrants were educated and skilled, and left for the cities as soon as they could.

Between 1946 and 1956, over 1.2 million immigrants came to Canada from Europe. Alberta received 95,000; roughly 10 per cent of these were political refugees. By 1956 the postwar movement of refugees had largely ended; however, between 1956 and 1966 another 1.4 million immigrants came to Canada, about 90,000 of them to Alberta. During the late 1950s, the displaced persons were followed by immigrants from Mediterranean countries, including Portugal, Greece, and especially Italy, who left overcrowded rural areas where there was little economic opportunity. Italian and Portuguese men worked primarily in the urban construction industry, and the Greeks worked mainly in the restaurant business. Many Greek, Portuguese, and Italian women worked in service industries.

Non-white immigration remained slight throughout the 1950s and 1960s. Most Albertans tacitly approved the federal government's policy of encouraging European immigration to promote economic development, while limiting non-whites. Despite lingering racist measures in the immigration act, which restricted non-white immigration, the repeal of the Chinese Exclusion Act in 1947 enabled Chinese Canadians to sponsor relatives and begin to establish more normal patterns of family life. Small quotas were also introduced in 1951 for the Commonwealth countries of India, Pakistan, and Ceylon (Sri Lanka). For the first time, Albertans began to meet Pakistanis, Indians, and Sri Lankans, most of whom came as professionals to the cities, although some of these South Asians began their careers as teachers in rural Alberta.

The economic boom in the cities during the 1950s created immense opportunities for skilled immigrant workmen, technicians, and professionals. The small construction industry was gradually taken over by Dutch, German, Mennonite, Austrian, Italian, and other immigrants, who found that language and cultural barriers meant little in construction. Many prospered in the extended postwar boom. Although housing styles were predominantly North American, they also often subtly reflected the influence of the European contractors and craftsmen.

"Displaced persons" encountered some adjustment problems. Those who came to Alberta as farm labourers, often in the sugar beet fields of southern Alberta, usually faced primitive living conditions. Once they moved to the cities, they often faced difficulties in having their European qualifications recognized. Many former professionals—army officers, civil servants, and skilled workers—experienced demoralizing periods of downward mobility. Few found management work in the oil industry. This was largely because they lacked a North American education and because the industry had a strong Anglo-Saxon bias.

Many newcomers found some solace in ethnic organizations and churches during the 1950s. The well-educated, energetic postwar immigrants revitalized the cultural organizations of many ethnic groups, and established many new ones. Tension often arose, however, between these immigrants and earlier ones, based on differing class and political backgrounds. Among the anti-communist central and eastern Europeans, small new nationalist ethnic organizations were established by Ukrainians, Russians, Estonians, Latvians, Lithuanians, Hungarians, Poles, Czechs, Slovaks, Croats, and Serbs. These organizations reflected the newcomers' dedication to the liberation of their homelands and their determination to keep their homeland cultures and languages alive.

In the postwar era, the political consensus among central and eastern European groups, including the numerically dominant Ukrainians, shifted decidedly to the right. Public opinion in the larger society was running against the left because of the Cold War, the Gouzenko affair (which revealed Soviet spying in Canada), and Canada's support for the Korean War. The economic prosperity of the 1950s, along with aging, softened the radical edge of many immigrant activists. While the presence and cultural life of postwar central and eastern European immigrants was, unfortunately, generally ignored by the larger society, their political perspectives were among the many factors that helped to shift Alberta's political culture to the right during the 1950s and 1960s.

Since British and Western European immigrants faced less discrimination than the displaced persons, and since their cultural adjustment was less traumatic, their organizations were usually less numerous and less active. Also, they lacked a political mission. However, they too tended to the conservative side of the political spectrum. They included British immigrants fleeing socialism, conservative rural Dutch Calvinist immigrants, and the small-business oriented Germans, Austrians, and Scandinavians, who were usually leery of government regulation.

The relatively few Americans who came to Alberta in the postwar era had a notable social and political impact. In the early years of the boom, a majority of the senior management of the major oil companies, most of which were American-owned, were from California, Oklahoma, Texas, and Louisiana. From 1955 to 1970, nine of the fifteen presidents of Calgary's exclusive Petroleum Club were Americans. Americans such as Charles Hetherington, president of Panarctic Oils (which helped open the Arctic to oil exploration), and Robert Campbell, president of Pan-Canadian Petroleums, also ran Canadian companies. Faced with growing pressure from Canadians in their ranks, and aware of growing Canadian nationalism, the American oil companies gradually Canadianized their personnel at the senior levels of management during the 1960s. Those Americans who remained usually took out Canadian citizenship so that they could vote. Like their counterparts in the United States, they often held strong right-wing views. The Americans also brought their enthusiasm for involvement in volunteer organizations; they helped give Calgary its volunteer activist orientation through participation in groups such as the prestigious Stampede Board (which ran the annual Calgary Stampede and related exhibitions and sports activities).

Large numbers of American professors were recruited to the province's universities in the 1960s, partly because of the rapid expansion of universities at a time when there was a limited number of qualified Canadian applications. During the late 1960s, American war resisters, opposed to the Vietnam War, began arriving. Most of them stayed only temporarily and had a fleeting impact. By contrast, most of the professors stayed on and integrated fully into Canadian university life even though they had intended to stay only a few years.

Urban Life and Popular Culture

The postwar oil boom led to dramatic urban growth and change. As the head-office centre of the oil industry, Calgary boomed. By 1965, it had 965 headquarters of companies that were involved in various phases of petroleum exploration, extraction, financing, processing, and marketing. Half of the city's workers owed their jobs directly to the oil and gas industry. Edmonton, which was closer to the major oil finds, developed as a major refining and petrochemical centre, as the main base of operations for oil-industry contractors, and as the dominant centre for the transmission of petroleum products. Both cities grew from just over a 100,000 in 1946 to over 400,000 in 1971, making them two of the fastest-growing cities in North America. New office towers transformed their skylines. Suburban housing developments and shopping centres sprang up, marking their outward expansion. In Edmonton highrise apartments and new elite residential neighbourhoods competed with each other along the edge of the valley for views of the river.

With a well-paid management class, the impact of oil wealth was particularly evident in Calgary. New exclusive suburbs in south Calgary, such as Eagle Ridge, gave visible expression to this wealth, along with a proliferation of exclusive golf clubs and riding stables. Oil wealth also made private philanthropy possible. The Ontario-born Calgary lawyer and oilman Eric Harvie, who owned extensive

When this photo of downtown Calgary was taken in 1964, Calgary had tripled in size since the end of World War II to over 300,000 people. Edmonton had more than tripled during the same time period. Although Calgary continued to service its agricultural hinterland, it became largely dependent on the oil and gas industry. (*Glenbow Archives NA 2864-1539*)

mineral leases in the Leduc area and Redwater oilfields, was fascinated by history and collecting. He endowed the Glenbow Foundation in 1955 to house his substantial collection of historical artifacts and artwork. During the 1960s and 1970s, the Glenbow Museum and Archives developed into western Canada's most important collection of material on the history of the West and served as southern Alberta's major museum and art gallery.

Many other centres were also transformed by the oil industry. The cities absorbed the off-farm migration, which resulted from better economic opportunities in the cities and the growth of mechanization on the farms. Red Deer developed beyond its roles in agricultural service and distribution to become the centre of oil and natural-gas developments in central Alberta. By 1971, it had replaced Medicine Hat as the fourth-largest city in Alberta. Although little influenced by oilfield development, Lethbridge remained the third largest city, reaching 41,000 by 1971. The closing of Lethbridge's coal mines in the late 1940s and early 1950s had a limited impact on its economy, because the completion of the St. Mary River Dam in 1951 doubled the irrigated acreage in the surrounding area, and this furthered the growth of the city as an agricultural distribution centre.

Alberta in the 1950s and 1960s was marked by the dominance of urban life, by affluence, and by consumerism. The baby boom and the pent-up desire for homes, appliances, and cars created a massive demand for consumer goods. By 1971 there were over 550,000 cars in the province, over five times more than in 1946. The popularity of the car transformed the urban landscape with more and more parking lots, gas stations, drive-in theatres, fast-food drive-ins, and motels.

These trends reflected the growing Americanization of Canadian society. The age of the consumer was also the age of television, which in Canada was made up mostly of American programs. During the 1950s, television replaced the movies as the main vehicle for American cultural influence in the province: Albertans were as taken as the rest of North Americans by I Love Lucy, The Ed Sullivan Show, and Father Knows Best, among many others. By the mid-1960s, fourteen television stations in Alberta broadcast to most of the province. Television, radio, magazines, and records brought the latest trends in North American popular culture and a bewildering succession of fads in clothing, music, hair fashions, slang, and dances, from the jive to the twist. The immense popularity of pop musicians, including Elvis Presley, swept the province. However, the impact of extreme elements in North American popular culture, such as the "beatniks," "hoods," and "hippies," was always limited by Alberta's relative isolation. While each of these three movements had Alberta imitators, more conservative cultural styles usually prevailed.

Affluence and mass-market catering to the baby boomers and city dwellers brought changes in social values and styles, and hence generational conflict. Beneath the cover of prosperity were many tales of painful adjustment from rural to urban life, of conflict between immigrant parents and their North-Americanized children, and of personal struggles over religious and ethnic identity—all reflections of rapidly changing social values.

Despite pockets of poverty, a generally contented population lost interest in politics; prosperity had softened class, religious, and ethnic conflict. Increasingly apolitical, Albertans accepted Manning's "chairman of the board" style of administration, and only a few voices lamented the absence of a real opposition or of political debate. European travel, summer cottages, and professional sports were much more on the minds of middle-class and upper-middle-class urbanites in the 1950s and 1960s than monetary reform or western alienation.

Prosperity did not prevail in rural Alberta to the same extent that it did in the cities, but farm incomes were kept up by good crops and by the Diefenbaker government's massive wheat sales to China and the Soviet Union, which began in the early 1960s. The standard of living of farm families improved with government-sponsored farm

Farms were further revolutionized by changing technology during the postwar era. Farmers could use these three self-propelled combines to do the work of dozens of farm hands. With new technology, and other economic trends, farms increased in size and the rural population declined. (*Glenbow Archives ND 10-235*)

income supports, rural electrification schemes, better telephone service, and the widespread conversion from coal to propane for home fuel. Those who remained on farms were generally better off than before, but there were fewer of them. The 41 per cent of the population living on farms in 1946 declined to 19 per cent by 1966. Towns that were centrally located on highways grew as farmers travelled farther to shop and socialize. Many other hamlets and villages, their social and economic life undercut, faded into oblivion.

Rapid growth and affluence in the cities brought a new era of confidence and assertiveness, which was best reflected in a renewed boosterism. City administrations, chambers of commerce, and service clubs experienced a renaissance in their aggressive self-promotion. Reflecting this trend during the 1950s was the fact that, in each of the province's largest cities, a flamboyant, self-made promoter was elected mayor. In Calgary, radio announcer and manager Don Mackay enthusiastically dealt with the problems of a rapidly growing city, with its new university, airport terminal, and sports facilities. Mackay popularized the white Stetson hat as the city's symbol. Medicine Hat's mayor, the Jewish athlete, rancher, and businessman, Harry Veiner, attracted widespread attention through his zany capers, challenging rival mayors at every conceivable sports and novelty contest, from boxing to dogsled races, and from Indian wrestling to skipping, milking, and twist dancing. His business promotion helped assure the development of a petrochemical industry in Medicine Hat. Theatre owner A. W. Shackleford in Lethbridge and William Hawrelak in Edmonton had similar capacities for promoting themselves and their cities.

Hawrelak, a young Ukrainian Canadian businessman with a farm background, served from 1951 to 1959. Hawrelak was an endless booster, and his projects included promoting the Yellowhead Highway, and building new libraries, hospitals, parks, and other recreational facilities. Hawrelak resigned in 1959 after a judicial inquiry concluded there had been misconduct and conflict of interest in his real estate dealings. Ever popular in northeast Edmonton with small businesspeople, and with the large number of Edmontonians of Slavic background who resented the longstanding Anglo-Canadian social and economic dominance of the city, Hawrelak was re-elected in 1964. However, he was again disqualified from office because of conflict of interest in 1965. Hawrelak had the final say though, winning overwhelmingly again as mayor in 1974. He died in office the following year. As noted by one author, Hawrelak's continuing

310

popularity among Slavs was part of a "need for a symbolic recognition of personal achievement for his own ethnic community that the dominant society never did come to understand."[1]

Alberta's cities cultivated their western image as a source of identity and pride and as a tourist attraction. Perhaps the Calgary Stampede, as well as Whoop-up Days in Lethbridge and Klondike Days in Edmonton, were attempts to stay close to western (and in Edmonton's case northern) roots at a time when the pioneer generation was passing away and the relevance of symbols of rural identity was fading.

The new urban confidence and affluence were reflected in the popularity of professional sports, particularly football, which indirectly encouraged other social changes. The Calgary Stampeders' Grey Cup victory in 1948 and the Edmonton Eskimos' football dynasty of the 1950s brought great excitement. Albertans idolized the Eskimos' American import quarterback, Jackie Parker. Professional football cut across ethnic and racial barriers, with football stars Normie Kwong (who was born in Calgary), Rollie Miles, Johnny Bright, "Sugarfoot" Anderson, and "Woody" Strode helping to provide a new, positive image of Chinese and blacks. Professional football in the 1950s proved to be something of a training ground for many Alberta politicians. Football provided both notoriety and contacts, and a number of Eskimo players eventually developed high profiles in Alberta public life. These included Premier Don Getty, MP Steve Paproski, and businessman Normie Kwong. Peter Lougheed also had a brief stint as a professional player for the Eskimos.

Postwar affluence encouraged the development and expansion of educational and cultural institutions. The two new twin Jubilee Auditoria, built by the province in Calgary and Edmonton in 1955, provided extensive new facilities for arts groups.

Postsecondary education expanded dramatically. Because of the needs of a highly technical oil industry and a young, growing population, Alberta came to have one of the best-educated populations in the country. The University of Alberta expanded rapidly, growing from 5,000 in 1959 to 17,500 a decade later, with a plethora a new buildings that altered the face of the campus, and a variety of new programs. The province also established a new university in Calgary during the 1950s and 1960s. It had a long gestation, going back to 1945 when the Normal School in Calgary became a branch of the Faculty of Education at the University of Alberta. Gradually, during the 1950s and 1960s, other programs were introduced, and the university developed as a branch of the University of Alberta. After 1966 the University of Calgary became fully autonomous. In 1956 Lethbridge Junior College began offering both university and vocational courses, and in 1967 the University of Lethbridge took over and expanded the academic section of the college. Athabasca, an innovative extension university, was established in 1970. Several junior colleges were also started. Edmonton's Grant MacEwan Community College, begun in 1970, was designed to exclusively offer vocational and other non-university programs.

Technical education received a boost because of the needs created by the oil boom. In 1962 the Northern Alberta Institute of Technology began operation and by 1966, with six thousand students, NAIT was the largest technical institute in Canada. The Provincial Institute of Technology and Art in Calgary became the Southern Alberta Institute of Technology (SAIT) in 1960.

The new and expanded universities and colleges attracted a cosmopolitan group of academics and instructors from across North America, Europe, and Asia. Creative writing, drama, music, dance, and the visual arts all received new impetus from academics who became involved in the local arts scenes.

One example of the new ferment in the arts in the urban centres was the activity promoted by the Allied Arts Council in Calgary. The Council began in 1946 when retired chief city librarian Alexander Calhoun and a small group saved and leased an old mansion, the Coste House, as their cultural home. Calhoun had long been a cultural force in Calgary, arriving from Ontario first in 1911. He had turned the library into a community centre, and though as an agnostic and socialist was somewhat isolated from mainstream thought in the city, he helped energize the city's intellectual and cultural life. The Allied Arts Council, with Calhoun as president, developed the Coste House as an art galley and centre for a sketch club, the Alberta Society of Artists, the Women's Musical Club, the Calgary branch of the Canadian Handicraft Guild, the Calgary Civic Theatre, and other groups.

By the 1960s, professional theatre began to overshadow amateur theatre in the two largest cities. The Citadel Theatre was started in Edmonton in 1965 by local lawyer, real estate developer, and arts promoter Joe Shoctor. The Edmonton-born Shoctor had studied at the University of Alberta. His interest in drama took him to New York, where he produced several plays before deciding to return home to help develop theatre in Edmonton. Theatre Calgary emerged in 1968, building on the work of a strong amateur theatre movement,

312

which had been led during the late 1940s, 1950s, and 1960s by local drama teacher Betty Mitchell. Her Workshop 14 group, which began as an adjunct to a high school drama program, helped raise the standard of amateur drama in the province and pave the way for professional theatre.

The Banff School of Fine Arts attracted leading writers, musicians, and artists from across Canada, the United States, and abroad, and furthered its reputation as a major Canadian cultural institution. Talented young Albertans found encouragement from a cosmopolitan group of faculty and students. Novelists W. O. Mitchell and Robert Kroetsch, pianist Marek Jablonski, and many other artists studied and taught at the centre.

Mitchell, who began teaching at the Banff School in the late 1960s, was born in Saskatchewan in 1912. After university, and a year as principal at a school in Castor, Mitchell moved to High River in 1944. He lived there until 1968, devoting himself to writing, but leaving for a stint of three years as fiction editor for Maclean's magazine. From 1968 to 1987, he was writer-in-residence at several universities in Alberta and Ontario. Mitchell is one of the most accessible and popular prairie novelists. His classic novel, *Who Has Seen the Wind*, published in 1947, powerfully portrays the landscape, characters, and society of a small prairie town. His "Jake and the Kid" stories, written during the 1950s for magazine and radio, and published as a book in 1961, introduced a national audience to the humour, eccentric characters, tall tales, and local dialect of the prairies.

The art department of the Provincial Institute of Technology and Art in Calgary developed further in the postwar years under the leadership of Illingworth "Buck" Kerr. A native of Saskatchewan, Kerr had studied in Toronto during the 1920s under members of the Group of Seven. After living several years in England, where he painted and wrote, he came to Calgary in 1947 and directed the art department for the next twenty years. (The art department was renamed the Alberta College of Art in 1960.) Anxious to capture the space and scale of the prairies, Kerr studied in the mid-1950s with leading exponents of abstract expressionism in the United States, and his subsequent work was influenced by them. Kerr had a strong impact on a whole new generation of Alberta artists.

The Manning Years

A farm boy from Saskatchewan, whose only formal education beyond grade eight was in Aberhart's Prophetic Bible Institute, presided over the dramatic economic, demographic, and social transformation of Alberta. After the oil discoveries, prolonged economic growth drastically reduced the appeal of radical economic reform. Ernest Manning subsequently transformed the Social Credit movement from one of fading principle to one that could claim credit for prosperity.

Throughout the late 1940s and 1950s, Manning cemented an alliance with business. His philosophy of individualism, strong opposition to socialism, Cold War rhetoric, and anti-unionism appealed to businessmen. They tolerated his strong commitment to generous social services, based on Social Credit's concern for the disadvantaged, because oil wealth made these services possible. Under Manning, Alberta's per capita spending on social services was well ahead of the national average.

In the energy field, the Social Credit government wanted the maximum production possible and encouraged investment and development to diversify the economy. They welcomed American capital and expertise, seeing no other option. Earlier they had tried to interest British and central Canadian capital in the oil industry, but with little success. While American investment poured into many Canadian industries during the 1950s, energy was the sector where it was greatest. By 1963, Americans controlled 62 per cent of the Canadian oil and natural gas industries.

Manning's natural resources policy was based on three main assumptions. First, he assumed that the resources belonged to the people of Alberta, and the Alberta government must get a fair return. Second, he assumed that sound conservation practices were essential. (Aberhart had first established the Petroleum and Gas Conservation Board in 1938 in response to concern about wasteful flaring of gas. Manning later renamed it the Energy Resources Conservation Board, making it responsible for regulating exploration and production.) Third, Manning assumed that the most efficient way of developing resources was through the private sector. He rejected government ownership, partly for ideological reasons. In addition, the petroleum industry was risky; Alberta oil was expensive to produce, and the government lacked the expertise to produce, refine, and market petroleum in a world where large companies controlled access to markets.

Critics charge that the Socred government didn't get a large enough return and failed to protect the resource from foreign ownership, but Socred policies were widely approved by the Alberta public. The many Americans and their children in Alberta, the Alberta government's reliance on American technical expertise, and the large numbers of Albertans who worked for American-owned companies reduced concern about American ownership. The ideological climate of the Cold War also predisposed Albertans to look favourably on American interests. During the late 1960s and 1970s, nationalists, such as the New Democratic Party (NDP, the successor of the CCF), and Edmonton bookseller and publisher Mel Hurtig (one of the founders and later chairman of the Committee for an Independent Canada), warned of the dangers to the Canadian economy, and cultural and political sovereignty, of excessive American ownership. While many Albertans had forebodings about the level of American ownership, at election time the majority usually voted on the assumption that American capital was necessary for continuing prosperity.

Manning had remarkable longevity as premier because of prosperity and the perception of his being a capable manager of the province's resources. He won seven elections over twenty-five years, usually with large, and often huge, majorities. Revenues from oil made possible an enviable network of roads, educational institutions, and social and health services. By 1957 Alberta was Canada's leading per capita spender. Social Credit was particularly generous in its treatment of pensioners. To the embarrassment of Alberta's CCF, the Alberta government's supplement to pensioners was considerably larger than that of the CCF government in neighbouring Saskatchewan. Spending on postsecondary education was also high, although there was little support for the Social Credit regime among university faculty or students.

Few Albertans listened to Manning's nationally broadcast weekly *Back to the Bible Hour*, but many found it reassuring that they had a premier who was a staunch Christian—a man of sobriety, purpose, and integrity. This meant that his government faced relatively few scandals.

Nonetheless, in 1955 charges of abuse of public trust by cabinet ministers and MLAs helped the opposition Liberals (led by combative ex-newspaperman Harper Prowse) win fifteen of twenty-four opposition seats. The Socred support dipped from 56 to 46 per cent of the popular vote. The issues involved government procurement policies regarding land and materials, tendering practices, and the Treasury Branch's alleged favouritism to MLAs in granting loans. Shortly after the election, Manning set up a Royal Commission to inquire into the allegations. The commission found no evidence of graft, though they did find slack management in land acquisition and in awarding contracts.

The success of the Liberal opposition was short-lived. The under-representation of urban areas in the electoral system, Manning's abolition in 1956 of the preferential voting system that had assured at least some opposition seats in urban areas, coupled with Liberal leadership difficulties, led to a rapid decline in Liberal support. In 1957 and 1958, Social Credit also paid out politically popular oil "dividends," harkening back to their famous dividend of 1935. (The government distributed $11 million in 1957 or $20 for every adult, followed by $10 million in 1958 or $17 per adult.) The Conservatives' national revival in the late 1950s under Diefenbaker also helped the provincial Tories and split the opposition vote, enabling the Socreds to rebound in the 1959 provincial election with sixty-one of sixty-five seats based on 56 per cent of the popular vote.

Manning's success depended partly on his ability to articulate and defend an emerging right-wing political consensus, but also to bend when necessary. During the 1960s there was a gradual relaxing of restrictions on movie censorship and drinking, despite Manning's personal views. This flexibility temporarily prevented urban voters from openly revolting against Social Credit's conservative social views.

During the 1960s, Manning became one of the country's leading proponents of free enterprise and a critic of the federal government's drift toward a welfare state. During the 1930s, the federal government had portrayed Social Credit as a dangerous experimenter with new social and economic policies. During the 1950s and 1960s, Manning returned the compliment. His opposition to Liberal national policies on medicare and bilingualism reflected a paradoxical right-wing political culture that combined a fervent belief in individualism and self-reliance with intense pressures for social and cultural conformity.

The Emerging Conservative Bastion

Manning was able to hang on to power provincially long after the conditions that first gave rise to Social Credit changed. Nevertheless, a major change was underway in federal politics in the late 1950s. Many Albertans, now relatively prosperous, were growing tired of the futility of third parties at the national level. They had been sending Social Crediters to Ottawa since 1935, but this had seemingly done little other than isolate Alberta. The national Conservatives chose a Westerner, John Diefenbaker, as leader in 1956. Alberta, which had been a wasteland for the Conservatives for decades, was ripe for change. Federally, change came decisively in 1958; provincially it came in 1971. Alberta became one of the main bastions of Conservative strength in Canada.

Throughout the late 1940s and early 1950s, the federal Liberals in Alberta had outpolled the Tories by a margin of two to one. However, the Liberals were associated in the public mind with central Canadian interests, and Albertans had no strong voices in successive cabinets of Liberal Prime Minister Louis St. Laurent. The 1958 election brought a swing to the Conservatives across western Canada. John Diefenbaker had shaped the Conservatives into what appeared to be a protest party against big business and big government. He appealed to small businessmen, farmers, ethnic minorities, and other status-deprived groups.

As the MP for a multi-ethnic riding in northern Saskatchewan, and partly of German background himself, Diefenbaker was sensitive to the feelings of many ethnic groups that they were discriminated against, and he actively courted the "ethnic" vote. His vision of One Canada, expressed eventually in his Bill of Rights (1960), stressed the need for equal rights for all. In addition, his strident anti-communism contributed to his success among central and eastern Europeans. He was able to attract the support of many groups, such as the Ukrainians, for whom the Conservative party had previously been anathema as the party of big business and the WASP establishment.

Symbolic of Diefenbaker's reaching out to new groups was his appointment to the Senate of Blood Indian James Gladstone, the first Treaty Indian in the upper house. Gladstone, a rancher from Cardston, was a former president of the Indian Association of Alberta, where he had fought for better education, greater government respect for treaty rights, and more participation by Indians in their own administration. Gladstone's appointment was a clear sign of Diefenbaker's commitment to equal rights. Status Indians obtained the right to vote in federal elections in 1960 and in provincial elections in Alberta in 1965.

In the 1958 federal election, ridings in Alberta where Conservatives had not run for decades returned Conservative candidates. All the Social Credit MPs were swept aside; national Social Credit leader Solon Low returned to his old job teaching social studies in Raymond. A new generation of politicians emerged, including Pollockville rancher Jack Horner and Peace River lawyer Ged Baldwin, two Conservatives who performed on the national stage for the next twenty years.

Though the Alberta Conservative party was very much a Diefenbaker party, veteran Conservative MP Douglas Harkness from Calgary proved to be a thorn in Diefenbaker's side. In 1963 he resigned from the Diefenbaker cabinet over defence policy. Nonetheless, Albertans generally remained loyal to Diefenbaker. Farmers felt they had a sympathetic ear in Diefenbaker's ministers of agriculture, and Diefenbaker's support for oil drilling in northern Canada won support in the oilpatch.

Social Credit experienced a limited come-back during the 1960s under their national leader, Robert Thompson, from Red Deer. Despite his varied background as pilot, chiropractor, civil servant, and missionary in Ethiopia (and adviser to Haile Selassie), Thompson had difficulty bridging the linguistic, cultural, and ideological gaps between the rump group of Social Crediters from English-speaking Canada and the sizable group of rural *Créditistes* from Quebec. Although they had political leverage in minority federal governments during the 1960s, the Social Crediters split irrevocably. Thompson abandoned the hope of developing Social Credit into a national party and defected to the Conservatives in 1967, finally ending Alberta's dream of convincing the rest of the country of the merits of Social Credit.

Protest and Urbanity: Social and Political Change in the Late 1960s

By the late 1960s, Albertans were in a mood for change. The early baby boomers were beginning to emerge from universities in record numbers. Student sit-ins, such as a University of Calgary library demonstration in 1966 demanding longer library hours, were pale imitations of their American counterparts, but did indicate a questioning of authority. In March 1968, 3000 students marched from the University of Alberta campus to the legislature, protesting rising tuition fees and asking for increased government grants for universities. Dramatic events in the United States—the protests against the war in Vietnam, political assassinations, and racial conflict—led Canadians to question and to distance themselves from American values. The new left, black and red power, and women's liberation all became topics of debate on university campuses, and American spokespersons for each of these movements brought their views to the province. Indian and women activists, who were developing a new consciousness and pride, began challenging racist and sexist laws and

318

practices. Twenty-four-year-old Cree activist Harold Cardinal, president of the Indian Association of Alberta (IAA), created waves with his book, *The Unjust Society* (1969). Cardinal was from the Sucker Creek Reserve near High Prairie, and in 1968 had become the youngest elected president of the IAA. His book attacked governments and churches for manipulation of Indians, and lambasted the federal government's 1969 "White Paper" (which proposed the ending of the Indians' special status) as a blueprint for cultural genocide. Cardinal thus began a long and active career in native politics at both the provincial and national levels.

Alberta by the late 1960s and early 1970s was also feeling the effects of the gathering feminist revolution. Women, particularly the growing number of younger women with postsecondary education, were influenced by the writing of early second-wave feminists such as Betty Friedan and Germaine Greer. Symbolized by the federal Royal Commission on the Status of Women begun in 1967, a heightened awareness was spreading among women of the ways in which sexist attitudes and institutions shaped their lives and limited their opportunities. Small groups of educated women throughout Alberta, particularly in the cities, met informally to discuss their problems in light of the new feminist insights. Some established formal organizations, such as the Calgary Birth Control Association, devoted to giving women more choice regarding their reproductive lives.

Patterns of female participation in the paid work force had undergone a largely unnoted but significant transformation, beginning in the 1950s and early 1960s. Farm women, both aided by increased mechanization and impelled by the growing cost of that mechanization, were becoming even more involved in the business and work of farming. At the same time, more urban women, enabled by technological advances and compelled by the higher costs of an ever-increasing standard of living, were staying in the paid workforce after marriage. The economic prosperity of the oil boom encouraged growing female participation in the workforce.

Though most often in traditionally female and low-paid jobs, women's increased participation in the work force, along with their increasing levels of education, contributed to their growing awareness of the discrepancy between their aspirations, their real-life experiences, and the still pervasive stereotypes concerning their "place" in society. While most women in Alberta in the mid to late 1960s would not have labelled themselves "feminists," they were becoming increasingly sensitized to issues of equality.

319

However, as late as the early 1970s, Alberta women's formal political voice was muted, a far cry from the activism of women politicians such as Nellie McClung and Irene Parlby prior to the Depression. Traditional social and political values still held sway among older, rural, and smalltown women, and those associated with conservative religious groups. A predominantly right-wing political culture largely discouraged women's political activism. When the "new look" Conservatives swept to power in 1971 under Peter Lougheed, there were only two women among seventy-five Conservative candidates. The Conservative platform gave only limited recognition to changes in Alberta women's lifestyles; of 120 campaign promises, four were directed toward women. They promised expanded support for daycare centres and an increased number of women on boards and task forces, and made non-committal pledges to implement the recommendations of the federal government's Royal Commission on the Status of Women if Alberta women supported the recommendations, and to "assess the need" of a women's rights protection act. Though Alberta women continued to play a significant role in local politics on schoolboards and as alderwomen throughout the 1960s and 1970s, at the provincial and federal levels, their chief political role was as party workers (in all parties) and as sacrificial candidates for the Liberals and NDP.

Some of the overall momentum for change in the late 1960s was expressed in the 1968 federal election, with Pierre Trudeau's Liberals capturing 35 per cent of the Alberta vote and four out of nineteen seats in the province, including strong support from urban youth. This was up substantially from the 20 to 25 per cent of the vote the Liberals under Lester Pearson had attracted in the province for most of the 1960s. Trudeau's freshness, style, Canadian nationalism, and his reputed ability to understand Quebec infected many urbanites with a mild form of Trudeaumania. While the Tories maintained overwhelming support with fifteen seats, and while support for Trudeau and the Liberals soon weakened, in 1968 the electorate was receptive to social and political change.

The desire of a new urban Alberta to break with the tried and the stodgy was capitalized on by a young Calgary lawyer, Peter Lougheed, grandson of the wealthy Tory Senator James Lougheed. Lougheed was born in Calgary in 1928 and educated in Alberta, graduating from the University of Alberta with a law degree in 1952. He played university football and was student body president. Lougheed earned a degree in business from Harvard in 1954, and practised law in Calgary before

320

joining an engineering and construction firm, Mannix Corporation. He left for an independent law practice in 1962, and began planning a political career that could recoup his family's prestige, which had been tarnished by financial ruin during the Depression. He won the leadership of the tiny Progressive Conservative party in 1965 with the strong support of longtime personal friends and business associates from Calgary, who would later assume high-profile duties in his administration. In 1963, the provincial Conservative party had won only 13 per cent of the vote. Lougheed aggressively began to rebuild the party, developing new policies and attracting potential candidates. Since the party was so weak, Lougheed met little resistance in impressing his image and ideas on the provincial Conservatives. However, his political breakthrough came only after Manning retired as premier in 1968.

With the collapse of Social Credit at the federal level, Manning sensed the changing political winds. He attempted to come to grips with new political realities in his book, *Political Realignment* (1967). The book, which was heavily influenced by his son, Preston Manning, advocated the reorganization of the existing political spectrum into two national parties. The right-wing party, which Manning favoured, would adopt a policy of "social conservatism," combining free enterprise and humanitarian concerns. It would emerge from a combination of the Conservatives and Social Credit, while the New Democrats and Liberals would unite to form the alternative.

While some suspected Manning's purpose in writing the book was to facilitate a run at the national Progressive Conservative leadership, it is more likely he was trying to salvage some future for Social Credit. Hard-line Social Crediters were, however, aghast at the idea of a merger with the Tories, and the new ideas served to confuse and divide Social Crediters. Manning's government won easily in the 1967 provincial election, but Lougheed's tireless organizational work garnered 26 per cent of the vote and six seats for the Conservatives, with Lougheed himself winning Calgary West.

When Manning retired in 1968, he was appointed to the board of directors of a national bank and a score of other corporations. This baffled old-line Social Crediters. However, it was an apt symbol of Manning's reconciliation with big business and his own personal political realignment.

Manning's leadership was so dominant in the party and had lasted so long that there was little room for other potential leaders to

Harry Strom was a rancher from Bow Island who replaced Manning as premier in 1968. Strom, who embodied rural Alberta, had difficulty reorienting Social Credit to the realities of a predominantly urban, middle-class, and secular society. Strom was premier from 1968 to 1971. (*Glenbow Archives NA 3326-2*)

emerge. When he stepped down, there were no popular replacements. In the 1968 leadership convention, a small group of young reformers in the party, aware of Social Credit's weakness among new voters, looked for a candidate who might help reorient the party. They came up with Harry Strom, a tall, soft-spoken rancher from Bow Island who had been minister of agriculture and minister of municipal affairs in Manning's cabinets. Strom had the tacit support of Manning, with whom he shared a common evangelical religious perspective.

Though a man of impeccable integrity, Strom had few leadership abilities. He was relatively inarticulate, did not give the impression of being decisive, and was at sea amidst the growing ideological cleavages within Social Credit. Strom seemed willing to try to move the party in new directions, but given his rural background and personal style, he was not the person to do it. He did make some changes, introducing progressive welfare policies and more liberally financed education. He also began to focus on environmental issues and "human resources" development. However, with a rural leader and after over thirty years in office, the party was unable to convince the electorate that it was keeping pace with the times. Veteran cabinet ministers were skeptical of new directions and Strom did not push the idea of change too hard for fear of alienating the aging Social Credit rank and file. Once Manning was gone, it was not hard for people who had supported Social Credit provincially, while voting for the Conservatives federally, to vote Conservative provincially as well.

In the provincial election of August 1971, the Tories took forty-nine seats compared to Social Credit's twenty-five and the New Democrats' one. New voting patterns were established that would endure for a generation. Many people who had formerly voted Social Credit now turned to the new-look Tories and their youthful leader, Peter Lougheed. The well-organized and media-wise Conservatives offered the electorate continued free-enterprise conservatism but with the added bonuses of urban middle-class respectability, a comfortably vague social conscience, and a little political excitement.

The Conservatives' campaign strategy emphasized the need for change without harshly criticizing the Socreds. The Conservatives made numerous election promises (120) that were broad enough to appeal to all sectors of society, and chose a slogan that was particularly apropos and persuasive: "Now!" Lougheed was the first Alberta politician to use television effectively. The campaign platform included seeds of Lougheed's later policies: the need to diversify the economy and move Alberta away from an over-reliance on oil and gas,

Peter Lougheed, a young Calgary lawyer, revived the provincial Progressive Conservative party in the mid-1960s, and in 1967 led a group of six Conservative MLAs into the legislature. They included, left to right, Len Werry, Lou Hyndman, Hugh Horner, Peter Lougheed, Dave Russell, and Don Getty. All but Horner represented Edmonton or Calgary ridings. This group was the nucleus of the Lougheed Conservatives, who defeated Social Credit in 1971, ushering in a new era in Alberta politics. (*Courtesy David Wood*)

the need to stimulate growth in smaller centres, and the need for a stronger voice in Ottawa.

Through hard work, personal charm, and appeals to elites who had been ignored by Social Credit, Lougheed was able to secure candidates from a wide range of social, ethnic, and religious backgrounds. He thus overcame the stigma that was still attached to the Conservatives of being an elitist, urban, Anglo-Canadian group. Among others, Lougheed recruited seven Ukrainian candidates and a postwar German immigrant, Horst Schmid. Schmid had worked as a ditch digger and foreman in a gold mine in Yellowknife and as an accountant, businessman, and restaurant owner in Edmonton. He became known as host of a radio program for the large German-speaking community. Schmid was later crucial in garnering and maintaining support among ethnic groups for the Conservatives during the election and later after his appointment as minister of culture.

In 1967 Lougheed attracted Dr. Hugh Horner away from federal politics. Horner, a doctor in Barrhead, had been elected to Parliament in the Diefenbaker sweep in 1958. He was one of the five Conservatives elected with Lougheed to the legislature in 1967 and helped give Lougheed credibility in rural Alberta. After the 1971 election, "Doc" Horner became deputy premier and minister of agriculture. With their broad range of candidates, the Tories were not only able to capture the cities, but also the non-Anglo areas of central and northern Alberta.

With the Conservative victory, power passed from a cabinet made up of teachers, farmers, and small businessmen from rural areas and small towns to a new, young, and largely urban middle class. Of the seventy-five Tory candidates in 1971, fifteen were business people and twenty-eight were professionals, including eleven lawyers. Among the lawyers who would hold key positions in Lougheed cabinets were Merv Leitch from Calgary; Lou Hyndman, Neil Crawford, and Julian Koziak from Edmonton; and Jim Horsman from Medicine Hat. Other key people included Don Getty, an Edmonton oil investment consultant, and Dave Russell, a Calgary architect. All were in their thirties or early forties. These seventy-five candidates, most of whom had been personally recruited by Lougheed, became the nucleus of the Conservative party throughout the 1970s and 1980s.

The Conservative victory marked the consolidation of social, demographic, and economic changes that had rapidly transformed Alberta in the postwar era. Social Credit had little chance of surviving in a society that was increasingly urban, middle-class, affluent, and secular. Ironically, Social Credit presided over and encouraged the affluence, high rates of urbanization, interprovincial migration, and high levels of education that ultimately undermined its base of support.

When Social Credit was defeated by the Conservatives after thirty-six years in power, most Albertans felt that a new era had arrived. However, no one knew just what the new era would bring; nor could observers predict the oil price increases that would accelerate economic and population growth, social change, western alienation, and political confrontation between Ottawa and Alberta.

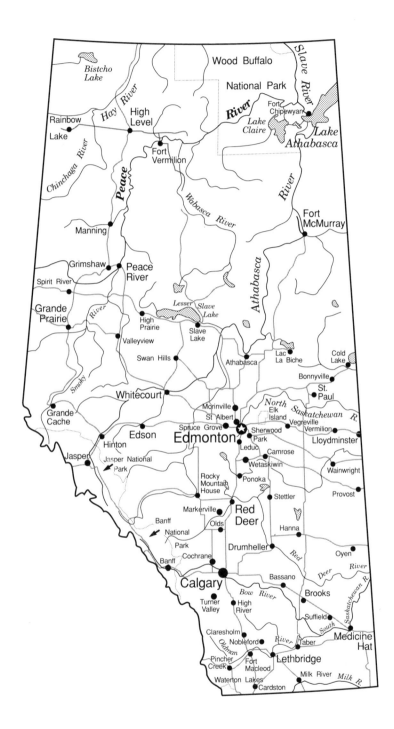

CHAPTER TWELVE

Boom and Bust: The Lougheed Years and After

Peter Lougheed led the Conservatives to power in 1971, shortly before the economic boom that shaped the mood and the events of the decade. That boom was the product not so much of local conditions, but of a decision by the Organization of Petroleum Exporting Countries (OPEC) to increase the price it was asking for oil. When, as a result, the price of oil skyrocketed, people and capital flooded into Alberta, overheating its economy. Between 1971 and 1981, Alberta's Gross Domestic Product increased six-fold from $7.9 billion to $47.2 billion in current dollars, or, in constant (1971) dollars, almost doubled to $14.6 billion. During the 1970s, the province became the wealthiest in Canada, with the highest per-capita income and a steadily mounting Heritage Fund. Boomtime Alberta exuded a sense of vigour, optimism, and brash confidence, although underneath the glitter and swagger, there were also nagging anxieties about the future. Cities grew rapidly. Social change was equally swift, particularly in the roles of religion and ethnicity, and in the status of women and natives. These economic and social changes were reflected in politics as yet another new Alberta found itself centrestage in a national debate over both energy policy and the nature of Confederation.

Premier Peter Lougheed, like his predecessors Brownlee, Aberhart, and Manning, emerged as a remarkably powerful presence, towering over his cabinets as the major architect and symbol of an entire era. The Lougheed Conservatives perpetuated the Alberta syndrome of one-party dominance, characterized by weak and divided oppositions and a tendency toward one-man rule. As the spokesman for a new Alberta, Lougheed gave voice to Albertans' frustrated pride and their determination to be taken seriously on the national stage.

During the Lougheed years, the fortunes and leadership of the national political parties, the dynamics of an activist "province-building" provincial government, western alienation, the power politics of oil, and massive economic and social change within the province combined to produce an explosive confrontation between Alberta and the Liberal federal government. One of the side effects during the early 1980s was the emergence of a small but angry and noisy separatist movement.

Economic developments during the 1970s and 1980s also brought a forceful, and painful, reminder of Alberta's susceptibility to boom-bust economic cycles. In 1982 and 1983, boom changed to bust, with widespread economic devastation. The economic and political mood of the mid to late 1980s differed from that of the previous decade. The frantic intensity of the 1970s gave way to slower growth and a more relaxed lifestyle. By the mid-1980s, with a new cast of political actors at both the federal and provincial levels, the western separatist movement collapsed, and western alienation temporarily subsided.

In the mid to late 1980s, the winds of political change were evident at both the provincial and federal levels. For the first time since their election, the provincial Conservatives found themselves facing new challenges from a revived opposition of New Democrats and Liberals. Under a new premier, Don Getty, the provincial Conservatives began to lose their aura of invincibility. Beginning in 1987, a new right-wing Reform Party began harnessing the tradi-tional mainstays of western alienation into a new political alliance that by 1989 was beginning to threaten the hegemony of federal Alberta Conservatives.

The Boom: Urban Growth, Migration, Immigration, and Multiculturalism

Alberta's population increased by over a third, from 1.6 million in 1971 to 2.2 million in 1981. Growth slowed dramatically with the bust in the early 1980s (from 1983 to 1988 there was net migration out of the province); but by the late 1980s, with continuing immigration and a relatively high natural increase, the population had increased to 2.4 million—almost 10 per cent of Canada's population. During the 1970s Calgary and Edmonton, where growth in absolute numbers was most dramatic, became classic boomtowns: new suburbs mush-roomed, housing and land values skyrocketed, and downtown highrise construction was ceaseless. The population of each city was over 500,000 by 1981 and grew to over 650,000 by the late 1980s. Calgary had become an important financial and computer centre, attracting investors from around the world. By 1978 total annual building permits in Calgary had reached a staggering one billion dollars. As a result, its skyline was transformed with sleek steel and glass. Several Calgary-based developers such as Trizec, Nu-West, and Carma also invested heavily elsewhere in Canada and in the United States.

Edmonton's growth was similarly dramatic as the provincial government expanded, the petrochemical industry developed, and the city furthered its role as a supply centre for major new oil developments in northern Alberta and the Arctic. The value of Edmonton's building permits eventually rose even higher than Calgary's to $1.7 billion in 1980. One of the chief symbols of the boom was the massive West Edmonton Mall, developed by the Ghermezian brothers, wealthy Iranian immigrants. The Ghermezians had come to Canada in the 1950s and opened a carpet shop before expanding into real estate and eventually into megamalls. West Edmonton Mall, a mecca of materialism, became one of Alberta's major tourist attractions.

Also indicative of the possibilities of boomtime Alberta was the career of a fervent, self-declared free-enterpriser, Ontario-born entrepreneur Peter Pocklington. He arrived in Edmonton in 1971 and turned his car dealerships into a multimillion-dollar real estate, food, and sport empire. His domain included ownership of another symbol of the new West, the Edmonton Oilers, a championship hockey team that moved from the World Hockey Association to the NHL in 1980. With their star Wayne Gretzky, the Oilers won a series of Stanley Cups in 1984, 1985, 1987 and 1988. Pocklington's status as public hero fell dramatically after a long and violent labour dispute with his employees in 1986 at the Gainers meat packing plant in Edmonton, after he sold Gretzky in 1988 to the Los Angeles Kings, and after financial difficulties at Gainers forced the provincial government (which had given Gainers substantial financial support) to take over the company in 1989.

The further development of a petrochemical industry, and oil and gas exploration, brought dramatic growth during the 1970s to Medicine Hat, Red Deer, and Grande Prairie. Grande Prairie's rapid expansion during the 1970s (from 13,000 in 1971 to 24,000 by 1981) was based partly on the discovery by Canadian Hunter Exploration of the huge Elmworth gas field in 1976, and strong activity from a large number of other oil and gas companies, but it was also based on further forestry development. The small seasonal sawmills in the Peace River region were joined in 1973 by a large pulp mill, owned by the American-based Proctor and Gamble. By 1979 the mill accounted for over half of Alberta's pulp production. The economic boom stretched Grande Prairie at the seams, but it also diversified its economy, now based on agriculture, forestry, and petroleum. In addition, the city was the administrative, cultural, and educational centre for the Peace River region.

The increasing price of oil also finally made extensive extraction of synthetic crude oil from the huge reserves of the Athabasca oil sands economically feasible. Fort McMurray, the most explosive boomtown in the province, grew from 1200 when the Great Canadian Oil Sands project (controlled by Sun Oil of Philadelphia) began construction in 1964 to over 10,000 by 1973, when the federal and provincial governments and several oil giants joined in the massive Syncrude project. In 1976 and 1977, a total work force of over 10,000 worked feverishly on the construction of the Syncrude project, which included a world-scale ore processing and refining plant. Huge open-pit oil mines made use of immense draglines (with booms the length of a football field) and bucketwheels to excavate and move the oilsands, which were then transported by conveyor belt to the plant for processing.

Once the $2.3 billion Syncrude plant opened in 1978, Fort McMurray grew to over 35,000 people, housed largely in new suburbs perched on the edge of the wilderness. The incredibly rapid growth of the community during the 1970s created social problems. As noted by one author, "Housing shortages were chronic, basic community services like medical care, fire fighting and education were insufficient to meet demand, crime increased beyond the initial capacity of the police to handle it, recreational facilities remained scarce, and service industries proved inadequate."[1] But the largely single, transient, and boisterous population during the construction phase of Syncrude quickly gave way to a highly family-oriented community. Fort McMurray quickly developed all the facilities of a modern city with a new city hall, courthouse, hospital, community college, and many active athletic, cultural, and ethnic organizations.

Alberta's prosperity attracted thousands of migrants—mostly young single people and young families—from across Canada. From 1971 to 1981, the proportion of Alberta's population born in other provinces increased from 21 per cent to over 29 per cent, with the Ontario-born the largest group, making up almost 8 per cent of the population. The newly arrived Maritimers and French Canadians established their own organizations and social networks.

French Canadians from Quebec, Ontario, and New Brunswick

Downtown Fort McMurray, 1983. After a fleeting life as a fur-trade post in the late 1700s and early 1800s, then as a transportation centre in the late 1800s and early 1900s, Fort McMurray exploded into life after 1964 with the development of the oil sands. (*Syncrude*)

both revitalized and introduced new perspectives and conflicts into the Franco-Albertan community. Alberta surpassed Manitoba in its number of francophones. Many improvements were occurring in the fields of French-language education and communication. These included, during the 1970s, French immersion schools, and new radio and television facilities run in French by *Radio-Canada,* CBC's French language division. These changes were mainly the result of federal government initiatives in response to the separatist threat in Quebec. Federal financial support through the Department of the Secretary of State also supported the activities of several francophone organizations, including the largest, the *Association canadienne-francaise de l'Alberta* (ACFA). The vitality of Alberta's francophone community was expressed through new theatre, choral, and dance groups. Because of relatively small numbers, urban dispersal, and occasionally unsympathetic attitudes on the part of the majority, francophones still fought an uphill battle in their struggle to preserve their language and culture. Of the 5 per cent of the Alberta population of French background, only a minority still speak French.

With Canada's liberalized immigration laws after 1967, the boom also brought for the first time significant numbers of people from Asia and other parts of the Third World. By the late 1970s and throughout the 1980s, immigrants from the Third World, especially Asia, made up well over half of Alberta's approximately 10,000 immigrants per year. Immigrants from Hong Kong and Southeast Asia substantially increased the size of Alberta's Chinese community to well over 50,000.

Chinatowns in Calgary and Edmonton changed markedly. In the late 1960s, urban renewal plans in Calgary that would have destroyed the existing Chinatown were opposed by the Sien Lok Society, which was composed of both Canadian-born Chinese and immigrant businesspeople and professionals. The organization helped to save Calgary's Chinatown from destruction, hoping to make it the focal point of Chinese cultural identity. Several other new organizations, including the United Calgary Chinese Association and the Chinatown Development Task Force, developed conflicting visions of the future of Chinatown. During the 1970s and 1980s, with the influx of immigrants and capital, several new towers and buildings with Chinese facades were built. These housed a wide range of new institutions, including cultural, sport, fraternal, and political societies; several Christian churches and a Buddhist temple, Mandarin and Cantonese schools, four newspapers, apartments for elderly Chinese, and a wide variety of other services offered by businesses and professionals. Similarly, by 1980 in Edmonton there were twenty-three different Chinese organizations. Edmonton's old Chinatown underwent major renovation, while a new commercial Chinatown developed farther north along 97th Street. A large Chinese arch on one of Edmonton's downtown streets provided striking evidence of the continuing Chinese presence in the city and of the links to Edmonton's sister city of Harbin, China.

The new immigration changed Alberta's Chinese community. Chinatowns were marked by new economic and cultural vitality but also by divisions and power struggles between the Canadian-born, mainland Chinese, and newcomers from Hong Kong. Small, family-run Chinese restaurants, which continued to spread throughout the suburbs, provided employment for many Chinese. A sizable Chinese professional class also developed, made up of the Canadian-born, graduating foreign students, and new immigrants from Asia. During the 1980s wealthy Hong Kong investors, eager to redirect their money in light of the expiration of Britain's lease on Hong Kong in 1997, began moving into Calgary and Edmonton. They bought condominiums, houses, businesses, and shopping plazas.

In contrast to the earlier stereotype of poverty-stricken Chinese, the Chinese in Alberta now included a professional and moneyed class. Signaling the changing status of Chinese Canadians, two Canadian-born Chinese were elected to the Alberta legislature— Calgary businessman George Ho Lem (a Social Crediter, elected in 1971), and civil servant Henry Woo (a Conservative, first elected in Edmonton in 1979).

West Indians, South Asians, Filipinos, Vietnamese, Koreans, and Latin Americans also injected an element of economic and cultural vitality, with the South Asians, Filipinos, and Koreans particularly visible in small, family-run businesses. Over 80 per cent of the new Third World immigrants who came to Alberta lived in Edmonton and Calgary, particularly in the northeast sections of each city, and in the southeast Mill Woods section of Edmonton. These neighbourhoods were close to the industrial sections and had slightly cheaper housing than other districts. By the 1980s, more than one out of ten residents in these two cities belonged to one of the "visible" minorities from the Third World. Alberta cities were not only multicultural, but increasingly multiracial.

Most of the newcomers came for economic reasons, but by the 1980s, 20 per cent were political refugees. The Asians expelled from Uganda in 1972 belonged mostly to the Ismaili Muslim sect. They made a very rapid and successful adjustment in urban small business. Approximately 6000 Chileans, supporters of the left-wing Allende regime overthrown in a military coup in 1973, were the first sizable group of Latin Americans. They faced a difficult period of adjustment because of their lack of English and limited job skills. Throughout the late 1970s and 1980s, Lebanese immigrants fled political chaos and civil war. They often used family networks to find a niche for themselves in service industries.

The largest group of political refugees came from Southeast Asia. The movement of "boat people" began in 1975 with the collapse of the American-backed regime in South Vietnam. By late 1978, the exodus of refugees from Vietnam, Cambodia, and Laos had become a major international concern. Both the federal government and many Albertans, usually through church groups, helped the refugees to adjust; nevertheless, they experienced a difficult period of cultural disorientation and periodic unemployment. The province received 7500 in the peak years of 1979 and 1980.

Throughout the 1980s there were roughly 2500 refugees each year, with equal portions from Southeast Asia, eastern Europe, Latin America, and other world areas, principally Africa and the Middle East. Some Albertans felt threatened by the new racial pluralism. In late 1989 some unscrupulous entrepreneurs began turning prejudice into a money-making business with the appearance of racist lapel pins and calendars. Those most often singled out for racist attention were South Asians—people who trace their origins to the Indian subcontinent.

The Sikhs, who made up about one-third of the 30,000 South Asians in Alberta, were visible because of their turbans and beards, and they experienced the most prejudice. They were victimized in several incidents of assault and vandalism in the late 1970s. During the 1980s, public unease about Canada's changing racial composition was reinforced by highly exaggerated fears of Sikh terrorism. By 1989, a strong symbolic public campaign had been initiated in Calgary to prevent religiously devout Sikhs from wearing turbans if they were recruited into the Royal Canadian Mounted Police. This issue crystalized growing anxiety about the shifting racial composition of Alberta, and forcefully recalled the centrality of the Mounted Police as a symbol of Canadian and Western identity. Individual Albertans and Alberta MPs led the unsuccessful national campaign on the turban issue.

Although prejudice was directed mostly against non-white minorities, there were two widely publicized incidents of anti-Semitism in the early 1980s involving isolated right-wing extremists who denied the Holocaust and warned of an international Jewish conspiracy. However, anti-Semitism in Alberta was relatively weak compared to other forms of racism directed against natives, blacks, and visible immigrant groups. Migration of Jews from central Canada, Israel, and South Africa brought new development to the Jewish community in the two largest cities, which together grew to over ten thousand people. Because of migration to the larger cities, the Jewish communities in smaller cities such as Lethbridge and Medicine Hat declined. In Calgary and Edmonton, however, with the support of the newcomers, the Jewish communities built new cultural, religious, recreational, and educational institutions.

Despite some fears of growing anti-Semitism, Alberta's Jews were achieving new levels of prominence and acceptance. As Albertans became urbanized and better educated and as urban values came to dominate the political culture, Jews seemed less distinctive than they once had. A predominantly Alberta-born generation of Jews excelled in education, the professions, and the arts. The Austrian-born refugee writer and professor Henry Kreisel, theatre promoter Joe Shoctor, university presidents Max Wyman and Myer Horowitz, Justice Tevie Miller, patrons of the arts such as Martha and Harry Cohen, lawyer/politicians Ron Ghitter and Sheldon Chumir, historian David Bercuson, and many others helped break down prejudice.

Although Third World immigrants faced adjustment problems, they were aided by a wide variety of governmental and voluntary organizations with material and social support, including English language classes. Their adjustment was eased by an array of cultural, sports, social, and religious organizations, and by the language schools they established.

The groups formed by the new immigrants quickly became part of a larger network of ethnic groups, whose activities were supported by the provincial and federal governments under multicultural policies introduced in 1971. The Alberta government also established an August holiday—Heritage Day—to celebrate Alberta's past and ethnic diversity. Ethnic culture finally emerged from church basements and ethnic halls. Despite lingering pockets of prejudice, most urban Albertans opened themselves to this diversity, and a variety of government agencies, educational institutions, and voluntary organizations helped with programs to fight prejudice and acknowledge diversity.

Many Albertans, particularly those of Ukrainian origin, helped develop multiculturalism at the national level. Several members of the Ukrainian Canadian Professional and Business Federation had substantial political influence. Working with other ethnic groups, they helped expand the concept of bilingual education to include not only French, but other languages, including Ukrainian. Alberta became a national pioneer in teaching "heritage" languages, boasting several Ukrainian-English and German-English schools in the Edmonton area. The province also sponsored programs in Cree, Mandarin Chinese, and Arabic in Edmonton. Ukrainian Canadian lawyer from Edmonton, Laurence Decore, son of former Liberal MP and judge John Decore, helped shape the multicultural clause in the 1982 Charter of Rights. His advocacy of multiculturalism provided part of the base of support that helped in his successful bid for Edmonton's mayoralty in 1983, and for the provincial Liberal leadership in 1988.

As urban politicians became aware of the strength of new immigrant groups, fierce battles emerged during nomination meetings and at election time in municipal, provincial, and federal elections in Calgary and Edmonton to capture the "ethnic vote." Politicians traded charges of corrupt practices in "rounding up" ethnic voters with free meals and transportation, and promises of future influence, grants for ethnic activities, or (in the case of federal politicians) help in immigration cases. Despite much talk of growing ethnic power, leaders of new immigrant groups, wary of prejudice and insecure in their status, usually served as brokers for Anglo politicians rather than running as candidates themselves. Though new immigrant groups had limited power and experienced some prejudice, successful politicians and other opinion leaders were aware that Alberta's society was changing, and that political as well as police, educational, social service, and health facilities would have to change to accommodate this growing diversity.

Social Change: The Perils and Promise of Affluence

The swiftly changing skylines and mainstreets of rapidly growing cities and towns had their counterparts in the less visible realm of social structures and values. Besides prosperity, the boom of the 1970s brought more crime, drug use, alcoholism, prostitution, and other social problems. Alberta came to have the highest rates of abortion, suicide, divorce, and teenage pregnancy in the country. Many individuals and couples, lacking family support systems, could not stand the stress of a boom-bust economy that fostered big dreams, and produced confused values and identities. Rapid urban growth also led to formidable transportation problems, troubled school systems, and severely strained municipal budgets.

Social change was also evident in the role of religion. In the 1960s, 1970s, and 1980s, mainline churches, such as the United, Presbyterian, and Anglican, gradually lost some of their numerical and social predominance. In contrast was the continued vitality, urban growth, and increasingly middle-class status of evangelical and unorthodox conservative groups, such as the Christian and Missionary Alliance, the Church of the Nazarene, Pentecostals, Jehovah's Witnesses, Mennonites, and Mormons. These latter groups, despite deep theological divisions and often antagonisms, nonetheless shared much in common in their conservative social values, including a dedicated belief in the family, and opposition to what they saw as immoral social trends including premarital sex, pornography, abortion, common-law marriage, and drug use. These groups represented only about 10 per cent of the population, but because of the relative decline in size and strength of the mainline denominations, they became more prominent in the province's religious mosaic.

Third World immigration added strength and new perspectives to the Roman Catholic Church, and brought several world religions previously absent from the province. With the support of new immigrants, new Muslim mosques and Sikh and Buddhist temples were built in the large cities during the 1970s and 1980s. Alberta gradually ceased to be predominantly Protestant. By the 1980s, almost half of Albertans either identified themselves as Catholic (28 per cent), Orthodox (2 per cent), other world religions (3 per cent), or professed no religion at all (12 per cent).

During the 1970s and 1980s, with growing urbanization, affluence, increasing education, and other social and economic changes, Alberta became more secular. Conservative religious institutions and values were still important, particularly to people living in smaller towns and cities. Private religious schools, pro-life, and anti-pornography movements all had devoted followers, and religious bookstores did a booming business. But religion no longer provided the unquestioned foundation of Alberta's society. Although Alberta's image as a "Bible Belt" lingered, average church attendance differed little from that in other parts of North America and was actually less than the Canadian average (only one-third of the population attended church once a month or more). Further, liquor laws were liberalized and the large cities introduced Sunday shopping (albeit only after much controversy).

Despite explosive urban growth during the 1970s, Alberta's urban landscape was dotted with reminders of the province's agrarian and smalltown past: the popularity of western style clothing, suburban sprawl reflecting a strong attachment to the single-family dwelling, backyard vegetable gardens, and acreages and hobby farms situated just beyond the urban perimeters. Despite these remnants, the way of life of most Albertans differed only marginally from people living in other metropolitan centres across Canada. A growing number were considerably less familiar with the smells of the barnyard and the work of the cowboy and farmer than they were with the Toronto and New York stock markets, international travel, and gourmet cuisine.

The rapid growth of urban areas brought many cultural developments—new art galleries; art centres; theatre, musical, dance, and artistic groups; and the development of a new generation of musicians, composers, architects, dancers, artists, and writers. The new cultural life was supported by a growing audience—urban Alberta had one of the best-educated and most affluent populations in the country—and by all levels of government. While most of the new artistic development was in Calgary and Edmonton and surrounding communities, lively theatre, music, and art groups also developed in smaller cities such as Grande Prairie, Fort McMurray, Lethbridge, Medicine Hat, and Red Deer. Bands, amateur theatre, and art and choral groups also maintained the cultural life of many smaller towns, though the popularity of television took its toll on amateur productions.

The explosion of artistic development involved all of the arts, including ballet and opera. Music fans and musicians in Calgary and Edmonton developed jazz and folk festivals. In the early 1970s, Alberta Theatre Projects in Calgary began producing plays by local writers on western themes. Beginning in 1982, Brian Paisley of Chinook Theatre in Edmonton developed the week-long summer Fringe Festival of experimental theatre, attracting performers from across North America and abroad. The Citadel Theatre expanded further with new facilities, a School for Performing Arts, and a travelling theatre company. Several new experimental theatre groups also provided Edmonton with a lively theatre scene.

A third generation of Alberta artists—photographers, printmakers, painters, and sculptors—emerged. Unlike most of their predecessors, many Alberta artists were now committed to abstract art. Expressionism came to Alberta from New York, partly through the influence of the Edmonton Art Gallery.

Though a fledgling film industry depended largely on Alberta serving as a location for foreign films, Alberta talent also emerged, including documentary filmmaker Tom Radford and award-winning film director Anne Wheeler. Her films *Loyalties* and *Bye Bye Blues* drew on Alberta settings and experiences. The provincial government also established the Alberta Motion Picture Development Corporation in 1981 to support the film industry, providing seed money for producers to get movies and television programs started. Banff's annual International Television Festival also attracted international television executives.

Some Alberta architects and musicians have also developed national and international reputations. Architect Douglas Cardinal developed his nonconformist vision of prairie curves and native spirituality (drawn from his Métis roots) to create strikingly original churches and public buildings in Alberta (such as Red Deer's St. Mary's Church, and Grande Prairie Regional College) and the Canadian Museum of Civilization in Hull, Quebec. A flamboyant young singer from Consort named k. d. lang moved from Red Deer College to Edmonton stages before emerging during the late 1980s as a major voice in the North American country music scene with her self-styled "cowpunk" image.

The 1970s and 1980s also saw a burst of new publications: business, political, literary, and lifestyle magazines, and academic journals. Edmonton developed as the publishing centre of the province. *NeWest Review*, a monthly review of the arts and politics founded by writer George Melnyk, and *Alberta Report*, Ted Byfield's neo-conservative and strident provincial-rights oriented weekly newsmagazine, gave competing left and right visions of a new West. Over twenty presses, supported by provincial and federal government funding, developed to meet the growing market for educational materials and books, predominantly on western themes. Hurtig Publishers became the first major English-language book publisher in Canada outside Toronto, and in 1985 published *The Canadian Encyclopedia*, one of the largest publishing projects in Canadian history.

Several Alberta fiction and nonfiction writers also gained national prominence, often by focussing on local settings. Popular historians James Gray, Hugh Dempsey, James MacGregor, Grant MacEwan, Tony Cashman, and John Charyk developed lively accounts of western Canadian history directed at both academic and popular audiences.

These historians were a remarkable group of westerners. After a long career as a journalist in Winnipeg and Ottawa, Gray came to Calgary in 1947 at age forty-one to edit the *Farm and Ranch Review*, and make it a strong voice for farmers and for Canadian interests in the face of a large influx of American oil money. From 1955 to 1963 he edited the *Western Oil Examiner* and worked in public relations for Home Oil before turning to historical writing. He drew extensively on his own experiences growing up in Winnipeg, as an unemployed relief worker during the Depression, and as a journalist. Gray wrote a series of outstanding books, beginning with *The Winter Years* (1966).

With the demise of the *Edmonton Bulletin* in the early 1950s, Alberta-born Hugh Dempsey left journalism to work for government and later as archivist for the Glenbow Foundation in Calgary. He then became Director of History and Associate Director of the Glenbow

Museum. He became editor of *Alberta Historical Review* in 1958 (five years after its founding), and continued as editor for over thirty years. His prolific writing included several insightful biographies of native leaders.

Scots-born James MacGregor came as an infant to Alberta in 1906. His family homesteaded in the Westlock area. MacGregor worked as an engineer for Canadian Utilities and travelled the province. In 1949, he published *Blankets and Beads: A History of the Saskatchewan River*. His part-time writing career eventually produced twenty books on Alberta history. MacGregor attempted to balance well-researched academic history with human interest and a sense of the Alberta landscape. He worked closely with Dempsey to build the Historical Society of Alberta into a broad-based, vital organization.

Grant MacEwan's remarkable career and accomplishments have made him virtually a provincial institution. Born in 1902, raised in Saskatchewan, and educated in animal husbandry, MacEwan taught at the University of Saskatchewan. Between 1936 and 1945 he began his writing career with four agricultural textbooks. A love for western history led to his first historical book, *Sodbusters* (1948). This was followed by nearly annual books on different aspects of western history. MacEwan was Dean of Agriculture at the University of Manitoba from 1946 until 1951 when, following his defeat as a Liberal candidate in a federal by-election, he moved from Winnipeg to Calgary. He was a Calgary alderman throughout the 1950s, was elected as a Liberal MLA in 1955, and succeeded Harper Prowse as Liberal leader in 1958. Never an avid partisan, he resigned two years later. MacEwan was mayor of Calgary from 1963 to 1966. As Lieutenant Governor of Alberta from 1966 to 1974, he shared his enthusiasm for western history through prolific public speaking and writing. He wrote extensively on agricultural, native, urban, and political history, producing by 1990 thirty-nine books. His biographies breathed life into many fascinating figures in western and Alberta history. MacEwan's frugal lifestyle and dedicated conservationism also provided a living witness to the pioneer virtues that he worked to keep alive.

These dedicated historians, along with a younger group of professional, university-trained historians in the 1960s, 1970s, and 1980s, helped Albertans and other Canadians explore the diversity and richness of Alberta's past.

Novelists Henry Kreisel, Rudy Wiebe, Robert Kroetsch, and Aritha van Herk and playwrights George Ryga, Sharon Pollock, and

John Murrell often drew on a western sense of place and history and their own roots to experiment with new forms of fiction. Guide-naturalist Andy Russell's books on cowboy life, wildlife, and wilderness; Myrna Kostash's books and articles on ethnic history, youth culture, and feminism; and Larry Pratt's books on the politics of oil also attracted national audiences.

A growing historical consciousness was nourished in part by the province's seventy-fifth anniversary celebrations in 1980. A new surge of community museums, archives, historical societies, community reunions, recreated historic parks, and literally hundreds of new local histories demonstrated an interest in preserving the past. Government aid through agencies such as the Alberta Historical Resources Foundation and the Historic Sites Service supported new research, and helped preserve and develop important historic sites such as Head-Smashed-In Buffalo Jump and the Ukrainian Cultural Heritage Village. These historical projects gave Albertans a new sense of pride and place: they had a history of their own.

The New West and the Politics of Alienation

Along with wealth, social change, and cultural development, the 1970s and early 1980s brought increased alienation from the federal government, and recurrent and protracted federal-provincial conflicts. One factor in Alberta's disaffection with central Canada was the sheer length of the Liberal régime in Ottawa. With the exception of a brief period from 1977 to 1979, when an angry and disenchanted Jack Horner crossed the floor to join Trudeau's cabinet, and during the short-lived Conservative government of Joe Clark in 1979, Alberta had no elected representatives in the ruling federal party from 1972 to 1984. Because the meteoric rise of Alberta's economic fortunes was not matched by a similar rise in political influence, many Albertans felt resentful that in the game of national politics, given the numerical dominance of Quebec and Ontario, the deck was stacked against them. Many also contended that the federal Liberals cynically used Alberta to maintain their power base in central Canada. They argued that because it did not need Alberta's votes, the Liberal government was able to buy eastern votes with Alberta oil, which it priced well below world oil prices. One economist later calculated that the loss of revenue to Alberta because of the policy of controlled oil prices and special federal taxes during the 1970s and 1980s amounted to over $50 billion.

Because of the lack of Liberal representation from Alberta in Ottawa, controversial policies on bilingualism, metrication, energy, and the constitution were introduced with little or no consultation with Albertans, and with few or no spokespeople in Alberta to explain or justify the policies. New Liberal policies were repeatedly seen as having been introduced without regard for the opinions of Albertans. Distrust of Pierre Trudeau and the Liberals deepened throughout the 1970s. Anti-French Canadian and anti-intellectual feelings also undoubtedly played a role in the hostility toward Trudeau.

Alienation was also the product of the class interests of oil wealth, and of a right-wing ideological revolt. Because of the vast sums of money that the high-risk oil industry both required and generated, a moneyed class flourished in Alberta. The growing number of white-collar professionals in the oil industry and of financier-developers bolstered the ranks and power of political conservatism. Their political ideology was built on a social-Darwinian faith in the efficiency and morality of an economy based on individualism and rooted in a

The Lougheed government fought numerous battles with the Liberal government of Pierre Trudeau over the control and pricing of oil, and over the constitution. Lougheed and Trudeau are shown here at an energy conference in Ottawa in April 1975. Hostility to Trudeau's policies contributed to a Conservative stranglehold on Alberta politics at both the provincial and federal levels throughout the 1970s and early 1980s. (*Courtesy David Wood*)

vision of western Canada, particularly Alberta, as one of the last frontiers of economic opportunity—a place and time that demanded the talents of risk-taking entrepreneurs. The election of Ronald Reagan to the American presidency in 1980 gave further credibility to conservative forces. Critics of this new elite noted, however, that they never refused government aid, and sometimes demanded it.

However, class interests and ideology alone cannot account for the depth of alienation, or for the fact that it permeated all social classes and all regions of the province. Historical memory, a deep-seated perception of continuing economic discrimination, and ideology (among other factors) combined to produce profound alienation from the federal government.

Lougheed in Power

Feeling powerless and ideologically alienated at the national level, most Albertans, including many of the new arrivals from elsewhere in Canada, turned to the provincial Conservatives under Peter Lougheed to protect them against perceived federal encroachment. Because the province's economy was so dependent on oil and gas, support for Lougheed came not only from petroleum executives and the businessmen and workers who serviced the industry, but also from a wide cross section of the population, including young Albertans whose future career plans were closely linked to the oil and gas industry. The oil and gas industry had resisted Lougheed's decision in 1973-74 to unilaterally increase provincial government royalties, but in the growing series of conflicts between the federal and provincial government, the industry usually sided with the latter.

The Lougheed government fought numerous battles with the federal government over the control and pricing of oil, particularly in 1973-74 and in 1980-81, shortly after steep rises in world oil prices. In September 1973, the federal government froze domestic oil prices and imposed an export tax on shipments to the U.S. Alberta responded by increasing its royalty charges for crown reserves, but Ottawa then escalated the conflict by declaring these royalty payments ineligible as deductions in calculating federal income tax. Lougheed reacted angrily to what he saw as a discriminatory policy, introduced by a federal government that had reneged on previous promises to the province. A bumper sticker declaring "Let the Eastern bastards freeze in the dark" suggested that Lougheed's reaction was moderate compared to that of some other Albertans. Some oil companies decided the revenue fight between the two levels of government left them too little profit, and sent their oil rigs south of the border. Subsequent negotiations between the governments led to shifting tax loads and rising oil and gas prices, which temporarily lessened the conflict. However, conflict escalated even further following the doubling of oil prices in 1979-80 in the wake of the Iran-Iraq war.

In the context of recurring federal-provincial conflict over energy policy, the provincial Conservative party subsequently won a series of one-sided electoral victories in 1975, 1979, and 1982, with roughly 60 per cent of the popular vote and over 90 per cent of the seats. Lougheed presented these elections as referendums on federal-provincial relations. He drew on Albertans' pride, historical regional grievances, and economic self-interest to convince them that the interests of Lougheed, the Conservative Party, the oil industry, and Alberta were synonymous. As in the past, federal-provincial conflict, the perceived interests of Alberta, and one-party dominance nourished each other. Also, through careful stage-management of public relations, the Lougheed Conservatives could usually count on media coverage being generally supportive.

The beginning of a new era in Alberta politics. Lieutenant Governor Grant MacEwan administers the oath of office to Alberta's new Conservative MLAs on September 10, 1971. Premier Peter Lougheed is on MacEwan's left. Lougheed had won 49 out of 75 seats in 1971, but in an atmosphere of federal-provincial battles over energy and the constitution, his majorities increased. In three subsequent elections, Lougheed increased the number of Conservative seats to over 90 per cent of the total. Social Credit disappeared, and the other opposition parties barely survived. (*Courtesy David Wood*)

Throughout the 1970s and early 1980s, the opposition returned to the weak state that had characterized it during the Manning years. Opposition weakness meant that Tory party nomination meetings became the main political battlegrounds in the province. After the 1971 election, the Social Credit party collapsed. Conflict over leadership and ideology sapped the party's energy, and it had difficulty explaining the need for two conservative parties. By the 1982 provincial election, the Social Credit party had virtually disappeared at the provincial level, receiving less than one per cent of the popular vote.

Social Credit was taken over by a tiny group of staunch Douglasites and other extreme right-wingers, who used it as a vehicle for their anti-Semitic views. James Keegstra, a high school social studies and shop teacher, mayor of Eckville, and the Alberta vice-president of the national Social Credit party, taught his students that the Holocaust was a hoax and that a Jewish conspiracy had ruled the world for two centuries. After his views came to public light in 1983, Keegstra was eventually dismissed from his job. He was subsequently convicted of violating federal hate laws. This conviction was later overturned in the Alberta Court of Appeal on the grounds that hate laws violated the guarantee of freedom of expression in the Charter of Rights. The provincial government in turn appealed this ruling, and in December 1989 the Supreme Court of Canada was asked to rule on the question of balancing the rights of minorities to freedom from hate with individuals' rights to freedom of expression.

The national media focussed a great deal of attention on the Keegstra affair. Although Keegstra had some defenders, there was no real evidence of an upsurge of anti-Semitism in Alberta. After his views became known, the voters of Eckville repudiated him as mayor, and his views were condemned by Alberta's religious leaders, newspapers, and political leadership. This episode did, however, bring to light the vestiges of Social Credit anti-Semitism that had been driven underground by Manning in the late 1940s, and illustrated the continuing connection between anti-Semitism and the extreme right in North America.

On the moderate end of the political spectrum, the leader of the provincial Liberals through most of the 1970s and 1980s was Nick Taylor, a witty Calgary oilman with rural roots in southeast Alberta. Taylor carried the albatross of the unpopularity of the federal Liberals. During the 1970s, his environmentalism and emphasis on "high tech" service industries rather than energy megaprojects had little appeal in boomtime Alberta, where bigger was better. The provincial

Liberals barely survived, garnering only 2 per cent of the vote in 1982. The provincial New Democratic Party (NDP) under the dedicated leadership of Grant Notley made little headway in Alberta's predominantly conservative political culture. They did, however, maintain a small but consistent base of support in working-class Edmonton and in northern rural Alberta, coupled with strong support from the province's labour unions. Notley, who came from a farm background, was a leader of the student CCF at the University of Alberta in the late 1950s, a peace activist, and eventually the provincial organizer and provincial secretary of the NDP (successor to the CCF), founded in 1961. In 1968 Notley, at age twenty-nine, became leader of the Alberta NDP. He was noted for his single-minded devotion to politics. As the sole New Democrat in the legislature from 1971 to 1982, representing the rural riding of Spirit River-Fairview in the Peace River district, Notley kept alive the ideal of more open, accountable, and democratic government while the provincial Tories adopted a boardroom style of politics that was secretive and averse to public debate.

Lougheed's main goals and strategies concerned the economy, particularly energy, and related constitutional issues. His economic goals were to insure a healthy petroleum industry in Alberta, to get maximum revenue for the provincial government from depleting petroleum resources, to increase local control over economic development, to expand industrialization and local processing, and generally to promote economic diversification. These were to be accomplished with a view to transferring some of the secondary industry, high income jobs, and decision-making from central Canada to the West. The Conservatives adopted a "province building" strategy of state support for private entrepreneurs, organized through an expanded bureaucracy in several agencies that were crucial to Alberta's economic development strategy. These agencies included the Department of Federal and Intergovernmental Affairs, the Ministry of Economic Development, the Treasury Department, the Department of Energy and Natural Resources, and the Premier's Office. Their strategy included support for an expanded petrochemical industry and for the development of heavy oil and oil sands. Their interventions in the economy included setting up the Alberta Energy Company (1973), purchasing Pacific Western Airlines (1974), and playing a significant part in the Syncrude project at Fort McMurray.

Syncrude was a massive synthetic oil project to extract oil from the oil sands. Following intensive negotiations from 1973 to 1975, the

A Dragline in the Oilsands. With increasing world oil prices, it became an economically viable proposition to extract synthetic crude oil from the huge reserves of the Athabasca oil sands. *(Syncrude)*

multi-billion dollar plan included both the Alberta and federal governments, and Imperial, Gulf, and Cities Services oil companies. Though there was some unease within Conservative ranks over the interventionism of the Lougheed government, the electorate generally accepted the premier's analysis that in a landlocked province, remote from markets, with an allegedly hostile federal government, the provincial government needed to play an activist role.

In 1976, in order to diversify the economy, maximize provincial revenues, and deal with embarrassingly large surpluses in the provincial treasury, Lougheed established the Alberta Heritage Savings Trust Fund (AHSTF). The fund put a portion of oil and gas revenues into capital assets and long-term investments. Its purpose was to save and invest a portion of the income from non-renewable resources for the future. The fund's rapid growth was a source of pride for many Albertans and a testament to the foresight of their government, although people in other parts of the country sometimes resented it. As economic conditions worsened in 1982–83, the fund also became a lightning rod of discontent for sectors of Alberta society hard hit by recession or by the underfunding of social, health, and educational services.

While Lougheed focussed on economic and constitutional issues, the riches of the Heritage Fund and other provincial revenues made

347

possible support for research, cultural, and recreational facilities, which strengthened his government's popularity. One of Lougheed's visions was Kananaskis Country. This four-thousand-square-kilometre region west of Calgary in the mountains was developed to accommodate a variety of recreational activities year-round. Like the national parks, Kananaskis became a focal point of debate between those who wanted development to promote tourism, and environmentalists who wanted to protect natural areas. The Lougheed government also tried to develop Alberta as a major centre for medical research. The Alberta Heritage Foundation of Medical Research began in 1979–80 with a $300-million endowment fund. In addition, the Heritage Fund financed the upgrading of irrigation facilities in southern Alberta. The government also promoted economic growth in smaller centres by relocating provincial government offices and, with an eye to rural voters, by scattering new airports and hospitals across rural Alberta.

Critics pointed to a range of problems as the downside of the Lougheed years. These included the tendency of the government to turn a blind eye to industrial polluters, the high degree of foreign ownership in Alberta, growing provincial control over municipal governments, neglect of educational and social services systems, manipulation of the media, and an indirect stifling of political dissent. Critics noted that the Tories opposed a freedom of information act and exercised tight control over information regarding the Heritage Fund. Although as leader of the opposition Lougheed had argued that MLAs should not be forced to vote along party lines, he quickly expelled Calgary MLA Tom Sindlinger from the Conservative caucus in 1981 when Sindlinger expressed qualified approval of Trudeau's plans to patriate the constitution. Critics also noted that economic diversification away from non-renewable resources did not materialize. By the early 1980s, Alberta was more dependent on the petroleum industry than ever. Those on the right saw the growth of the provincial civil service from 17,000 in 1971 to 40,000 in 1982 as evidence of excessive government size and power, and worried about high levels of government spending. Those on the left viewed Lougheed's sensitivity to the interests of big business and the multinational oil companies to be at the expense of "ordinary" Albertans and Canadian sovereignty.

Despite these criticisms, Lougheed was even more popular than Manning had been. He was able to give many Albertans a stronger sense of being an important part of Canadian political life, a feeling that what happened in Alberta was not peripheral but central to Canada's future. Like Aberhart and Manning, he commanded extraordinary deference from his followers. Despite his influential family and upper-middle-class urban roots, he gained the devoted support of a wide cross section, cutting across class, ethnic, regional, and religious lines. Lougheed Conservative candidates consistently defeated NDP candidates in working-class ridings. The well-financed and well-organized Tory political machine, built around a core of Lougheed's long-time friends and business acquaintances, delivered at the grass-roots level through committed volunteer effort. The party faithful were rewarded through widespread patronage appointments to an ever-increasing number of government boards and advisory councils.

Lougheed was pragmatic, a good organizer, a team builder, and a tough negotiator. Twice he was the object of campaigns to convince him to run for the leadership of the national Progressive Conservative Party. His leadership skills and his ability to convince Albertans (and other Canadians) of his policies were put to the test during the heated energy and constitutional battles with Ottawa in 1980 and 1981.

Energy and Constitutional Wars: the NEP, the Rise of Separatism, and Economic Bust

Conflict between the Alberta and federal governments reached its peak in 1980–81, following the unilateral introduction of new energy and constitutional policies by the reborn Liberal government of Pierre Trudeau. Trudeau had been defeated by the Conservatives under Albertan Joe Clark in the 1979 federal election, but Clark had only a minority government.

Clark, born in 1939, was the son of a newspaper editor in High River. He had played an active part in student politics and journalism while a political science student at the University of Alberta, before working full-time for the Progressive Conservatives. He worked as an organizer and ran unsuccessfully for the provincial Conservatives under Lougheed in 1967, and then went to work in Ottawa for prominent Conservatives, including leader Robert Stanfield. In 1972 he was elected MP for the Rocky Mountain constituency in Alberta. In 1976 Clark emerged as the surprise winner, a compromise candidate, at the national Conservative leadership convention. Although he had many political skills, and was knowledgeable about and sensitive to all of Canada's regions, he could not shake an image of inexperience and weakness. As prime minister, he left many wondering whether he could stand up to his old boss, Peter Lougheed, in the complex oil price negotiations that took place in the fall and winter of 1979.

Lougheed's determined and protracted negotiations with Clark over oil pricing contributed to the erosion of support for the Progressive Conservatives in central Canada. Clark's minority government was defeated in December 1979, when it tried to introduce an unpopular gasoline tax as part of its plan for steep increases in oil prices. Trudeau returned to power in early 1980, determined to get a larger share for the federal government from "windfall" oil profits, and to pursue his lifelong goal of constitutional reform.

The Lougheed government vehemently opposed the dramatic new constitutional and energy policies that the Trudeau government introduced in the fall of 1980. Western alienation quickly reached its highest peak since the 1930s. Lougheed unswervingly opposed the unilateral action of the federal government in patriating the constitution, and was one of the leaders of the "gang of eight" premiers who fought the federal action. After a protracted legal and public opinion battle, Canada's new Constitution Act (1982) included an amending formula, protecting provincial rights, that the Alberta government had developed and promoted. The formula required agreement for constitutional amendments from at least seven provinces (representing 50 per cent of Canada's population) and provided an opting-out provision designed to protect existing provincial powers against federal encroachment. It originated partly from Alberta's attempt to devise an amending procedure that left all provinces equal but did not have the inflexibility created by giving all provinces a veto. It also originated from oil-rich Alberta's nagging fear that the rest of the country might, at some future point, conspire to take away control of its resources. The final accord gave provinces the right to apply indirect taxes on natural resources and make laws in relation to interprovincial trade in natural resources.

The Trudeau constitutional moves in September 1980 aroused deep suspicion, but the National Energy Policy (NEP) announced shortly thereafter evoked unprecedented hostility and opposition. The NEP increased federal control over the oil and gas industry, and revenues from it. Through a variety of complicated measures, it attempted to direct activity to the frontier regions outside provincial jurisdiction, and to Canadianize the oil industry. The federal govern-

350

ment, through its crown agency, Petro-Canada, was a willing buyer for companies who didn't want to live with the new system. The goal was 50 per cent Canadian ownership by 1990.

A protracted legal contest and an intense battle for public opinion, nationally and in Alberta, followed between the two governments. In a dramatic gesture that stunned the country, the Alberta government cut oil production and withheld approval of large oil sands and heavy oil projects. Oil companies slashed their exploration budgets in what amounted to a capital strike, and oil rigs clogged the border crossings heading south. People throughout the province protested in large and noisy public meetings. Lougheed rallied his Alberta television audience: "Our forefathers fought hard to obtain these resources. . . We now have a responsibility to manage them well and preserve our ownership rights. . . the Ottawa government—without negotiation and without agreement—simply walked into our homes and occupied the living room."[2]

Albertans were swept up in the view that they had subsidized central Canadian consumers of oil by billions of dollars through receiving less than world price for oil while they had always paid more than world price for eastern manufactured goods, and that taxes on oil and gas exports were discriminatory since hydro-electricity exported from Ontario and Quebec did not have similar taxes. The NEP was widely interpreted not as an effort to Canadianize the oil industry, but as a much more insidious effort to nationalize it. Some Albertans boycotted Petro-Canada stations and a popular bumper sticker proclaimed, "I'd rather push this thing a mile than buy from Petro-Canada."

For many Albertans, Trudeau's policies and personal style had become a symbol of the sins of central Canada. Letters to the editor, graffiti, T-shirts, bumper stickers, political humour, and political meetings had dislike or hatred of Trudeau and the Liberals as their common theme. The few remaining Alberta Liberal faithful found themselves driving behind cars with bumper stickers proclaiming, "This Car Doesn't Brake for Liberals." The few Liberal cabinet ministers who ventured to Alberta to sell the new policies often came with security protection because audiences were so hostile.

In this tense political climate, tiny right-wing separatist parties sprang up. The Western Canada Concept (WCC) demanded either drastic changes in the Canadian political system or the separation of western Canada. Another quasi-separatist movement, known as "West Fed," was established by a wealthy Edmonton farm implement dealer, Elmer Knudsen, after the Trudeau victory in 1980. He drew crowds with his Ottawa-bashing and then confounded them with his bizarre theory that, since 1929, western Canada had not been part of Canada constitutionally. Many separatists firmly believed that the Trudeau government was using constitutional reform as a pretext for confiscating western oil and property and for establishing a socialist/communist state. Knudsen later revamped his organization as the "Confederation of Regions" Party, which dropped its explicit western separatism but spread its narrow anti-French vision of a unilingual Canada elsewhere in the country. Though he obtained very little support in the West, by the late 1980s Knudsen was garnering support in rural New Brunswick.

The WCC and West-Fed movements drew on many old grievances and remedies. The WCC revived the populist reforms of initiative, referendum, and recall. They also drew on all levels of society, bringing together farmers, ranchers, small businessmen, housewives, oil workers, and a few oil executives (usually from smaller Canadian companies). The most prominent supporter was Carl Nickle, a multi-millionaire oilman from Calgary and a former Conservative MP. Polls showed a consistent, hard-core support of around 8 per cent for separation. Throughout the early 1980s, many others were beginning to ponder the option seriously.

In February 1982, as economic storm clouds gathered, the leader of the Alberta WCC, Gordon Kesler, a rodeo rider and oil scout, won a surprise victory in a provincial by-election in Olds-Didsbury. This electoral upset aroused new hopes for the separatists and alerted the rest of the country to the depth of alienation in Alberta. Trudeau and Lougheed blamed each other for the separatist showing.

But support for separatism was short-lived. The separatists, plagued by infighting, could not decide whether the threat to separate was simply a bargaining ploy or if they really wanted to separate the West from the rest of Canada. In the November 1982 provincial election, the provincial Tories responded to political unrest with promises to spend more on consumers and farmers, and shield them from high interest rates. The WCC garnered 12 per cent of the popular vote, concentrated in rural central and southern Alberta, but won no seats. Kesler and the separatist movement went down to defeat.

After protracted negotiation, the federal and provincial governments had come to an energy pricing agreement in August 1981. It left major elements of the NEP intact, but increased the price of oil, transferred some control of the industry back to Alberta, and gave

Alberta greater revenues. An apparently satisfied Lougheed announced that the federal enemy was "sitting on the front porch and we're serving them coffee."[3] But world demand for oil was falling, and the optimism of the agreement, based on the assumption of ever-increasing oil prices, soon faced the harsh reality of falling prices. The psychological and economic impact of the NEP, high interest rates, softening world oil prices, and an economic recession throughout the western world led to distress throughout the Alberta economy.

The boom was over. During 1982 and 1983, many oil companies and related service businesses laid off employees. The Alsands mega-project for retrieving oil from the tar sands collapsed. The once high-flying Dome Oil (led by business folk-hero Jack Gallagher), which had been gobbling up other oil companies, experienced financial difficulties so spectacular that the federal government and the banks had to bail the company out. It limped on until it was finally purchased by the American company Amoco in 1988.

The malaise in Alberta's key industry was quickly reflected in other sectors of the economy. Housing and land prices plummetted. Land developers and contractors found themselves carrying debt loads they could not handle. In the big cities, many developers and contractors went bankrupt or closed down their businesses. Many urban Albertans, who had recently had paper fortunes in real estate and were accustomed to big homes, expensive cars, and luxury vacations, faced personal bankruptcy. Unemployment increased from 3.8 per cent in 1981 to 10.2 per cent in 1983. Many who had come to Alberta during the oil boom left for other parts of Canada, and for the first time in many years, the province's population did not increase. Following a string of mortgage company bankruptcies in the early 1980s, two new western banks, Canadian Commercial and North-lands, which had invested heavily in Alberta real estate, tottered precariously. In 1985 both failed. The provincial government had to step in to save the provincial credit unions and trust companies.

The Cast Changes: The Getty Government and the New Federal Scene

The Conservative victory at the national level in September 1984 temporarily changed Alberta's political climate. For the fifth straight time, Albertans returned all Conservatives to Parliament. At last they were on the winning side. Alberta Liberals had hoped that under a new English Canadian and pro-business leader, John Turner, their fortunes might improve. However, voters took their vengeance on the Liberals, and their share of the vote was only 13 per cent. Under a majority Conservative government, the strong sense of political alienation eased. Two Albertans, Joe Clark as minister of external affairs and Vegreville lawyer Don Mazankowski as deputy prime minister, took on senior cabinet posts. Albertans generally did not feel bitter about Brian Mulroney displacing Clark as Conservative leader since many Alberta Conservatives, including Lougheed, had supported Mulroney over Clark in the 1983 Tory leadership race.

The Conservative government quickly moved to ease resentment over the NEP. In March 1985 the "Western Accord" went most of the way to dismantling the NEP, with an end to special taxes and grants and a move to world prices for oil. As federal-provincial tensions eased, the separatist movement collapsed. Despite much sound and fury, Alberta right-wingers had decided, at least for the time being, to stick with the Conservatives.

The subsiding of the energy and constitutional wars contributed to Lougheed's decision to retire from politics in 1985. The race to replace him revealed some of the recurring regional, ethnic, and religious cleavages in the province that had been masked during his ascendancy. A determined battle was fought by Edmontonians Don Getty and Julian Koziak, both former cabinet ministers, and former Calgary MLA Ron Ghitter.

Don Getty, former athlete and oil company executive, was a key cabinet minister in the early Lougheed governments, and replaced Lougheed when he retired in 1985. Under Getty, the Conservative dominance in Alberta began to slip. Getty was committed to economic diversification, free trade, and the vision of Canada embodied in the 1987 Meech Lake constitutional accord. (*Courtesy Progressive Conservative Party*)

Getty was the candidate of the Tory party establishment. Born in Montreal in 1933, Getty spent part of his youth in London, Ontario, and quarterbacked for the University of Western Ontario football team while earning a degree in business administration. He moved to Alberta in 1955 to play football for the Edmonton Eskimos and work for Imperial Oil. One of Lougheed's original "team" in the 1967 provincial election, and minister of energy and intergovernmental affairs in the 1970s, he had left the Lougheed government in 1979 to head a small oil firm, but was lured back into politics when Lougheed retired.

Middle-aged, affluent males and the Tory party establishment formed the core of Getty's support in his well-financed drive for the leadership. Local Tory aldermen and MLAs also built up support for Getty among new immigrant groups in several east-end Calgary and Edmonton ridings. The Tory leadership race marked the first entry of the new "visible" minorities into Alberta politics. With implicit support from Lougheed, Getty won the leadership. He turned to Lougheed's former cabinet ministers for the key players in his first cabinet.

The waning of federal-provincial conflict and the end of Alberta's economic boom created an opportunity for the opposition. In the 1986 provincial election, for the first time since 1971 the province's place in the national political community was not the main focus of provincial politics. The relative absence of federal-provincial conflict, a deteriorating economy, and Getty's perceived weakness when compared to Lougheed, gave opposition parties an opening. Urban unemployment, labour conflict, and the province's continuing dependence on the shaky oil and gas industries led to discontent with the Tories. In May 1986 the opposition elected twenty-two members out of eighty-three, breaking a succession of lopsided Conservative majorities. The NDP under social worker Ray Martin (replacing Grant Notley, who died in a tragic plane accident in 1984) routed the Conservatives in Edmonton, and with added support from ridings in rural northern Alberta, returned sixteen members. The Liberals finally elected four members, including their leader Nick Taylor, who had been defeated in several previous elections.

The Getty government faced difficult economic circumstances. The world price of oil, which had been $44 dollars per barrel in 1981, had declined to $39 by March 1983. It unexpectedly collapsed to $10 in 1986. This led to further layoffs in the oil industry. Even firms that

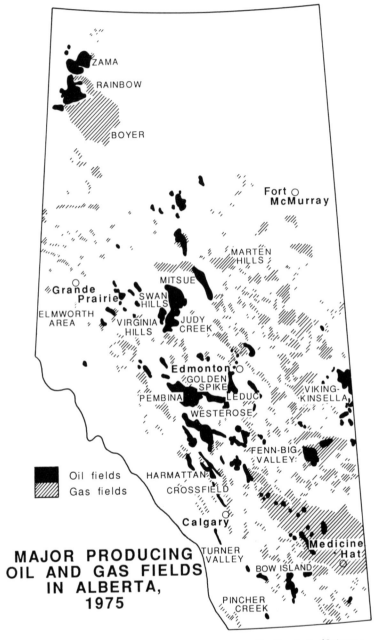

ZAMA

RAINBOW

BOYER

Fort O
McMurray

MARTEN
HILLS

MITSUE

Grande
Prairie SWAN
HILLS

ELMWORTH
AREA VIRGINIA JUDY
HILLS CREEK

Edmonton O

GOLDEN
SPIKE

VIKING-
KINSELLA

PEMBINA LEDUC

WESTEROSE

FENN-BIG
VALLEY

■ Oil fields
▨ Gas fields

HARMATTAN

CROSSFIELD

Calgary O

Medicine
Hat

MAJOR PRODUCING
OIL AND GAS FIELDS
IN ALBERTA,
1975

TURNER
VALLEY

BOW ISLAND

PINCHER
CREEK

Based on information from : *"Our Petroleum Challenge: The New Era"* (Calgary :
Petroleum Resources Communication Foundation, 1978).

had appeared as the pinnacle of success found their debt loads difficult to manage. For example, Nova (formerly Alberta Gas Trunk Line) had expanded rapidly during the 1970s (particularly in petrochemicals) under nationalist entrepreneur Bob Blair. Nova was forced to sell off part of Husky Oil to Hong Kong investors. With low prices for oil, planned expansion in tar sands and heavy oils had to be postponed.

Alberta agriculture also faced difficult years. The percentage of the population in agriculture had been steadily declining, affecting farmers' political influence and the viability of many small communities. By the 1980s less than 10 per cent of Alberta's workforce was employed in agriculture. In addition, agricultural prices fell as a result of world grain surpluses. Alberta farmers faced international subsidy wars, disappearing markets, and rising costs. A series of dry years in southern and eastern Alberta in the mid to late 1980s, with drought as severe as during the 1930s, brought many farmers to the brink of ruin. The average capital value of a farm declined from $634,000 in 1981 to $495,000 in 1986. The federal government stepped in to help the grain farmers, and Alberta's diversified agricultural base provided a backstop to overall collapse. Nonetheless, many farmers went under and many more were in trouble, particularly young ones just starting out and deeply in debt. The outstanding farm debt continued to rise from $4 billion in 1981 to $5.4 billion in 1987. The number of farm foreclosures brought memories of the bleak years of the Depression.

To offset the declines in the oil and gas industry and agriculture, the Getty government put even greater emphasis on economic diversification, stressing high technology, tourism, and forestry. In 1987, with economic woes slashing provincial government revenues, the Getty government implemented an austerity program. Cuts in health care, social services, and education, along with increased taxes, hurt many and provoked a negative public reaction.

Another major headache for the provincial government was the collapse of the Principal Group of Companies, an Edmonton-based financial empire owned by Donald Cormie. Provincial Treasurer Dick Johnston finally suspended the business licences and froze the assets of two Principal subsidiaries in June 1987. Principal's bankruptcy six weeks later hurt many Albertans and other Canadians, some of whom had invested their life savings. The Principal affair shook the view of the Tories as efficient overseers of the economy. As the government-appointed Code inquiry showed in 1989 in its report on the Principal affair, the Conservative government had been willing to overlook its own regulations in order to accommodate its business friends.

The Getty government invested a good deal of financial and political capital in its plans for economic diversification, particularly in forestry. A buoyant market for world pulp spurred development, and in 1988 and early 1989, Getty announced new or expanded sawmills, fibreboard, and pulp and paper plants in Grande Prairie, Peace River, Hinton, Whitecourt, Slave Lake, Manning, Lac La Biche, and Athabasca, among other locations. This multi-billion-dollar government-driven program, with its publicly funded infrastructure, loans, and guarantees, including major concessions to Japanese investors, was intended to create twelve thousand new jobs and lead to a development boom in northern Alberta. Though generally popular in northern Alberta, the projects aroused serious concerns among environmentalists, natives, federal officials, and others about the cumulative impact of the massive number of new projects on northern rivers, and among economists about the wisdom of relying on another industry prone to boom-bust cycles.

In the federal-provincial sphere, relations between the Alberta and federal governments were cordial from 1984 onward compared to the 1970s and early 1980s. The Conservative affiliation of both governments made this possible. On energy issues, the federal government's moves were seen as slow, but usually in accord with the views of the provincial government and the energy industry.

On the constitutional front, the Getty government supported the Meech Lake constitutional accord in the spring of 1987. This accord transferred more power to the provinces in return for Quebec's agreement to sign the 1982 constitution. Getty went into the Meech Lake talks with national Senate reform as his priority. A Canadian Committee for a Triple E Senate (Equal, Elected, Effective) began in Alberta in the early 1980s, arguing that a strong western voice at the national level would only come with an equal, elected, and effective Senate. Though started by Conservatives, the Triple E committee (headed by a tenacious Kathyrn farmer, Bert Brown) developed a non-partisan and broad-based appeal. Premier Lougheed had been unenthusiastic about an elected Senate, but Getty was convinced by the almost evangelical fervour of the Triple E committee. Getty emerged from the Meech Lake agreement with a guarantee of future talks on Senate reform. This was coupled, however, with a constitutional amending formula that gave a veto to all provinces. Critics argued that this made future Triple E Senate reform highly unlikely.

358

At one level, the Meech Lake Accord, passed by the Alberta legislature in November 1987, was greeted by Conservatives in Alberta as a statement of national unity, consistent with their longstanding views about the equality of provinces and the need for increased provincial power. The intense opposition in 1987 and 1988 of opponents of bilingualism to Bill C-72, the amendments to the federal government's Official Languages Act, temporarily channelled anti-Quebec feelings that otherwise might have been mobilized against the accord. By insisting in April 1987 that French Canadian NDP MLA Leo Piquette ask for permission before he could speak French in the Alberta legislature, and by introducing in June 1988 a French language policy (Bill 60) that seemed designed to not offend the sensitivities of those opposed to bilingualism rather than to respond to Franco-Albertans, the Getty government demonstrated to opponents of bilingualism that the accord provided little or no support for French language rights in Alberta.

However, by 1989 opponents of bilingualism had refocussed on the recognition in the accord of Quebec as a distinct society, and began opposing it. Opposition to the accord also came from many native, ethnic, and women's groups, who argued that it ignored or threatened their status, and from those who saw its provincial rights focus as ultimately destructive of Canadian federalism. The opposition to the Meech Lake Accord gradually extended to all ends of the political spectrum and included Franco-Albertans and Liberals as well as opponents of French Canadians and Quebec. By November 1989, three-quarters of Albertans wanted the accord reopened and renegotiated.

In one other major area of federal-provincial relations, the free trade initiatives with the United States in 1988, the Getty government and most Albertans strongly supported the Mulroney government. Lougheed had been one of the early enthusiastic advocates of a free trade deal. Many trade unionists and cultural and economic nationalists warned about the possible adverse impact of free trade on the economy, social programs, culture, and sovereignty. But the energy industry was enthusiastic in its support of free trade, believing it would bring assured markets and world prices, and remove the possibility of "interference" from Ottawa in setting prices. The agricultural sector also hoped for improved access to American markets. During the 1988 federal election campaign, the Alberta government and business interests launched a major advertising campaign in support of the deal. The Tories won twenty-five of the twenty-six Alberta seats in the election, while the NDP elected their first Alberta MP, Ross Harvey in Edmonton.

Anxious to take credit for new initiatives in oil, tourism, and forestry, and fearing political fallout from a looming unpopular federal sales tax and from the Code inquiry into the government handling of the Principal fiasco, in March 1989 Getty called a snap election, less than three years into his mandate. The Tories hoped to catch the opposition off guard. Getty attracted to the Conservative side Ray Speaker, a popular rural opposition MLA and ex-Social Credit cabinet minister, and Ralph Klein, Calgary's populist mayor, with promises of future cabinet posts. But the Tory strategy backfired. Though the Conservatives still won 59 of 83 seats, their popular vote fell from 51 to 44 per cent, and Getty lost his own seat in Edmonton. Tory support eroded further not only in Edmonton, but in their Calgary stronghold.

The increase in opposition strength had many causes. The election results partly reflected voter backlash against Tory austerity in 1987, which had deeply affected nurses, teachers, social workers, and social service recipients. This was followed by what were seen to be excessively lavish Tory campaign promises in the 1989 election with, among other promised programs, mortgage assistance and extensive rural road paving. Many voters were also disillusioned by Getty's seeming insensitivity to women's and environmental issues. The media, less awed than during Lougheed's tenure, turned a critical eye on the Tory record and promises. Campaigning on a platform of fiscal responsibility, with more attention to the environment, small business, and education, the Liberals garnered 29 per cent of the vote, and elected eight MLAs. The NDP maintained sixteen seats, primarily in Edmonton and surrounding area, though their popular vote declined from 29 to 26 per cent. Getty easily won a subsequent by-election in Stettler, but the provincial election undermined the myth of Tory invincibility. It also showed that at least in urban Alberta, there were serious deficiencies in the Tory party machine.

This trend in both the 1986 and 1989 provincial elections toward strong multi-party competition in urban Alberta reflected changing leadership and issues, and broader social and economic trends. The political solidarity of the Lougheed years had masked divisions in Alberta, between urban and rural Alberta, between north and south, and among social classes. These had been downplayed during the years of confrontation with Ottawa. The tight three-party races in the large cities in 1989 demonstrated that a young, heterogeneous, well-educated population could not be taken for granted by the Conservatives.

Though the provincial and federal Conservatives maintained their dominance throughout the late 1980s, both also began to feel increased disaffection among their own right-wing supporters. At the federal level, scandals in the Mulroney cabinet, economic patronage allegedly favouring Quebec over the West, and moderate as opposed to right-wing social policies alienated some long-time Conservatives. The Conservative political coalition between Quebec and Alberta, which provided a critical part of the federal government's power base, resulted in recurring tensions for many Alberta Conservatives.

In 1987, disaffected right-wingers, who felt that only constitutional and party reform could change a system that discriminated against the West, formed a new political party, the Reform Party of Canada. They elected Preston Manning, son of former Alberta premier Ernest Manning, as leader. Though drawing on many of the same grievances (such as bilingualism, alleged central Canadian domination, and government waste) that underlay the earlier right-wing separatist movements, the Reformers rejected separatism. They proclaimed that "The West Wants In!" and proposed reforms, in particular a Triple E Senate, and referenda on major public issues, to make Ottawa more responsive. The new party won a respectable 15 per cent of the popular vote in Alberta in the 1988 federal election, but no seats. The Reform Party was trapped by its strong support for the Conservatives' free trade initiative during what became an essentially one-issue federal campaign. Once the election was over, the Reform Party brought its agenda items of Senate reform and opposition to the Meech Lake Accord to the fore, and they elected their first MP, Deborah Grey, in a subsequent by-election in Beaver River in the spring of 1989.

By the fall of 1989, disaffected Conservatives were deserting both federal and provincial Tories for the new Reform Party. The growing strength of the Reform Party was strikingly revealed in the easy victory of the Reform Party candidate, Stan Waters, in Canada's first Senate election. After signing the Meech Lake Accord, Getty had remained undeterred in his view that the accord would help rather than hinder the cause of Senate reform. To prove his point, and under pressure from Triple E supporters, he took advantage of a provision in the Meech Lake Accord that allowed provincial governments to submit a list of names from which the prime minister would then choose new senators. In October 1989, over the objection of the federal Conservatives, he pushed ahead with a province-wide Senate election to provide a nominee for the federal government to appoint.

The results were an embarrassment for both the federal and provincial Tories. The voters used the opportunity to deal a stinging rebuke to both, while at the same time striking a blow for Senate reform. Retired lieutenant general and Calgary businessman Waters and the Reform Party tapped growing discontent with the Getty and Mulroney governments on a wide range of issues, including a controversial MLA pay hike of 30 per cent, the federal Conservatives' proposed Goods and Services Tax, and the Meech Lake Accord. They administered a humiliating defeat to the Conservative candidate, longtime Senate reformer Bert Brown, who finished a distant third. In no hurry to respond to this unprecedented election, the Mulroney government did not appoint Waters to the Senate until June 1990. This appointment, made in the aftermath of a renegotiated (though ultimately failed) Meech Lake agreement, was designed to reassure Albertans that the Conservative government was serious about Senate reform.

The results of the Senate election fed doubts among provincial Conservatives about Getty's leadership. Getty, however, was able to beat back a challenge to his leadership at the April 1990 Conservative party convention. Whether the results of the Senate election would enhance or hinder momentum for a Triple E Senate remained a question for the future. It was clear, however, that the Reform Party could draw on a strong current of discontent with both levels of government, and could alter the provincial political scene if they decided to contest future provincial elections. Provincial Conservatives were afraid that their party, already struggling in the large cities, could be wiped out if the Reform Party decided to challenge them in the rural strongholds. Public opinion, which showed strong support for the Reform Party among older voters in rural Alberta, supported this view. Alberta politics was entering a new, highly fluid, and likely an intensely competitive period.

Women

Throughout the 1970s and 1980s, women's status also changed as they became increasingly assertive of their rights and dignity. They became more visible in the work place, in traditionally male professions such as medicine, law, and journalism, and in the universities, labour unions, and politics. In keeping with national trends that had begun in the late 1950s, Alberta women were marrying later and having fewer children. In addition, a high divorce rate increased dramatically the number of single-parent families headed by women. Although family size, work, and divorce patterns varied greatly depending on a number of social factors, particularly ethnicity and religion, these trends meant that more women were in the paid workforce for longer periods of time than ever before.

Perhaps the most dramatic shift in women's work patterns was the increasing numbers of married women with preschool children in the workforce. By 1985 a higher percentage of Alberta women (60 per cent) were employed than anywhere else in the country, and over half of women with preschool children worked outside the home. One of the most dramatic effects of this change in women's work patterns was the emergence of a new institution and an increasingly volatile political issue—daycare. In contrast to the early 1970s, when institutionalized daycare was practically non-existent and working women with small children had to rely on informal arrangements for childcare, by the early 1980s, daycare facilities dotted the urban landscape. Some people called for higher standards, better pay for daycare workers, and a government-funded system of universal daycare; traditionalists felt that the tax system and increased public spending on daycare discriminated against parents (generally women) who stayed home to care for their children.

In addition to daycare, public debate over women's issues focussed on several key issues: equal rights, particularly with regard to equal opportunity and pay in the workplace, and abortion. A landmark Alberta legal case, that of farm wife Irene Murdoch, became a national rallying point for women's groups interested in improving the matrimonial and property rights of women. When Murdoch's marriage broke up in 1968, she claimed a share of the family ranch. Women across the country were shocked when in 1973 the Supreme Court of Canada granted Murdoch only a lump sum maintenance payment rather than her claim to partnership. This decision galvanized women into action. Their lobbying eventually helped to bring legislation in most provinces, including Alberta, requiring an equal division of family assets at the dissolution of a marriage. Women's rights were further bolstered in 1982 when an equal rights clause (section 28) was added to the Charter of Rights of the new Canadian constitution.

Several new feminist organizations helped to alter social attitudes and policy regarding women, children, and marriage. Groups such as the Alberta Status of Women Action Committee, established in the early 1970s, lobbied politicians and tried to raise public awareness on a wide range of issues, such as daycare, poverty, equal pay, violence

363

against wives and children, pornography, prostitution, and child sexual abuse. The new feminism undoubtedly influenced social policy and practices of educators, lawyers, social workers, psychologists, and police. Feminists also established new newspapers, magazines, and institutions, including rape crisis and birth control centres, and emergency shelters for battered women.

Women began making greater inroads in politics. In the 1979 provincial election, six women were elected to the seventy-nine-seat legislature, and in 1989 thirteen women were elected to the eighty-three seat legislature. Though at first women in politics tended to be given "minor" responsibilities, by the late 1980s Alberta had female cabinet members in important portfolios, such as Nancy Betkowski in Hospitals and Medical Care, and Elaine McCoy in Labour. In addition, both feminists and traditionalists, though often not fully acknowledging their common ground, had successfully pushed for greater recognition of the economic and social value of traditional "women's work" in the family, the household, and community organizations.

Nevertheless, in the late 1980s, women still faced substantial barriers to economic and social equality. In Alberta, as elsewhere in Canada, women continued to occupy low-paying, low-status, and often dead-end jobs. Even those women who had risen to positions of power and influence still found themselves barred in various ways from "old boy" networks.

Natives

Alberta natives were also affected by the economic, social, and political changes of the 1970s and 1980s. Provincial, regional, and national native organizations, under a new, often highly educated, native leadership, became increasingly vocal in their attempt to shape federal policy toward Indians and Métis. In the context of intense debates over reforming the Canadian constitution, and rapid social and economic change, natives addressed a new set of issues. Resource development in northern Alberta intruded on hitherto isolated groups, arousing volatile debate surrounding the issue of land claims, and the underlying questions of who should reap the benefits of resource wealth, and whether resource development could be made compatible with a traditional native way of life.

In 1969 the Indian leadership in Alberta opposed the recently proposed federal "White Paper" on Indian policy, which they saw as a blueprint for assimilation into Canadian society. Alberta Indian leaders replied with their own "Citizens' Plus Red Paper," which claimed that Indians were a distinct group who had special rights. They rejected the federal proposals to end the treaties and reserves. The fight against the federal "White Paper" led to greater unity among Alberta's Treaty Indian leaders, and together with natives elsewhere in Canada, they initiated a new constitutional and political dialogue with the federal government. Working with national Indian organizations such as the National Indian Brotherhood (and its successor organization, the Assembly of First Nations), Alberta Indians also undertook new initiatives in social services and education. They opposed sending native children out of their communities for adoption, and asserted more control over their own education. The federal government and natives both agreed that the church-administered residential school system (which had separated many students from their families, languages, and cultures) were costly, had resulted in emotional, cultural, and social devastation, and should be abolished. In 1973 the federal government agreed to native demands to transfer control and funding of education to Indian bands. The bands began to redesign curricula, and train and hire their own teachers. This led to a lower drop-out rate of native students from schools.

The revised curricula reflected a new approach to Indian culture and spirituality. Natives began presenting their culture in a different way from the traditionally negative approach of government agents and missionaries. By the 1970s, the federal bureaucracy and most Christian churches were beginning to adjust to the new realities of a world conscious of the evils of racism and internal colonialism.

The growing control of Indian and Métis organizations over social programs and education also led to a greater emphasis on native self-government. This concept was fraught with thorny practical and theoretical issues. Nonetheless, Indian and Métis leaders began seeking ways of achieving more self-government.

The Métis pioneered in the area of self-government. In 1975, the eight Métis settlement associations formed the Alberta Federation of Métis Settlement Associations to fight for land security, local legislative authority, and adequate financing. The Métis settlements wanted to take over administrative control from the provincial government's Métis Development Branch. Aided by the recognition of Métis aboriginal rights in the Canadian constitution in 1982, the Métis association began negotiating with the Lougheed and Getty governments to achieve more constitutional protection and more self-government. In June 1989, the residents of Alberta's eight Métis settlements overwhelmingly approved an agreement giving the Métis a measure of self-government and $310 million in land compensation, to be used for economic development.

These thrusts for more self-government occurred against a backdrop of a rapidly changing and growing native population. The estimated 72,000 natives in Alberta in 1981 (3 per cent of the Alberta population) included 35,800 status Indians, 8,600 non-status Indians, 27,100 Métis, and 500 Inuit. This predominantly youthful population was becoming increasingly urban: 40 per cent lived in urban centres. The native population was also becoming better educated, with a growing number of high school graduates, university students, and the beginnings of a professional class. However, most natives still experienced poverty and unemployment. High unemployment rates, coupled with cultural and psychological stresses stemming from decades of poverty, racism, and government paternalism, contributed to their having higher rates of incarceration, alcoholism, and a shorter life expectancy than the rest of the population.

Facing these problems, Alberta Indian bands struggled to improve their economic conditions. Almost half of Alberta's forty-two bands had oil and gas on their reserves and these bands used the oil wealth to develop commercial projects. By 1979 the resource-rich Samson Band at Hobbema had its own trust company, real estate and rental properties in Edmonton, a feed lot, thousands of head of cattle, and an elaborate grain handling system. Another northern band bought hotels in Fort McMurray and Jasper. The Enoch band in Edmonton and the Sarcee in Calgary developed large-scale real estate projects for non-Indians. The Bloods developed a large house-construction factory. In 1989 the Sturgeon Lake band, in partnership with a company from China and with support from the federal Native Economic Development Program, built a chopstick factory, using the aspen forests to supply the Asian market.

Economic development and growing political activism were closely related. Alberta native leaders joined the national battle for recognition of aboriginal rights in the constitution and fought for redress of land claims. Land claims often led natives into conflicts with other groups. For example, in 1980 the Bloods at Cardston demanded government action on their land claims, and blockaded access to some Cardston businesses. They also began boycotts of Cardston schools and businesses. In northern Alberta, as oil and forestry development pushed farther northward, groups previously largely isolated from white contact, such as the Cree of Lubicon Lake, fought to protect their way of life against encroachment by oil companies.

The Lubicon Indians' protest attracted national and international attention. Representatives of international organizations and church leaders came to investigate the longstanding claims of the Lubicon Cree. The Lubicons had been missed by the Treaty No. 8 commissioners in 1899, and it was not until 1939 that the federal government recognized them as a distinct band. However, World War II postponed the federal government's plans to establish a reserve. After the war, when the federal government gave no indication of proceeding with a reserve, the province began granting oil and gas exploration leases. During the 1970s, the provincial government built a resource road to open the area. Significant oil finds brought numerous oil companies to the region in the early 1980s; eventually four hundred wells were drilled within a ten-mile radius of their settlement. The Lubicons (who by the late 1980s numbered around 450) went to court in an unsuccessful effort to stop development until their land claim was resolved. In 1985 the federal government appointed Davie Fulton, a former federal minister of justice, to investigate, but the federal and provincial governments refused to accept his recommendations. The Alberta government continued to sell oil and forestry leases on land claimed by the Lubicons.

A boycott of the Calgary Winter Olympic Games in early 1988 drew national and international attention to the Lubicons' claims. In the fall of 1988, the band closed access to the disputed land. Premier Getty tried to break through the bureaucratic logjam and with the quiet, determined Lubicon chief, Bernard Ominayak, agreed in October on the size of the land claim. However, further negotiations between the Lubicons and the federal government resulted in stalemate. Ottawa feared the precedent of a too-generous settlement, since besides the Lubicons, there were six other isolated bands in northern Alberta who had also been missed by Treaty No. 8.

Throughout the protracted negotiations over land claims and a new constitutional status, the natives discovered they had allies in the general public. Though wary of native claims to special status, a 1986 survey indicated that half of Albertans believed that native land claims should be settled before resource projects proceeded. However, native land claims undoubtedly poisoned relations in some communities. In small towns and cities, prejudice and discrimination also continued in housing and the workplace. Many natives also charged that insensitive health care workers and police discriminated against them, denying them dignity. The lives of Alberta's native peoples are undoubtedly constrained by a continuing legacy of neglect, paternalism, and racism, yet there are also many signs of a new interest in and appreciation of native culture among non-natives.

The new native political, economic, and social initiatives during the 1970s and 1980s were all part of a drive for equality and self-respect. There were differences (and conflicts) in approach between tribes, and there were often contrasts between an aggressive, sophisticated, and educated native leadership, and a more cautious and traditional grass-roots community. Nonetheless, together they attempted to throw off the heavy hand of government bureaucracy and cope with a new set of complex circumstances. Natives turned more and more to their rich past, their culture, and native spirituality to help them cope with the problems of modern society and their increasing role in that society.

Alberta and the International Community

One of the consequences of the boom, growth, and wealth of the 1970s and 1980s was a new national and international stature for Alberta. International figures including Queen Elizabeth, Indira Gandhi, Sheik Yamani, Margaret Thatcher, King Hussein, and the Pope visited the province. International sporting events also symbolized this new stature. In Edmonton, the Commonwealth Games in 1978 and the Universiade Games in 1983 helped raise Alberta's international profile.

The Fifteenth Winter Olympic Games in Calgary in 1988 further enhanced Alberta's new status. Fears of an elitist Olympics, controlled by and for Calgary's wealthy males, gradually broke down as the city's populist mayor, Ralph Klein, insisted on mass volunteer participation in running the Games. The well-organized events showcased Alberta's friendliness, volunteer spirit, and cultural diversity.

The Olympics left a legacy of sports facilities and tourist interest. While the annual $2.4 billion worth of receipts from tourism was well behind the $4.4 billion from agriculture and $14.9 billion from oil, gas, and mineral production (1988), tourism provided a new hope for economic diversification. The Olympics symbolized the ways in which Alberta had changed from a remote frontier to a complex, modern society linked to the main economic and social trends of the rest of the world.

Paradoxically, the mood of Albertans entering the 1990s combined a striking confidence with profound insecurity. The confidence stemmed partly from a sense that Alberta was becoming increasingly visible on the regional, national, and international stages. The province's artists and writers, some known internationally, were developing an appreciative audience at home, and were no longer forced to leave the province to pursue their careers. Its sports teams had captured the major national hockey and football championships for several years running. Its universities were gaining national recognition as centres of excellence in many fields. Several of its businesses had expanded nationally and internationally. Its political voices were being heard throughout the country, if not always being listened to or appreciated.

By the late 1980s, despite continued uncertainty in the oil and gas industry and distress in agriculture, Alberta had begun to recover from the economic bust of the early part of the decade. Population growth and economic growth were slower, but confidence was returning. Nevertheless, an economy so dependent on fluctuating

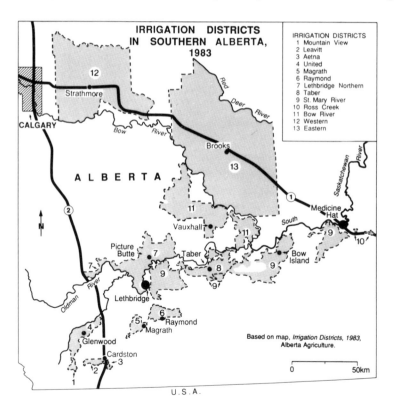

IRRIGATION DISTRICTS
IN SOUTHERN ALBERTA,
1983

IRRIGATION DISTRICTS
1 Mountain View
2 Leavitt
3 Aetna
4 United
5 Magrath
6 Raymond
7 Lethbridge Northern
8 Taber
9 St. Mary River
10 Ross Creek
11 Bow River
12 Western
13 Eastern

Based on map, *Irrigation Districts, 1983,*
Alberta Agriculture.

0   50km

U.S.A.

world prices for wheat, oil, and pulp generated anxiety, and tinged confidence with insecurity. The very nature of the oil and gas industry, which is based on a non-renewable resource, heightened uncertainty. Even though Alberta has huge oil sands, abundant natural gas, and heavy oil and coal deposits, in addition to its declining deposits of light and medium crude oil, there was a strong fear during the 1970s and early 1980s of what might happen when these resources are depleted. During the 1980s, business and political leaders became increasingly concerned about low prices and price volatility in the resource-based economy.

Albertans were agreed on the need to diversify the economy to avoid boom-bust economic cycles. But they were also uneasy that the price of diversification might turn out to be deterioration and over-exploitation of the forests and rivers, and a tourist industry that might compromise or destroy the province's wilderness.

Nor is it surprising that Albertans should feel insecure given the province's foreshortened development. Since the 1870s, Alberta has absorbed the impact of enormous economic, technological, and social changes. These have often occurred in such rapid succession that while reeling unsteadily in the aftermath of one change, Albertans have had to recoup quickly to deal with yet another barrage of shifting circumstances. All of this has occurred in a province that has had little time to develop a strong sense of identity, or even a strong awareness of its history and varied local regions.

Today's Alberta is youthful, vital, and energetic, a place generating both new urban landscapes and an upsurge of creative activity in the economic, social, and cultural spheres. It is also an unstable juxtaposition of historical, economic, political, and social forces, and neither the pattern of this convergence nor its outcome is easy to foresee. Clearly though, the overlapping central strands in Alberta's history—the native experience; the impact of the frontier; the legacy of the pioneer years; ethnic and religious pluralism; the subtle interplay among religion, ethnicity, and politics; its status as an economic and political hinterland, dependent on outside metropolitan centres; and its resource-based boom/bust economy—will continue to shape its destiny.

Despite the uncertainty of their economic prospects, Albertans face the future with pride in their past achievements. Alberta's relative prosperity, its diverse and enterprising population, vast wilderness and resources, and its natural beauty all combine to suggest much potential for the twenty-first century.

Notes

Chapter One
Native Peoples and the Encounter with the European Frontier
[1] Hugh Dempsey, *Crowfoot: Chief of the Blackfeet* (Edmonton: Hurtig, 1972), 24.
[2] Hugh Dempsey, *Indian Tribes of Alberta* (Calgary: Glenbow, 1978), 66.
[3] Ibid., 61.
[4] A. S. Morton, *A History of the Canadian West to 1870–71*, second ed., (Toronto: University of Toronto Press, 1973), 463.
[5] Ibid., 700.
[6] Quoted in J. G. MacGregor, *A History of Alberta* (Edmonton: Hurtig, 1972), 65
[7] Quoted in Isaac Mabindisa, "The Praying Man: The Life and Times of Henry Bird Steinhauer," unpublished Ph.D., University of Alberta, 1984, 416.
[8] Ibid., 418
[9] Hugh Dempsey, ed., *The Rundle Journalists, 1840–1848* (Calgary: Alberta Records Publications Board, 1977), 116

Chapter Two
"Civilizing" the Northwest: 1850–1885
[1] Quoted in Douglas Owram, *Promise of Eden: The Canadian Expansionist Movement and the Idea of the West, 1856–1900* (Toronto: University of Toronto Press, 1980), 49.
[2] Quoted in Lewis O. Saum, "From Vermont to Whoop-Up Country: Some Letters of D. W. Davis, 1867–1878," *Montana: The Magazine of Western History*, Vol. 35, No. 3 (Summer 1985), 67
[3] Quoted in Ronald Atkin, *Maintain the Right* (New York: John Day, 1973), 197.
[4] Quoted in Donald Smith, "The Original Peoples," in H. & T. Palmer, eds., *Peoples of Alberta* (Saskatoon: Western Producer, 1985), 61.
[5] Quoted in Hugh Dempsey, *Big Bear: The End of Freedom* (Vancouver: Douglas & McIntyre, 1984), 160.

Chapter Three
The Northwest Frontier: Economy and Settlement, 1880–1896
[1] Quoted in J. G. MacGregor, *Edmonton Trader* (Toronto: McClelland and Stewart, 1963), 201.
[2] Quoted in Douglas Leighton, "Banff is where it all began," *Canadian Geographic*, (Feb./March, 1985), 9. See also Sid Marty, *A Grand and Fabulous*

Notion: The First Century of Canada's Parks (Toronto: NC Press, 1984), Chapter 3.

[3] Maureen Ursenbach Beecher, "Mormon Women in Southern Alberta: The Pioneer Years," in Brigham Card, Howard Palmer, et al. *The Mormon Presence in Canada* (Edmonton: University of Alberta Press, 1990).

Chapter Four
Peopling the "Last Best West": 1896–1913

[1] Though originally known as Fort Macleod, the town was incorporated as Macleod in 1892. In 1952, the town restored its original name.

[2] *Lethbridge News*, June 26, Aug. 4, Jan. 29, 1889, quoted in Howard Palmer, "Responses to Foreign Immigration: Nativism and Ethnic Tolerance in Alberta," unpublished M.A., University of Alberta, 1971, 38.

[3] Quoted in Helen Evans Reid, *All Silent, All Damned: The Search for Isaac Barr* (Toronto: Ryerson Press, 1969), 46.

[4] Emma Curtin, "Daughters of Empire: British Gentlewomen in Alberta, 1880–1914," unpublished M.A. thesis, University of Calgary, 1990, iii, 54. I am indebted to Ms. Curtin for the insights on this topic.

[5] N. N. and H. N. Ronning, *The Gospel at Work* (Minneapolis: 1943), 88.

[6] Ibid.

[7] Although the name became officially known as Crowsnest Pass, this book uses the original Crow's Nest Pass since that is the preference of both historians of the region and local residents.

[8] Translation from brochure, "About the Founding and Settling of the German Swiss Colony, Blumenau," (1903, in author's possession). See also Edith Clark, ed., *Tales of Tail Creek Country* (1968), 81–84; Jessie Campbell, *Chatter Chips From Beaver Dam Creek* (Lacombe: Castor Old Timers' Association, 1975), 31–34.

[9] *Canadian Annual Review* (1907), 389.

[10] Charles Gordon, *Postscript to Adventure: The Autobiography of Ralph Connor*, second ed. (Toronto: McClelland and Stewart, 1975), 110.

Chapter Five
The Pioneer Moment: Building the Rural Core

[1] Gerald Friesen, *The Canadian Prairies: A History* (Toronto: University of Toronto Press, 1984), 304.

[2] Quoted in Helen Evans Reid, *All Silent All Damned* (Toronto: Ryerson Press, 1969), 85.

[3] Ernest B. Ingles, "The Custom Threshermen in Western Canada, 1890–1925," in David Jones and Ian MacPherson, eds., *Building Beyond the Homestead* (Calgary: University of Calgary Press, 1988), 135–160.

[4] W. J. C. Cherwinski, "In Search of Jake Trumper: The Farm Hand and the Prairie Farm Family," in David Jones and Ian MacPherson, eds., *Building Beyond the Homestead*, 111–134; Cecilia Danysk, "Showing These Slaves

Their Class Position: Barriers to Organizing Prairie Farm Workers," in ibid., 163–178.

[5] Quoted in Neil McDonald, "Canadian Nationalism and North-West Schools, 1884–1905," in Alf Chaiton and Neil McDonald, eds., *Canadian Schools and Canadian Identity* (Gage: Toronto, 1977), 173.

[6] Ibid., 171.

[7] M. R. Lupul, "Ukrainian Language Education in Canada's Public Schools," in M. R. Lupul, ed., *A Heritage in Transition* (Toronto, McClelland and Stewart, 1983), 232.

[8] The best accounts of this school crisis are M. R. Lupul, "Ukrainian Language Education in Canada's Public Schools," 228–233; and Orest Martynowych, *The Ukrainian Bloc Settlement in East Central Alberta* (Edmonton: Historic Sites Services, 1985), 211–215.

[9] Paul Voisey, *Vulcan: The Making of a Prairie Community* (Toronto: University of Toronto Press, 1988)

[10] J. W. Morrison, "Agricultural Achievements of the Prairie Experimental Farms, 1886–1986," *Prairie Forum*, Vol. 11, No. 2 (Fall 1986), 208.

[11] Quoted in E. C. Stacey, *Peace Country Heritage* (Saskatoon: Western Producer, 1974), 17.

[12] James Gray, *A Brand of Its Own: The 100 Year History of the Calgary Exhibition and Stampede* (Saskatoon: Western Producer, 1985), 9.

Chapter Six

The Boom Years (1896–1913): Politics, Cities, and Resource Development

[1] Quoted in Douglas Owram, ed., *The Formation of Alberta: A Documentary History* (Calgary: Historical Society of Alberta, 1979), 375.

[2] James Gray, *Talk to My Lawyer! Great Stories of Southern Alberta's Bar & Bench* (Edmonton: Hurtig, 1987), 19.

[3] Quoted in L. G. Thomas, *The Liberal Party in Alberta* (Toronto: University of Toronto Press, 1959), 51.

[4] Quoted in E. A. Corbett, *Henry Marshall Tory* (Toronto: Ryerson, 1954), 59.

[5] J. G. MacGregor, *Paddle Wheels to Bucket-Wheels on the Athabasca* (Toronto: McClelland and Stewart, 1974), 139.

[6] Ibid., 114.

[7] J. G. MacGregor, *A History of Alberta* (Edmonton: Hurtig, 1972), 205.

[8] Quoted in A. A. den Otter, *Civilizing the West: The Galts and the Development of Western Canada* (Edmonton: University of Alberta Press, 1982), 292.

Chapter Seven

The Great War and After: The Fervent Years, 1914–1921

[1] Glenbow Archives, quoted in Richard Cunniffe, "The Militia Regiments of Alberta, 1901–39," unpublished manuscript, 97.

[2] R. I. McLean, "Temperance and Prohibition in Alberta," unpublished M.A. thesis, University of Calgary, 1969, 44–45.

[3] James Gray, *Booze: The Impact of Whisky on the Prairies* (Toronto: Macmillan, 1972), 83–100.

[4] Barbara Nicholson, "Feminism in Western Canada to 1916," unpublished M.A. thesis, University of Calgary, 1972, 133.

[5] Nellie McClung, *The Stream Runs Fast* (Toronto: Thomas Allen, 1945), 112.

[6] W. L. Morton, *The Progressive Party in Canada* (Toronto: University of Toronto Press, 1950), 39.

[7] *Calgary Albertan*, Feb. 28, 1916.

[8] Stanley Gordon, "The History of Aviation in Alberta to 1955," unpublished background paper, Reynolds Museum and Alberta Culture, 1985, 16.

[9] David Jones, *Empire of Dust* (Edmonton: University of Alberta Press, 1987), 111.

[10] Quoted in Paul Sharp, *The Agrarian Revolt in Western Canada* (Minneapolis, University of Minnesota Press, 1948), 115.

Chapter Eight
The Transitional Twenties: Struggling with Change

[1] R. G. Moyles, ed., *Challenge of the Homestead: Peace River Letters of Clyde and Myrle Campbell, 1919–1924* (Calgary: Alberta Records Publications Board, 1988), 4.

[2] David Jones, *Empire of Dust* (Edmonton: University of Alberta Press, 1987), 132.

[3] Franklin Foster, "John Edward Brownlee: A Biography," unpublished Ph.D., Queen's University, 1981, 168.

[4] Ibid., 172.

[5] P. D. Smith, "The United Farmers of Alberta and the Ginger Group: Independent Political Action, 1919–1939," unpublished M.A. thesis, University of Alberta, 1973, 15.

[6] Stanley Gordon, "The History of Aviation in Alberta to 1955," Unpublished Study for Reynolds-Alberta Museum and Alberta Culture, 1985, 17.

[7] *Edmonton Journal*, May 2, 1922.

[8] W. E. Mann, *Sect, Cult, and Church in Alberta* (Toronto: University of Toronto Press, 1955), 74.

[9] Ibid., 121.

Chapter Nine
The Crisis Years and the Rise of Social Credit

[1] *Calgary Herald*, May 6, 1936; Jan. 19, 1937.

[2] Ben Swankey, "Reflections of an Alberta Communist: The Hungry Thirties," *Alberta History*, Vol. 27, No. 4 (Autumn 1979), 4.

[3] Premier's Papers, Provincial Archives of Alberta, Brownlee to N. Priestley, Aug. 15, 1932. Quoted in Susan Kooyman, "The Policies and Legislation of the United Farmers of Alberta Government, 1921–1935," unpublished M.A. thesis, University of Calgary, 1981, 106.

[4] On the relationship between the UFA and CCF see Carl Betke, "The UFA: Visions of a Cooperative Commonwealth," *Alberta History*, Vol. 27, No. 3 (Summer 1979):7–14.

[5] Quoted in John Irving, *The Social Credit Movement in Alberta* (Toronto: University of Toronto Press, 1959), 322.

[6] *Lethbridge Herald*, Oct. 3, 1935.

[7] Information on Jaques from interview by Norma Milton with his daughter, Nanette McKay, Calgary, 1979 (in author's possession).

[8] National Archives of Canada, Bennett Papers, Box 568, R. B. Bennett to J. Y. Card, Aug. 31, 1935.

[9] *Today and Tomorrow*, Aug. 5, 1937; quoted in J. A. Boudreau, *Alberta, Aberhart and Social Credit* (Toronto: Holt Rinehart Winston, 1975), 86.

[10] Glenbow Archives, *Calgary Herald* collector, Papers re: Social Credit Movement in Alberta, Box 2, f. 8.

[11] Alvin Finkel, *The Social Credit Phenomenon in Alberta* (Toronto: University of Toronto Press, 1989), 46.

Chapter Ten

World War II and the Beginnings of Transformation: 1940–1947

[1] P. C. Conrad, *Training for Victory: The B.C.A.T.P. in the West* (Saskatoon: Western Producer, 1989), 77.

[2] Murray Dobbin, *The One-And-A-Half Men* (Vancouver: New Star, 1981), 146.

Chapter Eleven

Oil and the Birth of Modern Alberta: 1947–1971

[1] James Lightbody, "'Wild Bill' Hawrelak: 'Let's Get Edmonton Rolling Again'," in Allan Levine, ed., *Your Worship!* (Toronto: Lorimer, 1989).

Chapter Twelve

Boom and Bust: The Lougheed Years and After

[1] Great Plains Research Consultants, "The Athabasca Oil Sands: A History, 1951–1983," Research Report for Historic Sites Service, March, 1984, 168.

[2] Transcript of Premier Lougheed's Address to the Province of Alberta in Reaction to the Federal Budget, Oct. 30, 1980.

[3] Lougheed's perception of the agreement and the Conservative's media strategy is discussed in David G. Wood, *The Lougheed Legacy* (Toronto: Key Porter, 1985), 180–181.

Annotated Bibliography

Introduction and Chapter One: **Native Peoples and the Encounter with the European Frontier**

For background on the biophysical regions of Alberta see L. D. Cordes and D. J. Pennock, "Biophysical Constraints of the Natural Environment on Settlement," in B. M. Barr and P. J. Smith, *Environment and Economy: Essays on the Human Geography of Alberta* (Edmonton: Pica Pica Press, 1984). On Alberta's natural environment, W. G. Hardy, *Alberta, A Natural History* (Edmonton: Hurtig, 1967).

For bibliographies of Alberta see Bruce Peel, *A Bibliography of the Prairie Provinces to 1953* (Toronto: University of Toronto Press, 1956); Supplement, Toronto, 1963; Alan Artibise, *Western Canada Since 1870: A Select Bibliography* (Vancouver: University of British Columbia Press, 1978); Pat Roome and Leslie Robinson, "Alberta", *Communique*, Vol. IV, No. 2 (Autumn 1980); and Gloria Strathern, *Alberta 1954–1979, A Provincial Bibliography* (Edmonton: University of Alberta Press 1982). For a listing of local histories, Joanna Krotki, ed., *Local Histories of Alberta: An Annotated Bibliography* (Edmonton: Division of East European Studies, University of Alberta, 1980). For a recent bibliography, Robert E. Brundin and Kathleen De Long, "Alberta Books, A Selected Western Bibliography, 1982–87," *Alberta* Vol. 1, No. 2 (1989):82–112.

For a journal that specializes in Alberta history and other aspects of Alberta see *Alberta History* (1953–). A *Cumulative Index: Alberta History* (Calgary: Historical Society of Alberta, 1981) covers the years 1953–1977. See also the interdisciplinary *Alberta* (1988–), and *Prairie Forum* (1976–).

Studies on the early archaeology of Alberta include H. M. Wormington and Richard Forbis, *An Introduction to the Archaeology of Alberta, Canada* (Denver: Denver Museum of Natural History, 1965); T. A. Moore, ed. *Alberta Archaeology: Prospect and Retrospect* (Lethbridge: Archaeological Society of Alberta, 1981); and the popular synthesis: Gail Helgason, *The First Albertans: An Archaeological Search* (Edmonton: Lone Pine, 1987). On the life cycle of the Plains Indians: George B. Grinnell, *Blackfoot Lodge Tales* (Lincoln: University of Nebraska Press, 1962, reprint of 1892 edition); and David C. Mandelbaum, *The Plains Cree* (Regina: Canadian Plains Research Center, 1979).

The biographies by Hugh Dempsey of *Red Crow* (Saskatoon: Western Producer, 1980), *Crowfoot* (Edmonton: Hurtig, 1972), and *Big Bear* (Vancouver: Douglas and McIntyre, 1984) are outstanding accounts of native life in the nineteenth century. His survey *Indian Tribes of Alberta* (Calgary: Glenbow, 1978) is a useful overview. Donald Smith's chapter, "The Original

Peoples of Alberta," in H. & T. Palmer, eds., *Peoples of Alberta* (Saskatoon: Western Producer, 1985) is a summary of new research with an extensive bibliography.

For general accounts of the fur trade see H. A. Innis, *The Fur Trade in Canada*, rev. ed. (Toronto: University of Toronto Press, 1962); and A. S. Morton, *A History of the Canadian West to 1870-71* (London: 1939), second edition, edited by L. G. Thomas (Toronto: University of Toronto Press, 1973). E. E. Rich, *The Fur Trade and the North West to 1857* (Toronto: McClelland and Stewart, 1967) provides a general survey of the fur-trade period. For a popular account of fur-trade history see Daniel Francis, *Battle for the West: Fur Traders and the Birth of Western Canada* (Edmonton: Hurtig, 1982). For a detailed account of Fort Chipewyan, see James Parker, *Emporium of the North: Fort Chipewyan and the Fur Trade to 1835* (Regina: Canadian Plains Research Center, 1987). See also two useful biographies, J. S. Galbraith, *The Little Emperor: Governor Simpson of the Hudson's Bay Company* (Toronto: Macmillan, 1976) and J. G. McGregor, *John Rowand: Czar of the Prairies* (Saskatoon: Western Producer, 1979).

Of particular importance on Indians and the fur trade are the books of Arthur J. Ray, including, among others, *Indians in the Fur Trade: Their Role as Trappers, Hunters and Middlemen in the Lands Southwest of Hudson Bay 1660-1870* (Toronto: University of Toronto Press, 1974).

For further information on family and community in the fur trade see Sylvia Van Kirk, *"Many Tender Ties": Women in Fur-Trade Society in Western Canada* (Winnipeg: Watson and Dwyer, 1980); and "'The Custom of the Country': An Examination of Fur Trade Marriage Practices," in L. H. Thomas, ed., *Essays on Western History* (Edmonton: University of Alberta Press, 1976): 49-68. Frits Pannekoek, *The Fur Trade and Western Canadian Society, 1670-1870*, Canadian Historical Association Booklet (Ottawa: Canadian Historical Association, 1987) provides a helpful synthesis and bibliography on fur trade social history. For a useful overview of the Métis see John Foster, "The Plains Metis" in R. Bruce Morrison and C. R. Wilson, eds., *Native Peoples: The Canadian Experience* (Toronto: McClelland & Stewart, 1986).

For a useful bibliography on the Blackfoot that contains many references to native religion, see Hugh Dempsey and Lindsay Moir, *Bibliography of the Blackfoot* (Metuchen, N. J.: Scarecrow Press, 1989). The missionary work of all major denominations is analyzed in John Webster Grant's *Moon of Wintertime: Missionaries and the Indians of Canada in Encounter since 1534* (Toronto: University of Toronto Press, 1984). On Rundle and Steinhauer see works cited in footnotes. On the McDougalls, among other works, James Nix, *Mission Among the Buffalo* (Toronto: Ryerson Press, 1960); Les Hurt, *The Victoria Settlement, 1862-1922* (Edmonton: Historic Sites Service, 1979), Chapter 2; and for a recent compilation of John McDougall's writing, Thomas Bredin, ed., *Parsons on the Plains* (Toronto: Longman, 1971). On

Catholics see Katherine Hughes, *Father Lacombe: The Black-Robe Voyageur* (Toronto: William Briggs, 1914); J. G. MacGregor, *Father Lacombe* (Edmonton: Hurtig, 1975). For an overview of past, and ongoing research on the Oblates, see Raymond Huel, "The Western Oblate History Project," *Alberta*, Vol. 1, No. 2, (1989): 63–69.

Chapter Two: "Civilizing" the Northwest: 1850–1885

On the expansionist movement, see Douglas Owram, *The Promise of Eden: The Canadian Expansionist Movement and the Idea of the West, 1856–1900* (Toronto: University of Toronto Press, 1980). On changing images of the northwest: Douglas Francis, "From Wasteland to Utopia: Changing Images of the Canadian West in the Nineteenth Century," *Great Plains Quarterly*, Vol. 7, No. 3, Summer 1987: 178–194. See also more generally, Francis' *Images of the West: Changing Perceptions of the Prairies, 1690–1960* (Saskatoon: Western Producer, 1989). On the Palliser Expedition: Irene Spry, *The Palliser Expedition* (Toronto: Macmillan, 1963).

For accounts of the whisky trade see Paul Sharp, *Whoop-Up Country* (Norman: University of Oklahoma Press, 1955); Georgia Green Fooks, *Fort Whoop-Up: Alberta's First and Most Notorious Whisky Fort* (Lethbridge: Whoop-Up Country Chapter Occasional Paper, 1983); and M. A. Kennedy and B. O. K. Reeves, "An Inventory and Historical Description of Whisky Posts in Southern Alberta," June 1984, unpublished study for Historic Sites Service.

For an account of the life of Jerry Potts, including his roles in the whisky trade, the Indian battle of 1870, and the NWMP see Hugh Dempsey, *Jerry Potts: Plainsman* (Calgary: Glenbow, 1966). Four major scholarly books on the history of the North-West Mounted Police are: Ronald Aitkin, *Maintain the Right: The Early History of The North West Mounted Police* (Toronto: Macmillan, 1973); Hugh Dempsey, ed., *Men in Scarlet* (Calgary: McClelland and Stewart and Historical Society of Alberta, 1974); S. W. Horrall, *The Pictorial History of the Royal Canadian Mounted Police* (Toronto: McGraw Hill Ryerson, 1973); and R. C. Macleod, *The North West Mounted Police and Law Enforcement 1873–1905* (Toronto: University of Toronto Press, 1975). The factors behind the establishment of the force are discussed in S. W. Horrall, "Sir John A. Macdonald and the Mounted Police Force for the Northwest Territories," *Canadian Historical Review* 53, 1972: 201–225.

For the Indian point of view regarding the treaties, consult Richard Price, ed., *The Spirit of Alberta Indian Treaties* (Toronto: Butterworth, 1979); and John Snow, *These Mountains are Our Sacred Places* (Toronto: Samuel Stevens, 1977).

George Stanley, *The Birth of Western Canada*, second ed. (Toronto: University of Toronto Press, 1960) provides an account of treaty making, the reserve system, and the participation of Indians in the North-West Rebellion. On Canadian government policy toward the natives see John L. Tobias, "Protection, Civilization, Assimilation: An Outline History of Canada's Indian Policy," *The Western Canadian Journal of Anthropology* VI, 1976: 13–30.

On the native and white reaction to the rebellion in Alberta, see Dempsey's biographies of native leaders cited in Chapter 1. See also Jack Dunn, "The Alberta Field Force of 1885," unpublished M.A. thesis, University of Calgary, 1979; and Bob Beal and Rod Macleod, *Prairie Fire: The 1885 North-West Rebellion* (Edmonton: Hurtig, 1984). For the life of Kootenai Brown see William Rodney, *Kootenai Brown: His life and Times, 1839–1916* (Sidney, B.C.: Gray's Publishing, 1969).

Chapter Three: **The Northwest Frontier**

For the major accounts of prairie settlement and dominion lands policy see A. S. Morton, *History of Prairie Settlement* (Toronto: Macmillan, 1938); and Chester Martin, *Dominion Lands Policy* (Toronto: Macmillan, 1938).

The major studies of ranching are David Breen, *The Canadian Prairie West and the Ranching Frontier, 1874–1924* (Toronto: University of Toronto Press, 1983); Simon Evans, "The Passing of a Frontier: Ranching in the Canadian West, 1882–1912," unpublished Ph.D., University of Calgary, 1976; and Lewis G. Thomas, (Patrick Dunae ed.) *Ranchers' Legacy* (Edmonton: University of Alberta Press, 1986). Also on the British impact on ranching, Patrick Dunae, *Gentlemen Emigrants* (Vancouver: Douglas & McIntyre, 1982) and Sheilagh Jameson, "Women in the Southern Alberta Ranch Community 1881–1914" in H. C. Klassen, ed., *The Canadian West: Social Change and Economic Development* (Calgary: Comprint, 1977): 63–78. There are also several good essays on ranching in A. W. Rasporich and Henry Klassen, eds., *Frontier Calgary* (Calgary: McClelland and Stewart West, 1975). Sheilagh Jameson's *Ranchers, Cowboys and Characters: Birth of Alberta's Western Heritage* (Calgary: Glenbow, 1987) is very useful. See also Grant MacEwan, *John Ware's Cow Country* (Edmonton: Institute of Applied Art, 1960) and Grant MacEwan, *Pat Burns, Cattle King* (Saskatoon: Western Producer, 1979). On the social life of early Calgary see H. C. Klassen, "Life in Frontier Calgary," in A. W. Rasporich, ed., *Western Canada: Past and Present* (Calgary: McClelland and Stewart West, 1975):42–57.

For a popular account of the building of the CPR, see Pierre Berton, *The National Dream: The Great Railway, 1871–1881* (Toronto: McClelland and Stewart, 1970); and *The Last Spike: The Great Railway, 1881–1885* (Toronto: McClelland and Stewart, 1971). On the overall impact of the CPR: Hugh Dempsey, ed., *The CPR West: The Iron Road and the Making of a Nation* (Vancouver: Douglas & McIntyre, 1984).

For the impact of the railway on urban development see David C. Jones et al., *The Weather Factory: A Pictorial History of Medicine Hat* (Saskatoon:

Western Producer, 1988); Max Foran, *Calgary: An Illustrated History* (Toronto: Lorimer, 1978); A. A. den Otter, *Civilizing the West: The Galts and the Development of Western Canada* (Edmonton: University of Alberta Press, 1982); John Gilpin, "Failed Metropolis: The City of Strathcona, 1891–1912," in Alan Artibise, ed., *Town and City: Aspects of Western Canadian Urban Development* (Regina: Canadian Plains Research Center, 1981). On Edmonton's history: Carl Betke, "The Development of Urban Community in Prairie Canada, Edmonton, 1898–1921," unpublished Ph.D., University of Alberta, 1981; Tony Cashman, *Best Edmonton Stories* (Edmonton: Hurtig, 1976); and J. G. MacGregor, *Edmonton: A History* (Edmonton: Hurtig, 1967). On the land office steal, J. G. MacGregor, *Edmonton Trader* (Toronto: McClelland and Stewart, 1963): Chapter 14.

On the early history of Banff see Douglas Leighton, "Banff is where it all began," *Canadian Geographic*, Feb./March 1985: 8–15; Sid Marty, A *Grand and Fabulous Notion: The First Century of Canada's Parks* (Toronto: NC Press, 1984), Chapter 3; David Smyth, "The Cave and Basin Hot Springs," *The Beaver*, Winter 1984–85: 46–51; E. J. Hart, *The Selling of Canada* (Banff: Altitude, 1983); and E. J. Hart, *Diamond Hitch: The Early Outfitters and Guides of Banff and Jasper* (Banff: Summerthought, 1979).

On Red Deer see Wellington Dawe, *History of Red Deer, Alberta*. On attitudes toward schools: Neil McDonald, "Canadian Nationalism and North-West Schools, 1884–1905," in Alf Chaiton and Neil McDonald, eds., *Canadian Schools and Canadian Identity* (Toronto: Gage, 1977): 151–183.

For the impact of Ontarians on Alberta see Douglas Francis, "'Rural Ontario West': Ontarians in Alberta," in H. & T. Palmer, eds., *Peoples of Alberta* (Saskatoon: Western Producer, 1985):123–142. On French Canadians and the West see A. I. Silver, "French Canada and the Prairie Frontier; 1870–1890," *Canadian Historical Review*, L, March 1969: 11–36; A. I. Silver, *The French-Canadian Idea of Confederation, 1864–1900* (Toronto: University of Toronto Press, 1982):Chapters 7 and 10. On the opposition to bilingualism and separate schools see Manoly R. Lupul, *The Roman Catholic Church and the North-West School Question: A Study in Church-State Relations in Western Canada 1875–1905* (Toronto: University of Toronto Press, 1974).

Canadian immigration policy is discussed in Norman Macdonald, *Canada: Immigration and Colonization 1842–1908* (Toronto: Macmillan, 1966). For Mormon immigration see Lawrence Lee, "The Mormons Come to Canada 1887–1902," *Pacific Northwest Quarterly* 59 (1968): 11–22; and H. Palmer, *Land of the Second Chance* (Lethbridge: Lethbridge Herald, 1972), Chapter 10. For the most recent scholarship see the collection of essays in Brigham Y. Card, Howard Palmer, et al., *The Mormon Presence in Canada* (Edmonton: University of Alberta Press, 1990). On Scandinavians, H. & T. Palmer, "The Icelandic Experience in Alberta," in *Peoples of Alberta*, Chapter 8; Jane McCracken, *Stephan G. Stephansson: The Poet of the Rocky Mountains* (Edmonton: Alberta Culture, 1982) and Gulbrand Loken, *From*

380

Fjord to Frontier: A History of the Norwegians in Canada (Toronto: McClelland and Stewart, 1980). On Germans, Edmund Heier, "The Immigration of Russo-German Catholics and Lutherans Into Canada," *Canadian Slavonic Papers* V (1960):160–75; E. Gerwin, "A Survey of the German-Speaking Population in the Province of Alberta," unpublished M.A. thesis, University of Alberta, 1938. On Ukrainians: Manoly R. Lupul, ed., *A Heritage in Transition: Essays in the History of Ukrainians in Canada* (Toronto: McClelland and Stewart, 1982); Myrna Kostash, *All of Baba's Children* (Edmonton: Hurtig, 1977) and Orest Martynowych, *The Ukrainian Bloc Settlement in East Central Alberta, 1890–1930: A History* (Edmonton: Alberta Culture, 1985).

Chapter Four: **Peopling the "Last Best West"**

For an overview of the settlement boom, see H. & T. Palmer, *Peoples of Alberta* (Saskatoon: Western Producer, 1985), Chapter 1; Jean Burnet with Howard Palmer, *'Coming Canadians': An Introduction to the History of Canada's Peoples* (Toronto: McClelland and Stewart, 1988):Chapter 3. For an overview of research in immigration and ethnic history: H. Palmer "Canadian Immigration and Ethnic History in the 1970s and 1980s" in *Journal of Canadian Studies*, Vol. 17 No. 1 (1982):35–50.

On Sifton's policy see David Hall, "Clifford Sifton: Immigration and Settlement Policy, 1896–1905" in H. Palmer, ed., *The Settlement of the West* (Calgary: Comprint, 1977):60–85. On public attitudes and racism, H. Palmer, *Patterns of Prejudice* (Toronto: McClelland and Stewart, 1982):Chapter 1.

On the Barr colonists see Helen Reid, *All Silent All Damned: The Search for Isaac Barr* (Toronto: Ryerson, 1969) and Kathryn Ivany, "The History of the Barr Colonists as an Ethnic Experience, 1903–23," unpublished M.A. thesis, University of Alberta, 1985. On the role of British "gentlewomen" see Emma Curtin, "Daughters of Empire: British Gentlewomen in Alberta, 1880–1914," unpublished M.A. thesis, University of Calgary, 1990; and S. Jackel, ed., *A Flannel Shirt and Liberty: British Gentlewomen in the Canadian West, 1880–1914* (Vancouver: University of British Columbia Press, 1982). For discussion of the British working class and the British role in the labour movement see Ross McCormack, "Cloth Caps and Jobs: The Ethnicity of English Immigrants in Canada, 1900–1914," in Jorgen Dahlie and Tissa Fernando, eds., *Ethnicity, Power, and Politics in Canada* (Toronto: Methuen, 1981):44–47; and David Bercuson, *Fools and Wise Men: The Rise and Fall of the One Big Union* (Toronto: Macmillan, 1978).

On immigration promotion in the U.S. see Harold Troper, *Only Farmers Need Apply* (Toronto: Griffin House, 1972). On the background to American immigration: Karel Bicha, *The American Farmer and the Canadian West, 1896–1914* (Lawrence, Kansas: Coronado, 1968); Paul Sharp, "The American Farmer and the Last Best West," *Agricultural History* (April 1947):65–

75; Paul Sharp, "When Our West Moved North" *American Historical Review*, Vol. 55 (1950):286–300. On blacks in Alberta see, H. & T. Palmer, *Peoples of Alberta*, Chapter 16 and works cited there.

On Scandinavians see K. O. Bjork, "Scandinavian Migration to the Canadian Prairie Provinces, 1893–1914," *Norwegian-American Studies* 26 (1974):63–75; William Wonders, "Scandinavian Homesteaders in Central Alberta" in H. Palmer and D. Smith, eds., *The New Provinces: Alberta and Saskatchewan, 1905–1980* (Vancouver: Tantalus, 1980):131–171; G. Loken, *From Fjord to Frontier* (Toronto, McClelland & Stewart, 1980):Chapter 5; Frank Paulsen, *Danish Settlements on the Canadian Prairies: Folk Tradition, Immigrant Experiences and Local History* (Ottawa: National Museum of Man, 1974). For background on Finnish immigration and causes of radicalism see Alan Kuitunen, "The Finnish Canadian Socialist Movement, 1900–1914," unpublished M.A. thesis, University of Calgary, 1982. On Finnish women see Varpu Lindstrom-Best, *Defiant Sisters: A Social History of Finnish Immigrant Women in Canada* (Toronto: Multicultural History Society of Ontario, 1988). On the Dutch and French, see H. and T. Palmer, *Peoples of Alberta*, Chapters 4 and 7; and Herman Ganzevoort, *A Bittersweet Land: The Dutch Experience in Canada, 1890–1980* (Toronto: McClelland and Stewart, 1988).

On Germans, Heinz Lehmann, *The German Canadians 1750–1937*, translated and edited by G. Bassler (St. John's: Jesperson Press, 1986) and Elizabeth Gerwin, "A Survey of the German-Speaking Population of Alberta," unpublished M.A. thesis, University of Alberta, 1938. On the Mennonites: Frank Epp, *Mennonites in Canada 1786–1920* (Toronto: Macmillan, 1974), Chapter 13; A. A. Sawatzky, "The Mennonites of Alberta and Their Assimilation," unpublished M.A. thesis, University of Alberta, 1964, Chapter 1; and H. Palmer, *Land of the Second Chance* (Lethbridge: Lethbridge Herald, 1972): Chapter 7. On the Hutterites, Robert Macdonald, "The Hutterites in Alberta," in H. & T. Palmer, eds., *Peoples of Alberta*, 348–364 and works cited there. For a general discussion of the causes of emigration from central and eastern Europe see Johann Chmelar, "The Austrian Emigration, 1900–1914" in Bernard Bailyn, ed., *Dislocation and Emigration: The Social Background of American Immigration, Perspectives in American History* VII (1973):275–378. See also the chapters on Hungarians, Romanians, Poles, and Ukrainians in H. & T. Palmer, eds., *Peoples of Alberta*. Also on Ukrainians consult John Lehr, "The Government and the Immigrant: Perspectives on Ukrainian Block Settlement in the Canadian West," *Canadian Ethnic Studies* 9, 2 (1977):42–52; J. Lehr, "The Landscape of Ukrainian Settlement in the Canadian West," *Great Plains Quarterly* 2, 2 (1982):94–105. On the ethnic left, Donald Avery, *Dangerous Foreigners: European Immigrant Workers and Labour Radicalism in Canada 1896–1932* (Toronto: McClelland and Stewart, 1979). On the Jews: Max Rubin, "Alberta's Jews: The Long Journey," in H. & T. Palmer, eds. *Peoples of Alberta*, Chapter 14. On the Doukhobors, George Woodcock and Ivan Avakumovic, *The Doukhobors* (Toronto: Oxford University Press, 1968) and

H. Palmer, *Land of the Second Chance*, Chapter 15. On Greeks, Peter Chimbos, *The Canadian Odyssey: The Greek Experience in Canada* (Toronto: McClelland and Stewart, 1980). On Arabs consult Baha Abu Laban, *An Olive Branch on the Family Tree: The Arabs in Canada* (Toronto: McClelland and Stewart, 1980); Mildred Duncanson, "Uncle Sam Jamha" in *Alberta History* 28, 3, Summer (1980):18–25 and Harold Barclay, "A Lebanese Community in Lac La Biche, Alberta" in Jean Elliott, ed., *Minority Canadians: Immigrant Groups* (Scarborough, 1971). On Italians, H. Palmer, *Land of the Second Chance*, Chapter 12.

On the Chinese and Japanese, Ed Wickberg, ed., *From China to Canada: A History of the Chinese Communities in Canada* (Toronto: McClelland and Stewart, 1982); Ken Adachi, *The Enemy That Never Was* (Toronto: McClelland and Stewart, 1976); Ban Seng Hoe, *Structural Changes of Two Chinese Comunities in Alberta*, Canada (Ottawa: National Museum of Man, 1976); H. Palmer, "Anti-Oriental Sentiment in Alberta, 1880–1920" in *Canadian Ethnic Studies* II, 2 (1970):31–57; H. Palmer, "Patterns of Prejudice: Attitudes toward Chinese and Japanese in Alberta, 1920–1950" in *Histoire Sociale/Social History* 13, 25 (1980):137–160; Brian Dawson, "The Chinese Experience in Frontier Calgary, 1885–1910" in A. W. Rasporich and H. C. Klassen, eds., *Frontier Calgary* (Calgary: McClelland and Stewart West, 1975):124–140. On the anti-Chinese riot, in addition to the studies above, see William Beahen, "Mob Law Could Not Prevail," *Alberta History*, Vol. 29, No. 3 (Summer 1981):1–7. See also on the Japanese, Ann and David Sunahara, "The Japanese in Alberta," in H. & T. Palmer, eds., *Peoples of Alberta*, Chapter 17.

Among the studies of native education, see E. Brian Titley, "Indian Industrial Schools in Western Canada," in Nancy Sheehan et al, *Schools in the West: Essays in Canadian Educational History* (Calgary: Detselig, 1986):133–153. On natives, Donald Smith, "The Original Peoples of Alberta," in *Peoples of Alberta*, 67–69 and works cited there. For fuller discussions of the interplay of immigration, ethnicity, and religion, see H. Palmer, *Land of the Second Chance*, 239–244; Jean Burnet with Howard Palmer, *Coming Canadians*: Chapter 7; and W. E. Mann, *Sect, Cult, and Church in Alberta* (Toronto: University of Toronto Press, 1955). For a discussion of the ideas and novels of Ralph Connor, see Patricia Roome, "Images of the West: Social Themes in Prairie Literature, 1898–1930," unpublished M. A., University of Calgary, 1976, Chapter 1. For an alternative interpretation of the role of religion in one region of rural Alberta: Paul Voisey, *Vulcan: The Making of a Prairie Community* (Toronto, University of Toronto Press, 1988):Chapter 8.

Chapter Five: **The Pioneer Moment**

For an overview of prairie agriculture, see Grant MacEwan, *Illustrated History of Western Canadian Agriculture* (Saskatoon: Western Producer,

1980). On rural society and the wheat economy see Gerald Friesen, *The Canadian Prairies: A History* (Toronto: University of Toronto Press, 1984), Chapter 13. David Jones, "'There is some Power About the Land'—The Western Agrarian Press and Country Life Ideology," *Journal of Canadian Studies*, Vol. 17, No. 3, Fall 1982:96–108 discusses the idealization of farm life. R. Douglas Francis, "The Ideal and the Real: The Image of the Canadian West in the Settlement Period," in Richard Davies, ed., *Rupert's Land: A Cultural Tapestry* (Waterloo: Wilfrid Laurier Press, 1988):253–273 and Anthony Rasporich, "Utopian Ideal and Community Settlement in Western Canada, 1880–1914," in H. Klassen, ed., *The Canadian West: Social Change and Economic Development* (Calgary: Comprint, 1977):37–62 discuss the image of a western agrarian utopia. For a thematic account of settlers' adjustment to the new landscape of the prairies, see Ronald Rees, *New and Naked Land: Making the Prairies Home* (Saskatoon: Western Producer, 1988).

For farm starting costs see Robert Ankil and Robert Litt, "The Growth of Prairie Agriculture: Economic Considerations," in Donald Akenson, ed., *Canadian Papers in Rural History* (Gananoque: Langdale Press, 1978) Vol. 1:35–64; Lyle Dick, "Estimates of Farm Making Costs in Saskatchewan, 1882–1914," *Prairie Forum*, Vol. 6, No. 2 (Fall, 1981):183–202. Among the many studies of Ukrainian pioneer life, see especially Orest Martynowych, *The Ukrainian Bloc Settlement in East Central Alberta, 1890–1930: A History* (Edmonton, Historic Sites Service, 1985):Chapter 3. On central and eastern European pioneer women: Ann Woywitka, "A Roumanian Pioneer," *Alberta Historical Review* Vol. 21 (Autumn, 1973):20–27. For a perceptive account of pioneer women, based on oral history, which also deals with many important themes not touched on in this chapter see Eliane Silverman, *The Last Best West: Women on the Alberta Frontier: 1880–1930* (Montreal: Eden Press, 1984). For an impressionistic overview of farm women, see Sara Brooks Sundberg, "Farm Women on the Canadian Prairie Frontier: The Helpmate Image," in Veronica Strong-Boag and Anita Clair Fellman, eds., *Rethinking Canada: The Promise of Women's History* (Toronto: Copp Clark, 1986):95–106.

On farm work and farm labourers, Ernest Ingles, "The Custom Threshermen in Western Canada, 1890–1925," in David Jones and Ian MacPherson, eds., *Building Beyond the Homestead* (Calgary: University of Calgary Press, 1988):135–160; John Herd Thompson, "Bringing in the Sheaves: The Harvest Excursionists, 1890–1929," *Canadian Historical Review* 54 (December 1978):467–489; W. J. C. Cherwinski, "In Search of Jake Trumper: The Farm Hand and the Prairie Farm Family," in David Jones and Ian MacPherson, eds., *Building Beyond the Homestead*:111–134; and Cecilia Danysk, "Showing These Slaves Their Class Position: Barriers to Organizing Prairie Farm Workers," in Ibid., 163–178. On farm mechanization see Ernest Ingles, "Some Aspects of Dry-Land Agriculture in the Canadian Prairies to 1925," unpublished M.A. thesis, University of Calgary, 1973; and Stanley Gordon, "Agricultural Tractors in Alberta Since 1925," unpublished research paper, Alberta Culture, 1983. Statistics from Alberta Department of Agriculture, *A Historical Series of Agricultural Statistics for Alberta* (Edmonton: Alberta Department of Agriculture, 1967?)

The accounts of pioneer institutions and social life are based on numerous local histories, a complete listing of which is in Joanna Krotki, ed., *Local Histories of Alberta: An Annotated Bibliography* (Edmonton: Division of East European Studies, University of Alberta, 1980). The ethnic dimension of pioneer life is discussed in detail in H. & T. Palmer, eds., *Peoples of Alberta* (Saskatoon: Western Producer, 1985). For rural education see John W. Chalmers, *Schools of the Foothills Province: The Story of Public Education in Alberta* (Toronto: University of Toronto Press, 1967); Robert Patterson, "Voices from the Past: The Personal and Professional Struggles of Rural School Teachers," in Nancy Sheehan et. al., *Schools in the West: Essays in Canadian Educational History* (Calgary: Detselig, 1986):99–112; David Jones, "Schools and Social Disintegration in the Alberta Dry Belt of the Twenties," in Nancy Sheehan et al, *Schools in the West* 265–284; and John Charyk, *The Little White Schoolhouse* (Saskatoon: Western Producer, 1968). On the Ukrainian school crisis: Manoly R. Lupul, "Ukrainian Language Education in Canada's Public Schools," in Manoly R. Lupul, ed., *A Heritage in Transition* (Toronto: McClelland and Stewart, 1982):Chapter 10 and Orest Martynowych, *The Ukrainian Bloc Settlement in East Central Alberta*:211–215. Details on Estonian settlement are from H. & T. Palmer, *Peoples of Alberta*:203–206, and Ukrainian halls from Orest Martynowych, *The Ukrainian Bloc Settlement in East Central Alberta*:229–236.

Details on Nanton are from Nanton and District Historical Society, *Mosquito Creek Roundup* (Altona: Friesen, 1975) plus a useful student research paper by Jean Moore, "Nanton, An Agricultural Community, 1880–1920," unpublished paper, University of Calgary, 1982. For discussion of social relations in other rural areas see Paul Voisey, *Vulcan: The Making of a Prairie Community* (Toronto: University of Toronto Press, 1988) Chapter 10, and Jean Burnet, *Next Year Country* (Toronto: University of Toronto Press, 1951).

On irrigation see E. A. Mitchner, "The Development of Western Waters, 1885–1930," unpublished manuscript, University of Alberta, 1973. On the career of William Pearce, see E. A. Mitchner, "William Pearce and Federal Government Activity in Western Canada, 1882–1904," unpublished Ph.D., University of Alberta, 1971. On irrigation in the Lethbridge area: A. A. den Otter, *Civilizing the Canadian West* (Edmonton, University of Alberta Press, 1982):Chapters 8 and 9; and in the CPR bloc, J. B. Hedges, *Building the Canadian West* (New York: Macmillan, 1939); and E. A. Mitchner, "CPR's Irrigation Block," in Hugh Dempsey, ed., *The CPR West* (Vancouver: Douglas & McIntyre, 1984):259–274. On the EID, Renie Gross and Lea Kramer, *Tapping the Bow* (Brooks: Eastern Irrigation District, 1985).

For the Lethbridge research station, Alex Johnston, *To Serve Agriculture* (Ottawa: Canada Department of Agriculture Historical Series, 1977). For a more general account of agricultural research, including discussion of research at Lethbridge, Lacombe, and Beaverlodge, J. W. Morrison, "Agricultural Achievements of the Prairie Experimental Farms, 1886–1986," *Prairie Forum*, Vol. 11, No. 2, (Fall 1986):195–214. On the relationship between experts and farmers, David Jones, *Empire of Dust* (Edmonton: University of Alberta Press, 1987):Chapter 8. On agricultural fairs see David Jones *Midways, Judges, and Smooth-Tongued Fakirs* (Saskatoon: Western Producer, 1983).

On the decline of ranching consult David Breen, *The Canadian Prairie West and the Ranching Frontier, 1874–1924* (Toronto: University of Toronto Press, 1983):Chapters 5–6. On the origins of the Calgary Stampede, L. V. Kelly, *The Range Men* (Toronto: William Briggs, 1913) and James Gray, *A Brand of its Own: The 100 Year History of the Calgary Exhibition and Stampede* (Saskatoon: Western Producer, 1985).

Chapter Six: **Politics, Cities, and Resource Development**

For an overview of political developments in the North-West Territories see L. H. Thomas, *The Northwest Territories: 1870–1905*, Canadian Historical Assocation booklet (Ottawa: Canadian Historical Association, 1970). See also L. H. Thomas, *The Struggle for Responsible Government in the Northwest Territories: 1870–1897* (Toronto: University of Toronto, 1956) and George Richardson, "The Conservative Party in the Provisional District of Alberta, 1887–1905," unpublished M.A. thesis, University of Alberta, 1977. J. W. Brennan, "The Autonomy Question and the Creation of Alberta and Saskatchewan" in H. Palmer and Donald Smith, eds., *The New Provinces: Alberta and Saskatchewan, 1905–1980* (Vancouver: Tantalus, 1980):43–63 analyzes the key questions related to Alberta becoming a province. Stan Gordon, "F. W. G. Haultain, Territorial Politics and the Quasi-Party System," *Prairie Forum*, Vol. 6, No. 1, Spring 1981; and Grant MacEwan, *Frederick Haultain* (Saskatoon: Western Producer, 1985) discuss the political career of an important figure. Douglas Owram, ed., *The Formation of Alberta: A Documentary History* (Calgary: Alberta Records Board Publication, 1979) contains a wealth of primary source materials. D. J. Hall, *Clifford Sifton: The Lonely Eminence 1901–1929* (Vancouver: UBC Press, 1985) discusses the Liberal party in the west and the autonomy issue. L. H. Thomas, *The Liberal Party in Alberta 1905–1921* (Toronto: University of Toronto Press, 1959) is the major study of the topic. Other valuable studies on autonomy and politics include Douglas Babcock, "Autonomy and Alienation in Alberta: Premier A. C. Rutherford," *Prairie Forum*, Vol. 6, No. 2 (Fall 1981):117–128, and Babcock's biography, *A Gentleman of Strathcona: Alexander Cameron Rutherford* (Edmonton: Occassional Paper No. 8, Alberta Historic Sites Service, 1980). On metropolitan rivalry see A. B. Kilpatrick, "A Lesson in Boosterism: The Contest for the Alberta Provincial Capital, 1904–06," *Urban*

History Review, Vol. 8, No. 3 (February 1980):47–109. For background on educational issues in the North-West Territories and in the autonomy debates consult Manoly R. Lupul, *The Roman Catholic Church and the North-West School Question: A Study in Church State Relations in Western Canada, 1875–1905* (Toronto: University of Toronto Press, 1974). For histories of Calgary and Edmonton during the boom period see J. G. MacGregor, *Edmonton: A History* (Edmonton: Hurtig, 1967); Carl Betke, "The Development of Urban Community in Prairie Canada: Edmonton, 1898–1921," unpublished Ph.D., University of Alberta, 1981; and Max Foran, *Calgary: An Illustrated History* (Toronto: Lorimer, 1978).

On public administration and the fiscal dilemmas of the provincial government see George Wright, "The Administration and Growth of the Government of Alberta, 1905–1921," unpublished M.A. thesis, University of Alberta, 1952. The best study of the origins and development of the University of Alberta is Maureen Aytenfisu, "The University of Alberta: Objectives, Structure and Role in the Community, 1908–1928," unpublished M.A. thesis, University of Alberta, 1982. On the development of the Peace River district, see Carl Dawson and R. W. Murchie, *The Settlement of the Peace River Country: A Study of a Pioneer Area* (Toronto: Macmillan, 1934); Carl Tracie, "Agricultural Settlement in the South Peace River Area," unpublished M.A. thesis, University of Alberta, 1967; John Eagle, "J. D. McArthur and the Peace River Railway," *Alberta History*, Vol. 29, No. 4 (Autumn 1981):33–39; Ena Schneider, *Ribbons of Steel: The Story of the Northern Alberta Railways* (Calgary: Detselig, 1989):7–91; and J. G. MacGregor, *Grande Prairie* (Grande Prairie: City of Grande Prairie, 1983). On the development of northeastern Alberta, Fort McMurray, and the Alberta and Great Waterways Railway, see J. G. MacGregor, *Paddle Wheels to Bucket-Wheels on the Athabasca* (Toronto: McClelland and Stewart, 1974); John W. Chalmers, ed., *The Land of Peter Pond* (Edmonton: Boreal Institute for Northern Studies, 1974); Barry Glen Ferguson, *Athabasca Oil Sands: Northern Resource Exploration, 1875–1951* (Regina: Canadian Plains Research Center, 1985):Chapter 1; and Morris Zaslow, *The Opening of the Canadian North, 1870–1914* (Toronto: McClelland and Stewart, 1971):Chapter 9.

On the origins and growth of the UFA, W. A. Macintosh, "The United Farmers of Alberta, 1909–1921," unpublished M.A. thesis, University of Calgary, 1971; and W. K. Rolph, *Henry Wise Wood of Alberta* (Toronto: University of Toronto Press, 1950).

On the history of coal see A. A. den Otter, "Railways and Alberta's Coal Problem, 1880–1960," in A. W. Rasporich, ed., *Western Canada: Past and Present* (Calgary: McClelland and Stewart West, 1975):84–98; A. A. den Otter, "Bondage of Steam: The CPR and Western Canadian Coal," in Hugh Dempsey, ed., *The CPR West: The Iron Road and the Making of a Nation* (Vancouver: Douglas and McIntyre, 1984):191–208; A. A. den Otter, *Civi-*

387

lizing the Canadian West (Edmonton: University of Alberta Press, 1982):Chapters 10 and 11. On specific regions see William James Cousins, *A History of the Crow's Nest Pass* (Lethbridge: Historic Trails Society of Alberta, 1981); Benn Gadd, *Bankhead: The Twenty Year Town* (Calgary: Coal Association of Canada, 1989); Alex Johnston et. al., *Lethbridge: Its Coal Industry* (Lethbridge: Lethbridge Historical Society, 1989); and Toni Ross, *Oh! The Coal Branch* (Calgary: 1974).

On the development of organized labour, particularly among the miners, consult Warren Caragata, "The Labour Movement in Alberta: An Untold Story," in David Leadbeater, ed., *Essays on the Political Economy of Alberta* (Toronto: New Hogtown Press, 1984):99–121; and his full-length study *Alberta Labour: A Heritage Untold* (Toronto: Lorimer, 1979); David Bercuson, *Fools and Wise Men, The Rise and Fall of the One Big Union* (Toronto: McGraw-Hill Ryerson, 1978); William Baker, "The Miners and the Mediator: the 1906 Lethbridge Strike and Mackenzie King," *Labour/Le Travailleur*, Vol. 11 (Spring 1983):89–117. The most complete study of coal and the coal miners is Allen Seager, "A Proletariat in Wild Rose Country: the Alberta Coal Miners, 1905–1945," unpublished Ph.D., York University, 1981. Some of his conclusions appear in "Socialists and Workers: The Western Canadian Coal Miners, 1900–21," *Labour/Le Travail*, Vol. 16 (Fall 1985):23–59.

On the early history of oil and gas see George de Mille, *Oil in Canada West, The Early Years* (Calgary: Northwest Printing, 1969) and David Breen, ed., *William Stewart Herron: Father of the Petroleum Industry in Alberta* (Calgary: Historical Society of Alberta, 1984). On the development of hydro-electric power: Christopher Armstrong and H. V. Nelles, "Competition vs. Convenience: Federal Administration of Bow River Waterpowers, 1906–13," in Henry Klassen, ed., *The Canadian West* (Calgary: Comprint, 1977):163–180.

Waterton and Jasper are discussed in Ian Getty, "The History of Waterton Lakes National Park, 1800–1937," research paper for National and Historic Parks Branch, 1971; William Rodney, *Kootenai Brown: his life and times, 1839–1916* (Sidney, B.C.: Gray's Publishing, 1969); and Brenda Gainer, "The Human History of Jasper National Park, Alberta," Manuscript Report 441 (Ottawa: Parks Canada, 1981).

Chapter Seven: **The Great War and After**

For an overview of the impact of the war on the prairie west see John Herd Thompson, *The Harvests of War: The Prairie West, 1914–1918* (Toronto: McClelland and Stewart, 1978). On pre-war attitudes toward militarism, Thomas Socknat, *Witness Against War: Pacifism in Canada, 1900–1945* (Toronto: University of Toronto, 1987):Chapter 1.

On comparative enlistment and casualty rates, C. A. Sharpe, "Enlistment in the Canadian Expeditionary Force 1914–1918: A Regional Analysis," *Journal of Canadian Studies*, Vol. 8, No. 4 (Winter 1983–84):15–29. On native reaction to the war, James Dempsey, "The Indians and World War One," *Alberta History* 31, No. 3 (Summer 1983):1–8. On Jim Cornwall see Harold Fryer, *Alberta the Pioneer Years* (Langley: Stagecoach, 1977):85–90. On immigrant minorities and the war, H. Palmer, *Patterns of Prejudice* (Toronto: McClelland and Stewart, 1982):Chapter 1; and Frances Swyripa and John Thompson, eds., *Loyalties in Conflict: Ukrainians in Canada During the Great War* (Edmonton: Canadian Institute for Ukrainian Studies, 1983). For Martin Nordegg's story, see Martin Nordegg, [T. D. Regehr, ed.] *The Possibilities of Canada are Truly Great* (Toronto: Macmillan, 1971).

For wartime conditions in the coalfields see Allen Seager, "A Proletariat in Wild Rose Country: the Alberta Coal Miners, 1905–45," unpublished Ph.D., York University, 1981, Chapter 5.

On the reform movements: Richard Allen, *The Social Passion: Religion and Social Reform in Canada, 1914–1928* (Toronto: University of Toronto Press, 1971); R. I. McLean, "Temperance and Prohibition in Alberta," unpublished M.A. thesis, University of Calgary, 1969; James Gray, *Booze* (Toronto: Macmillan, 1972); Nancy Sheehan, "Temperance, The WCTU, and Education in Alberta, 1905–1930," unpublished Ph.D., University of Alberta, 1980. For the political geography of the prohibition vote, Thomas Flanagan, "Political Geography and the United Farmers of Alberta," in S. M. Trofimenkoff, ed. *The Twenties in Western Canada* (Ottawa: National Museums of Canada, 1972):145–147. On the women's movement and suffrage, Paul Voisey, "The Votes for Women Movement, *Alberta History*, 23 (Summer 1975): 10–23; B. J. Nicholson, "Feminism in Western Canada to 1916," unpublished M.A. thesis, University of Calgary, 1972; and Carol Lee Bacchi, *Liberation Deferred? The Ideas of the English-Canadian Suffragists, 1877–1918* (Toronto: University of Toronto Press, 1983). Nicholson's thesis was particularly helpful with its biographical accounts of the "famous five." Among the biographical studies of the "famous five," Candace Savage, *Our Nell: A Scrapbook Biography of Nellie L. McClung* (Saskatoon: Western Producer, 1979). On women and the farm movement, Leslie Robinson, "Women and the Farm Movement in Alberta, 1905–1925," unpublished M.A. thesis, University of Calgary, 1979.

On the rise of the UFA, in addition to the Mackintosh and Rolph studies cited in Chapter 6, see W. L. Morton, "The Social Philosophy of Henry Wise Wood" in A. B. McKillop, ed., *Contexts of Canada's Past* (Toronto: Macmillan, 1980), Chapter 10; and W. L. Morton, *The Progressive Party in Canada* (Toronto: University of Toronto Press, 1950). For an analysis of Wood's and Irvine's ideas, C. B. Macpherson, *Democracy in Alberta* (Toronto: University of Toronto Press, 1953), Chapter 2. Paul Sharp, *The Agrarian Revolt in Western Canada* (Minneapolis: University of Minnesota Press, 1948) discusses the American influence on the farmers' movement. David Jones, *Empire of Dust* (Edmonton: University of Alberta Press, 1988) discusses the settlement of the drybelt and the disaster that befell. Thomas Flanagan, "Political Geography and the United Farmers of Alberta," in S. M. Trofimenkoff, ed., *The Twenties in Western Canada*: 138–169 shows the UFA bases of support. On the conscription issue see James Miller, "The Alberta Press and the Conscription Issue in the First World War, 1914–1918," unpublished M.A. thesis, University of Alberta, 1974. On the veterans' impact, Desmond Morton and Glenn Wright, *Winning the Second Battle: Canadian Veterans and the Return to Civilian Life, 1915–1930* (Toronto: University of Toronto Press, 1987). On the influenza epidemic: Janice Dickin McGinnis, "A City Faces an Epidemic," *Alberta History* Vol. 24, No. 4 (Autumn 1976):1–11. On the bush pilots, Stan McMillan and Mike Finland, eds., *Uncharted Skies: Canadian Bush Pilot Stories* (Edmonton: Reidmore, 1988).

For miners' living conditions, labour, and the rise of the OBU see David Bercuson, *Fools and Wisemen: The Rise and Fall of the One Big Union* (Toronto: McGraw Hill, 1978); Warren Carragata, *Alberta's Labour: A Heritage Untold* (Toronto: Lorimer, 1979):Chapter 5; Allen Seager, "A Proletariat in Wild Rose Country;" David Bercuson, ed., *Alberta's Coal Industry* (Calgary: Historical Society of Alberta, 1978); W. B. Askin, "Labour Unrest in Edmonton and District and its Coverage by the Edmonton Press: 1918–1919," unpublished M.A. thesis, University of Alberta, 1973. On immigrant radicalism and the Red Scare, Donald Avery, *Dangerous Foreigners: European Immigrant Workers and Labour Radicalism in Canada, 1896–1932* (Toronto: McClelland and Stewart, 1979):Chapters 1 and 2; David Bercuson, *Fools and Wisemen*, Chapter 4; and H. Palmer, *Patterns of Prejudice* (Toronto: McClelland and Stewart, 1982):53–56.

On the labour parties see Alvin Finkel, "The Rise and Fall of the Labour Party in Alberta, 1917–42," *Labour/LeTravail* 16 (Fall 1985):61–96.

Franklin Foster, "The 1921 Alberta Provincial Election: A Consideration of Factors Involved with Particular attention to Overtones of Millenialism," unpublished M.A. thesis, Queen's University, 1977; and H. Palmer, "William Irvine and the Emergence of Political Radicalism in Calgary, 1916–21," *Fort Calgary Quarterly*, Vol. 7, No. 2 (Spring 1987):1–19, discuss the background to the 1921 elections. Irvine's life and influence is discussed in detail in Anthony Mardiros, *William Irvine: The Life of a Prairie Radical* (Toronto: Lorimer, 1979).

Chapter Eight: **The Transitional Twenties**

For good overviews of the 1920s see James Gray, *The Roar of the Twenties* (Toronto: Macmillan, 1975); S. M. Trofimenkoff, *The Twenties in Western Canada* (Ottawa: National Museums of Canada, 1972); and John Herd Thompson with Allen Seager, *Canada 1922–1939* (Toronto: McClelland & Stewart, 1985). David Jones, *Empire of Dust* (Edmonton: University of Alberta Press, 1987) discusses social and economic collapse in the drybelt.

See also Wilfrid Eggleston, "The Old Homestead: Romance and Reality" in H. Palmer, ed., *The Settlement of the West*, (Calgary: Comprint, 1977):114–129 for a personalized account of the settlement and abandonment of the drybelt.

On Herman Trelle see Harold Fryer, *Alberta: The Pioneer Years* (Langley: Stagecoach, 1977):172–173. H. and T. Palmer, *Peoples of Alberta* (Saskatoon: Western Producer, 1985) Chapter 2 discuss population movements and ethnic groups. On immigrant domestics see Varpu Lindstrom-Best, *Defiant Sisters: A Social History of Finnish Immigrant Women in Canada* (Toronto: Multicultural History Society of Ontario, 1988):Chapter 5; and Norma Milton, "Essential Servants: Immigrant Domestic Servants on the Canadian Prairies, 1885–1930," unpublished M.A. thesis, University of Calgary, 1983. Helen Potrebenko, *No Streets of Gold: A Social History of Ukrainians in Alberta* (Vancouver: New Star, 1977) Chapter 5; and Benedykt Heydenkorn, ed., *Memoirs of Polish Immigrants in Canada* (Toronto: Canadian Polish Research Institute, 1979) discuss Ukrainian and Polish immigration. On the struggles of British immigrants see David Jones, "It's All Lies They Tell You: Immigrants, Hosts and the CPR," in Hugh Dempsey, ed., *The CPR West* (Calgary: Glenbow, 1984):107–124. For Mennonites in southern Alberta: Joanna Buhr, "Pursuit of a Vision: Persistence and Accommodation Among Coaldale Mennonites," unpublished M.A. thesis, University of Calgary, 1986. On Asian immigration: Edgar Wickberg, ed., *From China to Canada: A History of the Chinese Communities in Canada* (Toronto: McClelland and Stewart, 1982):Chapters 10 to 13 and Ann Sunahara, "The Japanese in Alberta," in H. & T. Palmer, eds., *Peoples of Alberta*, 399–400. H. Palmer, *Patterns of Prejudice* (Toronto: McClelland and Stewart, 1982):Chapters 2 and 3 discusses inter-ethnic relations during the 1920s, including the career of the Klan. See also Raymond Huel, "J. J. Maloney: How the West was saved from Rome, Quebec, and the Liberals," in John Foster, ed., *The Developing West* (Edmonton: University of Alberta Press, 1983).

On Turner Valley during the 1920s and 1930s: David Finch, "Turner Valley Oilfield Development, 1914–1945," unpublished M.A. thesis, University of Calgary, 1985; Douglas Cass, "Investment in Alberta Petroleum, 1912–1930," unpublished M.A. thesis, University of Calgary, 1985 and James H. Gray, *Talk to My Lawyer* (Edmonton: Hurtig, 1987):Chapter 8. On coal mining: Allen Seager, "A Proletariat in Wild Rose Country," unpublished Ph.D., York University, 1981, Chapter 7; A. A. den Otter, "Railways and Alberta's Coal Problem, 1880–1960," in A. W. Rasporich, ed., *Western Canada Past and Present* (Calgary: McClelland and Stewart West, 1975):91–92. On labour unrest and communists in the Drumheller Valley: Ann Capling, "The Communist Party of Canada in Alberta, 1922–29," unpublished M.A. thesis, University of Calgary, 1983; and Ann Capling, "Drumheller Strike of 1925," *Alberta History*, Vol. 31, No. 4 (Autumn 1983):11–19.

On the Stampede in the 1920s, James Gray, *A Brand of Its Own* (Saskatoon: Western Producer, 1985):Chapters 4 and 5.

Carl Betke, "The United Farmers of Alberta, 1921–35" in Carlo Caldarola, ed., *Society and Politics in Alberta* (Toronto: Methuen, 1979) and "Farm Politics in an Urban Age: The Decline of the United Farmers of Alberta after 1921," in L. H. Thomas, ed., *Essays on Western History* (Edmonton: University of Alberta Press, 1976):175–189, gives overviews of the UFA years. C. B. Macpherson, *Democracy in Alberta* (Toronto: University of Toronto Press, 1953): Chapter 3 shows UFA ideas facing political reality at the provincial level. Another good study of the UFA is Susan Kooyman, "The Policies and Legislation of the United Farmers of Alberta Government, 1921–35," unpublished M.A. thesis, University of Calgary, 1981. For background on UFA MLAs: H. C. Malliah, "A Socio-Historical Study of the Legislators of Alberta, 1905–1967," unpublished Ph.D., University of Alberta, 1970.

On the wheat pool see W. K. Rolph, *Henry Wise Wood of Alberta* (Toronto: University of Toronto Press, 1950):Chapter 7; and Phil Lewis, "The Alberta Wheat Pool 1923–35," unpublished M.A. thesis, University of Calgary, 1981.

On the liquor question and the UFA see Dianne Stretch, "From Prohibition to Government Control: The Liquor Question in Alberta, 1909–1919," unpublished M.A. thesis, University of Alberta, 1979. The best account of the Picariello case is in James Gray, *Talk to My Lawyer* (Edmonton: Hurtig, 1987):Chapter 4. See also Neil Watson, "John McKinley Cameron K.C." in Max Foran and Sheilagh Jameson, eds., *Citymakers: Calgarians After the Frontier* (Calgary: Historical Society of Alberta, 1987):117–130; and Harold Fryer, *Alberta: the Pioneer Years* (Langley: Stagecoach, 1977):51–55.

There is an excellent though as yet unpublished political biography of John Brownlee by Franklin Foster, "John Edward Brownlee: A Biography," unpublished Ph.D., Queen's University, 1981.

For the UFA at the federal level see W. L. Morton, *The Progressive Party in Canada* (Toronto: University of Toronto Press, 1950). See also P. D. Smith, "The United Farmers of Alberta and the Ginger Group: Independent Political Action, 1919–1939," unpublished M.A., University of Alberta, 1973. On Ukrainians and the UFA, Andrij Makuch, "In the Populist Tradition: Organizing the Ukrainian Farmer in Alberta, 1905–1935," unpublished M.A. thesis, University of Alberta, 1983. On the Conservative revival: Larry Glassford, "Winning the West: R. B. Bennett and the Conservative Breakthrough on the Prairies, 1927–1930," *Prairie Forum*, Vol. 13, No. 1 (Spring 1988):67–82.

A useful book that discusses the impact of technology on small town and rural social life is Paul Voisey, *Vulcan: The Making of a Prairie Community* (Toronto: University of Toronto Press, 1988). On Chautauqua see Sheilagh Jameson, *Chautauqua in Canada* (Calgary: Glenbow, 1979). On technology, movies, sports, and tourism see Donald G. Wetherell with Irene Kmet, *Useful Pleasures: The Shaping of Leisure in Alberta, 1896–1945* (Regina: Canadian Plains Research Center, 1990) and Donald Wetherell, "Some

Aspects of Technology and Leisure in Alberta, 1914–50," *Prairie Forum*, Vol. 11, No. 1 (Spring, 1986):51–69. On the history of aviation in the 1920s: Stanley Gordon, "The History of Aviation in Alberta to 1955," unpublished study for Reynolds-Alberta Museum and Alberta Culture, 1985.

For the impact of automobiles: Tony Cashman, *The Alberta Motor Association* (1968) and Tim Losey, "A History of the Automobile in Alberta, 1900–1955," unpublished Background Paper, Alberta Culture, 1984. On park policy and tourism consult Sid Marty, *A Grand and Fabulous Notion: The First Century of Canada's Parks* (Toronto: N.C.Press, 1984); Great Plains Research Consultants, "Banff National Park, 1792–1965: A History," unpublished study, 1984; E. J. Hart, *The Selling of Canada: The CPR and the Beginnings of Canadian Tourism* (Banff: Altitude Publishing, 1983); E. J. Hart, *Diamond Hitch: The Early Outfitters and Guides of Banff and Jasper* (Banff: Summerthought, 1979); Brenda Gainer, *The Human History of Jasper National Park, Alberta* (Ottawa: Environment Canada, 1981); and Ian Getty, "The History of Waterton Lakes National Park, 1800–1937."

Donald G. Wetherell with Irene Kmet, *Useful Pleasures: The Shaping of Leisure in Alberta, 1896–1945*, Chapter 5 discusses the history of radio. See also Bill McNeil and Morris Wolfe, *Signing On: The Birth of Radio in Canada* (Toronto: Doubleday, 1982) and Margaret Prang, "The Origins of Public Broadcasting in Canada," *Canadian Historical Review*, Vol. 46 (1965):1–31.

On the history of sport, William McLennan, *Sport in Early Calgary* (Calgary: Fort Brisebois Publishing, 1983); Patrick Lamb, "Deacon White, Sportsman," *Alberta History*, Vol. 37, No. 1 (Winter 1989):23–27; Carl Betke, "The Social Significance of Sport in the City of Edmonton in the 1920s," in A. R. McCormack and I. Macpherson, eds., *Cities in the West* (Ottawa: National Museums of Canada, 1975):211–236; and A. W. Rasporich and Elise Corbet, eds., *Winter Sport in the West* (Calgary: Historical Society of Alberta, 1990).

On women see Alison Prentice et. al., *Canadian Women: A History* (Toronto: Harcourt, 1988):Chapters 9, 10, 11; Veronica Strong-Boag, "Canadian Feminism in the 1920s: The Case of Nellie L. McClung," *Journal of Canadian Studies*, Vol. 12, No. 2 (Summer 1977):58–68; Veronica Strong-Boag, "Pulling in Double Harness or Hauling a Double Load: Women, Work and Feminism on the Canadian Prairie," *Journal of Canadian Studies*, Vol. 21, No. 3 (Fall 1986):32–52; and especially her *The New Day Recalled, 1919–1939* (Toronto: Copp Clark, 1988). On women and the left see Joan Sangster, *Dreams of Equality: Women on the Canadian Left, 1920–1950* (Toronto: University of Toronto Press, 1989); and Patricia Roome, "Amelia Turner," in Max Foran and Sheilagh Jameson, eds., *Citymakers: Calgarians After the Frontier*:225–246. On women and the peace movement, Donald Page, "The Development of a Western Canadian Peace Movement," in Susan Trofimenkoff, ed., *The Twenties in Western Canada*:75–106; and Thomas Socknat, *Witness Against War: Pacifism in Canada, 1900–1945* (Toronto: University of Toronto Press, 1987).

On rural women see Leslie Robinson, "Agrarian Reformers: Women and the Farm Movement in Alberta, 1909–1925," unpublished M.A. thesis, University of Calgary, 1979. For their legal and economic status see Elise Corbet, "Alberta Women in the 1920's: An Inquiry into Four Aspects of their Lives," unpublished M.A. thesis, University of Calgary, 1979. On the persons case, Rudy Marchildon, "The 'Persons' Controversy: The Legal Aspects of the Fight for Women Senators," *Atlantis* (Spring 1981):99–113; and Olive Stone, "Canadian Women as Legal Persons," *Alberta Law Review*, Vol. XVII, No. 2 (1979):331–371.

There are several useful discussions of the arts in the 1920s. On literature see Patricia Roome, "Images of the West: Social Themes in Prairie Literature, 1898–1930," unpublished M.A. thesis, University of Calgary, 1976. Donald G. Wetherell with Irene Kmet, *Useful Pleasures: The Shaping of Leisure in Alberta, 1896–1945*, Chapters 3 and 4 discuss music and drama. On the history of the Banff Centre see Donald Cameron, *Campus in the Clouds* (Toronto: McClelland and Stewart, 1956) and David Leighton, *Artists, Builders and Dreamers: 50 Years at the Banff School* (Toronto: McClelland and Stewart, 1982). On painting see Karen Wilkin, *Painting in Alberta: An Historical Survey* (Edmonton: 1980); Max Foran, "A. C. Leighton" in Max Foran and Sheilagh Jameson, eds., *Citymakers: Calgarians After the Frontier*:342–355; and Val Greenfield, *Founders of the Alberta College of Art* (Calgary: Alberta College of Art, 1986).

On church union see C. E. Silcox, *Church Union in Canada* (New York: NY Institute of Social and Religious Research, 1933) and James Gray, *The Roar of the Twenties*, Chapter 10. On fundamentalism, W. E. Mann, *Sect, Cult, and Church in Alberta* (Toronto: University of Toronto, 1955) and Donald Goertz, "The Development of A Bible Belt: The Socio-Religious Interaction in Alberta Between 1925 and 1938," unpublished Master of Christian Studies (Vancouver: Regent College, 1980). On Maxwell and the PBI, see David Elliott, "Studies of Eight Canadian Fundamentalists," unpublished Ph.D., University of British Columbia, Chapter 10. On the development of Aberhart's religious beliefs, David Elliott, "Anithetical Elements in William Aberhart's Theology and Political Ideology," *Canadian Historical Review*, Vol. 59, No. 1 (March 1978):38–58; and David Elliott, "The Devil and William Aberhart: The nature and function of his eschatology," *Studies in Religion*, Vol. 9, No. 3 (1980):325–37. On the history of the Prophetic Bible Institute see David Elliott and Iris Miller, "Aberhart and the Calgary Prophetic Bible Institute," *Prairie Forum*, Vol. 9, No. 1 (Spring 1984):61–77.

Chapter Nine: **The Crisis Years and the Rise of Social Credit**

For general studies of the Depression see Michael Horn, *The Dirty Thirties* (Toronto: Copp Clark, 1972); John Thompson with Allen Seager, *Canada 1922–39: Decades of Discord* (Toronto: McClelland & Stewart, 1985), and D. Francis and H. Ganzevoort, eds., *The Dirty Thirties in Prairie Canada*

(Vancouver: Tantalus, 1980). On the devastating impact of the Depression on the urban and rural west see James Gray, *The Winter Years* (Toronto: Macmillan, 1966) and *Men Against the Desert* (Saskatoon: Western Producer, 1967). For discussion of the impact of the Depression on ethnic relations: H. Palmer, *Patterns of Prejudice* (Toronto: McClelland and Stewart, 1982):Chapter 4. For accounts of ethnic support of the left, Myrna Kostash, *All of Baba's Children* (Edmonton: Hurtig, 1977) and Helen Potrebenko, *No Streets of Gold: A Social History of Ukrainians in Alberta* (Vancouver: New Star, 1977). Also on the communists, Ben Swankey, "Reflections of an Alberta Communist: the Hungry Thirties," *Alberta History*, Vol. 29, No. 4 (Autumn 1979):1–12 and Allen Seager, "Proletariat in Wild Rose Country," unpublished Ph.D., York University, 1981, Chapter 8. For a detailed account of the 1932 strike, Allen Seager, "The Pass Strike of 1932," *Alberta History*, Vol. 25, No. 1 (Winter 1977):1–11. On relief camps and marchers, Victor Hoar, ed., *Recollections of the On to Ottawa Trek* (Toronto: McClelland & Stewart, 1973) and Victor Howard with Mac Reynolds, *The Mackenzie-Papineau Battalion* (Ottawa: Carleton, 1986).

On the agricultural crisis, James Gray, *Men Against the Desert*; A. E. Palmer, *When the Winds Came* (Lethbridge: Lethbridge Herald, 1971); and Grant MacEwan, *Charles Noble: Guardian of the Soil* (Saskatoon: Western Producer, 1983).

On the reaction of the Brownlee government see F. L. Foster, "John Edward Brownlee: A Biography," unpublished Ph.D., Queen's University, 1981, Chapters 13–16. On internal conflict within the UFA, Carl Betke, "The UFA: Visions of a Cooperative Commonwealth," *Alberta History*, Vol. 27, No. 3 (Summer 1979):7–14. On labour politics and the roots of the CCF, Alvin Finkel, "The Obscure Origins of the CCF in Alberta," J. William Brennan, ed., *Building the Cooperative Commonwealth: Essays on the Democratic Socialist Tradition in Canada* (Regina: 1985) and Alvin Finkel, "The Rise and Fall of the Labour Party in Alberta, 1917–42," *Labour/Le Travail*, 16 (Fall 1985):61–96.

On the Brownlee scandal: Foster, "John Edward Brownlee," Chapters 17, 18; David Jones, "Fall of an Hon. Member," *Horizon Canada*, Vol. 10, No. 118:2822–2827; Tom Thorner, "A Study of Seduction: MacMillan vs. Brownlee," *Alberta Law Review*, Vol. 20, (1981):447; and James Gray, *Talk to My Lawyer* (Edmonton: Hurtig, 1987): Chapter 7.

On Social Credit there are a large number of exceptional studies. During the 1950s the University of Toronto published a series, including among others, John Irving, *The Social Credit Movement in Alberta* (1959) and C. B. Macpherson's *Democracy in Alberta: Social Credit and the Party System* (1953). Jean Burnet's *Next Year Country: A Study of Rural Social Organization in Alberta* (1951) looks at the impact of Depression in the Hanna area. W. E. Mann's *Sect, Cult, and Church in Alberta* (1955) discusses the religious background in Alberta that helped give rise to the Social Credit movement. The first major published biography of Aberhart is David Elliott and Iris

Miller, *Bible Bill: A Biography of William Aberhart* (Edmonton: Reidmore, 1987). Though critical, it perceptively portrays Aberhart's religious and political ideas and careers. A laudatory account, co-authored by one of Aberhart's daughters, is L. P. V. Johnson and Ola MacNutt, *Aberhart of Alberta* (Edmonton: Institute of Applied Art, 1970). For one insightful portrait: Harold Schultz, "Portrait of a Premier: William Aberhart," *Canadian Historical Review*, Vol. 45, No. 3 (1964):185–211. On the conflict between Ottawa and Alberta: J. R. Mallory, *Social Credit and the Federal Power in Canada* (Toronto: University of Toronto, 1954). For an overview of Social Credit economic measures: Hugh Whalen, "Social Credit Measures in Alberta," *Canadian Journal of Economics and Political Science*, Vol. 18, No. 4 (November 1952):500–517.

Useful documentary collections of material on Social Credit include Lewis H. Thomas, *William Aberhart and Social Credit in Alberta* (Toronto: Copp Clark, 1977) and Joseph A. Boudreau, *Alberta, Aberhart and Social Credit* (Toronto: Holt Rinehart, 1975). For discussions of the relationship between Social Credit, other reform movements, and the working class see Alvin Finkel, "The Rise and Fall of the Labour Party in Alberta, 1917–42;" Larry Hannant, "The Calgary Working Class and the Social Credit Movement in Alberta, 1932–35," in *Labour/Le Travail*, 16 (Fall 1985):97–116; and Alvin Finkel, *The Social Credit Phenomenon in Alberta* (Toronto: University of Toronto Press, 1989):Chapter 2. Alvin Finkel's "Alberta Social Credit Reappraised," *Prairie Forum*, Vol. 11, No. 1 (Spring 1986):69–86 and his *The Social Credit Phenomenon* stress the radical nature of the early Social Credit movement.

On the Social Credit drive into Saskatchewan, Ken Andrews, "Progressive Counterparts of the CCF: Social Credit and the Conservative Party in Saskatchewan, 1935–38," *Journal of Canadian Studies*, Vol. 17, No. 3 (Fall 1982):58–74. On Social Credit at the national level, Mary Hallett, "The Social Credit Party and the New Democracy Movement: 1939–1940," *Canadian Historical Review*, Vol. 47, No. 4 (December 1966); and Hugh Halleday, "Social Credit as a National Party in Canada," unpublished M.A. thesis, Carleton University, 1966.

Comparisons between the CCF and Social Credit are developed in John Conway, "The Prairie Populist Resistance to the National Policy: Some Reconsiderations," *Journal of Canadian Studies*, Vol. 14, No. 3 (Autumn 1979) and Alvin Finkel, *The Social Credit Phenomenon*. Also on comparisons between Alberta and Saskatchewan, David Smith, "A Comparison of Prairie Political Development in Saskatchewan and Alberta," *Journal of Canadian Studies*, Vol. IV (February 1969):17–25. For an alternative explanation to the one we offer see Nelson Wiseman, "The Pattern of Prairie Politics," *Queen's Quarterly*, 88 (Summer 1981):298–315. For comparisons between the UFA and Social Credit, C. B. Macpherson, *Democracy in Alberta*, Chapters 6 to 8.

Chapter Ten: **World War II and Transformation**

For background on the politics and economy of war, consult Robert Bothwell, Ian Drummond, and John English, *Canada: 1900-1945* (Toronto: University of Toronto Press, 1987), Chapters 19 to 22. On the BCATP, F. J. Hatch, *The Airdrome of Democracy: Canada and the British Commonwealth Air Training Plan 1939-45* (Ottawa: Department of National Defence, 1983). On the Alaska Highway, Ken Coates, ed., *The Alaska Highway: Papers of the 40th Anniversary Symposium* (Vancouver: University of British Columbia Press, 1985) and William Morrison, "Uncle Sam's Warpath," *Horizon Canada*, No. 76 (1986):1820-24. On biological and chemical warfare testing at Suffield: John Bryden, *Deadly Allies: Canada's Secret War, 1939-47* (Toronto: McClelland and Stewart, 1989). The POWs are discussed in David J. Carter, *Behind Canadian Barbed Wire: Alien, Refugee and Prisoner of War Camps in Canada 1914-46* (Calgary: Tumbleweed Press, 1980). On agriculture: John Herd Thompson and Ian Macpherson, "An Orderly Reconstruction: Prairie Agriculture in World War Two," *Canadian Papers in Rural History*, Vol. 4 (1984):11-32; and David Monod, "The End of Agrarianism: The Fight for Farm Parity in Alberta and Saskatchewan, 1935-48," *Labour/Le Travail*, Vol. 16 (Fall 1985):117-143.

On wartime and postwar coal: A. A. den Otter, "Railways and Alberta's Coal Problem, 1880-1960," in A. W. Rasporich, ed., *Western Canada: Past and Present* (Calgary: McClelland and Stewart West, 1975):84-98; and Allen Seager, "A Proletariat in Wild Rose Country: the Alberta Coal Miners, 1905-1945," unpublished Ph.D., York University, 1981, 467-485. On the oilsands, Barry Glen Ferguson, *Athabasca Oil Sands: Northern Resource Exploration, 1875-1951* (Regina: Canadian Plains Research Center, 1985), Chapters 2 to 5. On Social Credit: Alvin Finkel, *The Social Credit Phenomenon in Alberta* (Toronto: University of Toronto Press, 1989):Chapter 4; and David Elliott and Iris Miller, *Bible Bill* (Edmonton: Reidmore, 1987):Chapters 19 and 20.

On wartime nativism, H. Palmer, "Ethnic Relations in Wartime; Nationalism and European Minorities in Alberta during the Second World War," *Canadian Ethnic Studies*, Vol. XIV, No.3 (1982):1-23; H. Palmer, "Patterns of Prejudice: Attitudes toward Chinese and Japanese in Alberta, 1920-1950" in *Histoire Sociale/Social History*, Vol. 13, No. 25 (May 1980):137-160; and Ann Sunahara, *The Politics of Racism* (Toronto: Lorimer, 1982). On Mennonites, John Toews, *With Courage to Spare: The Life of B. B. Janz* (Winnipeg: 1978):Chapter 10; Aron Sawatzky, "The Mennonites of Alberta and Their Assimilation," unpublished M.A. thesis, University of Alberta, 1964; David Fransen, "Breaking Down the Barriers, Mennonites in Canada during the Second World War," in Norman Hillmer et. al., *On Guard for Thee: War, Ethnicity, and the Canadian State, 1939-45* (Ottawa: Canadian Committee for the History of the Second World War, 1989).

On Ukrainian Canadians and the war see Thomas Prymak, *Maple Leaf* and *Trident: The Ukrainian Canadians during the Second World War* (Toronto: Multicultural History Society of Ontario, 1988):Chapter 4. On natives during the war and the birth of the IAA, Murray Dobbin, *The One-And-A-Half Men* (Vancouver: New Star, 1981) Chapters 2, 10; Donald Smith, "John Laurie, A Good Samaritan," in Max Foran and Sheilagh Jameson, *City-makers: Calgarians After the Frontier* (Calgary: Historical Society of Alberta, 1987):263–274.

On women: Ruth Roach Pierson, *"They're Still Women After All": The Second World War and Canadian Womanhood* (Toronto: McClelland and Stewart, 1986); and Donna Alexander Zwicker, "Alberta Women and World War II," unpublished M.A. thesis, University of Calgary, 1985. On returning veterans, Barry Broadfoot, *The Veterans' Years: Coming Home from the War* (Vancouver: Douglas & McIntyre, 1985).

Chapter Eleven: **Oil and the Birth of Modern Alberta**

For national social, economic, and political trends during this period see Robert Bothwell, Ian Drummond and John English, *Canada since 1945: Power, Politics, and Provincialism* (Toronto: University of Toronto, 1981). For an overview of the oil industry see Earle Gray, *The Great Canadian Oil Patch* (Toronto: Maclean Hunter, 1970). On the impact of oil on the economy, Eric Hanson, *Dynamic Decade* (Toronto: McClelland and Stewart, 1958). For the national perspective, Hugh M. K. Grant, "The Petroleum Industry and Canadian Economic Development: An Economic History, 1900–1961," unpublished Ph.D., University of Toronto, 1986, Chapters 11 to 14, and John McDougall, *Fuels and the National Policy* (Toronto: Butterworths, 1982). For a brief overview of the post-Leduc years, A. W. Rasporich, "Leduc Plus Forty," CPA *Review*, Vol. 11, No. 1, (February 1987):3–5, 10–12. On the Trans-Canada Pipeline, William Kilbourn, *Pipeline: TransCanada and the Great Debate* (Toronto: Carke Irwin, 1970). G. Homer Durham, *N. Eldon Tanner: His Life and Service* (Salt Lake: Deseret, 1982) discusses the fascinating career of Manning's Minister of Lands and Mines.

On postwar immigration, H. & T. Palmer, eds., *Peoples of Alberta* (Saskatoon: Western Producer, 1985), Chapters 2, 7, 9, 10, 11, 12, 13. On urbanization in the postwar era, several studies edited by P. J. Smith and B. M. Barr, including *Environment and Economy: Essays on the Human Geography of Alberta* (Edmonton: Pica Pica Press, 1984); and Max Foran, *Calgary: An Illustrated History* (Toronto: Lorimer, 1978):Chapter 4. See also D. H. Breen, "Calgary: The City and the Petroleum Industry Since World War Two," *Urban History Review*, Vol. 2, No. 77 (October 1977):55–71. Among the few discussions of popular culture in the 1950s and 1960s, Alex Johnston and A. A. den Otter, *Lethbridge: A Centennial History* (Lethbridge: City of Lethbridge, 1985):Chapter 9. On urban politics: James Lightbody, " 'Wild Bill' Hawrelak: 'Lets Get Edmonton Rolling Again'," in Allan Levine, ed., *Your Worship!* (Toronto: Lorimer, 1990). On women in the 1950s and 1960s,

Alison Prentice et al., *Canadian Women: A History* (Toronto: Harcourt, 1988):Chapters 13 and 14.

On post-secondary education, Desmond Berghofer and Alan Vladicka, *Access to Opportunity, 1905–1980* (Edmonton: Alberta Advanced Education and Manpower, 1980), Chapters 3 to 5. On the arts in the postwar era, Donna Lohnes and Barbara Nicholson, *Alexander Calhoun* (Calgary: Calgary Public Library, 1987), Chapter 3; Lindsay Moir, "Dr. Betty Mitchell and the Development of Drama in Calgary" in Max Foran and Sheilagh Jameson, eds., *Citymakers: Calgarians After the Frontier* (Calgary: Historical Society of Alberta, 1987):366–374; and Illingworth Kerr, *Paint and Circumstance* (Calgary: Paperworks Press, 1987).

On Manning, oil, and politics, John Richards and Larry Pratt, *Prairie Capitalism: Power and Influence in the New West* (Toronto: McClelland and Stewart, 1979):Chapter 4; John Barr, *The Dynasty: The Rise and Fall of Social Credit in Alberta* (Toronto: McClelland and Stewart, 1974):Chapters 7 to 9, and Alvin Finkel, *The Social Credit Phenomenon in Alberta* (Toronto: University of Toronto Press, 1989), Chapters 5 and 6. On Manning and the opposition, Meir Serfaty, "Harper Prowse and the Alberta Liberals," *Alberta History*, Vol. 29, No. 1 (Winter 1981):1–9 and Bob Hesketh, "The Abolition of Preferential Voting in Alberta," *Prairie Forum*, Vol. 12, No. 1 (Spring 1987):123–143.

On background to the Diefenbaker sweep and Alberta Conservatives, Jack Horner, *My Own Brand* (Edmonton: Hurtig, 1980) Chapters 1 to 3. On the problems and decline of Social Credit at the national level, Hugh Halleday, "Social Credit as a National Party in Canada," unpublished M.A., Carleton, 1966. On Peter Lougheed and the rise of the provincial Conservatives, Meir Serfaty, "The Conservative Party of Alberta under Lougheed, 1965–71: Building an Image and an Organization," *Prairie Forum*, Vol. 6, No. 1 (Spring 1981):57–74; Alan Hustak, *Peter Lougheed: A Biography* (Toronto: McClelland and Stewart, 1979):Chapters 1 to 7, and David Wood, *The Lougheed Legacy* (Toronto: Key Porter Books, 1985):Chapters 3 to 5.

On the Strom administration, the last days of Social Credit, and the 1971 election: Alvin Finkel, *The Social Credit Phenomenon in Alberta*, Chapter 7; John Barr, *The Dynasty* (Toronto: McClelland and Stewart, 1974), Chapters 10 to 13; and Howard and Tamara Palmer, "The 1971 Election and the Fall of Social Credit in Alberta," *Prairie Forum*, Vol. 1, No. 2 (November 1976):123–134.

Chapter Twelve: **The Lougheed Years and After**

On Lougheed and the politics of the Lougheed years, see the journalistic account by Allan Hustak, *Peter Lougheed: A Biography* (Toronto: McClelland and Stewart, 1979); and the adulatory account by Tory insider David Wood, *The Lougheed Legacy* (Toronto: Key Porter Books, 1985).

For impressionistic studies of urban growth, oil wealth, and the politics of oil, see Peter Newman, *The Acquisitors* (Toronto: McClelland and Stewart, 1981):Chapter 7 to 9; and Peter Foster, *The Blue Eyed Sheiks: The Canadian Oil Establishment* (Toronto: Collins, 1979). On migration and the new immigration, H. & T. Palmer, *Peoples of Alberta* (Saskatoon: Western Producer, 1985):Chapters 2, 4, 6, 14, 18, and 19. On the development of Chinatowns in Alberta: David Lai, *Chinatowns: Towns Within Cities in Canada* (Vancouver: University of British Columbia Press, 1988), 135–141.

For a journalistic account of immigration from Hong Kong to Canada, Margaret Cannon, *China Tide* (Toronto: Harper and Collins, 1989). On multiculturalism and ethnic politics, see Jean Burnet with Howard Palmer, *"Coming Canadians": An Introduction to the History of Canada's Peoples* (Toronto: McClelland and Stewart, 1988):175–181. For empirical evidence for the decline of the mainline denominations see Reginald Bibby, "The State of Collective Religiosity in Canada: An Empirical Analysis," *Canadian Review of Sociology and Anthropology*, Vol. 16, No. 1 (1979):105–16. Discussion of the growth of "conservative" churches in Reginald Bibby, "Why Conservative Churches Really are Growing: Kelly Revisited," *Journal for the Scientific Study of Religion*, Vol. 17, No. 2 (June 1978):129–39.

For discussion of the broad changes that undermined regional differences on the prairies, though not political alienation or regionalism, see Roger Gibbins, *Prairie Politics and Society* (Toronto: Butterworths, 1980). Little has been written on the arts in Alberta during the 1970s and 1980s, though there are many interesting essays and reviews in *NeWest Review*, and some useful essays in A. W. Rasporich, ed., *The Making of the Modern West: Western Canada Since 1945* (Calgary: University of Calgary Press, 1984). For his autobiography, James Gray, *Troublemaker! A Personal History* (Toronto: Macmillan, 1978). On MacEwan, R. H. Macdonald, *Grant MacEwan* (Saskatoon: Western Producer, 1979).

For the historical background on federal-provincial conflict see David Elton, "Alberta and the Federal Government in Historical Perspective," in Carlo Caldarola, eds., *Society and Politics in Alberta* (Toronto: Methuen, 1979):108–30. On the Alberta economy, R. L. Mansell, "Texas and Alberta: A Comparison of Regional Economies," *Texas Business Review*, Nov./Dec. 1981:241–246; R. L. Mansell, "Energy Policy, Prices and Rents: Implications for Regional Growth and Development," in William Coffey and Mario Polese, eds., *Still Living Together: Recent Trends and Future Directions in Canadian Regional Development* (Montreal: Institute for Research on Public Policy, 1987) and R. L. Mansell and Michael Percy, *Strength in Adversity: A Study of the Alberta Economy* (C. D. Howe Research Institute, forthcoming). On the ideology and social organization of the oilpatch, J. D. Howse, *The Last of the Free Enterprisers* (Toronto: Macmillan, 1980).

On Keegstra, right-wing extremism, and anti-Semitism, Stanley Barrett, *Is God a Racist? The Right Wing in Canada* (Toronto: University of Toronto Press, 1987) and David Bercuson and Douglas Wertheimer, *A Trust Betrayed: The Keegstra Affair.* (Toronto: Doubleday, 1985). On the NDP, Larry Pratt,

"Grant Notley: Politics as a Calling," in Larry Pratt, ed., *Socialism and Democracy in Alberta* (Edmonton: NeWest Press, 1986):Chapter 1.

On Lougheed's economic strategy: Larry Pratt, "The Political Economy of Province-Building: Alberta's Development Strategy, 1971–1981" in David Leadbeater, ed. *Essays on the Political Economy of Alberta* (Toronto: New Hogtown Press, 1984):194–222, and John Richards and Larry Pratt, *Prairie Capitalism: Power and Influence in the New West* (Toronto: McClelland and Stewart, 1979):Chapter 9. For a summary of provincial economic initiatives during the Lougheed years, see the *White Paper Proposals for an Industrial and Science Strategy for Albertans: 1985–1990* (Edmonton: Government of Alberta, 1984):77–90. For an overview of the issues raised by the AHSTF: *Canadian Public Policy*, Vol. 6 Supplement (February 1980). For a critique of the Lougheed regime, Ron Chalmers, "Insults to Democracy during the Lougheed Era," in Larry Pratt, ed., *Socialism and Democracy in Alberta* (Edmonton: NeWest Press, 1986):Chapter 6 and Tom Sindlinger, *Senate Election: Alberta Sets the Pace* (Calgary: 1989):129–163. On Tory patronage, Jeffrey Simpson, *Spoils of Power* (Don Mills: Collins, 1988):Chapter 14.

David Humphreys' *Joe Clark: A Portrait* (Toronto: Deneau and Greenberg, 1978) is a campaign biography by a Tory friend. On the Clark Conservatives in power nationally see Jeffrey Simpson, *Discipline of Power: The Conservative Interlude and the Liberal Restoration* (Toronto: Macmillan, 1980). On the constitutional debate, David Milne, *Tug of War: Ottawa and the Provinces Under Trudeau and Mulroney* (Toronto: Lorimer, 1986) and Robert Sheppard and Michael Valpy, *The National Deal: The Fight for a Canadian Constitution* (Toronto: Fleet, 1982). On the oil industry, the NEP, and Ottawa-Alberta conflict: Michael Bliss, *Northern Enterprise: Five Centuries of Canadian Business* (Toronto: McClelland and Stewart, 1987):Chapter 18; Peter Foster, *The Sorcerer's Apprentices: Canada's Super-Bureaucrats and the Energy Mess* (Toronto: Collins, 1982), an angry book that shares oilmen's view of NEP bureaucratic bungling; and G. Bruce Doern and Glen Toner, *The Politics of Energy: The Development and Implementation of the NEP* (Toronto: Methuen, 1985).

For several discussions of alienation in Alberta, see Larry Pratt and Garth Stevenson, eds., *Western Separatism: The Myths, Realities and Dangers* (Edmonton: Hurtig, 1981). The degree of separatist support is discussed in Canada West Foundation, *Opinion Update*, Oct. 19, 1982, Report No. 14:3–4. See also Don Ray, "Western Separatism: Counter-elite of the Marginalized" in Chuck Reasons, ed., *Stampede City: Power and Politics in the West* (Toronto: Between the Lines, 1984):147–173. The Reasons book also contains other interesting essays on power and privilege in Calgary. For a comparative perspective: Harry H. Hiller, "Resources and Regional Rebellion: Western Australia and Western Canada," in B. W. Hodgins et al. eds, *Federalism in Canada and Australia* (Peterborough: Trent University and Broadview Press, 1989):381–398.

On the Mulroney government's energy policy see David Bercuson, J. L. Granatstein, and W. R. Young, *Sacred Trust? Brian Mulroney and the Conservative Party in Power* (Toronto: Doubleday, 1986). On the choice of Getty as leader, Margaret Hunziker, "Leadership Selection: The 1985 Alberta Progressive Conservative Leadership Convention," unpublished M.A. thesis, University of Calgary, 1986. On Getty and his government, Andrew Nikiforuk, Sheila Pratt, and Don Wanagas, eds., *Running on Empty: Alberta after the Boom* (Edmonton: NeWest Press, 1987). On the 1986 provincial election and shifting trends in Alberta politics: Allan Tupper, "New Dimensions of Alberta Politics," *Queen's Quarterly*, Vol. 93, No. 4 (Winter 1986):780–791 and Gurston Dacks, "From Consensus to Competition: Social Democracy and Political Culture in Alberta," in Larry Pratt, ed., *Socialism and Democracy in Alberta*, Chapter 9. On the foresty industry in Alberta: Michael Howlett, "The Forest Industry on the Prairies: Opportunities and Constraints to Future Development," *Prairie Forum*, Vol. 14, No. 2 (Fall 1989):233–257.

On the Getty government and the forestry initiatives: Andrew Nikiforuk and Ed Struzik, "The Great Forest Sell-Off," in *Report on Business Magazine* (November 1989):56–68.

On the Meech Lake agreement and Alberta: Roger Gibbins, with Howard Palmer, Brian Rusted, and David Taras, *Meech Lake and Canada: Perspectives from The West* (Edmonton: Academic Printing, 1988). On Alberta and Senate reform, Roger Gibbins, "Senate Reform: Always the Bridesmaid, Never the Bride," in Ronald Watts and Douglas Brown, eds., *Canada: The State of the Federation 1989* (Kingston: Institute of Intergovernmental Relations, Queen's University, 1989):194–210.

On women in the 1970s and 1980s, Alison Prentice et al. *Canadian Women: A History* (Toronto: Harcourt, 1988), Chapters 15, 16.

On natives, Donald Smith, "The Original Peoples of Alberta," in H. & T. Palmer eds. *Peoples of Alberta*:75–81; J. R. Miller, *Skyscrapers Hide the Heavens: A History of Indian-White Relations in Canada* (Toronto: University of Toronto Press, 1989), Chapters 12 to 14; Alberta Native Affairs, "A Demographic Overview of the Native Populations in Alberta," (Edmonton: Native Affairs Secretariat, 1985); J. Rick Ponting, "Profiles of Public Opinion on Canadian Natives and Native Issues," Module 3 (Calgary: Research Unit for Public Policy Studies, 1987); John Goddard, "Forked Tongues," *Saturday Night*, February 1988; and J. Rick Ponting, *Arduous Journey: Canadian Indians and Decolonization* (Toronto: McClelland and Stewart, 1986).

On the background to Calgary urban politics and the Olympics: Don Gillmor, "The People's Choice," *Saturday Night* (August, 1989):30–37.

Index

410

Murphy, Emily, 180, 236, 237
Murphy, Harvey, 248
music, 18, 88, 114, 222, 229, 235, 239, 312
musicians, 229, 230, 312, 313, 338, 339
Muslims, 98, 337
Myrnam, 94

Nacmine, 158
Nanton, 115-118, 196
Nanton, Augustus, 115, 160
Nanton News, 115
Naples, 98
National Energy Policy, 350, 352, 354
National Fuels Policy, 287
national parks, 48, 64-65, 165-166, 226-229;
  see also individual parks
National Parks Act, 227
national policy, 50, 59, 77, 136, 278, 279
nationalism, British Canadian, 104, 113,
  132, 168, 185, 203, 221; Canadian, 189,
  243, 281, 298, 302, 303, 306, 320, 348, 359
native land claims, 42, 367
native organizations, 295, 317, 319, 359,
  364, 365
native religion. *See* religion, native
natives, vii, vii, x, 3-10, 30, 31, 32, 39, 43,
  49, 101, 149, 236, 295-296, 364-368; *see
  also* Indians, Métis, and individual tribes
nativism, 78, 137, 160, 173, 174, 181, 186,
  203, 221, 250, 292; *see also* anti-
  Catholicism, anti-semitism, prejudice,
  racism
natural resources, provincial control of,
  130, 133, 216, 217; *see also* federal-
  provincial relations, energy policy
Nazarenes, 242
Neerlandia, 88, 89
Newcastle, 158
New Dayton, 86
New Democracy, 276
New Democrats, 315, 320, 321, 323, 346,
  349, 355, 359, 360
New Sweden, 71
newspapers, 57, 90, 105, 115, 123, 125, 137,
  152, 170, 174, 185, 229, 230, 231, 235,
  250, 260, 266, 272, 364; *see also*
  individual newspapers
Nickle, Carl, 352
Nielsen, Arne, 301
Noble blade, 252
Noble, C. S., 253
Nobleford, 88, 252, 253
Non-Partisan League, 86, 136, 180, 183,
  184, 194
non-partisanship, 130, 136, 178, 219, 278

Nordegg, 98, 156, 287
Nordegg, Martin, 158, 171
Norris, Malcolm, 295
North Dakota, 71, 184, 253
North Saskatchewan River, 31, 39, 48, 50,
  59, 60, 63, 108, 138
North West Coal and Navigation Co.
  (NWC&NC), 61, 94, 119
North West Company, 11, 12
North-West Mounted Police, vii, 25, 29, 35,
  38, 39, 41, 42, 43, 45, 46, 50, 53, 55, 61,
  63, 70, 100, 102, 126, 159, 160
North-West Rebellion, 43-49, 56, 68, 74, 80
North-West Territories (NWT), 31, 33, 44,
  66, 76, 77, 129, 131, 188, 224, 246;
  Assembly, 61, 67, 129, 135
Northern Alberta Institute of Technology
  (NAIT), 312
Northern Alberta Railway, 216, 284; *see
  also* Alberta and Great Waterways
  Railway, and Edmonton, Dunvegan and
  British Columbia Railway
Northwest Staging Route, 284
Norwegians, 71, 83, 87, 88, 150, 221, 235,
  238; *see also* Scandinavians
Notley, Grant, 346, 355
Nova, 357
nursing, 26, 182, 188, 234, 235, 297; *see also*
  hospitals
Nutcracker, 185

Oblate Order, 25, 26
O'Brien, Charles, 161
occupational specialization, 73, 96, 98, 203,
  304, 332, 333; *see also* class composition
Oddfellows, 84
Official Languages Act, 359
Oil City, 162
oil and gas companies, vii, viii, 162, 163,
  205, 273, 300, 301, 302, 306, 307, 343,
  344, 348, 351, 353, 369; *see also*
  individual companies
oil exploration, 144-146, 151, 163-164, 205,
  207, 300-308 *passim*, 329, 330, 367
Oil and Gas Conservation Act, 207
oil industry, 128, 146, 153, 162, 163, 164,
  205, 207, 285, 286, 243, 300-308 *passim*,
  329, 330, 350, 352, 354, 367; *see also*
  oilsands
oil prices, 325, 327, 330, 341, 343, 344,
  350, 353, 354, 355
oil sands, 144, 146, 286, 287, 329, 330, 346,
  351, 353, 357, 369
oilfield communities, comparison to coal
  towns, 207

415

419